D0162924

*Fundamentals
of Linguistic
Analysis*

Fundamentals of Linguistic Analysis

Ronald W. Langacker

University of California, San Diego

Harcourt Brace Jovanovich, Inc.
New York | Chicago | San Francisco | Atlanta

ISBN: 0-15-529455-5

Library of Congress Catalog Card Number: 70-190448

Printed in the United States of America

Preface

In reviewing another "problems" book some years ago, I made the comment that an adequate text to span the gap between linguistic theory and linguistic practice was still lacking. This comment was not altogether fair, for it is doubtful that any text can serve this function adequately. I fully expect the same criticism to be leveled at the present volume, and I wish to acknowledge its correctness in advance.

It is apparent nevertheless that books of this kind have an important role to play in linguistic pedagogy. Linguistics is a rather esoteric discipline that students find it hard to come to grips with. Explaining to them precisely what linguists do when they do linguistics is not easy, and showing them is not much easier. The best way for students to learn what linguistics is all about is by doing it themselves, by working with real language data and discovering for themselves regularities of the kind that linguists have come to expect. Materials that make linguistic analysis into a concrete reality for students instead of the mysterious abstraction that it tends to be thus have great pedagogical importance.

This book is intended to meet in part the need for such materials. It is meant for intermediate and advanced undergraduate students in linguistics and might also be used by graduate students who enter the field with little or no previous training. The book presupposes an introductory course in linguistics which covers the subject matter presented in my 1968 textbook, *Language and Its Structure*, or some comparable volume. Although there is no intrinsic connection between this book and *LAIS*, I have found it convenient to use the latter as a guide in determining what background material to present here in detail and what material to treat only briefly or omit altogether. For example, the basic phonetic symbols introduced in *LAIS* have been used here without comment, while others are explained in the text when they are first employed. The terminology and theoretical orientation of *LAIS* have also been adopted here, but for the most part the terms are standard ones and the theory is a general one that should prove compatible with the requirements of most instructors.

I have tried to make this text as general and flexible as possible, and it can be used in a number of ways. First, it can serve as the primary textbook for a course in linguistic analysis. As a supplementary text providing practical problems to accompany other course material, it should be appropriate for courses on various levels dealing with a variety of subject matter. Finally, teachers may find it useful as a reference manual, providing topics for class discussion and problems that can be adapted for exercises or examinations.

The book is intended for study rather than light reading, and it is contemplated that relatively few students will work through it without the guidance of an instructor. Problems with solutions are included in the text as pedagogical aids. They serve both to exemplify the substantive points under discussion and to show the student what to look for when working with linguistic data. These problems constitute an introduction to the series of problems without accompanying solutions that conclude each section. (Solutions to these problems are available, to instructors only, in a separate key.) The problems are arranged in increasing order of difficulty, but this gradation is highly subjective and should not be interpreted too rigorously.

One immediately faces a host of philosophical and practical decisions when conceiving and planning a book of this sort. Should the book concentrate on a single area, like syntax, or should it be more general? What theoretical orientation should be adopted? How much emphasis should be placed on procedural hints and "discovery procedures"? What format should be used for the problems? How should long vowels be written?

I cannot guarantee that I have made the correct philosophical decisions in all instances, nor can I hope to justify them fully in a few lines; but since these decisions directly determine the character of this book, it is appropriate that they at least be made explicit.

One or several volumes could easily be devoted to each of the topics covered here, namely lexical, syntactic, phonological, and diachronic analysis. The coverage of each of these topics is less inclusive and perhaps less satisfactory than it would have been had a whole book been devoted to it alone. However, a book dealing with just one area would have only limited usefulness, and it is questionable whether the degree of detail that could be presented in a book restricted to a single domain would really be appropriate at the undergraduate level. I believe, moreover, that there is some value to integrating all these facets of linguistic analysis in a single volume with a unified methodological and theoretical outlook.

The theoretical outlook adopted here requires some comment. The general orientation is transformational, and the version of transformational theory followed most closely is generative semantics; no distinction is made here between syntactic rules and semantic interpretation rules, and no special level of deep structure is posited between semantic and surface syntactic representations. I believe that this choice is justified on pedagogical grounds, and I have not made it solely on the basis of my own theoretical convictions, which do not coincide precisely with any current theory. Undergraduate instruction is not the place for detailed examination of competing linguistic theories, and close adherence to the controversial idiosyncrasies of any particular theory would be especially out of place in a book of this kind. Generative semantics is followed in its broad outlines primarily because this framework is conceptually the simplest. Nothing essential would be gained by the considerable expenditure of space and student credibility that would be required to introduce the distinction between syntactic and semantic rules or the notion of a level of deep structure distinct from semantic representations. In any event, the practical consequences of the choice from the instructor's standpoint should prove relatively minor. Problems that presuppose generative rather than interpretive semantics are confined almost entirely to the chapter on syntax, they are relatively few in number, and they are presented (I hope) in a reasonably non-provocative manner. Indeed, theory is de-emphasized to the point that most of the problems should be perfectly acceptable even to those of a non-transformational persuasion.

What has been emphasized here is the kinds of regularities found in language data and the importance of viewing this data in relation to underlying representations and rules that connect these representations with their surface manifestations. Unless the student is led to see the value of these abstract theoretical constructs, he cannot possibly appreciate the character of insightful linguistic analysis. Consequently, I have attached much more importance to the nature of linguistic argumentation and the nature of the evidence that can be adduced in support of rules and abstract structures than I have to specific procedures for manipulating data. Neither the problems nor the solutions follow a rigid format, and nothing resembling a battery of discovery procedures is offered. My personal conviction is that the intelligent student, left to his own devices with a collection of data that illustrates a structural regularity, is perfectly capable of finding this regularity on his own without having to be told how to proceed, especially when he has been given an idea of what to look for. While step-by-step procedures and hints about analytical techniques may help some students in the short run, in the long run the student is best served by being exposed to the powers of his own resourcefulness and creativity.

The noteworthy practical problems that attend the preparation of a book such as this all pertain to data: finding it, selecting it, organizing it, analyzing it, and transcribing it. In a book of this magnitude (190 problems involving some 90 languages), these problems are particularly acute.

I have taken data from many kinds of sources, including articles, monographs, practical grammars, dissertations, unpublished papers, personal communications, live informants, and my own intuitions. Naturally I cannot personally vouch for the full accuracy of every piece of data found in this book. However, I have used no sources whose validity was subject to serious question on my part, nor have I consciously altered or distorted the data my sources contain. I have rarely extrapolated from the data actually listed, and only in cases where explicit rules were given. In many instances I have used secondary sources even though primary sources exist. Secondary sources are convenient because of both their availability and their selectivity; very often they present interesting arrays of data culled from primary sources that would have remained buried and unnoticed had I employed only the latter. I have no reason to doubt the authenticity of the data obtained in this way, and the time and effort required to trace all the data back to its origins would have been prohibitive.

Many difficulties arise in dealing with data from so many sources, and even the data obtained from my own intuitions is not problem-free. One source of difficulty is dialectal variation. I am sure, for example, that not all users of this book will accede to all my judgments of grammaticality concerning English. I must ask students and instructors to accept as given the data from English (and any other language in which dialectal conflicts arise) for purposes of working the problems. Once they have been worked, it may prove profitable to discuss the dialectal differences and explore their consequences for the analysis.

Assuring the correctness of an analysis is never an easy matter. This problem has been compounded for me by the fact that I have had to handle data from a wide variety of languages with which I am not personally familiar and by the necessity of providing analyses that are simple enough and sufficiently self-contained to serve as solutions for problems in an undergraduate text. It is conceivable that some of the analyses, whether they are my own or have been adapted from the work of other linguists, are basically incorrect. It is certainly the case that some of these analyses will not prove fully general, though they are perfectly valid for the data presented. I have tried to convey to the student the notion that no problem is fully self-contained and that the adequacy of linguistic descriptions is consequently not a matter of absolutes but one of degree, and these remarks apply with special force to the analyses in this book. However, I have not knowingly adopted any solutions that are plainly wrong in major respects. My aim throughout has been to lead students to construct analyses which are defensible for the data presented and could in principle be fully general.

Transcription has been an especially difficult matter. Part of the difficulty lies in dealing with the variability and occasional indeterminacy of the transcriptions employed in the references I have consulted. Needless to say, every writer has his own transcriptional preferences. Moreover, many do not always state the values of the symbols they use, and some do not even make it clear whether their transcription is phonetic, phonemic, orthographic, or some combination thereof. The remainder of the difficulty lies in devising a unified system of transcriptions and notations sufficiently flexible to do the many different jobs required of it, yet sufficiently precise, simple, and straightforward to be pedagogically useful. My solution to these problems may not be optimal, but it certainly requires explanation.

I have employed two basic types of transcription, phonetic and orthographic. However, the phonetic transcriptions are not strictly phonetic, nor are the orthographic transcriptions strictly orthographic. The phonetic transcriptions are in general fairly broad, but they range from narrow phonetic through phonemic, and the amount of detail they specify varies in accordance with the requirements of individual problems. Phonetic distinctions marked in the data for one problem may be omitted in another. For example, I have generally omitted markings for stress in syntactic problems (for which lexical stress is seldom pertinent), even for those languages in which I have marked stress elsewhere. I have treated a transcription as orthographic when it represents a standard orthography or when I have not had sufficient information to determine how to translate it into the system of phonetic transcription adopted here.

Phonetic and orthographic transcriptions are not specially marked in tabular arrays of data, including in particular the list of data for each problem. In the text, however, phonetic transcriptions are included in square brackets ([]) while orthographic transcriptions are italicized. With the exception of commas to mark clause boundaries, I have used capitalization and punctuation only for standard orthographic representations with which the reader is likely to be familiar, such as those of English and French. Hyphens are often employed to mark morpheme boundaries in either type of transcription. In order to facilitate comprehension, I have sometimes included literal word-by-word or morpheme-by-morpheme glosses beneath the phonetic or orthographic transcription of an expression. When the transcription and literal gloss contain different numbers of elements, braces (‿ or ⁀) are used to group together the sequence of elements that corresponds to a single element in the other representation.

After complaining at some length about the difficulties involved in writing a book of this kind, I should like to conclude by acknowledging the various people who have contributed in one way or another to making the chore less onerous than it might otherwise have been. A number of people have been kind enough to supply me with problems, data, intuitions, or papers from which relevant data could be extracted; these include William Bright, Kenneth

Hale, Benjamin T'sou, Eric Hamp, S. -Y. Kuroda, and Jo-Ann Flora. Special thanks are due to Mrs. Villiana Hyde, from whom I have learned what little I know about Luiseño. More generally, I must acknowledge the many scholars on whose work I have drawn, as well as the students whom I have subjected to various problems. Arlene Jacobs is to be commended for her courage and patience in typing a substantial portion of the manuscript. Finally, my wife Peggy is to be cited for the same reason, and also for the many other ways in which she has helped.

R.W.L.

Contents

Notations

Most of the special notations used in this book are explained in the text when they first occur, but they are summarized here for ease of reference. The great majority are standard linguistic notations. However, no attempt has been made to include standard notations not employed in this book.

PHONETIC NOTATIONS

The phonetic symbols employed here are of three kinds: segmental symbols, diacritics, and boundary symbols. Diacritics accompany segmental symbols as subscripts or superscripts and qualify their phonetic values. Boundary symbols are written between segmental symbols.

Segmental Symbols

The precise value of the segmental symbols listed below may vary somewhat depending on the phonetic detail of the language and the requirements of individual problems. Some of the finer distinctions, such as the distinction between tense and lax vowels, are not always made notationally when they do not bear on the matter under consideration. [e], for example, always designates a tense mid front vowel when it is used in contrast to [ɛ], but when it is not contrasted with [ɛ], [e] may be either tense or lax. In some instances, the notational distinctions labeled tense versus lax in the vowel chart below may be used instead for gradations of height.

Vowel Symbols

		UN-ROUNDED	ROUNDED		UN-ROUNDED	ROUNDED
HIGH	Tense	i	ü		ɨ	u
	Lax	ɪ				ʊ
MID	Tense	e	ö	ə	ë	o
	Lax	ɛ	ɔ̈		ʌ	ɔ
LOW		æ			a	
		FRONT		CENTRAL	BACK	

In some instances, the notational distinctions labeled voiceless versus voiced in the consonant chart on p. xv may be used instead to differentiate tense and lax consonants.

Consonant Symbols

		BILABIAL	LABIO-DENTAL	DENTAL	ALVEOLAR	PALATAL	VELAR	UVULAR	PHARYNGEAL	GLOTTAL
STOP	Voiceless	p			t		k	q		ʔ
	Voiced	b			d		g			
FRICATIVE	Voiceless		f	θ	s	š	x	x̣	ħ	h
	Voiced	β	v	ð	z	ž	γ	ɣ		
AFFRICATE	Voiceless				c	č				
	Voiced				ʒ	ǰ				
LATERAL	Voiceless				L					
	Voiced				l					
NASAL		m			n	ñ	ŋ			
GLIDE		w				y				

Several consonant symbols cannot be adequately accommodated in the chart above:

r Any *r*-like sound (it has not been necessary to distinguish them in this book). It may be an alveolar flap or trill; a uvular trill or uvular friction; or a sound like the English *r*, which involves a special tongue configuration but no oral obstruction or friction.

ƛ Voiceless lateral affricate.

D Voiced stop produced by rapidly flapping the tongue against the alveolar ridge.

Diacritics

The special symbols *c* and *v* are used here to show the position of diacritics. They stand for consonant symbols and vowel symbols respectively.

    ç   Voiceless.
    c̦   Syllabic.
    c̣   Articulated farther toward the front than usual.
    y̨   Articulated as a glide.
    c̣   Retroflex. Articulated farther toward the back than usual.
    $c^{\text{ʔ}}$ Glottalized.
    c^{h} Aspirated.
    c^{y} Palatalized.
    c^{w} Labialized or rounded.
    c^{1} Unreleased.
    c′   Tense.
    $c^{\text{ə}}$ Offglide toward mid central position.
    c̃   Palatalized.
    ṽ   Nasalized.
    v̈   Opposite of usual value for front-back feature.
    c̄   Glottalized and implosive.
    v̄   Long.
    cc   Long.
    vv   Long.

Stress:

    v́   Primary stress.
    v̂   Secondary degree of stress.
    v̀   Tertiary degree of stress.
    v̆   Weakly stressed or unstressed.
    v̋   Focus stress.
    v‴   Emphatic or contrastive stress.

Tone (notations vary from language to language):

    v́   High. Rising. High rising.
    v̂   Mid. Falling. Mid-high trailing.
    v̆   Rising. Low falling-rising.
    v̀   Low. Mid. Falling. Low trailing.
    v̄   High.

Boundary Symbols

    +   Boundary between two elements of compound.
    -   Morpheme boundary.
    .   Syllable boundary.

NON-PHONETIC NOTATIONS

Lexical

=	Lexical rule.
$\emptyset$	Zero.
-	Morpheme boundary.

Syntactic

$\Rightarrow$	Syntactic (transformational) rule.
*	Ungrammatical.
[ ]	Subordinate clause.
S	Sentence. Clause. Proposition.
PRED	Predicate.
ARG	Argument.
N	Noun.
V	Verb.
ADJ	Adjective.
P	Preposition.
ART	Article.
ADV	Adverb.
PRON	Pronoun.
NP	Noun phrase or nominal.
VP	Verb phrase.
PP	Prepositional phrase.
REL	Relative clause marker.
ABS	Absolutive suffix.
NOM	Nominative case.
ACC	Accusative case.
ERG	Ergative case.
X, Y	Arbitrary symbols that can stand for any element or any sequence of elements.
$X_i \, Y_i$	X and Y are coreferential.
$X_i \, Y_j$	X and Y are non-coreferential.

Phonological

$\longrightarrow$	Phonological rule. (Also used in diagrams of rule ordering.)
C	Consonant.
V	Vowel.
/ /	Phonemic or phonological representation.
[ ]	Any phonological transcription, ranging in detail or abstractness from narrow phonetic through phonemic.

Diachronic

X > Y   X becomes Y historically.
Y < X   Y derives from X historically.
  *   Reconstructed.

Problems

Asterisks mark the numbers of problems whose solutions are included in the text.

Chapter 3

Chapter 4

Chapter 5

Fundamentals
of Linguistic
Analysis

1

Preliminaries

A language is a set of principles relating meanings and phonetic sequences. These internalized principles enable the speakers of a language to exchange ideas by means of speech sounds. Modern linguistics is based on the fundamental empirical fact that languages are elaborately and intricately structured. Linguistic analysis is the attempt to discover and describe language structure, to elucidate the pattern and regularity that inhere in the sound-meaning correlations of languages. Most basically, this is what linguistics is all about.

The purpose of this book is to enable you to share to some degree the experience of linguistic analysis. Only by personally struggling with language data can you come to appreciate the nature of linguistic investigation and its achievements; and only by winning some struggles, by discovering for yourself some of the regularities of language structure, can you begin to realize why linguists find enough satisfaction in the study of grammar to choose it over more lucrative professions such as jewel robbery or television repair. Reading about linguistics is no substitute for doing linguistics, and doing linguistics is what this book is all about. To be sure, linguistics is a rather specialized enterprise, one that is not likely to appeal to everybody. The analysis of grammatical systems is in no immediate danger of replacing professional football as the national pastime.

Naturally, there are limits on what a single book can accomplish in this regard. To be pedagogically useful, problems must be simplified and isolated artificially from the total linguistic system. Certain facets of linguistic investigation, such as the discovery of language universals, are simply not amenable to treatment in problem form. Furthermore, practical considerations make it necessary to exclude any examination of the problems and methods of many linguistic subdisciplines, such as psycholinguistics, applied linguistics, phonetics, etymology, the study of writing systems, and so on.

This book will be concerned solely with selected aspects of descriptive and historical linguistics. The problems will therefore pertain to the structure of individual languages at a given point in time or to the historical relationships obtaining between related languages or between different historical stages of the same language. The emphasis throughout will be on discovering the regularities that underlie linguistic data, on recognizing pattern and structure. No attempt will be made to examine the intricacies of any particular version of linguistic theory; consequently, these exercises should prove compatible with a wide spectrum of theoretical viewpoints.

If this book is successful, it will teach you how linguists think when they analyze linguistic data. It will help you to understand how linguistic discoveries are made, by allowing you to make such discoveries. Moreover, it will introduce you to the nature of linguistic argumentation and show you how claims regarding the structure of a language can be justified. Finally, it will teach you something substantive about how languages are put together.

1.1   *Language Structure*

Languages are elaborately structured. Neither the character of a language nor its historical evolution can be adequately described or understood unless its structure is taken into account. These facts are obvious to anyone who has studied descriptive and historical linguistics in depth, but the linguistic novice is sometimes puzzled. "What does it mean to say that languages are structured?" "How are they structured?" "I don't see any structure." "Aren't you interested in the derivation of words?" The difficulty is simply that the novice does not know what to look for. The structured character of language will be apparent to him once the nature of this structure is pointed out. We will begin therefore by looking at some examples of language structure.

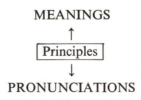

MEANINGS

↑

Principles

↓

PRONUNCIATIONS

Figure 1.1–1

A language is a set of principles that relate meanings and pronunciations, as shown in Figure 1.1–1. Because the speaker of a language has internalized this set of principles, he is able to translate his thoughts into observable utterances and to deduce the intended meaning of the utterances of others.

It is customary and helpful to discuss the structure of a language in terms of *components,* though any such division represents an oversimplification. We will speak of the *lexical, syntactic,* and *phonological* components of a language. Each component consists in a series of *rules* or *principles*—two terms that will be used more or less interchangeably in this book. A rule or principle is a regularity in the structure of a language. These terms also designate the statements linguists make to describe linguistic regularities; since no confusion is likely to result, the terms will be used here in both senses. The speaker of a language is able to create and understand novel sentences, that is, sentences that have never before occurred in his linguistic experience, just because the sound-meaning correlations of his language are governed by rules rather than being random and arbitrary.

LEXICAL RULES

Some rules are quite general and come into play in determining the form of virtually every sentence in a language. (A syntactic rule requiring that a verb agree with its subject is an example.) Other rules are less general and function in the derivation of some sentences but not others. There is no sharp dichotomy between general and non-general rules, but only a continuum from the fully general to the highly idiosyncratic. *Lexical items* (such as words, morphemes, compounds, and idioms) can be viewed as rules of very limited generality.

A lexical item pairs a meaning with a pronunciation. In the case of morphemes and some complex lexical items (idioms in particular), such pairings are arbitrary or conventional—there is no way to predict, on the basis of other regularities in the language, which meaning will be paired with which pronunciation. There is nevertheless an important sense in which a lexical item embodies a linguistic regularity and can therefore be viewed as a rule. Namely, the sound-meaning correlation that it represents in the language is constant; it does not vary randomly from one sentence to the next. Roughly speaking, a given meaning can be represented by the same phonological form in any sentence in which the meaning figures. This is a special sort of regularity, and a lexical item can consequently be viewed as a special sort of rule. In accordance with standard practice, however, the term *lexical item* will often be used in preference to *lexical rule.*

Let us consider one simple example, from Spanish. The following sentences are given in a very broad (non-detailed) phonetic transcription, and their meanings are represented by English glosses.

unómbreestábaakí	'A man was here.'
béoadósómbres	'I see two men.'
éstosómbressónintelixéntes	'These men are intelligent.'
elómbrenótrabáxa	'The man isn't working.'

These four sentences all have a component of meaning in common, which we can symbolize as 'man'. Examining these sentences, we find that they also share a component of pronunciation—the phonetic sequence [ómbre] occurs in all four sentences. On the basis of these observations, we can hypothesize the following lexical rule:

'man' = ómbre

That is, the meaning 'man' may be manifested phonologically as [ómbre]. The hypothesized rule may or may not turn out to be correct. Only by testing a hypothesis over a much wider range of data can we determine its validity. In the relatively simple case of lexical items and their meanings, the intuitions of a native speaker can generally be trusted; any speaker of Spanish can affirm that [ómbre] means 'man'. However, the validity of rules, even of lexical rules, cannot always be established on the basis of native intuition alone. We will return many times to the matter of justifying hypothesized rules.

Lexical regularities of the sort just illustrated are so ubiquitous and so obvious that speakers tend to take them for granted. Thus it is important to emphasize that the constancy of sound-meaning correspondences at the lexical level is not a logical necessity but rather an empirical fact of great consequence. It would be logically possible for 'man' to be manifested as [ómbre] in one sentence, as [gáto] in another, as [árboles] in a third, and so on indefinitely. We may speculate as to why lexical sound-meaning correlations do not vary randomly from sentence to sentence (for instance, we could observe that this would make languages tremendously difficult if not impossible to learn), but our speculations in no way diminish the fundamental importance of this empirically determined fact.

Lexical items will be considered more fully in Chapter 2.

SYNTACTIC RULES

The meaning of a sentence is referred to as its **semantic representation** or its **conceptual structure.** Although relatively little is known about semantic representations, some facts are quite evident. It is clear, for example, that the semantic representation of a sentence is a structured entity in which the meanings of individual lexical items function as components. Thus the meanings of *the*, *girl*, *believe*, and *PRESENT* (the present tense morpheme) all figure in the semantic representation of sentence (1).

(1) The girl believes.

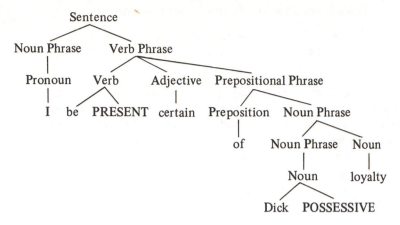

Figure 1.1–2

It is equally apparent that the meanings of individual lexical items are not exhaustive of the conceptual structure of a sentence. For instance, (2) and (3) contain the same lexical items, and the meaning of each item is the same in both sentences, but the two sentences have very different senses.

> (2) The boy knows the girl believes.
> (3) The girl believes the boy knows.

To account for this, it is necessary to assume that the meaning of a sentence is greater than the sum of the meanings of its parts; in addition to the meanings of individual lexical items, the semantic representation of a sentence includes the configuration of these components, the way in which they are arranged with respect to one another. Semantic representations will be discussed in more detail at the beginning of Chapter 3.

Much more is known about the surface form of sentences. The *surface structure* of a sentence consists in a string of lexical items grouped into hierarchically arranged units called *constituents*. Figure 1.1–2, for instance, represents the surface structure of (4).

> (4) I am certain of Dick's loyalty.

Although many details are open to question, diagrams like Figure 1.1–2 must be at least approximately correct.

Even in the absence of a detailed characterization of semantic representations, it is evident that the conceptual and surface structures of sentences are not congruent. Ambiguous sentences, such as (5), show this quite clearly; since two or more distinct conceptual structures are associated with the same surface structure, the conceptual and surface structures cannot be identical.

Paraphrases like (6) and (7) lead to the same conclusion.

> (5) Martha likes Elvin more than Sue.
> (6) That he breathes often is true.
> (7) It is true that he breathes often.

Further indication of the discrepancies between surface structures and the semantic representations that underlie them is provided by sentences in which meaningless elements appear in surface structure, in which certain components of meaning have no surface manifestation, or in which semantic units are split up into non-contiguous surface constituents. All three phenomena are illustrated in sentence (8).

> (8) There are three letters on the table which you should answer before leaving.

There is generally analyzed as a meaningless element that appears in certain sentences which would otherwise have indefinite surface subjects. The suffix *ing* of *leaving* is likewise a meaningless element, one that marks subordinate clauses. *You* is understood semantically to be the subject of both *answer* and *leaving*, but it occurs overtly only with the former. Finally, *three letters which you should answer before leaving* constitutes a semantic unit, but in surface structure it appears split up into two non-contiguous constituents, *three letters* and *which you should answer before leaving*. Compare (8) with its paraphrase, (9).

> (9) Three letters which you should answer before you leave are on the table.

The semantic representation of these sentences is reflected much more directly in (9) than in (8).

Two kinds of rules serve to relate meanings and surface structures: lexical rules and syntactic rules. By virtue of lexical rules, components of the meaning of a sentence are associated with phonological forms; thus the meaning component 'man' can be associated with the form [ómbre] in Spanish. Syntactic rules, on the other hand, account for the configurational differences between surface structures and semantic representations. This scheme is depicted in Figure 1.1–3.

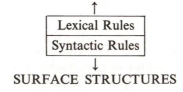

SEMANTIC REPRESENTATIONS

↑

| Lexical Rules |
| Syntactic Rules |

↓

SURFACE STRUCTURES

Figure 1.1–3

Syntactic rules modify semantic representations in various ways and there-by determine the surface configuration of sentences. In (8), for example, syntactic rules of English are responsible for inserting *there* and *ing*, for deleting the subject *you* of *leaving*, and for splitting up the nominal *three letters which you should answer before leaving* into two parts. The surface structure of a sentence is thus the cumulative product of a series of lexical and syntactic rules, each of which modifies an underlying representation in some way, making it more like its ultimate surface form.

We see, then, that the surface structure of a sentence is most insightfully viewed in relation to the structures that underlie it. These include both the conceptual structure and a sequence of intermediate structures representing the "outputs" of the various rules that apply in the derivation of the ultimate surface form. Not all syntactic rules introduce radical differences between the semantic and surface structures of sentences; many just specify the fine detail of surface structures, including such things as agreement and word order. It follows that some underlying representations are not appreciably more ab-stract than surface structures and do not reflect semantic representations much more directly than do surface forms. It is often possible to justify hypothesized underlying representations of this sort on the basis of purely syntactic evidence.

Consider the following data from English. An asterisk marks a sentence as ungrammatical.

(10) (a) I am certain of Dick's loyalty.
    (b) I am certain of Dick's being loyal.
    (c) I am certain of it.
    (d) *I am certain Dick's loyalty.
    (e) *I am certain of that Dick is loyal.
    (f) I am certain that Dick is loyal.

(11) (a) He is disturbed at Dick's loyalty.
    (b) He is disturbed at Dick's being loyal.
    (c) He is disturbed at it.
    (d) *He is disturbed Dick's loyalty.
    (e) *He is disturbed at that Dick is loyal.
    (f) He is disturbed that Dick is loyal.

(12) (a) My aunt is ecstatic over Dick's loyalty.
    (b) My aunt is ecstatic over Dick's being loyal.
    (c) My aunt is ecstatic over it.
    (d) *My aunt is ecstatic Dick's loyalty.
    (e) *My aunt is ecstatic over that Dick is loyal.
    (f) My aunt is ecstatic that Dick is loyal.

On the basis of sentences (10)(a)–(10)(c), it appears that the adjective *certain* can be followed by a prepositional phrase consisting of the preposition *of* and a noun phrase (*NP*). (The embedded clauses in this data, *Dick's being loyal* and *that Dick is loyal*, function syntactically as noun phrases. See Chapter 3, p. *144* .) The ungrammaticality of (10) (d) seems to indicate that *certain* cannot be followed directly by a noun phrase; *of* must intervene. Similarly, in example (11) *disturbed* can be followed by *at NP* but not by *NP* alone, and in (12) *ecstatic* allows *over NP* but not *NP* by itself. The (a)–(d) sentences therefore follow a consistent pattern: The sequence *ADJ P NP* is grammatical, but **ADJ NP* is ungrammatical.

However, the (e)–(f) sentences seem to upset this regularity. In the (e) sentences the sequence **ADJ P NP* is ungrammatical, and the (f) sentences are well formed (that is, grammatical) despite the fact that they contain the sequence *ADJ NP*. Must we therefore give up the generalization that adjectives allow prepositional phrases as complements but do not allow naked noun phrases? Must we admit that the occurrence of prepositions with adjectives is random and does not follow any pattern?

Clearly not. The distribution of prepositions in examples (10)–(12) is anything but random, for the violations of the general pattern established above are themselves quite regular. Both discrepancies in the general pattern are consistently associated with the presence of a subordinate clause headed by the subordinating particle *that;* when a *that* clause is present in surface structure, the preposition is not permissible, and the preposition can be omitted only when the noun phrase consists of a *that* clause.

$$
\text{ADJ P} \left\{ \begin{array}{l} \text{Dick's loyalty} \\ \text{Dick's being loyal} \\ \text{it} \\ \text{*that Dick is loyal} \end{array} \right\} \qquad \text{ADJ} \left\{ \begin{array}{l} \text{*Dick's loyalty} \\ \text{*Dick's being loyal} \\ \text{*it} \\ \text{that Dick is loyal} \end{array} \right\}
$$

Because this pattern holds regardless of the identity of the adjective and preposition, it represents a syntactic rule rather than lexical idiosyncrasies.

One way to express this regularity is to posit for English a syntactic rule which deletes the preposition that normally accompanies an adjective when this preposition occurs directly before the subordinating particle *that*. The double arrow symbolizes the application of a syntactic rule.

ADJ P that X $\Rightarrow$ ADJ that X

By positing this preposition deletion rule, we can account for both apparent anomalies simultaneously, the deviance of **ADJ P that X* and the grammaticality of *ADJ that X*. When the *NP* in the pattern *ADJ P NP* happens to be a *that* clause, preposition deletion elides the preposition; for this reason, **ADJ P that X* does not occur in surface structure. However, as the output of the preposition deletion rule, *ADJ that X* does occur in surface structure. The deviance of **ADJ P that X* constitutes a gap in an otherwise regular pattern, and *ADJ that X* fills this gap. In terms of this analysis, the two surface discrepancies are seen to be automatic consequences of the application of a single general rule. We have replaced two apparent irregularities with a general principle.

Let us therefore postulate for English an obligatory syntactic rule that deletes a preposition when it precedes the subordinating particle *that*. For each of the (f) sentences above, we will hypothesize an underlying structure containing an appropriate preposition; the obligatory application of the preposition deletion rule will account for the failure of the preposition to show up in surface structure. The derivation of sentence (10) (f) from its underlying

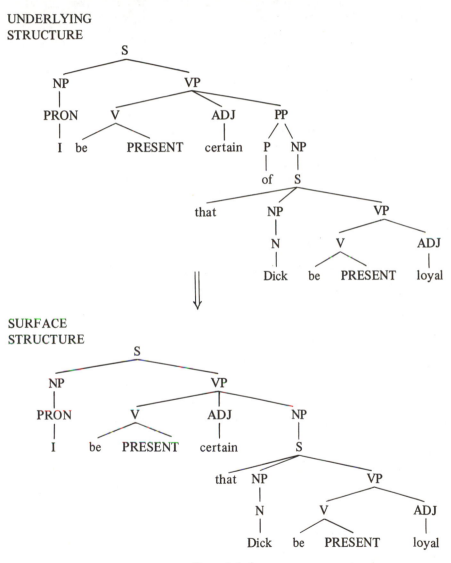

Figure 1.1–4

structure is sketched in Figure 1.1–4, in which the double arrow symbolizes the rule of preposition deletion. The surface structure of sentence (10) (f) is said to **derive from** the underlying structure by the rule of preposition deletion. (Once the preposition is deleted, there is no longer any reason to speak of a prepositional phrase—consequently there is no constituent labeled *PP* in the surface structure.)

The underlying structure postulated for sentence (10) (f) is not to be equated with the semantic representation of this sentence; the phenomenon of preposition deletion is a fairly superficial one, and the underlying structure does not reflect the semantics of the sentence much more directly than the surface structure does. By setting up underlying structures and the rule of preposition deletion, we have accomplished only a minute portion of the syntactic analysis of sentences like (10) (f), (11) (f), and (12) (f). Many other syntactic and lexical rules function in the derivation of such sentences from their semantic representations.

However, we have attained the more limited goal of accounting for the regularities in the distribution of prepositions in sentences like (10)–(12). Our analysis captures the following generalizations: (i) The grammatical sentences in (10)–(12) all have analogous underlying structures; in particular, the (f) sentences, like the (a), (b), and (c) sentences, have prepositions in their underlying structure (compare Figures 1.1–2 and 1.1–4). (ii) The pattern *ADJ P NP* is permissible, but the pattern *ADJ NP is not. This generalization does not hold at the level of surface structure, but it does hold at the level of underlying representations. (iii) Two apparent anomalies—the unexpected deviance of *ADJ P that X and the unexpected acceptability of *ADJ that X*—are shown to be consequences of the fact that an obligatory rule deletes prepositions before *that*. Hence postulating this one simple rule has the highly desirable effect of regularizing underlying representations and explaining two separate distributional anomalies.

The rule of preposition deletion can therefore be strongly supported. It is justified, not because native speakers are consciously aware of it (for they are not), but because it is a simple and natural rule that allows us to establish order in what previously appeared to be an unordered set of facts. When linguists resort to abstract rules and underlying representations, it is always in the attempt to capture the regularities implicit in linguistic data.

PHONOLOGICAL RULES

The surface structure of a sentence consists of a sequence of lexical items grouped into constituents. Despite its name, a surface structure is a highly abstract entity. When we hear the sentence *I am certain of Dick's loyalty*, we do not hear the tree structure in Figure 1.1–2; all we hear is a sequence of sounds reflecting the **phonetic manifestation** or **phonetic representation** of this sentence. The relationship between surface structures and phonetic representations is specified by phonological rules. Figure 1.1–5 summarizes the organization of linguistic systems. This sketch (which supersedes Figure 1.1–1) is still oversimplified in various ways, but it will serve for present purposes.

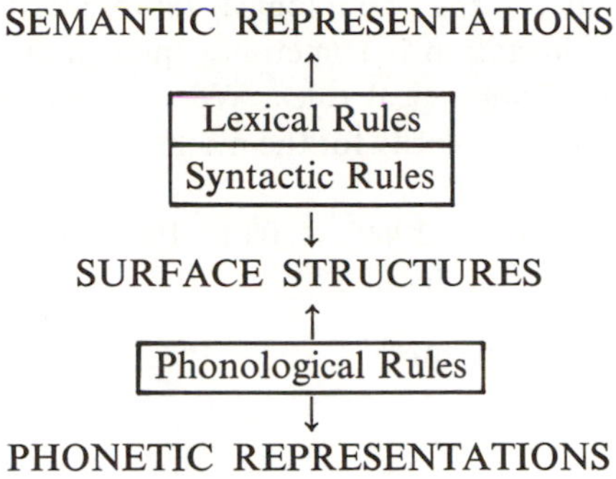

SEMANTIC REPRESENTATIONS

↑

| Lexical Rules |
| Syntactic Rules |

↓

SURFACE STRUCTURES

↑

| Phonological Rules |

↓

PHONETIC REPRESENTATIONS

Figure 1.1–5

Each of the lexical items in the surface structure of a sentence consists in the association of semantic, syntactic, and phonological properties. We may speak of the **semantic, syntactic,** and **phonological representations** of a lexical item. The semantic representation of a lexical item is simply its meaning. The syntactic representation of a lexical item is the set of properties that determine how it interacts with the syntactic rules and structures of the language; for example, the English word *certain* functions as an adjective and allows an accompanying prepositional phrase with *of*—these are two properties in the set that constitutes its syntactic representation. The phonological representation of a lexical item comprises the idiosyncratic phonological characteristics that have to be learned individually for that lexical item. It consists of **contrastive** or **distinctive** phonological properties, properties that are not predictable on the basis of general rules and that serve to distinguish lexical items from one another in the language. (Consequently, the lexical rule cited earlier for Spanish is not entirely correct; the meaning 'man' is directly associated not with the phonetic representation [ómbre] but rather with the more abstract phonological representation that underlies it, as well as with the syntactic properties of this morpheme.) For example, the information that *certain* begins with a fricative is part of its phonological representation; there is no way to predict this on the basis of general rules. On the other hand, the information that this fricative is non-pharyngealized is not included in its phonological representation, because it is a general principle of English phonology that no segments are pharyngealized.

The phonetic manifestation of a lexical item depends on three things: its phonological representation, the surrounding environment, and the phonological rules of the language. Phonological rules are regularities that hold not just for individual lexical items but for all the lexical items of the language (or at least for a whole class of items—not all phonological rules are fully general). They modify the phonological representations of individual lexical items in various ways, sometimes taking into account the phonological properties of adjoining lexical items or certain characteristics of the syntactic structure. The relation between the phonological representation of a lexical item and its phonetic manifestation is sometimes quite indirect, being mediated by a whole chain of phonological rules. We will consider only one simple example of phonological regularity for the moment, returning to phonological rules in Chapter 4.

The data below (Saxton, 1969) is from Papago, an American Indian language of the Uto-Aztecan family.

čɨposid	'to brand, mark'
čikpan	'to work'
takui	'yucca leaves'
toha	'white'
čɨwagi	'cloud'
čuk	'black'
tohono	'desert'
čuawi	'ground squirrel'
tatk	'roots'
čia	'hail'

The symbol [ɨ] stands for a vowel sound like the English [u], except that the lips are not rounded (that is, it is a high back unrounded vowel); the other symbols have, at least approximately, their standard phonetic values.

Examining this data, we discover a correlation between the consonants [t] and [č] and the segments that follow. [č] occurs only before high vowels (that is, before [i ɨ u]), and [t] never occurs before high vowels. We find [t] before the non-high vowels [a o] and also before the consonant [k], but never before [i ɨ u]; on the other hand, we find [č] before [i ɨ u], but never before [a o] or a consonant. [t] and [č] appear to be in ***complementary distribution;*** that is, they never occur in the same phonetic environment. Since we have examined only ten words, this regularity might very well be an accident due to our small range of data. In fact, however, it proves to be perfectly typical of the whole language.

It is apparent from these observations that the difference between [t] and [č] is not distinctive in Papago. Since the two consonants never occur in the same environment, the difference between them can never be the sole difference distinguishing two lexical items. Moreover, the regularity in their distribution indicates that we are dealing with a phonological rule rather than lexical idiosyncrasies. The information that a given lexical item is pronounced with [č] rather than [t] need not be included as part of the phonological representation of that item because it is possible to formulate a general rule that predicts when [č] will occur instead of [t]—namely, before high vowels. This represents a general phonological principle of Papago that holds true for all forms in the language.

The segment [č] can be analyzed as the phonetic variant of [t] that occurs when the following segment is a high vowel. In their underlying phonological representations, all the morphemes given above will have [t] as their initial segment. In order to account for the phonetic facts, we can postulate the following phonological rule: [t] is manifested as [č] before a high vowel. This means that [čia] 'hail', to take just one example, will have the derivation shown in Figure 1.1–6. The arrow symbolizes the rule changing [t] to [č].

PHONOLOGICAL   PHONETIC
REPRESENTATION   REPRESENTATION

tia   ⟶   čia

Figure 1.1–6

By postulating these abstract underlying representations and a phonological rule that derives their phonetic manifestations, we express the regularities found in the data. Instead of positing two different underlying segments, [t] and [č], each with defective distributions that just happen to be complementary, we only have to set up one underlying segment, [t], with no unusual restriction on the environments in which it can occur. We would surely be missing a generalization if we were to claim that the complementary distribution of [t] and [č] is mere coincidence; we capture this generalization by means of the rule changing [t] to [č] before high vowels. The hypothesized rule thus makes underlying phonological representations more uniform and serves to express regularities of linguistic structure that would otherwise go unnoted. To the extent that this is the case, such theoretical constructs are justified.

There are two reasons why it seems preferable to posit [t] rather than [č] in the underlying representations. First, [t] is phonetically simpler and more common than [č], and the rule changing [t] to [č] before high vowels is not an unusual one viewed in cross-linguistic terms (the word *tune* is pronounced [čun] in some dialects of English, to cite just one parallel instance). Second, in terms of environment it is simpler to state a rule changing [t] to [č] than a rule changing [č] to [t]; [t] becomes [č] before high vowels. A rule changing [č] to [t] would have to be made to apply before either non-high vowels or consonants. A simple rule is always preferable to a more complex rule, other things being equal.

DIACHRONIC INVESTIGATION

Synchronic linguistic investigation involves analyzing and describing the structure of a language at a single point in time; the rules discussed above were all synchronic rules. **Diachronic** investigation concerns the historical changes that occur in the structure of a language. Ultimately, diachronic investigation presupposes synchronic investigation, but the reverse is not necessarily true. In order to appreciate the historical changes that affect a linguistic system, it is essential to know and compare the structure of the system at two or more points in time. However, it is not necessary to know the history of a language in order to be able to describe it. After all, children learn to talk despite their complete ignorance regarding the historical origins of their native tongue.

A language is a system of rules, and historical changes in the structure of a language are therefore changes in a system of rules. Some linguistic changes affect non-general rules and consequently have only minimal effect; a change in the meaning of a lexical item is an example. Other changes affect general rules and may have sweeping effect. When change takes place through the addition, loss, or modification of general rules, differences between earlier and later stages of a language will tend to follow regular patterns. We will examine regularities of this sort in Chapter 5.

Let us consider the following data from Burmese (Burling, 1967). The forms in the first column below are from Proto Burmish, from which modern Burmese derives; they were reconstructed by comparing Burmese forms with their cognates in related languages (see Problem 5.4–11, p. 347). The forms in the second column are the Burmese descendants of the older forms. [c] stands for an alveolar affricate and tones are left unmarked, being irrelevant to the point at hand.

Proto Burmish	Burmese	
cin	si	'drum'
ca	sa	'eat'
cun	sun	'kite (bird)'
cum	soun	'pair'
co	souzan	'rule'
cu	su	'thorn'
cwe	swe	'tooth'

It is apparent from a glance at the data that the corresponding forms in the two columns are related in a regular way. Wherever Proto Burmish has [c], the corresponding Burmese form has [s], and conversely (we will ignore the other differences). This correspondence is not idiosyncratic to individual lexical items; rather it holds true for all lexical items represented at both stages of the language. The historical change responsible for the Burmese forms involved a general phonological rule and was not restricted to a single lexical item. We can hypothesize that the change consisted in the addition of the following rule to the phonological system of the language:

$$[c] \rightarrow [s]$$

That is, the underlying segment [c] is manifested phonetically as [s]. The correspondence is regular because the change involved the adoption of a general rule.

It is not necessarily the case that [c] → [s] is still a synchronic rule of Burmese. Somewhere along the line, children learning Burmese may have stopped postulating underlying phonological representations with [c] and the rule changing [c] to [s] and started to postulate underlying representations with [s]. Such a development depends on whether or not phonological regularities of Burmese continued to dictate the need for underlying representations with [c] and the hypothesized rule, and this can be determined only by a synchronic analysis of the language. In any event, the addition of this general rule to the phonology of Burmese has left its trace in the regularity of the correspondence.

1.2 Linguistic Analysis

If the purpose of this section were to describe a set of sure-fire techniques or procedures for discovering the rules of a language, these pages would have to be left blank. There are no mechanical procedures guaranteed to yield insightful results, no algorithms that would make it possible to replace linguists with computers. The conception and evaluation of scientific theories is an art that requires a combination of imagination and intellectual discipline, and this is just as true of linguistic investigation as of any other science. For this reason no attempt will be made here to present a recipe or manual of hints and procedures to follow in analyzing linguistic data; our time will be better spent examining some of the factors that come into play when one goes about the very complex business of linguistic analysis.

DATA

The linguistic description of a language is called a ***grammar***. A grammar can be regarded as a theory of the structure of a language. Synchronic analysis therefore involves the formulation and evaluation of theories about how languages are put together, while diachronic analysis involves theories pertaining to the evolution of linguistic systems. A theory must be based on the data it purports to explain, but the relationship between data and theory is not necessarily direct or simple. It is thus appropriate for us to examine the nature of linguistic data and its relation to theories that purport to account for it.

Three basic kinds of data may be available to the linguist when he analyzes a language: spoken utterances, written texts, and the intuitive or introspective judgments of native speakers. As in any empirical science, the data is necessarily incomplete and imperfect; consequently, it must be approached with a certain degree of skepticism and cannot always be taken at face value.

The incompleteness of the data available to the linguist should require little comment. No matter how many utterances he manages to capture with his tape recorder or with pencil and paper, no matter how many written texts he scans, the sentences he observes will never exhaust the grammatical expressions of the language. The observed data on which a grammar is based is necessarily finite, as is the grammar itself, but the rules of a language project to an infinite number of sentences. Moreover, the number of sentences is not the only source of incompleteness in linguistic data. Regardless of how many sentences are examined, the linguist can never be sure that he has come across all the lexical items of the language or all the sentence types that exist. These limitations hold even when the linguist is analyzing his native language and serving as his own informant; no matter how thorough he tries to be, some lexical items and some grammatical constructions are bound to escape his attention.

The imperfection of language data should also be apparent. Speakers and writers often make mistakes and fail to correct them; sometimes they consciously distort the linguistic system for stylistic effect. When transcribing utterances, a linguist—or even a tape recorder—is capable of mucking things up. Finally, it is important to observe that even the intuitive judgments of native speakers are susceptible to error. For instance, a speaker of English might maintain that the sentence *The horse raced past the house fell down* is ungrammatical, until it is pointed out to him that this is a shortened version of *The horse that was raced past the house fell down.* Or he might fail to perceive that the sentence *I had a car stolen* is ambiguous in at least three ways (it can mean 'Someone stole a car from me', 'I engaged someone to steal a car', or 'I was almost successful in stealing a car'—compare *I had the car stolen, but they caught up with me just when I was about to cross the border*).

These shortcomings of linguistic data do not constitute grounds for despair; it is still possible to formulate linguistic theories, just as it has proved possible to make theoretical advances in chemistry and physics despite incomplete and occasionally spurious data. Errors in the data may prove troublesome, but in most cases they can eventually be spotted and corrected. The incompleteness of linguistic data is not usually so bothersome as one might think, for the simple reason that a complete description of any language is far beyond our present capabilities. A language is a vastly complicated system, and although we have learned a tremendous amount about the structure of certain languages, even the most comprehensive grammars we possess are limited and fragmentary. At present, the problem is not so much one of insufficient data as one of figuring out what to do with all the data we have.

It is apparent, then, that a grammar—a theory of the structure of a language—will describe a range of data that cannot be identified with any corpus of recorded utterances. If a grammar is formulated correctly, it will characterize an infinity of sentences that have never been uttered but that would nevertheless be perfectly acceptable to a native speaker, and it will exclude as ill-formed numerous sentences that have occurred but that would nevertheless be disavowed by a native speaker. This is one of the senses in which the relation between data and theory is indirect. It does not mean that the data can be ignored or taken lightly, only that it must be handled judiciously and with perspective. Data for its own sake is of limited interest. It becomes truly interesting only when it is explicated by a coherent and insightful theory.

There is a second sense in which the relationship between data and theory is indirect: Possession of an adequate collection of data in no way ensures success in formulating a theory that will account for the data insightfully. A linguistic description must characterize the rules of a language—the psychological principles that enable a speaker to pair meanings and sound sequences. However, these rules are not part of the data; in particular, they are not accessible through introspection (if speakers could look inside their heads and see the rules of their language, there would be little need for linguists). Nor is it possible to deduce the rules simply by thumbing through the data or submitting it to any mechanical program of analytical procedures. The situation is quite analogous to that obtaining in the physical sciences; one could observe countless chemical reactions without ever arriving at a theory of atomic and molecular structure that would explain these reactions. Perseverance at shuffling data does not ensure success in the construction of a revealing theory in any science; a certain amount of cleverness is also required.

A word is in order about the nature and limitations of a speaker's intuitive judgments about his language. Intuitive judgments are very important to a linguist, since a native speaker has immediate introspective access to information that is not represented overtly in spoken or written texts. A speaker can judge whether or not a sentence is grammatical, and he can sometimes furnish clues about the source of the deviance of a sentence. A speaker can often determine whether or not a certain sound sequence constitutes an independent word, and he may even be able to isolate morphemes. Furthermore, by asking a native speaker whether he judges two sounds to be the same or different, a linguist can sometimes ascertain whether the two sounds are distinctive in the language.

Of all the introspective judgments made by a native speaker, judgments concerning meaning are perhaps the most important, for a linguist can make very little progress in analyzing a language unless he can somehow determine the approximate meaning of sentences and lexical items. Meaning is important in discovering lexical items, as the Spanish example given earlier clearly indicates. It can also be important in phonological analysis, since the difference between two sounds is considered contrastive by virtue of its potential for distinguishing forms with different meanings.

The importance of meaning for syntactic analysis should be quite evident. The syntactic rules of a language relate surface structures and semantic representations; clearly, only limited progress can be made unless the syntactic investigator can obtain at least a rough idea of the semantic properties of sentences. Judgments of ambiguity and paraphrase are especially helpful. If a sentence has more than one meaning, the rules of the language must make it possible to derive the sentence from more than one semantic representation. Similarly, if two different sentences are paraphrases, they must be derivable from the same semantic representation or at least from semantic representations that can be shown in a principled way to be equivalent. A proposed set of rules that fails to accommodate native judgments of ambiguity and paraphrase stands in need of revision.

The limitations of intuitive data must always be kept in mind. As noted earlier, the intuitive judgments that a native speaker makes—like every other aspect of linguistic performance—are susceptible to error and oversight. It is especially important to realize what types of data speakers have intuitions about. Speakers have intuitions about sentences, but they do not, for the most part, have intuitions about the rules that account for these sentences. (Lexical rules are at best only a partial exception. While a speaker can isolate a word from its surroundings, he is not likely to be able to give a very precise characterization of the meaning of that word. Moreover, he may very well fail to perceive the existence of lexical units smaller than a word, let alone their sense.) A native speaker of English can tell you that the sentence *My aunt is ecstatic that Dick is loyal* is grammatical, but unless he is a born linguist who has reflected on such sentences, he will not be able to tell you about the rule of preposition deletion. Not many Papago Indians can tell you that [t] becomes [č] before high vowels. The linguist has to discover such rules—they are not part of the available data.

INTEGRATION

A language is a tightly integrated system (the French, seldom at a loss for words, say *Tout se tient*). The force of this observation quickly becomes apparent when one tries to analyze or describe a language. It is rarely if ever possible to discover and formulate a rule without taking other rules into account. A linguist cannot successfully postulate underlying structures without considering the rules that apply to these structures, nor can he postulate rules without knowing something about the structures they apply to and the structures they must yield. Every claim a linguist makes about the structure of a language bears upon, and is borne upon by, the validity of other claims.

Consider, for example, the Papago data cited earlier. In order to account for certain regularities in the data, we hypothesized that [t] occurs in the underlying phonological representations of Papago forms, but never [č], and that the phonological component of Papago contains a rule changing [t] to [č] before high vowels. Two theoretical constructs are involved here, the underlying representation and the rule, and it is evident that the choice of one is inextricably bound up with the choice of the other. If [t] is chosen for the underlying representation, [t] → [č] is the necessary rule, and conversely. On the other hand, the rule [č] → [t] is required if [č] rather than [t] is posited at the level of phonological representations. The linguist cannot worry first about rules and then about underlying representations; he must worry about both simultaneously.

The analysis of a language does not involve a predetermined series of steps leading inexorably from start to finish—taking a language apart is not analogous to unraveling a knitted sweater. Instead, the linguist must conduct concurrent investigations of several different aspects of the linguistic system. Each investigation proceeds at its own individual pace, and developments in one investigation both influence and are influenced by developments in others. Continued progress is never guaranteed; every linguist dreams up many hypotheses that eventually prove to be false. There is no unique starting point for analyzing a language, nor is there any definite stopping point. An exhaustive and definitive analysis of any language is far beyond the bounds of our present capabilities.

When a linguist examines an array of data, he typically brings to bear on the task a set of hypotheses that he has already formulated to account for other facts about the language he is working with. However tentative and sketchy these hypotheses may be, whether they exist on paper or only in the back of the linguist's mind, they already constitute a partial theory of the structure of that language. Thus the linguist is dealing not with an isolated set of facts but with a set of facts viewed in relation to a previously conceived system of rules and underlying representations. His inchoate theory will naturally influence his analysis of the new data, by narrowing the range of possibilities he is likely to consider and even by suggesting specific hypotheses. The linguist hopes that the new data will be consistent with his incipient theory and that it will prove possible to integrate the rules and underlying representations he must now postulate with those he has already formulated to account for other phenomena. If everything fits together smoothly and things start to fall into place, he is probably justified in thinking that he has been on the right track.

Let us return to the Papago forms cited earlier for an illustration. Suppose that a linguist has examined the data and has come to the same conclusions that we reached: [t] occurs in phonological representations in Papago, but [č] does not; and [t] is changed to [č] before high vowels by a phonological rule. These hypotheses constitute a partial theory of Papago phonology. Suppose now that this linguist elicits some more data from a Papago Indian, including these two forms:

    doakam   'living creature'
    jiwia   'to arrive'

Linguists being what they are, we can expect our friend to jump immediately to the following tentative conclusion: "Aha! [d] never occurs before high vowels, and [ǰ] occurs only before high vowels. Only [d] occurs in underlying representations, and a phonological rule changes [d] to [ǰ] before high vowels."

Admittedly, this is a lot to conclude on the basis of only two forms. However, our linguist did not pull this hypothesis out of thin air; it was suggested to him by his incipient theory of Papago phonology. He knows that the palatal affricate [č] occurs only before high vowels and is a predictable variant of [t]; he also knows that similar sounds often behave in similar ways in a phonological system. Thus it is natural for him to speculate that the palatal affricate [ǰ] has the same distribution as [č] and that [ǰ] is related to [d] in the same way that [č] is related to [t]. His tentative hypothesis is not based solely on the new data but also on what he already knows about the rules and underlying representations of the language and on what he knows about languages in general. Naturally, he will have to check this hypothesis out against a much larger array of facts. In this particular instance, he will be pleased to find that his hypothesis is correct.

Such hypotheses do not always turn out to be correct, but they often do. It is possible to make successful predictions of this sort precisely because a language is a tightly integrated system. In the case at hand, the properties of [t] and [č] do not stand in isolation from the properties of the phonetically similar sounds [d] and [ǰ]. On the contrary, the two sets of sounds follow the same distributional pattern, and a generalization will be missed if they are not treated together. In fact, a rule affecting both [t] and [d] will actually be simpler than a rule affecting only [t]. By expanding his analysis to handle a larger array of data, the linguist can sometimes simplify it and render it more insightful.

The Papago segments [t č] are *tense* consonants; [d ǰ] are *lax* consonants. (The difference between tense and lax sounds is that tense sounds are pronounced with greater distinctness and muscular tension, causing the vocal tract to deviate farther from its neutral position.) To account for the relation between [t] and [č] in Papago, rule (A) must be postulated, leading to derivations such as the first line of Figure 1.2–1; and to account for the relation between [d] and [ǰ], rule (B) must be postulated, along with derivations such as the second line of Figure 1.2–1.

(A) A tense dental stop becomes a palatal affricate before a high vowel.
(B) A lax dental stop becomes a palatal affricate before a high vowel.

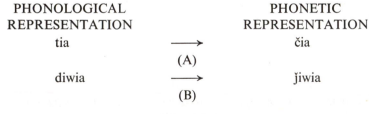

Figure 1.2–1

When rules (A) and (B) are compared, it immediately becomes clear that we are dealing not with two separate rules of limited generality but with a single general rule of which (A) and (B) are special cases. The significant generalization, the deeper regularity, is expressed in rule (C).

(C) A dental stop becomes a palatal affricate before a high vowel.

Rule (C) does the work of both (A) and (B). It is preferable to (A) and (B) because of its greater simplicity and generality.

The moral of the story is that the regularities underlying one body of data are very often intimately related to the regularities implicit in other bodies of data. Linguistic analysis therefore tends to be most fruitful when the investigator approaches new data in terms of the partial, inchoate theory he has previously formulated to account for other phenomena. If his theory leads him to uncover further regularities, and if these new findings can be integrated with his theory to capture still deeper generalizations, he can be confident that he has discovered something of significance.

UNIVERSALS

Descriptive linguistics has two fundamental goals. One goal is to formulate adequate theories of the structure of individual languages; these theories, whether complete or fragmentary, are usually called grammars. The second goal is to devise a **general linguistic theory** or **linguistic metatheory**. A linguistic metatheory is one that characterizes the structural properties shared by all human languages, and as such it constitutes the only really meaningful definition of the notion **language**. Despite many significant advances, neither goal has been fully achieved, nor is either likely to be achieved in our lifetime.

Our concern in the following chapters will be with the analysis of individual languages. However, the construction of grammars and the formulation of a linguistic metatheory are intimately related, and they cannot effectively be divorced in either theory or practice. That a metatheory describing grammatical universals presupposes a certain amount of progress in the analysis of individual languages is perhaps quite obvious. It may be somewhat less obvious that the opposite is also true. When a linguist formulates a syntactic rule, he is presupposing a theory of language that makes it meaningful for him to speak of syntactic rules. When he posits a phonological representation, he is presupposing a metatheory that allows abstract theoretical constructs of this sort. When he speaks of tense dental stops and palatal affricates, he is implicitly committing himself to the metatheoretical view that sound segments can be analyzed as bundles of phonological properties. In short, every step he takes draws upon metatheoretical assumptions, be they implicit or explicit. Consequently, we must devote some attention to general linguistic theory, even though the formulation of a linguistic metatheory is not our primary concern.

The term *language universal* has often been a source of confusion. In the strictest sense, a language universal is a structural property characteristic of every human language without exception. Many universals of this sort could be cited; here are just a few: Every language has lexical, syntactic, and phonological rules. Every language has some way of expressing negation. The phonological inventory of every language contains vowels, some of which are oral (that is, non-nasal). The phonological inventory of every language also contains consonants, including stops and non-stops. Every language has syntactic rules that delete elements (such as the preposition deletion rule of English). Every language has units which "modify" other units. Coordinate and subordinate structures are exploited to some degree in every language. And so on.

In a weaker sense, we can speak of *universal language tendencies*. Many structural traits which are not universal in the strict sense described above are nevertheless so widespread in languages of the world that their existence in all these languages cannot be merely a matter of chance. For example, many languages have a syntactic rule that moves question words to the beginning of a sentence (thus *what* occurs initially in the English question *What does he want?* even though it functions syntactically as the direct object of *want*), but this is by no means true of all languages. Besides stops, languages typically have fricatives, nasals, liquids, and glides, but some languages lack one or more of these classes. When a verb consists of a root followed by a series of suffixes, there is a strong tendency for inflectional suffixes to follow derivational suffixes (as in the English word *pressurizes*), but this pattern is far from exceptionless.

It is the position of this writer that universal tendencies of this sort have general linguistic significance and must be accommodated in linguistic metatheory. In the view adopted here, therefore, any linguistic metatheory must enumerate not only the properties that all languages have without exception but also those properties that they are normally expected to have. It is difficult to discern any clear boundaries between the universal, the probable, and the merely possible, and it is likely that they exist in a continuum. A linguistic metatheory characterizes the innate structural expectations that a child brings to bear in learning his native language, and it is perfectly natural to suppose that both absolute and non-absolute properties are included in the range of structural possibilities the child is equipped to deal with. In this book the term *language universal* will be used to designate both absolute universals and universal tendencies.

The importance of language universals for linguistic analysis is difficult to exaggerate. Virtually every move the linguist makes, every hypothesis he conceives, is directly influenced by what he knows to be possible or likely in the structure of a language. The more a linguist knows about language universals, the greater his knowledge of what to expect and what to look for when confronted with a body of data. Of the infinity of hypotheses that could in principle be formulated on the basis of a finite amount of data, he knows that only a handful have any real chance of proving correct, and he may have a pretty good idea which ones.

Consequently, the linguist conducts his investigation within the bounds of the linguistically possible and the linguistically probable, insofar as he knows what these bounds are. His limited knowledge of universals makes his job much easier than it might otherwise be, for universals very often suggest likely hypotheses and allow him to reject impossible ones out of hand. The preposition deletion rule will suggest itself to a linguist confronted with the English data considered earlier, for he knows that all languages have deletion rules which can lead to apparent anomalies in otherwise regular patterns. The fictitious linguist who analyzed Papago for us was not shooting in the dark when he hypothesized that the lax consonants [d ǰ] might pattern like the tense consonants [t č]; languages being what they are, it would be somewhat surprising if the tense and lax consonants did not behave analogously. And a linguist studying the history of Burmese would not hesitate on grounds of plausibility to claim that a rule changing [c] to [s] was added to the phonological component of the language during its historical development; a change of this kind is perfectly natural and not at all unprecedented. After all, the same thing happened in medieval French.

MOTIVATION

By now it should be apparent that linguistic analysis is an exceedingly complex problem-solving activity in which many different factors must be considered simultaneously. At every step in the analysis, the linguist must be concerned with the data before him, with its relationship to many other facets of the linguistic system, with its consequences for the partial theory he has constructed, and with its relationship to linguistic metatheory. His job is to bring all these considerations together, to perceive the regularities implicit in the data, to formulate and test hypotheses that will account for these regularities, to integrate his new findings with the rest of the grammar (making adjustments where necessary), and to consider any consequences his discoveries may have for linguistic metatheory. Once the complexity of the enterprise is recognized, it is easy to understand why any mechanical routine for the analysis of a language is likely to prove to be of limited value, as is any manual of procedural hints. The best way to analyze a language is to work hard, know what you are doing, and have brilliant insights.

There is one crucial aspect of linguistic investigation that has not as yet been accorded the attention it merits in this discussion. Once the investigator comes up with a set of rules, how does he know that they are the right ones? If he has two alternative analyses under consideration, how does he know which one to choose? The question, then, is how the investigator goes about justifying claims concerning the structure of a language, to himself and to others. In the linguist's jargon, how does one *motivate* an analysis?

The first thing to realize is that no theory can ever be completely adequate. Given the limitations of our present knowledge of language structure, it is never possible to claim with full assurance that a proposed set of rules is totally correct or that it handles the data in the most revealing way conceivable. All existing grammars are necessarily incomplete and leave a tremendous amount of data out of consideration. Consequently, it is always possible that an analysis which looks unimpeachable today will look quite dubious tomorrow. Further evidence may show that the analysis is basically wrong or that it stands in need of modification. Theories that incorporate deep and valid insights are very often superseded by theories that express still deeper insights.

At this stage in the game, therefore, linguists are dealing not with theories that are totally right or totally wrong but rather with a continuous scale on which some theories are more nearly adequate than others. Constructing a grammar is a matter of building successive models that are closer and closer approximations to linguistic reality. This does not mean that the discarded models have served no function, for any theory derives from the insights incorporated by its predecessors and could not have come into existence without them. Nor does it mean that grammars are arbitrary and that it does not matter what rules we postulate. All grammars are wrong, at least in the sense that they are incomplete, but some are clearly wronger than others. The object of linguistic description is a set of psychological principles, and an analysis is valid just to the extent that it makes true claims about these principles. The fact that linguistics deals with psychological rather than physical objects does not invalidate its status as an empirical science. Psychological structure may be elusive, but so is the structure of the atom.

Granted that no present theory can possibly give a fully adequate account of the structure of a language, how does one go about determining whether a proposed theory is at least on the right track? How does a linguist know when he has discovered something of value? How is an analysis motivated? Many different factors come into play in evaluating a proposed analysis. We will consider them under the headings *Adequacy, Convergence*, and *Insightfulness*, but it should not be supposed that this trifurcation represents anything more than a convenient way of organizing the discussion.

Adequacy. The term *adequacy* will be used here in a slightly narrower sense than it has been up until now. We may distinguish between internal and external adequacy. *Internal adequacy* refers to the compatibility of a theory with the data that it purports to describe. *External adequacy* pertains to a theory's compatibility with other facts and theories.

The validity of a theory is clearly open to question if it does not meet a fairly stringent condition of internal adequacy. However, the character of this condition must be properly understood. For one thing, no linguist works under the delusion that he can describe a language fully; when he proposes a set of rules, he offers them as a theory of only certain facets of the linguistic system; perhaps he has restricted the analysis to phonology, or to verb inflection, or to a subclass of declarative sentences. It should be evident that the failure of a theory to account for data outside its intended domain does not in itself count as evidence against it.

Even when the intended scope of the analysis is taken into account, the requirement of internal adequacy is not a mechanical one that can be imposed without the exercise of careful judgment. Since the data is seldom completely free of errors, any discrepancy between the observed data and the predictions of a theory may turn out not to be the fault of the theory. Furthermore, it is normally not realistic or desirable to require that an analysis be exhaustive in its coverage of the intended domain. Suppose, for example, that a linguist proposes an analysis of interrogative sentences in English. There are many different kinds of questions in English, each with its own subtle properties, and there is no clear line of demarcation between interrogative and non-interrogative sentences (compare the following: *How extensive are your troubles?*, *Tell me how extensive your troubles are*, *Tell me the extent of your troubles*). If this linguist is brave enough to posit a set of explicit rules to account for English questions, it is inevitable that some types of interrogatives will be left out altogether or at least be treated in a superficial manner. While this may be regrettable, it does not necessarily diminish the value of his analysis. If he has shed some light on matters of central concern, he may be forgiven for failing to clarify certain peripheral matters. An analysis that adds to our understanding of fundamental problems is to be preferred to one that achieves an exhaustive but superficial coverage of the data.

Despite these qualifications, the condition of internal adequacy is an important one. A theory whose predictions contradict reliable data clearly stands in need of modification, and a massive conflict between what a theory predicts as well formed in a language and what is in fact well formed raises the possibility that the theory is fundamentally in error. Other things being equal, a theory whose predictions accord closely with the data is certainly to be preferred to one that conflicts with the data. It should be noted, however, that the factual accuracy of a theory does not in itself guarantee its correctness. A theory might be in perfect accord with the data but be totally devoid of insight.

Considerations of external adequacy arise because linguists are concerned with more than just the synchronic analysis of individual languages. They are also interested in linguistic metatheory and diachronic analysis, both of which may bear on the evaluation of synchronic grammatical descriptions. These considerations are not necessarily the only areas with respect to which questions of external adequacy might be raised, but they are the only two we will consider here.

The close connection between grammatical description and linguistic metatheory has already been commented upon. In analyzing a language, the linguist is unavoidably influenced by what he knows (or thinks he knows) about linguistic universals. He has a rough conception of what constitutes a **natural** analysis—that is, an analysis which is in accord with universal tendencies. He approaches the data with a fairly elaborate set of expectations, and he will tend to favor an analysis that meets these expectations over one that does not. He will prefer a natural description to an unnatural one.

To take a simple example, the rule posited for Papago changing [t] to [č] before high vowels is a natural rule. It is natural in the sense that similar or identical rules are attested in numerous other languages, and also in the sense that it can be partially explained on articulatory grounds (high vowels are palatal sounds, pronounced with the tongue approaching the palatal region of the roof of the mouth; hence when [t] is pronounced before a high vowel, there is a tendency for it to be palatalized in anticipation of the following sound). By contrast, a rule changing [č] to [t] everywhere except before high vowels would not be natural in either of these two senses. Confronted with the choice between a rule changing [t] to [č] before high vowels and a rule changing [č] to [t] elsewhere, a linguist would thus incline to choose the former alternative. In this case, the natural rule also turns out to be the simpler one, since it is easier to state its environment—"before high vowels" is a simpler specification than "before consonants and non-high vowels." The two considerations of naturalness and simplicity converge to favor the rule [t]→[č].

Although universals are quite important in the evaluation of a proposed set of rules, most universals are not so well established that one should feel constrained to let them take precedence over other considerations. Languages do contain rules that are not natural, at least with respect to our present conception of naturalness, and we must make allowance for this simple fact, however much we would like to tidy up the linguistic picture. (For example, the phonological component of Aztec once contained a rule changing [t] to [ƛ] (a voiceless lateral affricate) only before the vowel [a]. Such a rule is not widely attested in languages of the world, to say the very least, nor is there any obvious articulatory explanation for it.) Moreover, it must be kept in mind that our present knowledge of language universals is at best crude and sketchy; since a linguistic metatheory must be empirically based, we must always be prepared to modify it when the claims it makes conflict with well-established facts.

In principle, the synchronic analysis of a language is carried out without regard to its historical evolution. Linguists have discovered, however, that the structure of a language is sometimes closely correlated with historical changes that have affected it. Structures that are manifested overtly at one stage in a language may be quite similar to the underlying representations of a later stage. Furthermore, synchronic rules are sometimes directly analogous to diachronic changes. These correlations are not a priori speculations but rather empirically determined facts. Questions of external adequacy therefore arise in regard to diachronic considerations.

The reason for the frequent reflection of diachronic changes in synchronic structure is not hard to discern; we may take the Burmese forms discussed earlier as a concrete illustration. Language change is change in a system of rules. When [c] changed to [s] in Burmese, this change consisted in the addition of the phonological rule [c]→[s] to the linguistic system. The segment [c], which was manifested overtly before the change occurred, assumed the status of an underlying representation once the new rule was adopted. As long as regularities in the structure of Burmese led children learning it natively to postulate [c] in underlying representations, the rule [c]→[s] remained a synchronic rule. The synchronic rule mirrors a historical change simply because the change consisted in the addition of this rule to the linguistic system.

It should not be concluded that synchronic and diachronic analyses always dovetail in this way. Subsequent modifications in the rules and underlying representations of a language may have the effect of obscuring the relationship between synchronic rules and historical changes, and over a long enough period of time the correlation between them is certain to disappear. At this point, linguists really do not know to what extent such correlations typically prevail. For this reason, diachronic evidence is never sufficient in itself to justify a synchronic analysis.

Suppose, for example, that a linguist working on modern Burmese makes the claim that the phonetic segment [s] derives synchronically from the underlying phonological segment [c] by virtue of the rule [c]→[s]. He might consider the fact that this derivation is historically accurate to be evidence in favor of his analysis, since the analysis minimizes the differences between early and modern Burmese and thus promises to simplify the diachronic theory that will account for these differences. If he can provide strong internal, synchronic evidence that his analysis is correct, its historical accuracy can indeed be counted as a point in its favor. However, any argument based on diachronic evidence alone must be rejected, for there is no assurance that the linguistic system has not been radically revised since the historical changes in question took place. The history of a language may furnish the linguist with valuable clues as he begins a synchronic analysis, and it may provide evidence to corroborate an analysis proposed and justified on other grounds, but it cannot stand alone as the sole motivation for a system of rules and underlying representations. Historical accuracy is neither a necessary nor a sufficient condition for adopting a synchronic theory.

Convergence. When dealing with a restricted range of data, a linguist can often conceive of several alternative ways, all fairly plausible, of accounting for the facts. What is needed in such a situation is some way to avoid having to choose arbitrarily among alternative analyses. Presumably, only one analysis is correct, and the linguist would like to have a principled basis for determining which one.

Because a language is a tightly integrated system, rules and representations postulated to account for one range of data frequently turn out to be useful in the description of other data that previously seemed unrelated to it. A rule or underlying representation that has this property is said to be *independently motivated*. The independent motivation of rules and representations is a powerful criterion for choosing among alternative analyses. Faced with a choice between two analyses that account equally well for a given body of data, a linguist will not hesitate to choose the one that involves rules and underlying representations that are independently motivated by virtue of helping to account for other data. By considering the consequences of competing analyses for the rest of the grammar he is constructing, the linguist is thus able to choose among them on a principled basis.

The independent motivation of rules and underlying representations is an extremely important component of linguistic argumentation. To justify a proposed set of rules and representations, it is not sufficient merely to show that they work, that they account for the data—in most instances, there are other analyses that will also work. Finding an analysis that works is of limited interest unless there is some reason to believe that the analysis makes true claims about the language. There are grounds for believing this when the proposed rules and underlying representations are shown to be independently motivated, for this means that evidence from different facets of the language converges to favor one particular analysis. If an analysis formulated to account for one group of facts were incorrect, there would be no reason to expect it to be of any value in expressing the regularities implicit in other data.

Let us consider some examples. The rule changing [t] to [č] before high vowels in Papago turned out to have independent motivation. The rule was originally postulated to account for distributional regularities in a set of forms beginning in the tense consonants [t č]. When the distribution of the lax consonants [d ǰ] was examined, it was found that [ǰ] could be considered the variant of [d] that occurs before high vowels. If [ǰ] is regarded as a variant of [d], a rule is required that changes [d] to [ǰ] in the proper environment. However, given the existence of the rule [t]→[č], there is no need to add to the complexity of the grammar by positing an entirely separate rule [d]→[ǰ]; it is sufficient to generalize the previously established rule to cover all dental stops instead of only tense dental stops. The grammar is actually simplified when the analysis is extended to handle the new class of data, and this is a strong indication that the original analysis was on the right track. The rule [t]→[č] is seen to be independently motivated because it serves not only its original function but an additional function as well.

The syntactic regularity in English discussed earlier provides further examples of independent motivation. Recall that underlying representations containing a preposition were postulated to account for expressions of the form *ADJ that X;* the preposition is erased by the rule of preposition deletion and consequently does not appear in surface structures. The analysis is illustrated in Figure 1.2–2. The proposed rule deletes a preposition when it immediately precedes the subordinating particle *that.* (Since *of* does not precede *that* in *I am certain of Dick's loyalty*, preposition deletion does not apply in the derivation of this sentence; hence its surface structure is identical to its underlying representation.) Postulating the rule and underlying representations of the form *ADJ P that X* allowed us to capture certain generalizations. Both of these theoretical constructs turn out to be independently motivated.

UNDERLYING REPRESENTATION	SURFACE STRUCTURE
I am certain of Dick's loyalty	I am certain of Dick's loyalty
I am certain of that Dick is loyal $\Longrightarrow$ (preposition deletion)	I am certain that Dick is loyal

Figure 1.2–2

The preposition deletion rule was formulated on the basis of sentences such as the following.

(1) (a) I am certain of Dick's loyalty.
    (b) *I am certain of that Dick is loyal.
    (c) I am certain that Dick is loyal.

In (1) (a) the prepositional object is an ordinary noun phrase. In (1) (b) and (1) (c), on the other hand, the noun phrase functioning as the prepositional object consists of an embedded clause headed by the subordinating particle *that*. Although (1) (b) is directly analogous to (1) (a), it is ungrammatical; this is accounted for by preposition deletion, which derives (1) (c) from (1) (b).

There is another type of subordinate clause in English that functions as a noun phrase; it is marked by the subordinating particle *to*, as in the following sentence, in which the *to* clause functions as the subject.

(2) To pull out of the war now would be a tragic mistake.

To clauses provide independent motivation for preposition deletion, since prepositions are deleted before *to* as well as *that*.

(3) (a) I am ready for my presents.
    (b) *I am ready for to open my presents.
    (c) I am ready to open my presents.
(4) (a) I am anxious for my presents.
    (b) *I am anxious for to open my presents.
    (c) I am anxious to open my presents.

The distribution of prepositions in sentences like (3)–(4) can be regularized by claiming that preposition deletion derives the (c) sentences from underlying structures like the (b) sentences. A separate new rule is not needed; it is only necessary to generalize preposition deletion so that it deletes a preposition immediately before any subordinating particle, not just *that*. Preposition deletion, posited to account for the absence of prepositions before *that* clauses, is seen to be independently motivated when *to* clauses are taken into consideration. Preposition deletion does not affect sentences with the subordinating elements *POSSESSIVE . . . ing*, as in *I am certain of Dick's being loyal;* this is because the preposition does not directly precede the subordinator, but rather the subject noun.

Underlying representations such as the (b) sentences above were posited to make it possible to state the generalization that the sequence *ADJ P NP* is grammatical in English to the exclusion of sequences of the form **ADJ NP*. The fact that this broad generalization can be captured at the expense of only one simple rule is fairly persuasive evidence that such underlying structures are valid; if the situation were not basically regular, it would not be possible to make it appear regular by the addition of a single natural rule. However, the desire to capture this generalization is not the only motivation for positing underlying representations with *ADJ P that X* and *ADJ P to X;* there are other constructions of English whose description is simplified if underlying structures of this form are postulated. Consequently, these underlying representations are independently motivated.

Consider the data in (5)–(7).

(5) (a) $\boxed{\text{I am certain of}}$ $\boxed{\text{Dick's loyalty.}}$

   (b) What $\boxed{\text{I am certain of}}$ is $\boxed{\text{Dick's loyalty.}}$

(6) (a) $\boxed{\text{I am certain}}$ $\boxed{\text{that Dick is loyal.}}$

   (b) What $\boxed{\text{I am certain of}}$ is $\boxed{\text{that Dick is loyal.}}$

(7) (a) $\boxed{\text{I am ready}}$ $\boxed{\text{to open my presents.}}$

   (b) What $\boxed{\text{I am ready for}}$ is $\boxed{\text{to open my presents.}}$

The sentences in (5) bear a special relationship to each other, a relationship that must somehow be expressed in a grammar of English. Although the particulars of this relationship are not our immediate concern, we can observe that (5) (a) is semantically a component of the more complex (5) (b); a person who claims that (5) (b) is true is automatically committed to the claim that (5) (a) is true. We can further observe that the surface structure of (5) (b) contains that of (5) (a), but split up into two parts. A noun phrase, *Dick's loyalty*, occurs after *is*, and the rest of (5) (a) occurs between *what* and *is*. The corresponding portions of the (a) and (b) sentences are enclosed in boxes.

(6) and (7) are exactly analogous, except for one detail. Although neither of the (a) sentences contains a preposition in its surface structure, a preposition shows up before *is* in the (b) sentences. In terms of surface structures, therefore, the relationship between the (a) and (b) sentences is irregular. The pattern in (6) and (7) does not follow precisely the more general pattern illustrated by (5); the two boxed portions of (5) (b) add up exactly to (5) (a), but there is a preposition in the (b) sentences of (6) and (7) that is not to be found in the

corresponding (a) sentences. If (6) (a) and (7) (a) contained prepositions, the relationship between the (a) and (b) sentences would be completely regular. However, we have argued on other grounds that sentences like (6) (a) and (7) (a) must have prepositions in their underlying representations. Consequently, the relation between the (a) and (b) sentences is completely regular; it is simply necessary to state this regularity at the level of underlying representations rather than at the level of surface structure. Underlying representations containing prepositions before *that* and *to* are thus independently motivated, since they make it possible to capture generalizations implicit in data other than that for which they were originally postulated.

There are still other grounds for adopting underlying representations with *ADJ P that X* and *ADJ P to X*. Consider (8)–(10).

(8) (a) What are you certain of?
    (b) I am certain of Dick's loyalty.
    (c) Are you certain of Dick's loyalty?
    (d) Yes, I am certain of it.
(9) (a) What are you certain of?
    (b) I am certain that Dick is loyal.
    (c) Are you certain that Dick is loyal?
    (d) Yes, I am certain of it.
(10) (a) What are you ready for?
    (b) I am ready to open my presents.
    (c) Are you ready to open your presents?
    (d) Yes, I am ready for it.

In each example the (b) and (d) sentences answer the (a) and (c) questions respectively. When a person answers an (a) question, he does so by replacing the question word *what* with a noun phrase, such as *Dick's loyalty* or *that Dick is loyal*. *What* functions as a prepositional object in the (a) sentences, and the answer *Dick's loyalty* is a prepositional object in (8) (b). The answers *that Dick is loyal* and *to open my presents* are not prepositional objects in the surface structures of (9) (b) and (10) (b), but the pattern can be regularized if prepositions are posited for the underlying structures of these sentences. The (c) and (d) sentences provide still further independent motivation for underlying prepositions. In (8) (c) and (8) (d) both *Dick's loyalty* and its pronominal replacement *it* function as prepositional objects. In (9) and (10), on the other hand, *it* is preceded by a preposition, but not the noun phrases it replaces, *that Dick is loyal* and *to open your presents*. Once more, a pattern is regularized by hypothesizing underlying representations with prepositions.

We see therefore that evidence from several different facets of English grammar converges to motivate the claim that surface expressions with the sequence *ADJ NP* derive by the rule of preposition deletion from underlying representations of the form *ADJ P NP*. A number of regularities in the structure of English that could not be captured by an examination of surface structures alone can be expressed in terms of underlying representations. The rule and underlying representations might be considered somewhat arbitrary if they served only one function; however, since these simple and natural theoretical constructs in fact allow us to express at least four different kinds of regularities that would otherwise be obscured, we can conclude that they are very strongly motivated.

The linguist is always looking for analyses favored by the convergence of several different kinds of evidence, and he is always delighted when he finds one. If the theoretical constructs he sets up for one facet of a language bear no particular relation to those he sets up for any other, he is likely to suspect that his analysis does not reflect linguistic reality. When, on the other hand, the rules and underlying representations postulated for one body of data have the effect of clarifying or resolving other problems, when one discovery leads to another and the pieces start to fall into place, then the linguist knows that he is on to something. Because of the tightly integrated character of language structure, theoretical constructs that make true claims about a language should in general have consequences for the system that reach beyond the confines of the data for which they were postulated. The convergence of evidence from several different aspects of the linguistic system thus constitutes strong evidence for the validity of an analysis.

Insightfulness. Although the contention that a linguistic analysis should be insightful is hardly controversial, it is no easy matter to specify what it is that distinguishes an insightful analysis from one that merely works. Perhaps we can say that an insightful analysis is one that discerns a regular pattern in a mass of seemingly disparate facts, one that shows apparent idiosyncrasies to follow from general principles, one that accounts for a great deal of data by means of a few simple statements, one that captures significant generalizations —or better yet, one that does all these things simultaneously. The key notions are regularity, generality, simplicity, and significance. It should not necessarily be assumed that these notions are any more self-evident than the notion of insightfulness, but discussing them will at least serve to raise some of the considerations that bear on the matter.

It should be apparent by now that the search for regularities pertaining to the structure and evolution of languages is fundamental to modern linguistics. It should also be apparent that linguistic regularities cannot always be discovered merely by collecting and categorizing data. Many regularities can be discovered and accounted for only when the data is viewed in relation to a system of abstract rules and underlying representations. These theoretical constructs do not follow directly from the data by means of any mechanical inductive procedures; they are achieved through the insights of an investigator who sees through to the essentials of a problem and perceives the "trick" that will make everything fall into place. For example, underlying representations such as *I am certain of that Dick is loyal* are not part of the linguist's data. They arise only when he is clever enough to see that positing such abstract representations will enable him to capture generalizations that could not otherwise be expressed.

The rules that embody the regularities of a language vary greatly in their generality. In the following rules for Papago, for instance, rule (C) is more general than rule (A) or (B), since it applies to a more inclusive class of segments.

(A) A tense dental stop becomes a palatal affricate before a high vowel.
(B) A lax dental stop becomes a palatal affricate before a high vowel.
(C) A dental stop becomes a palatal affricate before a high vowel.

General rules are considered more insightful than non-general rules, since the regularities they express are less obvious and more pervasive. A linguist would therefore adopt rule (C) for a grammar of Papago in preference to the two separate rules (A) and (B). Similarly, the insightfulness of the preposition deletion rule of English is enhanced when the rule is generalized to delete prepositions before all subordinating particles, not just *that*.

Simplicity and generality can very nearly be regarded as two sides of the same coin. For example, rule (C) above is simpler than either (A) or (B); being more general, it applies to a wider class of elements and thus requires a less detailed specification of its applicability. By the same token, the rule of preposition deletion, which eliminates any preposition before a subordinating particle, is simpler than a rule deleting some prepositions but not others, since the latter rule would have to incorporate a list of the prepositions it could apply to. In linguistics, as in any science, a theory is considered elegant and insightful if it is able to account for a wide range of variegated data with economy of statement and sparseness of conceptual apparatus. Other things being equal, a linguist will therefore tend to prefer one analysis over another if it involves fewer rules, simpler rules, or fewer distinct types of elements. An analysis of Papago that incorporates rule (C) wins on all three counts: Rule (C) takes the place of the two separate rules (A) and (B); it is simpler than (A) or (B); and it allows us to reduce the number of distinct segment types in phonological representations, since [č ǰ] are treated as predictable variants of [t d].

Most linguists would agree that the essence of their profession is the discovery and description of **significant linguistic generalizations**, though some would be hard-pressed to state just what they mean by the term. Significant linguistic generalizations can perhaps be characterized as generalizations that reveal something about the structure of a language. On the basis of a finite amount of data, an indefinite number of generalizations can be made, but only a few promise to shed any light on matters of intellectual concern. For instance, it might be true of a given body of data that no sentence contains more than seventeen words, that the sound [a] occurs at least once in each clause, that no sentence constitutes a palindrome, and so on. Under normal circumstances, a linguist would never even notice such facts; rather his attention would be drawn to structurally significant facts of the sort discussed in previous examples. It might prove difficult to give explicit criteria for determining when a generalization is significant and when it is not, but for all practical purposes it is sufficient to rely on personal judgment. The notion of a significant linguistic generalization is basically an intuitive one, as are all our notions of what constitutes an insightful analysis. There is no reason to be disturbed about this conclusion; it simply reflects our position in the universe.

Conclusion. It should be evident by now that linguistic analyses are not arbitrarily chosen. A linguist tries to make true claims about a language (or the evolution of a language), and there are several ways in which he can demonstrate to himself and to the linguistic world that the claims he makes are true or at least on the right track. To motivate an analysis, a linguist tries to show that it meets several or all of the following conditions: (1) The analysis accords with the data, including both recorded texts and intuitive judgments. (2) It is natural, in the sense that it conforms to universal tendencies. (3) It dovetails with the historical evolution of the language. (4) The rules and underlying representations of the analysis are independently motivated. (5) The rules express regularities that are not obvious through casual inspection of the data. (6) The rules are general. (7) The analysis is simple relative to any available alternative. (8) The analysis captures significant linguistic generalizations. No one condition is of overriding importance. It is only when a number of separate considerations converge in favor of a particular analysis that it can be regarded as well motivated.

LINGUISTIC PROBLEMS

In view of the tremendous complexity of the process of linguistic analysis, any set of practical problems devised for pedagogical purposes must fall short of recreating for the student the complicated situation the linguist finds himself in when he sets out to analyze a language. One factor that detracts from the realism of a set of problems is that the student cannot be expected to bring to the task the sophisticated knowledge of grammar and language universals that the professional linguist possesses. The need to choose relatively self-contained problems (or at least problems that can be simplified so as to make them appear to be self-contained) adds another dimension of artificiality to the situation that a book of this sort offers the student. Some attempt will be made in the following chapters to alleviate these difficulties, but it is impossible to overcome them altogether.

The most important sense in which a pedagogically oriented problem is artificial is that it is guaranteed to have a solution. The data is preselected and organized in problem form because it exemplifies a linguistic regularity and is sufficient to reveal that regularity to the perspicacious student. However, a language does not come prepackaged as a series of discrete problems; the linguist encounters it in the form of fragmentary and distorted data, with no indication of what sort of regularities to look for or of which constellations of data will yield insights when examined carefully. The most fundamental and difficult aspect of linguistic investigation is the recognition and isolation of problems that are susceptible to insightful analysis, and the recognition and isolation of a problem is often simultaneous with the discovery of its solution. It is not really possible, in a book of this sort, to expose the student to this aspect of linguistic investigation—merely by marshaling the data relevant to a solvable problem one accomplishes the task for him.

These shortcomings should not be underestimated, and you should not work through the problems under the delusion that they can teach you everything there is to know about linguistic investigation. Nevertheless, the following chapters may prove to be of some value to you in making the experience of linguistic analysis accessible.

2

Lexical Analysis

This chapter concerns the identification of lexical units, their structure, and their relationship to the rest of the grammatical system. In the course of the discussion, it will become apparent that lexical analysis is by no means as simple and straightforward as it might at first appear to be. Lexical items, though much more "concrete" and easier to discover than syntactic and phonological rules, must still be regarded as theoretical constructs rather than directly observable entities. Basic concepts like the notions word and morpheme turn out to be surprisingly problematic when examined in detail. Furthermore, the lexical analysis of a language is intimately connected with its syntactic and phonological analysis and cannot be completed without considerable progress in these other domains. For all these reasons, lexical analysis merits careful consideration.

2.1   *The Isolation of Words*

The existence of words as linguistic units is indicated by both structural and intuitive evidence. Structurally, numerous phonological and syntactic generalizations could not be stated without reference to the notion of the word. The intuitive reality of the word is witnessed by the fact that most writing systems break sentences up into word-sized units (typically marking word boundaries by spaces). Moreover, native speakers often have an intuitive grasp of what constitutes a word in their language, even if that language has never been committed to writing.

The fact that words are real entities should not lead us to assume that it is always an easy matter to determine what is a word and what is not. The linguist cannot normally rely on orthographic conventions, for most languages have no writing system until a linguist comes along and invents one. He cannot depend totally on the intuitive judgments of native speakers, valuable as they are, because full consistency cannot be presumed for these judgments and because speakers may have no firm opinion in many instances. Nor is it always possible for the linguist to segment an utterance into words on the basis of its phonetic characteristics, since speakers usually do not pause at word boundaries. Phonetically, a sentence typically consists of a continuous stream of sound with lexical boundaries left unmarked; even the representation of a sentence as a series of discrete sound segments constitutes a significant abstraction from phonetic reality (one that will be taken for granted in the transcriptions in this book).

The word is a difficult notion to define, and no formal definition will be attempted here. Instead we will examine one by one the various factors of which an adequate definition must take cognizance. Numerous considerations bear on the problem of locating the word boundaries in phonetic sequences, and no one consideration is sufficient by itself to isolate words correctly in all instances. Word boundaries are postulated on the basis of the convergence of different kinds of evidence.

RECURRENCE

A word can be partially defined as a phonological form that recurs with constant meaning. One step in the isolation of words therefore consists in finding recurrent phonetic sequences and checking to see if the occurrence of these apparent units is correlated with a constant component of meaning.

Finding phonological sequences that recur with constant meaning is not enough, of course, because the units obtained by this criterion alone may be too small or too large. Consider the English word [kæt], which recurs with a constant meaning component that for convenience can be symbolized 'cat'. Every time the sequence [kæt] occurs associated with the meaning 'cat', so do smaller sequences such as [kæ] or simply [æ]. However, if [kæ] or [æ] were posited as the word meaning 'cat', we would be left with residues such as [k] and [t] that could not be attributed a meaning. In an adequate analysis the word units postulated must be large enough to avoid any such proliferation of meaningless elements. By the same token, sequences larger than the word meet the condition of recurrence with constant meaning; phrases, clauses, and even entire sentences have this property. Larger units of this sort can be excluded by virtue of the fact that they contain smaller sequences that themselves meet the condition of recurrence with constant meaning; roughly speaking, the units posited as words should be the smallest units meeting the condition. (We will consider the distinction between words and morphemes below—for the moment we will restrict our attention to examples in which the distinction can be ignored.)

This characterization of the criteria for identifying words is of course only a first approximation; other considerations which come into play will be discussed after the following two problems, which illustrate the points covered so far.

Problem 2.1–1   Spanish

Isolate the words in the following sentences and state their meanings. For purposes of this problem, words can be defined as the smallest phonological units that recur with constant meaning. Your analysis should be such that every segment of every sentence is assigned to some word; that is, when a sentence is broken up into words, there should be no residues.

(1)	unómbreestáakí	'A man is here.'
(2)	elgátoestáenférmo	'The cat is ill.'
(3)	elómbreestáenférmo	'The man is ill.'
(4)	ungátoestáenférmo	'A cat is ill.'
(5)	elgátoestáakí	'The cat is here.'
(6)	ungátoestáakí	'A cat is here.'
(7)	unómbreestáenférmo	'A man is ill.'
(8)	elómbreestáakí	'The man is here.'

Discussion

Units of various sizes that seem to recur with constant meaning can be isolated. For example, [ómbre] occurs in sentences (1), (3), (7), and (8), which share the meaning component 'man'; [í] occurs in (1), (5), (6), and (8), which share the component 'here'; [ungátoestá] occurs in (4) and (6) and is apparently correlated with the meaning 'a cat is'.

Some of these units can be broken up into smaller units and are consequently too large to qualify as words in terms of the working definition given above. For example, [gáto] recurs with the meaning 'cat', which entails that [ungátoestá] must be divided into the smaller units [un gáto está]. Other units will prove to be too small to qualify as words under our provisional definition. For instance, [í] occurs only in the larger sequence [estáakí], which recurs with the meaning 'is here'. Since we have already found reason to believe that [está] is a separate word (meaning 'is'), we must consider [akí] alone. If [í] were postulated as a separate word meaning 'here', we would be left with the residue [ak], to which no meaning could be assigned; the word for 'here' is thus [akí].

Solution

'a' = un	'man' = ómbre	'here' = akí
'the' = el	'cat' = gáto	'ill' = enférmo
'is' = está		

Problem 2.1–2   *Luiseño*

Luiseño is a Uto-Aztecan language spoken in southern California. Isolate the words in the following sentences and state their meanings. Use the same provisional definition of the word you used in Problem 2.1–1, avoiding residues as before. The symbol [ʔ] stands for a glottal stop, and [q] for a postvelar voiceless stop (that is, [q] is like [k] except that it is articulated farther back in the mouth). A long vowel is written as a sequence of two vowel symbols, and stress is marked only on the first; [óo], for instance, stands for a mid back rounded vowel that is both long and stressed.

(1)	nawítmalqáywukálaqpokíik	'The girl is not walking home.'
(2)	yaʔášpolóov	'The man is good.'
(3)	yaʔášwukálaqpokíik	'The man is walking home.'
(4)	nawítmalwukálaqpokíik	'The girl is walking home.'
(5)	yaʔášqáywukálaq	'The man is not walking.'
(6)	nawítmalqáypolóov	'The girl is not good.'
(7)	yaʔášwukálaqpokíik	'A man is walking home.'

Discussion

Lexical units can be identified by comparing sentences that are very similar but not quite identical. (3) and (4), for example, share the meaning component 'is walking home' and the phonetic sequence [wukálaqpokíik]. The difference between [yaʔáš] and [nawítmal] must therefore be responsible for the semantic distinction 'man' versus 'girl'. (1) and (4) are identical except for the presence of [qáy] in (1), which evidently contributes the meaning 'not'. By contrasting (4) and (5), we find that [wukálaqpokíik] consists of the smaller units [wukálaq] 'is walking' and [pokíik] 'home'. Finally, the unit [polóov] 'is good' can be isolated by subtracting from (2) or (6) units that have already been identified.

The data provides no evidence for dividing any of these elements into smaller units. [polóov] 'is good' and [pokíik] 'home' happen to share the phonetic sequence [po], but there is no apparent meaning component that could reasonably be attributed to this sequence in both combinations. There is no basis for dividing [wukálaq] 'is walking' into, say, [wu] 'is' plus [kálaq] 'walking', because neither [wu] nor [kálaq] ever appears without the other; any segmentation of this recurrent unit would be purely speculative, given only the data at hand. Nor can [yaʔáš] 'man' or [nawítmal] 'girl' be divided non-arbitrarily into a noun and an article 'the'; indeed, (3) and (7) suggest that 'a' and 'the' are not overtly expressed in Luiseño.

Solution

'man' = yaʔáš	'is good' = polóov	'not' = qáy
'girl' = nawítmal	'is walking' = wukálaq	'home' = pokíik

In Problem 2.1–1 the Spanish sentences and their English glosses correspond word for word. This will not always be the case, as Problem 2.1–2 shows, even when related languages are compared. Sentences (2) and (6) demonstrate that Luiseño can express with an adjective alone what English expresses with the sequence *be ADJ*. Similarly, the single word [wukálaq] can be glossed as 'is walking'. A further difference is the absence in the Luiseño sentences of any word corresponding to the English article; Luiseño has no word meaning 'the' or 'a', so that [yaʔáš] can mean either 'the man' or 'a man'. The differences between corresponding sentences in two languages can of course be much more radical than these. The point of such examples is that when analyzing an unfamiliar language one never knows for certain precisely what meaning components to anticipate in a sentence on the basis of a rough translation; nor does one know precisely how the meaning components will be grouped into words. When checking for phonological units that recur with constant meaning, therefore, one must avoid imposing on the data the lexical and semantic structure of a more familiar language.

WORDS VERSUS MORPHEMES

The characterization of a word as a minimal phonological unit that recurs with constant meaning is insufficient by itself on a number of counts. One difficulty is that not every word has a meaning, although the vast majority of them certainly do. In the sentence *It is true that all politicians are not virtuous*, both *it* and *that* appear to be devoid of meaning, yet on intuitive grounds they must be called words. Some linguists have claimed that the word *be* has no meaning. In expressions of the form *be ADJ*, for instance, it can be argued that *be* contributes no meaning that is not already part of the meaning of the adjective. The plausibility of this proposal is further enhanced by the fact that many languages lack any word corresponding to *be* before adjectives; sentence (6) in the Luiseño problem above translates literally as 'girl not good'. The claim that *be* has no meaning may or may not be true, but it is clear from other examples that recurrence with constant meaning cannot be the sole consideration employed in the demarcation of words.

Other considerations come into play when we try to distinguish between words and morphemes, both of which typically (but not invariably) meet the condition of recurrence with constant meaning. We previously characterized words as the smallest units of this type, in order to distinguish them from larger units such as phrases and clauses, but this characterization is valid only as a first approximation. For instance, it is intuitively clear that *houses* is an English word, yet it can be broken down into the smaller meaningful units *house* and *s*. The smallest phonological units that recur with constant meaning are morphemes (see section 2.2). Words are the smallest such units that meet certain additional criteria as well. Many words (such as *house*) contain only one morpheme, but many others (such as *houses*) are polymorphemic. To distinguish adequately between words and morphemes, we must find criteria that judge the singular noun *house* to be a word while precluding the postulation of a word boundary between *house* and *s* in *houses*.

One additional criterion that is often used in isolating words is the possibility of pausing at word boundaries. Another is the ability of a word to constitute a complete utterance. Although speakers do not normally pause between words, it is much more natural to pause between words than within a word. Similarly, a single word often constitutes an entire utterance (as the answer to a question, for instance), but smaller units normally do not. Both these considerations militate against dividing *houses* into *house* plus *s*, since a pause between *house* and *s* would be unnatural, and since *s* cannot stand alone as a complete utterance. Neither of these criteria is ironclad, of course, any more than is the criterion of recurrence with constant meaning; the following dialogue shows that a non-word can occasionally occur bounded by pauses and can even constitute a complete utterance, though such cases are exceptional:

> "He is my employ . . . ER."
> "Your employER or employEE?"
> "EE."

It is evident, then, that no single criterion can be applied mechanically and in isolation from other considerations.

PHONOLOGICAL CRITERIA

Phonological evidence may also bear on the demarcation of words. Suppose, for instance, that a linguist who knows nothing about Luiseño is presented with the sentence [nawítmalqáywukálaqpokíik] 'The girl is not walking home'. Although his ignorance of the phonological system of this language will prevent him from drawing any definite conclusions until more data is available, his knowledge of universal phonological tendencies will at least enable him to engage in some shrewd speculations. He knows, for example, that in languages which make systematic use of stress there is a tendency for a word to contain only one stressed vowel. He also knows that sequences or *clusters* of consonants do not occur in many languages, particularly within a word, and that the last consonant of one word and the first consonant of the following word often form a cluster that could not occur within a single word. He might speculate on grounds such as these that the above sentence should be segmented into words as either [nawítmal qáy wukálaq pokíik] or [nawít malqáy wukálaq pokíik]. Until he uncovered more data, however, he could not determine which segmentation was correct, nor could he be sure that he was not completely off base.

Any systematic use of phonological evidence in determining the location of word boundaries therefore presupposes a partial knowledge of the phonological system of the language in question. By the same token, the phonological analysis of a language can advance only so far until numerous word and morpheme boundaries have been located. (See Chapter 4, pp. 280-82.) This situation illustrates the mutual dependence of different facets of a linguistic system. The investigator cannot first complete lexical analysis, then move on to phonology, then to syntax; rather he must investigate all these areas simultaneously, using the regularities he discovers in one area to help him solve problems in other domains.

Several kinds of phonological evidence may prove relevant in the demarcation of words. We have already seen that stress may be relevant, and sometimes it can serve as a fairly precise indicator of word boundaries. In French, for example, lexical stress can fall only on the last vowel of a word (not counting the reduced vowel [ə]); under normal circumstances, the occurrence of a stressed vowel in a French sentence thus points to the existence of a word boundary somewhere before the next vowel. Knowing this, one can conclude that the sentence below contains at least five words, and that one word boundary comes directly after [ɔ̃], another after either [í] or [íš], a third after either [έ] or [έs], and a fourth after either [ἔ] or [ἔg]. (A tilde over a vowel symbol marks nasalization—hence [ã] is a nasalized [a], and so on.)

ãríšeršéségarsɔ̃̄ẽteližá
'Henry was looking for five intelligent boys.'

Stress can help to delimit words in any language where it occurs a fixed number of syllables before or after word boundaries.

Any other phenomenon revealed by the phonological analysis of a language to be consistently associated with word boundaries may also prove relevant to the identification of words. For instance, stops in Luiseño are usually unaspirated, but aspiration (marked by the diacritic [ʰ]) can optionally accompany a word-final stop. The word for 'blanket' could thus be pronounced [táanat] or [táanatʰ], but the initial [t] could not be aspirated. The occurrence of a strongly aspirated stop in a Luiseño sentence therefore indicates that a word boundary follows. A somewhat different example is provided by Chumash, an American Indian language, now extinct, of the Hokan family (see Beeler, 1970). Within a word, two occurrences of [s] or two occurrences of [š] are possible, but [s] and [š] cannot both occur in the same word; this restriction is an instance of what is called *harmony*, the requirement that certain kinds of sounds within a word (or other unit) be similar in specified ways. The forms [ksaqutinánʔus] 'I tell him a story' and [šaqutinanʔiš] 'story' are Chumash words, but [saqutinanʔiš] is not well formed ([nʔ] symbolizes a glottalized [n]). If both [s] and [š] appear in a phonetic sequence, therefore, one can deduce that a word boundary must be present somewhere in between. The two problems that follow illustrate the use of phonological evidence in the isolation of words. Syntactic considerations also come into play.

Problem 2.1–3 *Papago*

Stress is regular in Papago and can be used in the location of word boundaries. In Part A you will determine the regularity in stress placement, and in Parts B and C you will isolate words.

PART A   Formulate a rule that accounts for the regularity in the placement of stress in the examples below. [ñ] symbolizes a palatal nasal (very much like the sound written *ny* in *canyon* or the Spanish sound written with the letter *ñ*).

dóʔag	'mountain'	táatam	'tooth'
ʔáañi	'I'	híwagid	'smell'
móʔo	'head'	náak	'ear'
háʔasa	'quit'	ʔáačim	'we'
bán	'coyote'	ñíid	'see'

Solution

Stress falls on the first vowel of a word.

Discussion

This regularity in stress placement should not be taken as implying that all Papago words are stressed. The occurrence in sentences of weakly stressed or unstressed elements that otherwise function like words is quite common. For example, *the* and *are* tend to occur without stress in the sentence *The frogs are insane*.

PART B   Locate the word boundaries in the following sentences. For purposes of this problem, assume that no word ends in a consonant cluster (that is, every word ends in a vowel or in a single consonant) and that no word is longer than three syllables. [ḍ] stands for a lax retroflex stop, articulated with the tip of the tongue against the palate just behind the alveolar ridge.

(1) máaginaʔomíḍ   'The car is running.'
(2) wákialʔočíkpan   'The cowboy is working.'
(3) wísiloʔohúhuʔidgmíistol 'The calf is chasing the cat.'

Discussion

The recurring sequence [ʔo] must be considered a separate word. In (1), for instance, [ʔomíḍ] cannot be a word, since it would violate the stress rule; nor can [máaginaʔo] be a word, since it would have four syllables. The sequence [huhuʔidgmíistol] in (3) must contain a word boundary somewhere between [i] and [íi], for the latter, being stressed, must be the first vowel in a word. The word boundary cannot come after [húhuʔidgm] or [húhuʔidg], because (by assumption) no word can end in a consonant cluster. The segmentation [húhuʔi dgmíistol] is most unlikely; [dgm] is highly unnatural as an initial consonant cluster, and it is especially out of place in Papago, which seems to have relatively few clusters. The proper segmentation is probably [húhuʔid gmíistol].

Solution

    (1) máagina ʔo míḍ
    (2) wákial ʔo číkpan
    (3) wísilo ʔo húhuʔid gmíistol

PART C   Using the results of Parts A and B, isolate the words in sentences (4)–(8). Then list all the words in (1)–(8) with their meanings.

    (4) míḍʔogmáagina   'The car is running.'
    (5) číposidʔogwákialgwísilo   'The cowboy is branding the calf.'
    (6) míistolʔohúhuʔidgwákial   'The cat is chasing the cowboy.'
    (7) číposidʔogʔáaligmíistol   'The child is branding the cat.'
    (8) ʔáaliʔočíkpan   'The child is working.'

Solution

    (4) míḍ ʔo gmáagina
    (5) číposid ʔo gwákial gwísilo
    (6) míistol ʔo húhuʔid gwákial
    (7) číposid ʔo gʔáali gmíistol
    (8) ʔáali ʔo číkpan

'is' = ʔo	'cowboy' = wákial, gwákial
'work' = číkpan	'calf' = wísilo, gwísilo
'run' = míḍ	'cat' = míistol, gmíistol
'chase' = húhuʔid	'child' = ʔáali, gʔáali
'brand' = číposid	'car' = máagina, gmáagina

Discussion

The meaning of [ʔo] cannot be determined precisely on the basis of this data alone; it may mark present tense, it may be equivalent to English *is . . . ing*, or it may have some other function. The lexical rule 'is' = [ʔo] is only one possible hypothesis.

The status of the element [g] is even more problematic. It may mean 'the', but the data is insufficient to show this one way or the other. The data also fails to make it clear whether [g] should be considered a separate word. [g] regularly appears before every noun, except at the beginning of a sentence; depending on its position, therefore, a noun can occur either with [g] or without it. Nouns like [wákial] have the same meaning regardless of whether or not [g] is present; however, both words and morphemes can be partially characterized as phonological units that recur with constant meaning, so it is not clear on these grounds alone whether the boundary between [g] and [wákial] is a word or morpheme boundary. It happens that a pause between [g] and [wákial] is not possible, nor can [g] constitute an entire utterance in Papago. Although not included in the data for the problem, these observations motivate the decision to treat sequences such as [gwákial] as single words.

The forms [mị́ḍ] and [máagina] appear only in sentences (1) and (4). Nothing in these two sentences alone indicates which means 'run' and which means 'car'. However, the rest of the data reveals that [g] only occurs prefixed to nouns. Since [g] precedes [máagina] in (4), this must be the form meaning 'car'.

Problem 2.1–4   Turkish

Turkish is a language with vowel harmony, meaning that all the vowels in a word must be similar in a certain way. Since words are the units relevant to Turkish vowel harmony, this phenomenon can be used to determine the placement of word boundaries. In Part A you will discover the basic vowel harmony rule; you will use this rule to isolate words in Part B and will complete the analysis in Part C. (The data is from Lewis, 1953. The problem is oversimplified in various ways; for one thing, many Turkish words, particularly those of foreign origin, are exceptions to vowel harmony. For further discussion of Turkish vowel harmony, see Chapter 4, pp. 271-72.)

PART A   Turkish has eight vowels, which can be distinguished in terms of three phonological *features*, as in the table given on the following page. The three distinguishing features are high versus non-high, front versus back, and rounded versus unrounded. A vowel can be characterized in terms of its value for each of these three features; [ü], for instance, is a high front rounded vowel, and [a] is a non-high back unrounded vowel.

	UNROUNDED			
		ROUNDED		
HIGH	i	ü	u	ɨ
NON-HIGH	e	ö	o	a
	FRONT		BACK	

One of these features functions in Turkish vowel harmony, in the sense that all the vowels in a word must have the same value for this feature. Examine the following words and state the rule of vowel harmony in terms of this relevant feature.

evde	'in the house'	aldɨm	'I took'
ankara	'Ankara'	odun	'wood'
verdim	'I gave'	odasɨ	'his room'
köprü	'bridge'	göstermek	'to show'

Discussion

Vowel harmony cannot depend on the feature high versus non-high, because high and non-high vowels can occur in the same word (for example, [verdim] 'I gave', [aldɨm] 'I took'). Rounding is not the crucial feature (for this data at least), because rounded and unrounded vowels co-occur in [odasɨ] 'his room' and [göstermek] 'to show'. Front versus back must be the relevant feature.

Solution

The vowels in a word must all be front vowels, or else they must all be back vowels.

PART B Once the rule of vowel harmony has been discovered, it can be used in the location of word boundaries. Divide the following sentences into words, making the words as large as possible consistent with the requirements of the vowel harmony rule. Assume that no word begins or ends in a cluster of two consonants, and that a consonant between two vowels at a word boundary belongs to the second word.

(1) čayiičtik   'We drank the tea.'
(2) odadabirčojukgördüm   'I saw a child in the room.'

Solution

    (1) čayɨ ičtik
    (2) odada bir čojuk gördüm

PART C Using the results of Parts A and B, isolate the words in sentences (3) and (4). Then list all the words in (1)–(4) with their meanings.

    (3) kɨzlarɨgördüm   'I saw the girls.'
    (4) biradamgördüm 'I saw a man.'

Discussion

The word [gördüm] has already been isolated in (2); it recurs in (2)–(4) with the meaning 'I saw'. The rest of (3), [kɨzlarɨ], may consist of just one word, since it contains only back vowels. The remainder of (4), [biradam], must consist of two words, since [i] is front and [a] is back. The proper segmentation is [bir adam], since [bir] has already been isolated; it evidently means 'a', so [adam] must mean 'man'.

    In determining the meanings of the other words, syntactic considerations come into play. In (4) [bir] 'a' precedes the noun it modifies; tentatively assuming that this order is constant, we can hypothesize that [čojuk] is the word for 'child' in (2), leaving [odada] as the word for 'in the room'. The verb comes last in sentences (2)–(4); if this is regularly true of Turkish, the verb in (1) must be [ičtik], meaning 'we drank'. [čayɨ] consequently means 'the tea'.

Solution

    (3) kɨzlarɨ gördüm
    (4) bir adam gördüm

'I saw' = gördüm	'child' = čojuk	'the girls' = kɨzlarɨ
'we drank' = ičtik	'man' = adam	'the tea' = čayɨ
'a' = bir	'in the room' = odada	

SYNTACTIC CRITERIA

As Problems 2.1–3 and 2.1–4 show, syntactic evidence is relevant to lexical analysis at the word level. In the Papago problem we were able to use a syntactic rule—namely, that [g] precedes any noun (except at the beginning of a sentence)—to determine that [máagina] is a noun and [mɨḑ] a verb. In the Turkish problem we used certain assumptions regarding word order to assign tentative meanings to units that had been isolated on phonological grounds. By assuming that [bir] always precedes the noun it modifies, we identified [čojuk] as the word for 'child'; [ičtik] was assigned the meaning 'we drank' by virtue of the hypothesis that the verb is regularly final in Turkish sentences.

In both problems syntactic evidence was used to assign meanings to lexical units that had been isolated by phonological criteria. Syntactic considerations are by no means restricted to this auxiliary role in lexical analysis; they are just as important as phonological considerations for determining the location of word boundaries. For example, once it is discovered that [g] is regularly prefixed to non-initial nouns in Papago, the occurrence of [g] in a phonetic sequence can be regarded as a clue that a word boundary may immediately precede. For a linguist unfamiliar with English, the segmentation of phonetic sequences into words will be facilitated by the discovery that the verb suffix *ing* virtually always occurs in word-final position.

Words can be partially defined in terms of their cohesiveness as syntactic units. One syntactic indicator that two elements cohere to form a word is the impossibility of inserting another word between them. For instance, the fact that no word can be inserted between the *house* and *s* of *houses* reinforces the intuitive judgment that *houses* is one word. (Expressions like *housemaids* do not violate this generalization; the *s* of *housemaids* indicates the plurality of the whole compound *housemaid*, not the plurality of *house* per se.) Similarly, Spanish [akí] 'here' is one word, since no other word can be inserted between [ak] and [í]. On the other hand, [elómbre] 'the man' can be considered two words because of the possibility of expressions like [el bwén ómbre] 'the good man'. In Papago no word can be inserted between [g] and the noun in expressions like [gwákial] 'the cowboy', indicating that [g] must be analyzed as a prefix rather than as a separate word.

The words of a sentence can very often be permuted, with or without a change in meaning, and the cohesiveness of phonological sequences under permutation is another syntactic consideration that enters into the process of isolating words. For example, comparison of the Spanish sentences [elómbreestáakí] 'The man is here' and [akíestáelómbre] 'Here is the man' reveals three sequences, [akí], [está], and [elómbre], that behave as units with respect to permutation. If permutability were the only consideration brought to bear on the segmentation of these sentences into words, one would have to conclude that exactly three words were involved. (Other considerations lead to the segmentation of [elómbre] into [el] plus [ómbre].) Larger word units such as [estáakí] could not be postulated, since [está] and [akí] can be permuted and thus do not cohere as a fixed lexical unit. Smaller word units such as [ak] and [í] could not be postulated, since the two smaller sequences cannot be separated or reversed.

Problem 2.1–5 German

Isolate the words in the sentences below and state their meanings. Pay particular attention to syntactic evidence.

    (1) ɛ́rhátdífráwgɛšlágɛn
       'He has beaten the woman.'

(2) zíhátdénmángɛštósɛn
'She has pushed the man.'

(3) zíhátdénknábɛgɛnŭslixgɛtrágɛn
'She has carried the boy with pleasure.'

(4) gɛnŭslixhátérdénmángɛšlágɛn
'He has beaten the man with pleasure.'

(5) dényúŋgɛnknábɛhátzígɛnŭslixgɛštósɛn
'She has pushed the young boy with pleasure.'

(6) dénáltɛnmánhátérgɛtrágɛn
'He has carried the old man.'

(7) dénmánhátérgɛšlágɛn
'He has beaten the man.'

(8) zíhátdíyúŋgɛfráwgɛnŭslixgɛštósɛn
'She has pushed the young woman with pleasure.'

Discussion

The sequences [érhát] and [zíhát] must be divided into two words, because [hátér] and [hátzí] in sentences (4)–(7) demonstrate the possibility of permutation. [gɛnŭslix] is apparently a single word; it permutes as a unit, as sentence pairs like (3) and (4) demonstrate, and there is no indication that it can be separated into two parts by the insertion of another word. Article plus noun sequences such as [dénmán] 'the man' might at first appear to cohere as units, since they can be permuted together, as in (2) and (7). However, sentences (5), (6), and (8) show that an adjective can be inserted between the article and noun, which means that they should probably be treated as separate words. The main verb is uniformly sentence-final in the data presented, and every main verb begins in [gɛ] and ends in [ɛn]. This pattern may prove useful in analyzing other sentences; if a phonetic sequence of the form [gɛ . . . ɛn] occurs at the end of an utterance, it can tentatively be identified as a verb word.

Solution

'he' = ér	'woman' = fráw
'she' = zí	'man' = mán
'the' = dí, dén	'boy' = knábɛ
'old' = áltɛn	'with pleasure' = gɛnŭslix
'young' = yúŋgɛ, yúŋgɛn	'has' = hát
'beaten' = gɛšlágɛn	'pushed' = gɛštósɛn
'carried' = gɛtrágɛn	

CONCLUSION

To summarize, many different factors are relevant in determining whether or not a phonetic sequence is a word: recurrence with constant meaning; the naturalness of a pause; the possibility of constituting a complete utterance; interaction with phonological rules; the impossibility of inserting another word in the sequence; behavior as a unit with respect to permutation; and last but not least, native intuition. No one criterion, mechanically applied, is sufficient to yield acceptable results in all instances. In fact, different criteria will often imply different segmentations, and to the extent that this is true the concept of the word is somewhat vague. For example, the sequence *it is* in sentences like *It is true that all politicians are not virtuous* could be analyzed as one word on the basis of some criteria (*it*, being meaningless, cannot be said to recur with constant meaning, nor can it occur as a complete utterance). But the same sequence can be analyzed as two words on the basis of other criteria (the possibility of pause, permutability, the possibility of inserting another word, and native intuition). Furthermore, the placement of word boundaries may vary according to style or rate of speech. For instance, although the preponderance of evidence favors the segmentation of *it is* into two words in the sentence above, all the criteria judge the stylistic variant *it's* to be a single word. Nevertheless, we should not conclude that the small measure of indeterminacy in the isolation of words invalidates the use of structural and intuitive evidence for the location of word boundaries in the large majority of relatively clear cases.

FURTHER PROBLEMS

Problem 2.1–6   Luiseño

Isolate the words in the sentences that follow and state their meanings. The symbol [x] stands for a voiceless velar fricative, and [ş] indicates a voiceless retroflex fricative, pronounced with the tip of the tongue approaching the palate just behind the alveolar ridge.

(1) húuʔunikatqáyčipómkat
    'The teacher is not a liar.'

(2) háxşuxéčiqşuŋáali
    'Who is hitting the woman?'

(3) tóowqşuşuŋáalihúuʔunikat
    'Does the teacher see the woman?'

(4) ʔivíşuŋáalnonáayixéčiq
    'This woman is hitting my father.'

(5) nonáayiṣuxéčiqʔivíṣuŋáal
'Is this woman hitting my father?'

(6) ʔivíhúuʔunikatqáynonáayitóowq
'This teacher does not see my father.'

(7) húuʔunikatṣučipómkat
'Is the teacher a liar?'

(8) ṣuŋáaliṣutóowqhúuʔunikat
'Does the teacher see the woman?'

(9) ʔivíṣuŋáalxéčiqnonáayi
'This woman is hitting my father.'

(10) húuʔunikatčipómkat
'The teacher is a liar.'

(11) ṣuŋáalitóowqhúuʔunikat
'The teacher sees the woman.'

(12) xéčiqṣuṣuŋáalʔivínonáayi
'Is this woman hitting my father?'

(13) háxṣučipómkat
'Who is a liar?'

(14) ʔivíhúuʔunikatnonáayitóowq
'This teacher sees my father.'

(15) húuʔunikatṣutóowqṣuŋáali
'Does the teacher see the woman?'

Problem 2.1–7 *French*

Isolate the words in the following sentences and state their meanings.

(1) ãríšɛršéséĝgarsɔ̃ɛ̃tɛližắ
'Henry was looking for five intelligent boys.'

(2) pyéršɛršéséĝgarsɔ̃stüpíd
'Peter was looking for five stupid boys.'

(3) leséĝgarsɔ̃kirəgardéãrísɔ̃bɔ̃
'The five boys who were looking at Henry are good.'

(4) ãrírəgardépyér
'Henry was looking at Peter.'

(5) pyérɛstüpíd
'Peter is stupid.'

(6) sɛ́bɔ̃garsɔ̃rəgardépyɛ́r
'Five good boys were looking at Peter.'

(7) ãríɛbɔ̃
'Henry is good.'

(8) pyɛ́rrəgardélebɔ̃garsɔ̃kišɛršɛ́ãrí
'Peter was looking at the good boys who were looking for Henry.'

Problem 2.1–8   Palauan

The data below (courtesy of Jo-Ann Flora) is from Palauan, a Malayo-Polynesian language spoken in Micronesia.

PART A   Use the criterion of permutability to divide expressions (1)–(6) into words.

(1) aʔádelmeŋitákl   'the man that sings'
(2) amálkelmerrós   'the chicken that crows'
(3) akemáŋetelráel   'the road that is long'
(4) amerróselmálk   'the chicken that crows'
(5) ameŋitáklelʔád   'the man that sings'
(6) aráelelkemáŋet   'the road that is long'

PART B   Isolate the words in (1)–(10) and give their meanings. Bear in mind that it is natural for all the elements of a relative clause to be contiguous. In English, for example, it is possible to say *anxious women* or *women (who are) anxious to have children*, but the expression **anxious women to have children* is ungrammatical because the relative clause *anxious to have children* has been broken up into two non-contiguous parts.

(7) auŋílelʔád   'the man that is good'
(8) aklówelmerrós   'the chicken that is big'
(9) auŋílelráel   'the road that is good'
(10) ameŋitákleldíl   'the woman that sings'

Problem 2.1–9   Classical Aztec

The data below is from Classical Aztec (the Aztec dialect spoken in the area of Mexico City at the time of the Spanish conquest in the sixteenth century). The symbol [λ] designates a voiceless lateral affricate. This sound is produced by forming a stop closure with the tip and sides of the tongue and releasing the closure, with fricative turbulence, at the sides only. [kʷ] stands for a labialized [k].

PART A The placement of stress is regular in Classical Aztec and can be used in the location of word boundaries. Examine the words below and formulate the rule that accounts for the placement of stress.

sénka	'very'	némi	'live'
íwan	'and'	tewántin	'we'
nakáyoλ	'body'	λakʷálli	'food'
nawaλatóa	'speak clearly'	sasanílli	'story'

PART B Using the stress rule postulated in Part A, segment sentences (1)–(3) into words. Assume for purposes of this problem that no word begins or ends in a consonant cluster.

(1) yéwaλsíwaλkiλasóλa   'He loves the woman.'
(2) kimiktíaskóyoλ   'He will kill the coyote.'
(3) íninλatoánikimiktíassíwaλ   'This ruler will kill the woman.'

PART C Isolate the words in (1)–(14) and state their meanings.

(4) yéwaλkíttakóyoλ   'He sees the coyote.'
(5) íninkóyoλkíttaλatoáni   'This coyote sees the ruler.'
(6) λatoánikiλasóλasíwaλ   'The ruler loves the woman.'
(7) íninλatoánisíwaλkimiktías   'This ruler will kill the woman.'
(8) kíttaλatoáni   'He sees the ruler.'
(9) kiλasóλaíninsíwaλ   'He loves this woman.'
(10) íninkóyoλλatoánikítta   'This coyote sees the ruler.'
(11) λatoánikítta   'He sees the ruler.'
(12) kíttakóyoλ   'He sees the coyote.'
(13) yéwaλkiλasóλasíwaλ   'He loves the woman.'
(14) λatoánisíwaλkiλasóλa   'The ruler loves the woman.'

Problem 2.1–10   Latin

Latin is a classic example (pardon the pun) of a language that permits many variations in word order. Permutability is therefore highly relevant to the location of word boundaries in Latin sentences. Keeping this in mind, isolate the words in the sentences that follow and give their meanings.

(1) réeksmágnushóminiiférrumdát
    'The great king gives a sword to the man.'

(2) hóminiidátférrummágnusréeks
    'The great king gives a sword to the man.'

(3) míilessápieenspúeroopekúuniammíttit
    'The wise soldier sends money to the boy.'

(4) pekúuniamsápieensmíilesmíttitpúeroo
'The wise soldier sends money to the boy.'

(5) mágnusmíilespekúuniamhóminiidát
'The great soldier gives money to the man.'

(6) púeroomíttitférrumréekssápieens
'The wise king sends a sword to the boy.'

(7) férrummíilesmágnusdátpúeroo
'The great soldier gives a sword to the boy.'

(8) hóminiidátférrummágnusmíiles
'The great soldier gives a sword to the man.'

(9) pekúuniamdátpúerooréekssápieens
'The wise king gives money to the boy.'

(10) réeksmágnusmíttithóminiiférrum
'The great king sends a sword to the man.'

Problem 2.1–11   Ayutla Mixtec

This problem concerns tone in the Ayutla dialect of Mixtec, a language of Mexico (Pankratz and Pike, 1967). Each vowel in Ayutla Mixtec occurs with one of three tones: high, mid, or low. These tones are indicated below by the respective diacritics [' ^ `]. When [a] occurs with high tone, for instance, it is marked [á]; when it occurs with mid tone, it is marked [â]; and it is symbolized [à] when it occurs with low tone. The symbol [tʸ] indicates a palatalized [t]—that is, a [t] articulated with regular stop closure and in addition a closure along the palate, the former being released first.

Ayutla Mixtec has a phonological rule that affects the form of two adjacent words if the first ends in a glottal stop: The glottal stop is deleted and the first three vowels of the second word receive the respective tones high, high, low ([' ' `]). For example, the word meaning 'son-in-law' is [kàsáʔ], and the word [kâkȧkàrà] means 'will ask for more'. When these two words combine to form the expression 'the son-in-law will ask for more', [kàsáʔ] loses its final [ʔ] and the tone pattern of the second word changes from [^ ` `] to [' ' `].

PHONOLOGICAL REPRESENTATION	PHONETIC REPRESENTATION
kàsáʔkâkȧkàrà $\longrightarrow$	kàsákákȧkàrà

The occurrence of the tone sequence [' ' `] can therefore be taken as a clue that a word boundary may immediately precede.

Using this phonological information where appropriate, isolate the words in the expressions below and state their meanings.

(1) kùmísášîî	'four nephews'
(2) yàtáíkáàʔ	'The basket is old.'
(3) nâmàášíkǎrà	'He asked for soap.'
(4) kòòtíkàčíʔ	'There are no blankets.'
(5) nâmàváʔà	'the good soap'
(6) kùmíčítʸáàyàtáʔ	'four old bananas'
(7) kòòkáčîîʔ	'There is no cotton.'
(8) kâkǎûnámáàʔ	'You will ask for soap.'
(9) šàkùtíkàčíʔ	'a few blankets'
(10) dîvìváʔà	'The egg is good.'

Problem 2.1–12   Swahili

PART A   The list of words given below (Perrott, 1951) illustrates two phonological regularities of Swahili that can serve in the demarcation of words; one involves the placement of stress and the other concerns the character of the final segment of a word. State these two regularities.

asubúhi	'morning'	karatási	'paper'
fuatíša	'to copy'	hurúma	'mercy'
wokóvu	'salvation'	edašára	'eleven'
ušínde	'defeat'	dámu	'blood'
utóto	'childhood'	fikíre	'to consider'

PART B   Using the rules discovered in Part A, determine the location of word boundaries in (1)–(3).

(1) kibándakínamilángomiwíli
'The hut has two doors.'

(2) mtumíšiánamšaháramkúbwa
'The servant has a big wage.'

(3) mwingerézaáánawatumíšiwánne
'The Englishman has four servants.'

PART C   Isolate the words in (1)–(10) and state their meanings.

(4) ndégewánamíguumiwíli	'Birds have two legs.'
(5) nyúmbaínamilángomiwíli	'The house has two doors.'
(6) mzúnguánamizígomikúbwa	'The European has big loads.'
(7) mézaínamíguumínne	'A table has four legs.'
(8) kibándakínavyúmbavitátu	'The hut has three rooms.'
(9) vyúmbaviwílivínavitánda	'Two rooms have beds.'
(10) wéviwánavísuvikúbwa	'The thieves have big knives.'

2.2 *The Isolation of Morphemes*

Sentences transcribed phonetically can be segmented into structurally significant sequences of various sizes. *Morphemes* are the smallest of these units that
have constant semantic value. Individual sound segments (such as the [k] of
cat) do not qualify as morphemes because they cannot properly be said to
have any meaning, except indirectly by virtue of belonging to a meaningful
sequence of segments. Clauses, phrases, and many words (for example, *houses*)
fail to qualify as morphemes because they can be divided into smaller meaningful units. The distinction between segments, morphemes, and larger units is
clearly valid despite the fact that some words consist of only one morpheme
and some morphemes consist of only one segment.

RECURRENCE

Like the concept of the word, the concept of the morpheme turns out to be
somewhat problematic when its application to linguistic data is examined in
detail. The definition of a morpheme as a minimal phonetic sequence that
recurs with constant meaning can only be regarded as a first approximation if
the definition is meant to include all the sorts of elements that linguists typically designate by the term. Still, this characterization is appropriate for a
great many morphemes, perhaps a majority, and it provides a convenient
point of departure. The following two problems illustrate this basic conception of the morpheme.

Problem 2.2–1   English

Isolate the morphemes that make up the following words.

carefully	humorless	fearful
hopeless	carelessly	fearlessness
wrathful	untruthfully	tastefully
harmlessly	dumbness	rapidly
stupidly	care	senseless
cleverness	shamefully	blamelessly
careful	harmful	truthfulness

Solution

care	humor	taste	ful
hope	fear	rapid	ly
wrath	truth	sense	less
harm	dumb	blame	ness
stupid	shame	clever	un

Discussion

Although the morphemic analysis of these words should be intuitively obvious to most speakers of English, it can also be established on the basis of the definition of a morpheme as a minimal phonetic sequence that recurs with constant meaning. For example, *care* recurs with constant meaning in *care*, *careful*, and *carefully*. By contrasting these three words, we are led to postulate three morphemes, *care*, *ful*, and *ly;* roughly speaking, *ful* means 'with' or 'having' (*careful* = 'having care'), and *ly* means 'in a . . . manner' (*carefully* = 'in a careful manner'). *Ful* and *ly* recur with the same meaning in other words, such as *harmful* and *harmlessly*, from which the further elements *harm* and *less* (meaning something like 'without') can be extracted. Since *less* is a morpheme, *fearlessness* must be divisible into *fear*, *less*, and *ness*, all of which recur in other words. Subtracting *ful* and *ness* from *truthfulness*, we isolate the apparent morpheme *truth*, which also occurs in *untruthfully*. Since we know *truth*, *ful*, and *ly* to be morphemes, none of which has negative meaning, the *un* of *untruthfully* is apparently a morpheme with the approximate sense 'not'. The remaining morphemes can be isolated in a similar manner.

Larger recurrent units, such as *fully* or *truthful*, do not qualify as morphemes because they contain smaller units (*ful*, *truth*, *ly*) that recur in association with a constant component of meaning. Smaller recurrent sequences, such as the *ess* of *less* and *ness*, are not morphemes because they are not meaningful. *Less* and *ness* have no obvious component of meaning in common that could be attributed to *ess*, and positing *ess* as a morpheme would leave the residues *l* and *n*, which also appear to be meaningless by themselves. The phonetic similarity between *less* and *ness* is evidently fortuitous.

Problem 2.2–2   Luiseño

Isolate the morphemes in the following sentences and state their meanings.

(1)	nóo wukálaq	'I am walking.'
(2)	nóo páaʔiq	'I am drinking.'
(3)	temét čáami páaʔivičunin	'The sun will make us want to drink.'
(4)	nóo póy wukálavičuniq	'I am making him want to walk.'
(5)	nóo páaʔin	'I will drink.'
(6)	nóo páaʔivičuq	'I want to drink.'
(7)	temét póy wukálavičuniq	'The sun is making him want to walk.'

Discussion

Morphemes can be isolated by comparing sentences that are almost but not quite identical. (2) and (5), for example, differ only in their final segments; the difference between [q] and [n] must therefore be responsible for the semantic distinction between 'PRESENT' and 'FUTURE'. By contrasting (1) and (2), we discover that [wukála] means 'walk' and [páaʔi] means 'drink'. Comparison of (2) and (6) shows that [vičú] contributes the meaning 'want'. Sentences (4) and (7) reveal that [nóo] and [temét] mean 'I' and 'sun' respectively.

The other morphemes are easily identified. [ni] recurs in (3), (4), and (7), which are the only sentences to share the meaning component 'make'; we can conclude that [ni] means 'make' by the criterion of recurrence with constant meaning. [čáami], found only in (3), must mean 'us', since all the other elements of (3) have been accounted for. For the same reason, the element [póy] that occurs in (4) and (7) must mean 'him'.

Solution

'I' = nóo	'sun' = temét
'him' = póy	'want' = viču
'us' = čáami	'make' = ni
'walk' = wukála	'PRESENT' = q
'drink' = páaʔi	'FUTURE' = n

We have characterized a morpheme as consisting in the association of a component of meaning and a sequence of sound segments. Implicit in this characterization is the assumption, not entirely justified, that the meaning components and recurring phonetic sequences of a language line up neatly and correspond in a one-to-one fashion. Although this conception of minimal lexical units is valid for a large number of cases, it is far too restrictive to serve as an accurate model of linguistic reality.

When linguists speak of morphemes, they may be referring to either phonological or semantic units. When morphemes are viewed as recurrent phonetic sequences, it is not always possible to associate these sequences with constant components of meaning. When morphemes are viewed as components of meaning, it is not always possible to isolate unique phonetic sequences that regularly manifest these meanings. The discrepancy between morphemes as phonological units and morphemes as semantic units remains even when we ignore the existence of **homonyms** (like *bear* and *bare*) and **synonyms** (*work* and *labor*).

MORPHEMES AS PHONOLOGICAL UNITS

Recurring phonetic sequences, even those that appear to have grammatical significance, cannot always be associated with a constant meaning. One type of example is provided by "complex" lexical items, lexical items containing more than one morpheme. The morphemes of a complex lexical item do not always carry the semantic value that they have when they occur in other combinations. For example, the word *understand* is constructed phonologically from the morphemes *under* and *stand*, but semantically *understand* appears to have nothing in common with either of its component parts. Nevertheless, there is grammatical motivation for dividing *understand* into *under* plus *stand* and for considering the latter to be, in some sense of the term, "the same morpheme as" the independent verb *stand*. Both of these units are irregular, having *stood* (rather than *standed*) as their past tense form. The fact that these two units share this morphological idiosyncrasy is evidence that they are related, not just separate morphemes that happen to be pronounced alike (such as *bear* and *bare*). Many other complex lexical items could be cited which have special meanings not derivable from those of their component morphemes. For purposes of semantic description, they must be treated as unanalyzable units. For phonological and morphological purposes, however, generalizations will often be missed unless they are analyzed into smaller components.

Occurrence in a complex lexical item is not the only circumstance in which a morpheme may fail to display its normal meaning. Morphemes are sometimes commandeered by the syntax of a language and pressed into service as sentence "trappings", losing their usual semantic value in their role as grammatical markers. For example, *that* and *it* are meaningful in the sentence *That's it*, but not in *It is true that all politicians are not virtuous, It's raining*, or *It's Penelope that I really love*. Similarly, *do* and *to* are meaningful in *They went to Vietnam with the intention of doing their duty*, but they are meaningless trappings in *What do they want me to say?*

Sentence trappings are not always totally meaningless; sometimes they are meaningful in the sense that they duplicate semantic information represented elsewhere in the sentence. Consider the following Spanish sentences, which illustrate the agreement of adjectives in gender with the nouns they modify.

(1) Él está contento.   'He is happy.'
(2) Ella está contenta.   'She is happy.'

The ending *o* is used on the adjective when the subject is masculine, and *a* when it is feminine.

The gender of a Spanish noun is not determined fully by the sex of the entity the noun designates—the distinction between masculine and feminine nouns is a grammatical one whose relation to natural gender is often totally arbitrary. However, the correlation is fairly consistent with respect to human nouns, and for these the distinction between masculine and feminine can reasonably be considered meaningful; *él* 'he' is appropriate when a male is referred to, and *ella* 'she' is appropriate when the referent is a female. However, the adjective endings *o* and *a* are not meaningful in the same way that the difference between *él* and *ella* is. The choice between the endings *o* and *a* is completely determined by the subject and hence conveys no information not conveyed by the subject itself. These endings are sentence trappings, grammatical embellishments that contribute no meaning of their own but are required by the syntax of Spanish. They are meaningful only in the derivative sense that they agree with elements that are independently meaningful.

Of course, subject pronouns can optionally be omitted in Spanish, as in the following sentences.

(3) Está contento.   'He is happy.'
(4) Está contenta.   'She is happy.'

In sentences like these, the distinction between *o* and *a* signals a difference in meaning, since the gender of the subject is indicated only by the adjective ending. The endings *o* and *a* can still be regarded as syntactic embellishments that contribute no meaning of their own to a sentence, but the redundancy represented in these trappings makes it possible to determine the gender of the subject even in surface structures from which the subject has been deleted.

If we view morphemes as recurring phonetic sequences having structural significance, therefore, we find that the units so obtained are not always associated with constant meaning; they may have no independent meaning at all or they may be meaningful only in certain uses. These possibilities should be kept in mind for the next two problems.

Problem 2.2–3   English

Isolate the morphemes in the following words and discuss their semantic value.

receive	respect	perceive
concur	deceive	inspect
expect	report	deport
transport	conceive	incur
recur	export	

Solution

re	in	ceive
con	ex	cur
per	trans	(s)pect
de		port

Although these morphemes could be given glosses appropriate to their use in Latin, for all practical purposes they can be said to be meaningless by themselves in modern English. Words such as *receive* and *expect* have fairly specific meanings, but individual morphemes such as *re*, *ceive*, *ex*, and *(s)pect* have no constant meaning associated with all their uses. *Export*, for example, can be attributed the meaning 'carry out' on etymological grounds, but this analysis fails to receive synchronic justification from related words. *Port* perhaps has the value 'carry' in *transport* and *deport*, but at best only metaphorically in *report;* and the word *expect* does not involve the semantic component 'out' in modern English. Similar remarks could be made with respect to the other morphemes.

Discussion

The claim that these units are meaningless by themselves, or at least that they lack consistent meaning in all their uses, might seem to call into question the decision to regard them as morphemes; an alternative would be to analyze *receive, export,* and so on as single morphemes. However, at least two considerations (besides intuition) motivate the claim that these words should be broken down into smaller units. First, elements such as *re, con, (s)pect,* and *port* recur with such frequency (particularly in combination with one another) that it is necessary to consider them real structural units, not accidentally recurring sequences. Second, the unit *ceive* has grammatical significance, since it has the special form *cept* in adjectives derived from the verbs in which it appears: *receptive, deceptive, conceptual, perceptive, perceptual.* If *ceive* were not a morpheme, there would be no reason to expect all the words with *ceive* to have derived adjectives with *cept;* this regularity would have to be treated as a mere coincidence. Furthermore, the fact that *ceive* is a morpheme entails that *re, de, con,* and *per* must be morphemes in *receive, deceive, conceive,* and *perceive*; it is normally assumed that the division of words into morphemes must be exhaustive. Once these units are isolated, the isolation of the others is only a matter of following this line of thought to its logical conclusion.

Problem 2.2–4 Papago

Isolate the morphemes in the sentences below. State the meaning or syntactic function of each one.

(1)	ʔáañi ʔañ číkpan	'I am working.'
(2)	mį́d ʔo hígay	'He is running.'
(3)	ʔáapim ʔam číkpan	'You (PLURAL) are working.'
(4)	číkpan ʔo hígam	'They are working.'
(5)	ʔáapi ʔap mį́d	'You (SINGULAR) are running.'
(6)	číkpan ʔač ʔáačim	'We are working.'
(7)	hígay ʔo mį́d	'He is running.'
(8)	číkpan ʔañ	'I am working.'
(9)	hígam ʔo číkpan	'They are working.'
(10)	ʔáačim ʔač číkpan	'We are working.'

Discussion

The words [číkpan] 'work' and [míḍ] 'run' are easily identified and apparently consist of only one morpheme apiece. Of the pronouns, the two third person forms [hígay] 'he' and [hígam] 'they' stand out from the rest. The latter contains the ending [m], which occurs in all the plural pronouns; however, forming the third person plural involves more than just adding this ending to [hígay], since the plural form does not contain [y]. The other four pronouns are all of the form [ʔáaCi(m)], with *C* standing for a consonant. The [m] occurs only in the plural forms [ʔáačim] 'we' and [ʔáapim] 'you (PLURAL)'. The difference between the consonants [ñ č p] and the presence or absence of [m] serve to distinguish the four pronouns. Except for [m], the segmentation of the [ʔáaCi(m)] forms into morphemes is somewhat arbitrary. It would be possible to posit the morpheme [ʔáa] as indicating a non-third person pronoun together with the morphemes [ñi] 'FIRST PERSON SINGULAR', [či] 'FIRST PERSON PLURAL', and [pi] 'SECOND PERSON'. Another alternative would be to make [ʔáa . . . i] a "discontinuous" morpheme, leaving [ñ], [č], and [p] as morphemes differentiating the pronouns of the first two persons. There is no obvious basis for preferring either analysis. This indeterminacy is not untypical of pronominal systems, and it would be a mistake to rigidly impose an arbitrary segmentation on such forms in the interest of maintaining an artificially simple conception of the morpheme.

In Problem 2.1–3 [ʔo] was tentatively assigned the meaning 'is'. The data for the present problem is compatible with this decision; the English word *is* marks present tense and agreement with a third person (singular) subject, and both tense and person are apparently involved in the unstressed particles in sentences (1)–(10). [ʔ] may mark present tense, but this must remain a speculation until sentences in other tenses are examined for comparison. [o] accompanies [ʔ] when the subject is third person, and [a] otherwise. The endings [ñ], [č], [p], and [m] agree with the non-third person subject pronouns. Since the form of the unstressed particle is completely determined by the subject, these particles are not independently meaningful (except for indicating present tense) and can be considered sentence trappings. However, they make it possible to determine the person of the subject in sentences from which the subject has been deleted, such as (8).

Solution

      'work' = číkpan   'run' = míḍ

Pronouns
      'THIRD PERSON' = híga(y)
      'NON-THIRD PERSON' = ʔáa
      'FIRST PERSON SINGULAR' = ñi

'FIRST PERSON PLURAL' = či
'SECOND PERSON' = pi
'PLURAL' = m

Particles marking tense and agreement with subject
'PRESENT' = ʔ
'THIRD PERSON' = o
'NON-THIRD PERSON' = a
'FIRST PERSON SINGULAR' = ñ
'FIRST PERSON PLURAL' = č
'SECOND PERSON SINGULAR' = p
'SECOND PERSON PLURAL' = m

MORPHEMES AS SEMANTIC UNITS

As noted earlier, morphemes can be viewed either as phonetic sequences or as components of meaning. We have already considered morphemes as recurring phonetic sequences and have found that such sequences cannot always be associated with a constant component of meaning. Let us now consider the morpheme as a component of meaning. We will find several kinds of examples which show that it is not always possible to isolate a unique phonetic sequence that regularly manifests a given meaning.

Synonyms, such as *work* and *labor* or *sweat* and *perspire*, show that it is possible for a component of meaning to be associated with more than one phonetic sequence. For the most part, the existence of synonymous lexical items has no structural significance and holds only limited interest. Sometimes, however, the choice among alternative lexical items to manifest a certain component of meaning is determined entirely by grammatical considerations and is therefore structurally significant. For example, the English morpheme *go* is used in the present tense, but the phonologically unrelated form *went* is used in the past tense. Whereas *killed* represents a simple modification of the verb *kill*, *went* can just as well be regarded as a lexical item separate from *go* that is used in place of *go* in the past tense. The use of alternate lexical items to represent the same component of meaning in different grammatical circumstances is called **suppletion**. The suppletive variants of the verb *be* (*am, is, are, was*) provide further illustration. The distinction between suppletion and other kinds of morphological irregularity is not always a sharp one (consider *buy* and *bought*, *sell* and *sold*, *will* and *would*), but the important point here is that a given meaning may be represented by several different phonetic sequences.

Because raw linguistic data often takes the form of utterances transcribed phonetically, it is convenient for purposes of pedagogical problems dealing with morphemic analysis to regard morphemes (and other lexical units) as consisting in the association of meanings and phonetic sequences. However, it is more accurate to discuss morphemes in terms of phonological rather than phonetic representations. Lexical items, including morphemes, consist in the association of a semantic representation, a syntactic representation, and an underlying phonological representation. The phonological representation of a morpheme may be constant despite certain variations in its phonetic realization in different environments. These phonetic variations in the shape of a morpheme are very often the result of the application of general phonological rules, which obscure at the phonetic level the underlying phonological uniformity of morphemes.

The Ayutla Mixtec data of Problem of 2.1–11 provides a good example. The form for 'soap' appears phonetically as either [nâmàá] or [námáà?]. (To simplify matters, a third variant, [nâmà], will be omitted from consideration.) Actually, neither of these phonetic sequences is identical to the phonological representation, which (for purposes of this discussion at least) can be taken to be [nâmàá?]. In Problem 2.1–11 we noted the existence in Ayutla Mixtec of a rule that applies to a combination of two words the first of which ends in a glottal stop. In such combinations the glottal stop of the first word is deleted and the tone sequence of the first three vowels of the second word changes to [′ ′ ˋ]. This general rule is responsible for deriving the two phonetic variants of the form for 'soap' from the single phonological representation. When [nâmàá?] occurs as the first word of an expression, as in [nâmàášíkǎrà] 'He asked for soap', this phonological rule causes the final [?] to be deleted. When [nâmàá?] occurs as the second word of an expression, as in [kâkǎǔnámáà?] 'You will ask for soap', the final [?] remains, but the tone sequence changes from [^ ˋ ′] to [′ ′ ˋ]. The surface phonetic variation in the form for 'soap' is therefore not irregular but simply reflects the application of a general phonological rule to uniform phonological representations.

Suppletion and phonetic variation due to the operation of general phonological rules are but two of the sources of difficulty in determining the segmental representation of components of meaning. Another source is **syncretism**, the use of a single, non-divisible phonetic sequence to manifest more than one component of meaning. To some degree, almost any form can be considered syncretistic, since virtually any meaning encoded by a phonological form can be broken down into smaller meaning components; 'run', for instance, involves such components as 'move', 'rapidity', and so on. However, some cases of syncretism stand out because the components of meaning that are merged at the phonetic level also have a grammatical function and are frequently manifested by separate phonological forms.

The French form *au* [o] 'to the' is a simple and oft-cited example. The meaning components 'to' and 'the' are sometimes manifested separately in French, as in the expression *à l'enfant* [alãfǽ] 'to the child', in which [a] stands for 'to' and [l] for 'the'. However, the single segment [o] in the phrase *au garçon* [ogarsɔ̃] 'to the boy' represents both 'to' and 'the'. In this particular example, the syncretism holds at the level of phonetics but not at the phonological level;

the underlying phonological sequence [al] is realized phonetically as [o] by virtue of a general phonological rule of French that changes [al] to [o] before a consonant. However, many syncretistic phonetic sequences do derive from phonological representations that are themselves syncretistic. The Luiseño form [q], which was found in Problem 2.2–2 to mark present tense, also indicates that the subject is singular, and there is no evidence for any underlying representation in which the two morphemes 'PRESENT' and 'SINGULAR' have separate phonological shapes. When a present tense verb has a plural subject, [wun] is used instead of [q]. The form [wun] is also syncretistic (manifesting the meaning components 'PRESENT' and 'PLURAL') and stands in a suppletive relationship to [q].

The phonological manifestation of components of meaning involves still further complexities. Most morphemes are represented phonologically as sequences of sound segments, but some have more abstract manifestations. For example, components of meaning are sometimes represented, not by sound segments, but rather by **suprasegmental** phenomena (length, stress, tone, and the like). In many languages intonation alone may distinguish questions and declarative sentences; thus the French sentences *Il est là* 'He is there' and *Il est là?* 'Is he there?' differ phonetically only in that the latter is pronounced with rising intonation. Problem 2.2–5, Diegueño, offers another kind of example.

Still more abstract are the entities referred to as **process morphemes** and **zero morphemes**. Process morphemes have no segmental representation of their own; they are manifested instead through the phonological modification of other morphemes. In English, for instance, one way of forming the past tense of a verb is to change the vowel of the verb stem. *Sang* is the past tense of *sing*, *rode* the past tense of *ride*, and so on. It would be somewhat artificial to point to any segment of *sang* as the past tense morpheme (if *a* were called the past tense marker, we would be left with *s . . . ng* as the verb root, but in forms like *sings*, *will sing*, and *singing* the root is apparently *sing*). More accurate would be the claim that the past tense morpheme is realized through the phonological process of changing the root vowel from *i* to *a* (that is, from [ɪ] to [æ]). Process morphemes show that the distinction between lexical rules on the one hand and syntactic and phonological rules on the other hand is not at all a sharp one.

As the name implies, zero morphemes are morphemes with no phonological shape whatsoever. The notion of the zero morpheme might at first seem self-contradictory, but the conceptual difficulty is resolved when we note that the absence of an element can convey just as much information as its presence. In Classical Aztec, for example, a verb normally contains a prefix that agrees with its subject (see Problem 2.2–11 below). When the subject is first or second person, the prefix is overtly manifested by means of a sequence of sound segments. However, there is no such segmental manifestation when the subject is third person. Given this situation, the absence of a prefix marking agreement is significant; it indicates that the subject of the verb is third person. To maintain the generalization that verbs agree with their subjects in Aztec, we can analyze verbs with third person subjects as containing agreement morphemes whose phonetic realization is zero. The notion of a zero morpheme is thus a coherent one in terms of a paradigmatic arrangement of forms such as a verb conjugation. In such a system, one slot in the paradigm may be characterized by the absence of some element overtly manifested in all the others; zero, in other words, may have contrastive value. To be sure, there are other ways of describing situations such as these—one does not have to speak of zero morphemes. Nevertheless, the concept is for many purposes a useful one.

Problem 2.2–5   Diegueño

This problem concerns the formation of plural verbs in Diegueño, an American Indian language of the Hokan family (Walker, 1970). A verb is marked plural in Diegueño if its subject or object is plural or if it designates a repeated or continuing activity. The symbol [L] stands for a voiceless lateral, and ['] for palatalization. Examine the singular and plural verb forms below, and discuss the phonological manifestation of the plural morpheme.

Singular	Plural	
Lʸap	Lʸaap	'burn'
muL	muuL	'gather'
čuupuL	čuupuuL	'boil'
saaw	saw	'eat'
wiṛ	wiiṛ	'be hard'

Solution

The singular and plural forms of these verbs are identical except for the length of the final vowel. If the final vowel of the singular is short, the corresponding vowel is long in the plural, and vice versa. The plural morpheme is thus not manifested as a sequence of sound segments. Rather it is a process morpheme that affects the suprasegmental properties of the singular form. The plural form of a verb is derived from the singular form by changing the length of the final vowel.

Problem 2.2–6   Italian

Isolate the morphemes in sentences (1)–(8) and state their meanings. [z̧] stands for a voiced alveolar affricate (the voiced counterpart of [c]); this sound occurs in English and is usually written *ds* (as in *bids*).

(1) lo skoláro e studióso	'The male pupil is studious.'
(2) le ʑíe sono amerikáne	'The aunts are American.'
(3) li ʑíi sono studiósi	'The uncles are studious.'
(4) la skolára e amerikána	'The female pupil is American.'
(5) li skolári sono amerikáni	'The male pupils are American.'
(6) la ʑía e studiósa	'The aunt is studious.'
(7) le skoláre sono studióse	'The female pupils are studious.'
(8) lo ʑío e amerikáno	'The uncle is American.'

Solution

'is' = e	'the' = l
'are' = sono	'MASCULINE SINGULAR' = o
'pupil' = skolár	'MASCULINE PLURAL' = i
'parent's sibling' = ʑí	'FEMININE SINGULAR' = a
'American' = amerikán	'FEMININE PLURAL' = e
'studious' = studiós	

Discussion

The forms for 'is' and 'are' are suppletive; that is, they are not directly related to each other phonologically. Moreover, they are syncretistic, although the data is not sufficient to establish this conclusively. The form [e] indicates the present tense of 'be' and also marks agreement with a third person singular subject; [sono] indicates the present tense of 'be' and also marks agreement with a third person plural subject. The endings [o], [i], [a], and [e] are syncretistic too, each representing both gender and number. They are independently meaningful on the subject nouns, since only the ending in words like [skoláro] and [ʑíe] indicates how many individuals are being referred to and whether these individuals are male or female. The same four endings occur as sentence trappings on the article [l] and the adjectives [studiós] and [amerikán]; here they merely agree with the subject and hence contribute no meaning of their own.

CONCLUSION

The concept of the morpheme is a problematic one, for linguists group together under this rubric many different kinds of entities. The clearest examples of morphemes are minimal sequences of phonological segments associated with a constant meaning and a syntactic representation. We have seen, however, that the term is also used more generally to designate minimal structural units

of various kinds that do not meet this condition. Structurally significant phonological sequences are considered morphemes even when they have no independent meaning or are meaningful only in certain uses; sentence trappings and
minimal units that figure in the construction of large numbers of words (such
as *per*, *ceive*, and (*s*)*pect*) qualify as morphemes in this way. By the same token,
components of meaning may be considered morphemes even when they have
no consistent segmental representation; morphemes may be manifested phonetically through suppletive variants, syncretism, suprasegmental phenomena, or
phonological processes, and sometimes they have no phonetic realization at
all.

It is apparent, then, that morphemic analysis involves a great deal more
than merely chopping up phonetic sequences and pinning semantic labels on
the chunks. Both syntactic and phonological considerations bear on the isolation of minimal lexical units, and the morphemic analysis of a language
cannot be successfully concluded in the absence of at least a modicum of
progress in the analysis of its syntax and phonology.

FURTHER PROBLEMS

Problem 2.2–7   Serbo-Croatian

Isolate the morphemes in the Serbo-Croatian sentences below (Javarek and
Sudjić, 1963) and give their meanings. Comment on sentence trappings, zero
morphemes, and other matters treated in this section.

(1)	yá čítam	'I read.'
(2)	óni píyu	'They drink.'
(3)	púšiš	'You smoke.'
(4)	ví čítate	'You (PLURAL) read.'
(5)	púšim	'I smoke.'
(6)	mí píyemo	'We drink.'
(7)	tí píyeš	'You drink.'
(8)	ón číta	'He reads.'
(9)	píyem	'I drink.'
(10)	púšite	'You (PLURAL) smoke.'
(11)	čítamo	'We read.'
(12)	óni púše	'They smoke.'
(13)	čítayu	'They read.'
(14)	púši	'He smokes.'
(15)	ví píyete	'You (PLURAL) drink.'
(16)	ón píye	'He drinks.'
(17)	mí púšimo	'We smoke.'
(18)	tí čítaš	'You read.'

Problem 2.2–8 Luiseño

Isolate the morphemes in sentences (1)–(20) and state the meaning or syntactic function of each. For suppletive morphemes, state the conditions in which each form is used.

(1)	nóo kwótaq	'I am getting up.'
(2)	húnwutum ʔehéŋmayumi qeʔéewun	'The bears are killing the birds.'
(3)	čáam tóowwun ʔehéŋmayi	'We see the bird.'
(4)	húnwutum ŋóoraan	'The bears are running.'
(5)	čáam wuváʔnawun ʔehéŋmayumi	'We are hitting the birds.'
(6)	nóo pókwaq	'I am running.'
(7)	ʔehéŋmay wíilaq	'The bird is flying.'
(8)	čáam móqnawun húnwuti	'We are killing the bear.'
(9)	húnwut wuváʔnaq čáami	'The bear is hitting us.'
(10)	čáam waráavaan	'We are getting up.'
(11)	nóo húnwuti móqnaq	'I am killing the bear.'
(12)	húnwut néy tóowq	'The bear sees me.'
(13)	čáam wótiwun húnwuti	'We are hitting the bear.'
(14)	nóo qeʔéeq húnwutumi	'I am killing the bears.'
(15)	ʔehéŋmayum wáapaan	'The birds are flying.'
(16)	nóo húnwuti wótiq	'I am hitting the bear.'
(17)	húnwutum čáami tóowwun	'The bears see us.'
(18)	nóo húnwuti tóowq	'I see the bear.'
(19)	čáam ŋóoraan	'We are running.'
(20)	húnwut pókwaq	'The bear is running.'

Problem 2.2–9 Turkish

Isolate the morphemes in the Turkish expressions below (Lewis, 1953) and state their meanings. Recall the rule of vowel harmony discussed in Problem 2.1–4.

(1)	gelmek	'to come'
(2)	adamlarin	'of the men'
(3)	almazsin	'you do not take'
(4)	gelmezsiniz	'you (PLURAL) do not come'
(5)	almamak	'not to take'
(6)	kizlardan	'from the girls'
(7)	ankarada	'in Ankara'
(8)	gelsin	'let him come'
(9)	almayiz	'we do not take'
(10)	gelmem	'I do not come'
(11)	köprülere	'to the bridges'
(12)	gelmez	'he does not come'

(13)	almazlar	'they do not take'
(14)	adama	'to the man'
(15)	almak	'to take'
(16)	evden	'from the house'
(17)	alsinlar	'let them take'
(18)	gelmezsin	'you do not come'
(19)	almam	'I do not take'
(20)	köprüde	'on the bridge'
(21)	gelmemek	'not to come'
(22)	almaz	'he does not take'
(23)	gelmezler	'they do not come'
(24)	köpeyin	'of the dog'
(25)	gelsinler	'let them come'
(26)	almazsiniz	'you (PLURAL) do not take'
(27)	adamlara	'to the men'
(28)	gelmeyiz	'we do not come'
(29)	alsin	'let him take'
(30)	köprülerde	'on the bridges'

Problem 2.2–10 Swahili

One of the most characteristic features of Swahili syntax is the occurrence with nouns of a set of prefixes that are used for purposes of agreement. Every noun has a particular prefix that regularly occurs with it, and every prefix has a special form that is used when the noun is plural. Isolate the morphemes in the data below (Perrott, 1951) and state their meanings. List the noun prefixes and state the rules governing their use.

(1)	tulirúdi	'We returned.'
(2)	kitábu kimója kitanitóša	'One book will be enough for me.'
(3)	ananiulíza	'He is asking me.'
(4)	utasóma	'You will read.'
(5)	watóto walirúdi	'The children returned.'
(6)	wanasóma	'They are reading.'
(7)	vísu vitátu vinatóša	'Three knives are enough.'
(8)	nitawajíbu	'I will answer you (PLURAL).'
(9)	mtumíši alisóma	'The servant read.'
(10)	walisóma kitábu	'They read (PAST) the book.'
(11)	mtarúdi	'You (PLURAL) will return.'
(12)	tutawaulíza	'We will ask them.'
(13)	mtóto mmója anawatóša	'One child is enough for them.'
(14)	mlisóma	'You (PLURAL) read (PAST).'

(15) vísu vidógo vitatóša   'Small knives will be enough.'
(16) ninakujíbu   'I am answering you.'
(17) watumíši watátu watatutóša   'Three servants will be enough for us.'

(18) kísu kimója kilitóša   'One knife was enough.'
(19) atasóma   'He will read.'
(20) tutawaulíza   'We will ask you (PLURAL).'
(21) ninarúdi   'I am returning.'
(22) vitábu vidógo vitátu vilimtóša   'Three small books were enough for him.'

(23) tulimjíbu   'We answered him.'
(24) mtumíši mmója atanitóša   'One servant will be enough for me.'

(25) walirúdi   'They returned.'
(26) vísu vitátu vinatutóša   'Three knives are enough for us.'

Problem 2.2–11   Classical Aztec

Isolate the morphemes in sentences (1)–(25) and state their meanings. Comment on any peculiarities or variations in the phonetic manifestation of components of meaning.

(1) tikimpoowáyaʔ   'We were counting them.'
(2) ninóca   'I call.'
(3) titečλasóλas   'You will love us.'
(4) óomik   'He died.'
(5) annémiʔ   'You (PLURAL) live.'
(6) óonoc   'He called.'
(7) ninoλasóλa   'I love myself.'
(8) tinémi   'You live.'
(9) nikimnocáya   'I was calling them.'
(10) míki   'He dies.'
(11) micλasóλaʔ   'They love you.'
(12) amečnocáyaʔ   'They were calling you (PLURAL).'
(13) ooníknoc   'I called him.'
(14) tinémiʔ   'We live.'
(15) annečλasóλaʔ   'You (PLURAL) love me.'
(16) mikíyaʔ   'They were dying.'
(17) ootíkpoow   'You counted it.'
(18) tečλasóλaʔ   'They love us.'
(19) moλasóλa   'He loves himself.'
(20) amečnócas   'He will call you (PLURAL).'

(21)	némiʔ	'They live.'
(22)	ankinocáyaʔ	'You (PLURAL) were calling him.'
(23)	timíkis	'You will die.'
(24)	tikpóowaʔ	'We count it.'
(25)	nečnócas	'He will call me.'

Problem 2.2–12   *Navaho*

This problem (Hale, *to appear*, a) illustrates the close connection between lexical and phonological analysis. For purposes of this problem, assume that the phonology of Navaho contains the following three rules.

(A) [l] is deleted when it occurs between two consonants.
(B) [i] is inserted at the beginning of a verb word that contains no vowels except in the verb root.
(C) If a word begins in [i], [y] is inserted directly before this vowel.

Because of the operation of these and other rules, the morphemic analysis of Navaho words is more regular at the underlying phonological level than at the phonetic level. The symbol ['] marks high tone. [γ] indicates a voiced velar fricative (the voiced counterpart of [x]), and [tʔ] stands for a glottalized [t].

Isolate the morphemes in the sentences below and state their meanings. Comment on the different phonetic manifestations of the morphemes meaning 'about' and 'walk along'. Give the underlying phonological representations of the verbs in sentences (1), (7), (9), and (16) and describe the derivation of their phonetic manifestations.

(1)	ší naašniš	'I work about.'
(2)	naabé	'He swims about.'
(3)	yiidloh	'We laugh.'
(4)	niča	'You cry.'
(5)	diné naalniš	'The man works about.'
(6)	nihí yiitʔaš	'We (two) walk along.'
(7)	ší yišγoL	'I run along.'
(8)	naniʔá	'You carry it about.'
(9)	neiilniš	'We work about.'
(10)	ʔaškii yilγoL	'The boy runs along.'
(11)	diné yiča	'The man is crying.'
(12)	naašbé	'I swim about.'
(13)	ni nanilniš	'You work about.'
(14)	ší yišááL	'I walk along.'
(15)	naalniš	'He works about.'
(16)	yiiča	'We cry.'
(17)	yišdloh	'I laugh.'

(18) nanibé   'You swim about.'
(19) ʔaškii naalniš   'The boy works about.'
(20) nihí yiikah   'We (more than two) walk along.'
(21) naašʔá   'I carry it about.'
(22) yišča   'I cry.'

2.3   Complex Lexical Items

The exercises in section 2.2 make it clear that languages abound in lexical items that are "complex" in the sense that they can be broken down into smaller units of structural significance. In this section we will examine the internal structure of complex lexical items and the principles that govern their composition.

We may distinguish several facets of the internal structure of complex lexical items. One is the linear ordering of the component morphemes. Another is the analysis of complex lexical items into roots, stems, and affixes. Still a third facet is a constituent structure not unlike that of sentences. The construction of complex lexical items from smaller units proceeds in accordance with rules having varying degrees of generality. These principles are intimately connected with the syntax of a language and may be considered (using the term somewhat broadly) syntactic rules. To the extent that such rules are general, the internal structure of the complex lexical items of a language will be regular.

LINEAR ORDERING

The morphemes which constitute a complex lexical item must occur in a fixed order. The three morphemes of *carelessness*, for instance, cannot be rearranged —*lessnesscare*, *nesscareless*, and so on are all impossible. The words of a sentence can often be permuted without any change in meaning or grammaticalness, but when the morphemes of a lexical item are permuted, the result is almost always an ungrammatical expression or one with a different meaning.

Restrictions on the ordering of morphemes in complex lexical items are sometimes quite general in their application. Consider, for instance, the Swahili word [tutawaulíza] 'we will ask them'. This word comprises the four morphemes [tu] 'we', [ta] 'FUTURE', [wa] 'them', and [ulíza] 'ask'; the first indicates the person of the subject, the second marks tense, the third indicates the person of the object, and the fourth is the verb root. If these elements were arranged in any other order, the resulting expression would be ungrammatical. The following formula summarizes the required linear ordering abstractly.

SUBJECT MARKER + TENSE + OBJECT MARKER + ROOT

This formula holds not just for this one word but for virtually any Swahili verb (restricting our consideration to simple sentences of the sort examined in Problem 2.2–10). The ordering of these four elements is therefore not an idiosyncratic trait of a single lexical item. Instead, the formula above can be regarded as a syntactic rule of considerable generality.

Problem 2.3–1   Navaho

Examine the verbs in sentences (1)–(22) of Problem 2.2–12. Construct a formula, such as the one given above for Swahili, that describes the order in which the elements of a Navaho verb must occur. Under each position of the formula list the items exemplified in Problem 2.2–12 that can occur in that position. Consider the verbs in terms of their underlying phonological representations rather than their phonetic shapes.

Solution

ADVERB + SUBJECT MARKER + ROOT

na	š	lniš
	ni	bé
	ii	dloh
		ááL, tʔaš, kah
		lɣoL
		ʔá
		ča

Discussion

In the data under consideration the adverbial element [na] 'about' does not occur with every verb root listed, but when it does occur it precedes the morpheme that agrees with the subject. The third person subject marker is zero, as in [naabé] 'He swims about'. The initial [y(i)] of words such as [yišɣoL] 'I run along' is not included, since it is introduced by phonological rules and does not figure in underlying phonological representations.

ROOTS, STEMS, AND AFFIXES

Most complex lexical items are formed by attaching *affixes* to a basic morpheme called the *root*. Affixes that precede the root are called *prefixes*, and those that follow the root are called *suffixes*. In the word *houses*, for instance, *house* is the root and *s* is a suffix. The word *carefully* is derived by suffixing *ful* and *ly* to the root *care*. *Unable* consists of the root *able* and the prefix *un*.

It is customary to distinguish between ***inflectional*** and ***derivational*** affixes. Inflectional affixes are those that mark number, gender, case, tense, and certain other categories; derivational affixes are those that are non-inflectional. Although the distinction is not a sharp one, inflectional and derivational affixes do tend to have certain contrasting properties. For one thing, derivational elements are in general independently meaningful, whereas inflectional categories are frequently introduced as sentence trappings by agreement rules. Second, derivational affixes have the potential to change the grammatical class of the elements to which they are attached. For example, the addition of the derivational suffix *ful* to the noun *care* results in an adjective, and the addition of *ly* to the adjective *careful* results in an adverb, *carefully*. By contrast, an adjective inflected to agree in gender and number with the noun it modifies remains an adjective.

Third, there is a universal tendency for derivational affixes to occur closer to the root than inflectional affixes; in words that contain a sequence of prefixes or suffixes, derivational elements tend to be central, and inflections peripheral. The root and derivational affixes (if there are any) constitute the kernel of a word, usually referred to as the ***stem***, and it is to the stem that inflectional affixes are attached. This schema is depicted in Figure 2.3–1, in

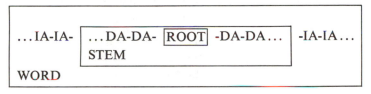

Figure 2.3–1

which *DA* stands for a derivational affix, *IA* for an inflectional affix, and hyphens for morpheme boundaries. In the English word *books*, for instance, *book* is both the root and the stem (there being no derivational element), and the plural *s* is an inflectional ending. In the word *unkindnesses*, the root is *kind*, the stem is *unkindness*, and it is to this entire stem that the plural ending *es* is added. Languages vary greatly in the number and kinds of affixes they allow, so Figure 2.3–1 should not be read too literally. Moreover, the tendency for the derivational affixes of a word to sink toward the root is only a tendency, not an absolute universal. The Navaho word [naašniš] 'I work about' is one exception. The root is [niš] 'work'. [naa] 'about' would probably be considered a derivational element, but it is farther from the root than [š], an inflectional affix that agrees with a first person singular subject.

Several kinds of syntactic rules serve to introduce inflections. Some inflectional affixes are introduced by rules that mark constituents in accordance with their syntactic function in the sentence. A syntactic rule of Papago introduces the prefix [g] on any noun that is not in sentence-initial position, for instance. The direct object of a verb in Latin is marked for accusative case, the subject for nominative case, and so on. Other inflectional affixes are induced by syntactic agreement rules. One example is the Navaho rule which requires that a verb contain a marker that agrees with its subject. An agreement rule of Spanish requires that an adjective agree in number and gender with the noun it modifies. Syntactic rules are also responsible for determining the position in a sentence of independently meaningful inflectional affixes, such as the plural endings on English nouns. Thus a syntactic rule of English specifies that the plurality of nouns is marked (in regular cases) by a suffix rather than by some other device.

Derivational affixes are in general independently meaningful. Frequently, rules of some generality govern the attachment of derivational affixes to roots in the formation of complex stems. In Turkish, for instance, negation can be expressed by the addition of the derivational suffix [ma] or [me] to the verb root. The word [almam] 'I do not take' consists of the root [al] 'take', the derivational suffix [ma] 'not', and the inflectional suffix [m], which agrees with the subject; [gelmem] 'I do not come' has a similar analysis. Consequently, we can say that Turkish manifests the following derivational pattern (*V* stands for a verb root).

> The meaning 'not to *V*' can be expressed by a complex verb consisting of *V* plus the suffix [ma] (or [me]).

A derivational regularity of this kind can be regarded as a special sort of syntactic rule, because it specifies the relationship between a semantic configuration and the particular syntactic pattern that manifests it.

Problem 2.3–2 Luiseño

State the derivational and inflectional rules that account for the occurrence of the suffixes on the verbs in sentences (1)–(6). Show the structure of the verb in (6) by means of a diagram analogous to Figure 2.3–1.

(1) nóo ŋéeq	'I am leaving.'
(2) nóo ŋéevičuq	'I want to leave.'
(3) nóo póy ŋéeniq	'I am making him leave.'
(4) nóo póy ŋéevičuniq	'I am making him want to leave.'
(5) nóo póy ŋéenivičuq	'I want to make him leave.'
(6) nóo póy ŋéevičunivičuq	'I want to make him want to leave.'

Solution

(A) The meaning 'want to *V*' can be expressed by a complex verb consisting of *V* plus the suffix [viču].

(B) The meaning 'make ... *V*' can be expressed by a complex verb consisting of *V* plus the suffix [ni].

(C) Present tense can be expressed by adding the suffix [q] to the verb stem.

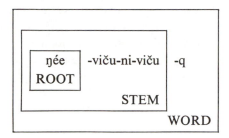

COMPOUNDS

Not all complex lexical items are single words consisting of a root flanked by affixes. Idioms and compounds are two exceptions to this common pattern. An **idiom** is a lexical item whose meaning is irregular given the meanings of its component morphemes. Some individual words are idioms (*understand*, for example), but many idioms consist of whole phrases (*shoot the bull, bite the dust, stick to the straight and narrow*). **Compounds** are lexical units formed by juxtaposing more than one stem. For instance, the compound *valve lifter* contains the two stems *valve* and *lifter*. *Valve* is both a root and a stem, since it has no derivational affixes. *Lifter* consists of the root *lift* and the derivational affix *er*.

Compound formation tends to follow certain patterns and can often be described by means of derivational rules analogous to those discussed above. However, many rules of compound formation turn out not to be very productive. Moreover, both compounds and other derived lexical items, even those that appear to follow regular derivational rules, are capable of taking on special senses that cannot be predicted from the meanings of the morphemes they contain or the rules that derive them. Compounds in particular are susceptible to idiomaticity.

Consider English compounds formed from two nouns such that the first is possessed by the second; examples are *armchair* ('chair with arms'), *rattlesnake* ('snake with rattles'), *family man* ('man with a family'), *ice water* ('water with ice'), *picture book* ('book with pictures'), and so on. On the basis of examples such as these, one can postulate for English a derivational rule roughly of the following form, where *N* stands for a noun.

The meaning 'N_1 with N_2' can be expressed by a compound noun of the form N_2N_1.

However, one quickly notices that this derivational pattern is only slightly productive; only for relatively few expressions of the form 'N_1 with N_2' is the corresponding compound an accepted lexical item of English. Thus a dog with a tail cannot be referred to as a *tail dog*, whisky with a cherry in it cannot be referred to as *cherry whisky*, and a man with an aunt cannot be referred to as an *aunt man*. Should lexical items such as these come into general use, they could be recognized as conforming to an existing derivational pattern, but at present they are only "potential" lexical items, not actual ones. Furthermore, some compounds that superficially appear to exemplify this derivational pattern are semantically irregular, having meanings not strictly equivalent to 'N_1 with N_2'. Thus a *lighthouse* is not simply a house with a light, and *ice cream* is not cream with ice in it (compare *ice water*). The derivational rule, as formulated, does not even exhaustively describe the meanings of all the "regular" compounds cited above. The generality and regularity of derivational patterns vary widely from pattern to pattern and from language to language.

Problem 2.3–3 French

State a derivational rule that will account for the compounds listed below. Regular French orthography is used.

(1) bracelet-cuir   'copper bracelet'
(2) boîte métal   'metal box'
(3) sauce tomate   'tomato sauce'
(4) cabane bambou   'bamboo hut'
(5) boîte acier   'steel box'
(6) pneu nylon   'nylon tire'
(7) bouteille verre   'glass bottle'

Solution

The meaning 'N_1 made out of N_2' can be expressed by a compound noun of the form $N_1 N_2$.

CONSTITUENT STRUCTURE

We have seen that complex lexical items must be attributed internal structure. For one thing, their component morphemes must occur in a particular linear order. Furthermore, complex words can be broken down into a stem plus a series of inflectional affixes, and a stem can be analyzed as consisting of a root and a series of derivational affixes. The notions root, stem, and affix imply that the internal structure of words is at least in part hierarchical; this hierarchical or "layered" structure is clearly revealed in Figure 2.3–1.

In addition, words and other complex lexical items can be attributed internal constituent structure analogous to that of sentences. This is most obviously true in the case of certain idioms, like *tip the scale at, break the ice, red herring, shoot the bull, sit on pins and needles,* and *kick the bucket.* The internal structure of these lexical items is conveniently described in terms of syntactic "tree" structures (like Figure 1.1–2 of the first chapter; see p. 5). *Shoot the bull,* for instance, can be attributed the constituent structure of Figure 2.3–2, whether it is taken in its literal or in its idiomatic sense. Even

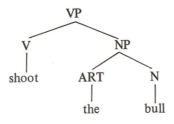

Figure 2.3–2

when *shoot the bull* is taken figuratively, *shoot* is a verb, *the bull* is a noun phrase, *the* is an article, and so on. Besides being intuitively correct, this analysis is supported by syntactic and phonological considerations. Syntactically, *shoot* functions like a verb in that it can be marked for tense (for example, *The two girls are shooting the bull, They shot the bull all day*). On the phonological side, the *shoot* of the idiom *shoot the bull* has the same irregular past tense form (*shot*) as the regular verb *shoot;* moreover, *the* has the same phonetic shapes as the regular article *the*—[ði] in very deliberate speech, [ðə] in normal speech, and [ð] in fast speech. To be sure, the idiom *shoot the bull* cannot undergo all the syntactic operations that non-idiomatic verb phrases can; *The bull was shot* can only refer to an assault on a male bovine, not to a bull session. But this lack of syntactic flexibility is characteristic of complex lexical items.

Words and compounds can also be attributed internal constituent structure. The structures of *unkindnesses* and *armchair* are depicted in Figures 2.3–3 and 2.3–4 respectively. The root *kind* of *unkindnesses* is an adjective, as is the derived form *unkind.* When *ness* is added to an adjective, the resulting constituent is a noun, in this case *unkindness.* Finally, the addition of the plural suffix *es* results in *unkindnesses,* which is also a noun. Both constituents of *armchair, arm* and *chair,* are nouns. Moreover, the compound *armchair* also functions syntactically as a noun, and Figure 2.3–4 reflects this fact.

The internal constituent structure of a word or compound is a direct reflection of the syntactic rules in accordance with which it is constructed. Figure 2.3–4, for instance, reflects the operation of derivational rule (A), which was discussed earlier.

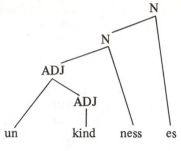

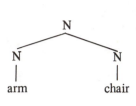

Figure 2.3-3   *Figure 2.3-4*

(A) The meaning 'N_1 with N_2' can be expressed by a compound noun of the form N_2N_1.

Similarly, Figure 2.3–3 mirrors the operation of derivational rules (B) and (C), as well as inflectional rule (D), which specifies how the plural of a noun is expressed (in regular cases).

(B) The meaning 'not *ADJ*' can be expressed by a complex adjective consisting of *ADJ* plus the prefix *un*.
(C) The meaning 'act of being *ADJ*' can be expressed by a complex noun consisting of *ADJ* plus the suffix *ness*.
(D) The plural of a noun can be formed by adding the suffix (*e*)*s*.

Knowledge of the derivational and inflectional rules of a language can therefore be used in determining the internal structure of lexical items to the extent that their formation follows general patterns.

Problem 2.3–4   English

State the derivational rules involved in the construction of the words listed in Problem 2.2–1. Diagram the internal constituent structure of the words *fearlessness*, *harmlessly*, and *untruthfully*.

Solution

(A) The meaning 'having *N*' can be expressed by a complex adjective consisting of *N* plus the suffix *ful*.
(B) The meaning 'in an *ADJ* manner' can be expressed by a complex adverb consisting of *ADJ* plus the suffix *ly*.
(C) The meaning 'without *N*' can be expressed by a complex adjective consisting of *N* plus the suffix *less*.
(D) The meaning 'the quality of being *ADJ*' can be expressed by a complex noun consisting of *ADJ* plus the suffix *ness*.
(E) The meaning 'not *ADJ*' can be expressed by a complex adjective consisting of *ADJ* plus the prefix *un*.

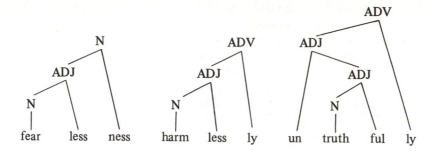

FURTHER PROBLEMS

Problem 2.3–5   Classical Aztec

Examine the verbs in Problem 2.2–11. Construct a formula describing the order in which the elements of an Aztec verb must occur (as you did in Problem 2.3–1 for Navaho). For each position in the formula, list the items exemplified in Problem 2.2–11 that can occur in that position.

Problem 2.3–6   Luiseño

Diagram the internal structure of the verbs in sentences (2), (4), and (6) of Problem 2.3–2. This structure should reflect the operation of the derivational and inflectional rules posited in Problem 2.3–2.

Problem 2.3–7   Urdu

Isolate the roots in the Urdu infinitival forms below (Bailey, 1956) and give their meanings. State the two basic derivational rules that account for these forms. Diagram the internal constituent structure of (5) and (9).

(1)	gana	'to sing'
(2)	bʊlana	'to cause to speak'
(3)	pɪgʰlana	'to melt' (transitive)
(4)	kʰelna	'to play'
(5)	gɪrna	'to fall'
(6)	jʌlana	'to burn' (transitive)
(7)	ʊlʌṭna	'to turn upside down' (intransitive)
(8)	čʌlna	'to move' (intransitive)
(9)	gɪrana	'to knock down'

(10) sʌmʌĵʰna   'to understand'
(11) gʌvana   'to cause to sing'
(12) bolna   'to speak'
(13) ʋlṭana   'to turn upside down' (transitive)
(14) ĵʌlna   'to burn' (intransitive)
(15) pɪgʰʌlna   'to melt' (intransitive)
(16) kʰɪlana   'to cause to play'
(17) čʌlana   'to cause to move'
(18) sʌmĵʰana   'to explain'

Problem 2.3–8   *Esperanto*

Esperanto is an artificial language invented by L. L. Zamenhof in the nine-teenth century to facilitate international communication. The following words (Connor *et al.*, 1959) illustrate some of the derivational rules of Esperanto. They are given in regular Esperanto orthography. Isolate the roots of these words and give their meanings. State the derivational rules in accordance with which the words are constructed. Diagram the internal constituent structure of (6) and (13).

(1) bono   'goodness'
(2) portistino   'female porter'
(3) instrua   'instructive'
(4) pura   'pure'
(5) malfacila   'difficult'
(6) malbone   'badly'
(7) patrino   'mother'
(8) facile   'easily'
(9) instruisto   'teacher'
(10) bona   'good'
(11) porti   'to carry'
(12) malgranda   'small'
(13) instruistino 'female teacher'
(14) instruo   'instruction'
(15) facila   'easy'
(16) bone   'well'
(17) patro   'father'
(18) facilo   'easiness'
(19) portisto   'porter'
(20) granda   'big'
(21) malbona   'bad'
(22) instrui   'to instruct'

Problem 2.3–9   Indonesian

The data below (Kwee, 1965) illustrates the use of four derivational affixes in Indonesian. Isolate these morphemes and comment on the phonological effect of adding them to a root. State the derivational rules that account for the complex words in the data. A single affix may enter into more than one derivational pattern. list stem + affixes

(1)	pəŋgunuŋ	'mountaineer'
(2)	bɔdɔh	'stupid'
(3)	pəkubʊran	'cemetery'
(4)	lawt	'sea'
(5)	pənčuri	'thief'
(6)	kəčuraŋan	'dishonesty'
(7)	baŋsa	'standing, position'
(8)	wartawan	'reporter'
(9)	lʊkis	'paint' (verb)
(10)	pəlayaran	'navigation'
(11)	rɪmba	'forest'
(12)	kəbɔdɔan	'stupidity'
(13)	bʊrʊk	'bad'
(14)	ajaran	'teaching, instruction'
(15)	hukʊm	'punish'
(16)	pənəmʊan	'find, invention'
(17)	lari	'run'
(18)	hartawan	'one who is wealthy'
(19)	pənʊlis	'writer'
(20)	čuraŋ	'dishonest'
(21)	kubʊr	'bury'
(22)	gunuŋ	'mountain'
(23)	baŋsawan	'one with standing, nobleman'
(24)	layar	'sail' (verb)
(25)	lʊkisan	'painting'
(26)	harta	'wealth'
(27)	tʊlis	'write'
(28)	hukʊman	'punishment'
(29)	pəlari	'runner'
(30)	pəlawt	'seaman'
(31)	ajar	'teach'
(32)	pərɪmba	'forester'
(33)	čuri	'steal'
(34)	kəbʊrʊkan	'badness'
(35)	təmʊ	'find'
(36)	warta	'news'

Problem 2.3–10   English

Postulate three derivational rules that will account for all the complex lexical items listed below. Give the internal constituent structure of (8), (17), and (20).

(1) floor wax
(2) gambler
(3) bird watcher
(4) auto polish
(5) stamp collector
(6) auto polish can label
(7) window washer
(8) garbage can collector
(9) girl fancier
(10) window shade
(11) lion tamer admirer
(12) painter
(13) toothbrush seller
(14) lighter fluid
(15) ticket taker
(16) hairbrush bristle tester
(17) lion tamer costume
(18) animal trainer
(19) birdcage bottom cleaner
(20) auto polish can label collector admirer

Problem 2.3–11   Warao

Warao is a language of Venezuela. Isolate the roots in the data below (Osborn, 1966 and 1967) and state their meanings. Formulate rules to account for the derivational and inflectional patterns that these complex words illustrate.

(1) niporaira — 'giant' (literally: large man)
(2) kapatamoana — 'has not yet cut'
(3) yapurukuna — 'would climb'
(4) hakakomoni — 'cannot run'
(5) noruhupute — 'they will sit down individually'
(6) ahimuroko — 'anteater' (literally: one who likes ants)
(7) inaminatu — 'teacher'
(8) narumeherete — 'will want (him) to go'
(9) nakopuhu — 'can swim'
(10) nahororoko — 'one who likes eating'
(11) mitu — 'one who sees'
(12) kahotapukuna — 'would command'

(13) narukomoni	'cannot go'
(14) nisamo	'buyers'
(15) wahipakatuma	'dugout canoes'
(16) mipumeherepute	'they will want them to see'
(17) narukuna	'would go'
(18) hanaira	'large stream'
(19) nakoroko	'one who likes swimming'
(20) narumehere	'want (him) to go'
(21) mimo	'witnesses' (literally: those who see)
(22) kapatakomoniyanaka	'it's not that (he) cannot cut'
(23) naomoana	'has not yet come'
(24) ruhupuhu	'can sit down'
(25) hoyoiratuma	'large rocks'
(26) rokoturoko	'one who likes song'
(27) kapatameheremoana	'has not yet wanted (him) to cut'
(28) nahoropuhu	'can eat'
(29) narupumoana	'they have not yet gone'
(30) hanokotuma	'houses'
(31) yapurumeherekuna	'would want to climb'

2.4   *Lexical Classes*

The lexical items of a language, both simple and complex, can be divided into classes on the basis of their syntactic and phonological properties. Traditional grammatical categories such as noun, verb, and adjective are classes in this sense. These and other lexical classes differ from one another in their inflectional properties, the derivational affixes they allow, the positions they can occupy in a sentence, the applicability of syntactic and phonological rules, and so on. Determining the class membership of lexical items is an important aspect of lexical analysis.

SYNTACTIC AND PHONOLOGICAL CLASSES

Lexical classes are not restricted to those for which there are traditional terms. In fact, any syntactic or phonological property which is not characteristic of all the lexical items of a language can be said to define a lexical class—namely, the class of lexical items sharing the property in question. For example, some English verbs allow direct objects, but others do not.

(1) (a) Felix built a house.
    (b) Felix lifted the rock.
    (c) Felix tripped his grandmother.
    (d) Felix killed a marijuana plant.

(2) (a) *Felix existed a house.
  (b) *Felix arose the rock.
  (c) *Felix stumbled his grandmother.
  (d) *Felix died a marijuana plant.

The verbs in (1) are but a few of the English verbs that tolerate a direct object. The verbs in (2) do not tolerate a direct object, and the sentences in (2) are consequently ungrammatical. The verbs allowing a direct object thus constitute a special class from which many verbs are excluded, and any adequate description of English must indicate which verbs are in this class and which are not. There happens to be traditional grammatical terminology for this classification; verbs that tolerate a direct object are said to be **transitive**, and verbs that do not allow a direct object are **intransitive**.

The applicability of syntactic and phonological rules is an especially important consideration in establishing lexical classes. Any rule that applies to some lexical items to the exclusion of others imposes an implicit classification on the lexical items of the language, one that will not necessarily coincide with the classification defined by any other property. For instance, a phonological rule of English changes [ɪ] to [æ] to indicate the past tense of a verb. This rule is of very limited generality, applying only to *sing, swim, begin, ring, drink, sink,* and a few others. This class of verbs must be enumerated in any complete description of English, and it does not coincide exactly with the lexical class defined by any other syntactic or phonological trait. Nor is there a traditional grammatical term for this class.

Classifying lexical items on the basis of their syntactic and phonological properties is an aspect of lexical analysis whose intimate connection with the syntactic and phonological analysis of a language should be self-evident. In describing the properties of a lexical item, one must specify how it interacts with the rules and structures of the language, and this is equivalent to specifying the syntactic and phonological classes to which it belongs. Insofar as it pertains to syntax, this information constitutes the syntactic representation of a lexical item. Insofar as it pertains to phonology, this information constitutes one part of its phonological representation, the other part being the sequence of segments which underlies its pronunciation. (This sequence of underlying segments has itself been referred to as the phonological representation in previous discussions—the term will normally be used in this narrower sense, as it has been up to now.) Lexical items belong to many different classes simultaneously, reflecting their numerous syntactic and phonological peculiarities. *Drink*, for instance, belongs to the class of English verbs that tolerate a direct object, to the class of verbs whose past tense is formed by changing [ɪ] to [æ], to the class of verbs that can be passivized (for example, *His blood was drunk by a milk-thirsty vampire*), and to many others. In some instances, the members of a class may share a number of special traits unique to that class.

More typically, however, classes overlap and cross-cut, and a class defined on the basis of one property will not coincide precisely with the class defined on the basis of any other.

Problem 2.4–1   English

The sentences below point to the existence of a special subclass of verbs within the class of transitive verbs in English. Determine the syntactic trait that defines this subclass and list the members of the subclass that are represented in the data.

   (1) The cat was startled by a loud noise.
   (2) Harriet's new hairpiece resembles this mop.
   (3) *Five dollars is cost by this shirt.
   (4) Sheila licked my fingers.
   (5) *Lots of troubles are had by him.
   (6) A milk-thirsty vampire drank his blood.
   (7) A loud noise startled the cat.
   (8) This new jacket suits me.
   (9) This shirt costs five dollars.
 (10) My pet elephant weighs four tons.
 (11) He has lots of troubles.
 (12) *I am suited by this new jacket.
 (13) His blood was drunk by a milk-thirsty vampire.
 (14) *This mop is resembled by Harriet's new hairpiece.
 (15) My fingers were licked by Sheila.
 (16) *Four tons is weighed by my pet elephant.

Solution

Among the transitive verbs of English are some that cannot occur in passive sentences. The members of this subclass include at least the following: *cost, have, suit, resemble, weigh.*

SEMANTIC CORRELATION

The members of a lexical class posited on syntactic or phonological grounds sometimes turn out to share a component of meaning. There is, for example, a subclass of English nouns which are identical in the singular and the plural; *deer, fish, moose, quail, antelope, trout, bass,* and *sheep* are some of the members of this subclass. These nouns are semantically similar in that they all designate types of animals. The division of nouns into gender classes also tends to follow natural semantic boundaries in many instances. Within the subclass of French nouns that designate humans, most nouns that refer to males are grammatically masculine, and most nouns that refer to females are grammatically feminine. For example, *homme* 'man', *père* 'father', *garçon* 'boy', *frère* 'brother', and *chanteur* 'male singer' are all masculine, while *femme* 'woman', *mère* 'mother', *jeune fille* 'girl', *soeur* 'sister', and *chanteuse* 'female singer' are all feminine.

The correlation between semantic and grammatical classes is important, but it must be noted that the correlation is seldom perfect. It is not always the case that every lexical item having the semantic trait in question also has the correlated grammatical property; thus *dog*, *cat*, and *horse* designate types of animals, but all have regular plurals rather than "zero" plurals. By the same token, every member of a grammatical class does not always possess the semantic property which seems to characterize the class as a whole. The French word *sentinelle* 'sentinel' is grammatically feminine, but most sentinels are male.

Problem 2.4–2   French

The past tense in French is expressed by the use of an "auxiliary" verb plus the past participle of the main verb. French intransitive verbs can be divided into two classes with respect to past tense formation. On the basis of the sentences below, determine the character of this classification and any semantic correlation the classification may have.

(1)	Il a chanté.	'He sang.'
(2)	Il est venu.	'He came.'
(3)	Il a couru.	'He ran.'
(4)	Il est allé.	'He went.'
(5)	Il est arrivé.	'He arrived.'
(6)	Il a pensé.	'He thought.'
(7)	Il a fini.	'He finished.'
(8)	Il a nagé.	'He swam.'
(9)	Il est monté.	'He went up.'
(10)	Il est descendu.	'He came down.'
(11)	Il a dansé.	'He danced.'
(12)	Il est parti.	'He left.'

Solution

Some verbs take the auxiliary verb *a* (literally: has), and others the auxiliary *est* (literally: is). The verbs which occur with *est* are the ones meaning 'come', 'go', 'arrive', 'go up', 'come down', and 'leave'. They are all verbs that indicate change of location but not the manner of locomotion. Verbs lacking this semantic property take *a* instead.

FURTHER PROBLEMS

Problem 2.4–3   English

The italicized verbs in the sentences below can be divided into two syntactic subclasses. Determine the basis for this subclassification and note any semantic correlation it may have.

(1) I *believe* that lettuce causes cancer.

(2) My doctor *dislikes* it that the AMA is so radical.

(3) Abernathy *resents* it that nobody wants to pet his alligator.

(4) Do you *promise* that you will put the garbage out faithfully?

(5) We *feel* that it would be improper for us to snap the senator's suspenders.

(6) I *despise* it that milkshakes are so fattening.

(7) That curvaceous blonde over there *loathes* it that her husband shows no interest in nuclear physics.

(8) Herschel *hopes* that Raquel will leave some food for him.

(9) Most decent people *abhor* it that the crime rate continues to soar.

(10) She *knows* that sex isn't everything.

(11) Herschel *detests* it that everyone thinks he is chubby.

(12) Marvin *says* that professional football will never become popular.

(13) I *hate* it that Zelda always beats me at three-dimensional chess.

(14) I *think* that something should be done about her.

Problem 2.4–4   Luiseño

On the basis of the words below, comment on the classification of Luiseño verbs with respect to the forms of their present tense endings.

(1) sámsawun	'are buying'
(2) ʔáamoq	'is hunting'
(3) héelaq	'is singing'
(4) téetilawun	'are talking'
(5) wáapaan	'are flying'
(6) munáa	'is going'
(7) lóʔxaq	'is cooking'
(8) ʔowóʔaan	'are working'
(9) móqnawun	'are killing'
(10) náqmaq	'is listening'
(11) ŋóoraan	'are running'
(12) tóowq	'is seeing'

(13) ŋéewun	'are leaving'
(14) héelaan	'are singing'
(15) móqnaq	'is killing'
(16) ŋéeq	'is leaving'
(17) waráavaan	'are getting up'
(18) lóʔxawun	'are cooking'
(19) téetilaq	'is talking'
(20) ʔáamowun	'are hunting'
(21) sámsaq	'is buying'
(22) munáa	'are going'
(23) tóowwun	'are seeing'
(24) náqmawun	'are listening'
(25) ʔowóʔaq	'is working'

Problem 2.4–5 *Maltese*

The verb forms below (Aquilina, 1965) are from Maltese, a Semitic language spoken on the island of Malta. These words include past tense forms and imperatives, the forms used in giving commands (indicated in the glosses by an exclamation point). Assume for purposes of this problem that imperative forms are derived by means of a phonological modification of the corresponding past forms, and divide the verbs into classes on this basis. The symbol [ħ] stands for a voiceless pharyngeal fricative. The constriction for this fricative sound is produced by drawing back the body of the tongue toward the rear wall of the pharynx.

(1) ilħʌʔ	'reach!'
(2) bʌrʌm	'twisted'
(3) ħʌrʌʔ	'burned'
(4) dʌħʌk	'laughed'
(5) omšot	'comb!'
(6) ʌħʔʌr	'oppress!'
(7) sʌhʌr	'worked overtime'
(8) obroš	'scratch!'
(9) ʌħrʌʔ	'burn!'
(10) lʌʔʌt	'hit'
(11) ičħʌd	'deny!'
(12) ħʌbʌt	'struck'
(13) ʌʔsʌm	'divide!'
(14) lʌħʌʔ	'reached'
(15) ʔʌsʌm	'divided'
(16) mʌšʌt	'combed'
(17) olʔot	'hit!'

(18) idħʌk   'laugh!'
(19) bʌrʌš   'scratched'
(20) ʌħbʌt   'strike!'
(21) čʌħʌd   'denied'
(22) ishʌr   'work overtime!'
(23) obrom   'twist!'
(24) ħʌʔʌr   'oppressed'

Problem 2.4–6   *Swahili*

Several sets of noun prefixes, singular and plural, are illustrated in the data from Swahili given below (Perrott, 1951). Divide the noun roots into classes on the basis of which prefix set they occur with. State any semantic correlation these classes may have. Standard Swahili orthography is used.

(1)	miti	'trees'	(19)	kikapu	'basket'
(2)	ukubwa	'size'	(20)	mikono	'arms'
(3)	mtumishi	'servant'	(21)	watumishi	'servants'
(4)	vibanda	'huts'	(22)	mtende	'date palm'
(5)	wazee	'old men'	(23)	mtoto	'child'
(6)	mkono	'arm'	(24)	mti	'tree'
(7)	kiti	'chair'	(25)	urefu	'length'
(8)	vikapu	'baskets'	(26)	kitabu	'book'
(9)	mtu	'man'	(27)	mchungwa	'orange tree'
(10)	michungwa	'orange trees'	(28)	wageni	'strangers'
(11)	umoja	'unity'	(29)	visu	'knives'
(12)	watoto	'children'	(30)	watu	'men'
(13)	kisu	'knife'	(31)	viti	'chairs'
(14)	miguu	'legs'	(32)	mguu	'leg'
(15)	mgeni	'stranger'	(33)	kibanda	'hut'
(16)	mitende	'date palms'	(34)	uzee	'old age'
(17)	vitabu	'books'	(35)	mzee	'old man'
(18)	udogo	'smallness'			

Problem 2.4–7   *Diegueño*

Five different phonological rules serve to derive plural verbs from singular verbs in Diegueño (Walker, 1970); one of them was illustrated in Problem 2.2–5. For some verbs, more than one of these rules applies in the formation of the plural. State these five rules and list the class of verbs that undergo each. Is it possible to predict on semantic or phonological grounds whether any of the rules will apply to a given verb?

Singular	Plural	
tuuñaa	tuuñaač	'pound'
naL	uunaaL	'fall'
wiṛ	wiiṛ	'be hard'
aam	naam	'go'
uuxʷay	uučxʷay	'kill'
Lʸap	Lʸaap	'burn'
čan	nčan	'step'
maa	mač	'eat soft things'
wiw	uuwiw	'see'
šmay	šuumay	'find'
muL	muuL	'gather'
saaw	saw	'eat'
aakuuxap	aačkuuxaap	'catch up with'
iimaa	iimaač	'dance'
pap	uupaap	'bake'
čuupuL	čuupuuL	'boil'
sii	sič	'drink'
aayiw	aačuuyiw	'bring'
aačpay	aačuupay	'believe'
aasip	aačuusip	'smoke'
ʔux	uuʔuux	'cough'

3

Syntactic Analysis

The syntactic and lexical rules of a language specify the relationship between the meanings of sentences and their surface structures. Lexical rules, which determine the phonological realization of components of meaning, were discussed in Chapter 2. Let us turn now to syntactic rules, the non-lexical principles of a language which function in connecting conceptual and surface structures. Any given surface structure reflects the operation of many different lexical and syntactic rules, which "derive" it from the underlying semantic structure. At least in part, these rules can be regarded as applying sequentially, each one modifying the underlying structure to some degree, making it less abstract and more like the ultimate surface structure.

It is evident that insightful syntactic analysis cannot be divorced from the problem of determining, with some degree of accuracy, the nature of the semantic representations that underlie sentences. Unfortunately, the character of semantic representations is very difficult to determine, and linguistic knowledge concerning this domain of grammar is at best fragmentary. Progress in the elucidation of semantic structure is nevertheless being made, and certain properties of semantic representations can be postulated with some confidence. We will begin our examination of syntactic analysis with a brief discussion of underlying representations and some of the grounds for positing them.

3.1 Underlying Representations

The semantic representation of a sentence is a cognitive structure susceptible to being encoded in linguistic form by the syntactic and lexical principles of a language. Two kinds of considerations therefore bear on the matter of postulating and motivating these underlying representations. First, semantic representations, as cognitive entities, are to some degree accessible to conscious introspection by native speakers. Second, structural evidence provided by syntactic and lexical analysis can sometimes be adduced to support certain hypotheses regarding semantic structure. For the moment we will be primarily concerned with aspects of semantic structure for which relatively clear introspective judgments seem obtainable. We will return shortly to the use of structural evidence in motivating underlying representations.

SEMANTIC INTUITIONS

Even linguistically sophisticated native speakers do not have the ability to routinely translate their semantic intuitions into detailed and fully explicit descriptions that linguists can use unquestioningly in the formulation of syntactic theories. Life is not that simple. Semantic intuitions are subtle and elusive. In pursuing these intuitions, one does not know beforehand quite what to look for, and progress in semantic analysis is revealed primarily by a growing realization of the many subtle complexities that await satisfactory description. Linguists have not yet devised a fully adequate way of talking about meanings or representing their structures in symbolic form; nor do they possess a comprehensive semantic theory that successfully integrates the various insights that have accrued concerning semantic structure.

Nevertheless, careful introspection can reveal a great deal about semantic representations. It is intuitively clear in sentence (1), for instance, that *not* negates the clause *Rex will . . . eat lettuce* but does not negate the clause *Terry will eat anything*. The former clause is said to be in the **scope** of *not*, since it is subject to the semantic force of this morpheme; the latter clause is outside the scope of *not*.

(1) Rex will not eat lettuce, but Terry will eat anything.

In (2), similarly, *the nurse broke the bottle* is semantically in the scope of *claims*, while *I say she didn't* is outside the scope of this verb; that is, only the former is claimed by Harvey.

(2) Although Harvey claims the nurse broke the bottle, I say she didn't.

It is intuitively clear that the semantic relation between *the nurse* and *broke* in (2) is quite similar to the relation holding between *the planes* and *devastated* in (3).

(3) The planes devastated a defenseless village.

Moreover, the semantic relation between *broke* and *the bottle* is constant in (2) and (4), despite their different surface structures; the two sentences describe the same change of state affecting a glass container.

(4) The bottle broke.

Countless examples such as these make it apparent that introspection can reveal many important properties of semantic representations. To be judged adequate, any comprehensive description of the semantic representations of a language must properly characterize these properties.

PROPOSITIONS

One important property of semantic representations which is revealed by linguistic intuition is that the meaning of many (if not all) sentences is decomposable into component ***propositions***. Sentence (1), for example, can be decomposed semantically into at least three component propositions, one concerning donkeys, one concerning seals, and one concerning elephants.

(1) Donkeys bray, seals bark, and elephants trumpet.

Sentence (2) decomposes into at least four component propositions. One proposition is that Alex makes a certain claim; another that Susan knows something; a third that George has a cat; and a fourth that this cat has two heads.

(2) Alex claims that Susan knows that George has a cat with two heads.

(3) contains at least two component propositions, one to the effect that lettuce is wholesome and the other to the effect that this state of affairs is unfortunate.

(3) Unfortunately, lettuce is wholesome.

It may not always be intuitively obvious exactly how many component propositions should be posited for a given sentence. Nor is it always clear how these propositions combine to form the semantic representation of the entire sentence (notice that the component propositions of (1) are joined together semantically in a very different way from those of (2)). However, there would seem to be little doubt concerning the correctness of the fundamental claim that some or all semantic representations are "complex" in the sense that they can be decomposed into component propositions.

A proposition is traditionally viewed as consisting of a ***predicate*** and its ***arguments***. Roughly speaking, a predicate is a semantic unit that describes an action, state, quality, relation, or the like. Arguments are the semantic units about which these predications are made. In sentence (1) above, for instance, *bray*, *bark*, and *trumpet* are predicates; *donkeys*, *seals*, and *elephants* are their respective arguments. (More precisely, these surface units "manifest" or "derive from" semantic predicates and arguments; predicates and arguments are semantic—not surface—entities, and we may speak of lexical items as "being" predicates and arguments only to avoid more cumbersome circumlocutions.) Similarly, in sentence (4) the phrase *is black* constitutes the predicate, of which *tar* is the argument; tar is what blackness is predicated of.

> (4) Tar is black.

In (5) the predicate is represented in surface structure by *resembles*. The two arguments of this predicate are *Spiro* and *George*.

> (5) Spiro resembles George.

As these examples show, predicates are typically manifested in surface structure by verbs or adjectives, while nominals normally manifest arguments. However, it is also possible for nominals to represent predicates. Consider the following sentences.

> (6) My father is a teacher.
> (7) My father sees a teacher.
> (8) My father teaches.

In (6) *is a teacher* (in which the nominal *a teacher* is the only clearly meaningful element, apart from tense) constitutes the predicate; *my father* is an argument of this predicate. It would be inappropriate to view *is* as stating a relationship between *my father* and *a teacher*, as the predicate *sees* does in (7). (6) is more similar semantically to (8) than to (7); the enterprise of teaching, of being a teacher, is predicated of *my father*. It is pertinent to note that in many languages—Luiseño, for instance—sentences like (6) contain no verbal element at all:

> (9) no-naʔ huuʔuni-kat
>   my-father teach-er
>   'My father is a teacher.'

The syntactic peculiarities that are frequently associated with the second nominal in sentences like (6) and (9) further suggest that this nominal derives from a semantic predicate. In French, to take just one example, this second nominal lacks an article when it constitutes a predicate, though the same nominal is ungrammatical without an article when it derives from an argument:

> (10) Mon père est professeur.
>   my father is teacher
>   'My father is a teacher.'

(11) Mon père voit un professeur.
      my father sees a teacher
      'My father sees a teacher.'

(12) *Mon père voit professeur.
      'My father sees teacher.'

(Compare example (5) of Problem 3.7–10, Maori.)

To facilitate comparison, it is convenient to depict semantic representations by means of tree diagrams similar to those employed to represent surface structures. For example, Figures 3.1–1 and 3.1–2 depict, though crudely, the respective semantic representations of (6) and (7). In these figures *PRED* of course stands for predicate, and *ARG* for argument. (The left-to-right order of elements is not significant in indicating semantic representations; it is customary to show the predicate as the leftmost or rightmost element in structures such as these.) The symbol *S*, which is used in diagrams of surface structures to symbolize clauses or sentences, is used here to stand for a proposition, because propositions are the semantic counterparts of surface clauses.

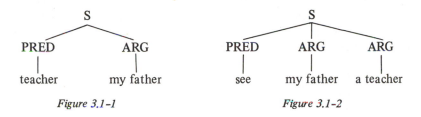

Figure 3.1–1   *Figure 3.1–2*

Figure 3.1–1 states that the proposition consists of a predicate, (*be a*) *teacher*, and its argument, *my father*. (Since we are dealing with semantic representations, *teacher*, *my father*, and so on do not stand for lexical items, but rather for some characterization of the meanings of these lexical items. *Be* and *a* are parenthesized here and omitted from Figure 3.1–1 because these elements are not clearly meaningful.) Similarly, Figure 3.1–2 depicts a proposition consisting of the predicate *see* and its two arguments, *my father* and *a teacher*. To be sure, Figures 3.1–1 and 3.1–2 show only selected aspects of the meanings of (6) and (7). For example, tense is not represented. Moreover, the nature of the semantic relations between the arguments and their predicates is not explicitly indicated. In a fully adequate description, it would be necessary to show somehow that the semantic relation between *my father* and *sees* is different from the relation between *sees* and *a teacher* in (7); that the relation between *broke* and *the bottle* is the same in (13) and (14); and so on.

(13) The nurse broke the bottle.
(14) The bottle broke.

PROPOSITIONAL STRUCTURE

Many if not all semantic representations can be decomposed into more than one component proposition. The way in which these component propositions combine with one another is an important aspect of the semantic representations of sentences. The term *propositional structure* will be used in this book to designate the way in which the semantic representation of a sentence is organized in terms of its component propositions.

The fundamental observation to be made in this regard is that some propositions function as arguments of other propositions. Consider (1) and (2).

    (1) Peggy believes the story.
    (2) Peggy believes babies are noisy.

In (1) *Peggy* and *the story* are arguments of the predicate *believes*. It is intuitively clear that in (2) the semantic relation between *believes* and *babies are noisy* is similar or identical to the relation between *believes* and *the story* in (1). To account for this similarity, we must analyze *babies are noisy*, like *the story*, as an argument of *believes*. This analysis is given in Figures 3.1–3 and 3.1–4. However, *babies are noisy* is itself a semantic proposition, indicating that propositions can function as arguments. The proposition *babies are noisy* is in the scope of *believes*—that is, this proposition is what is believed. To show that an element is in the scope of a predicate, we can represent it as an argument of that predicate, as in Figure 3.1–4.

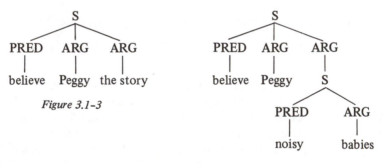

Figure 3.1–3

Figure 3.1–4

In cases where underlying propositions and surface clauses largely coincide, the propositional structure of sentences is readily apparent on the basis of introspection. Thus there is no real doubt that Figure 3.1–4 is correct as a first approximation to the propositional structure of (2), which contains two surface clauses, each corresponding to an underlying proposition. Introspective judgments are more subtle (and hence analyses based on them are more subject to controversy) when the propositional structure is significantly different from the surface clause structure. Figure 3.1–5, for instance, is clearly appropriate as the propositional structure of (3), whose clause structure reflects this propositional structure directly.

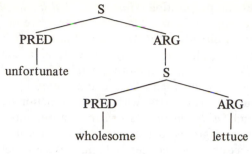

Figure 3.1–5

(3) That lettuce is wholesome is unfortunate.

But it is not immediately evident on intuitive grounds whether Figure 3.1–5 is also valid as the semantic representation of (4).

(4) Unfortunately, lettuce is wholesome.

While Figure 3.1–5 does not seem unreasonable as the underlying representation of (4), it might equally well be argued that (4) is a closer paraphrase of (5) and (6), which presumably have a more elaborate propositional structure.

(5) Lettuce is wholesome, and that lettuce is wholesome is unfortunate.
(6) Lettuce is wholesome, which is unfortunate.

It is generally agreed that the surface clause structure of a sentence sometimes differs in major respects from its underlying propositional structure. For example, (7) and (8) have the same propositional structure, shown in Figure 3.1–6.

(7) That Martin will fail his linguistics course is likely.
(8) Martin is likely to fail his linguistics course.

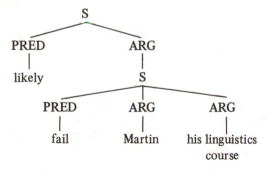

Figure 3.1–6

For both sentences the proposition *Martin . . . fail his linguistics course* is semantically in the scope of *likely*. The surface structure of (7) reflects this semantic organization directly; *that Martin will fail his linguistics course* is a subordinate clause which functions syntactically as a constituent of the clause containing *likely*. In (8), on the other hand, *Martin . . . fail his linguistics course* is not even a constituent. By the application of syntactic rules, it has been broken up into two parts, with *Martin* functioning as the surface subject of *likely* and *fail his linguistics course* as an infinitival complement. Primitive as they are, diagrams such as Figure 3.1–6 reveal some of the configurational differences between conceptual and surface structures and make it possible for us to begin talking about some of the rules that derive the latter from the former.

The differences between these two levels of structure are still more radical if we accept the somewhat controversial claim that elements such as modals, tense, negation, and conjunctions are to be analyzed as underlying predicates. For example, it is not unreasonable to argue that the modal *may* in (9) bears the same semantic relation to the clause containing it in surface structure that *possible* bears to the subordinate clause in (10).

(9) The mare may win the race.
(10) For the mare to win the race is possible.

If *may* has *the mare . . . win the race* in its scope semantically in (9), as *possible* does in (10), then an underlying representation like Figure 3.1–7 is perfectly appropriate for (9).

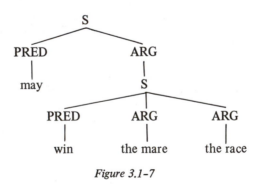

Figure 3.1–7

By the same token, it is not unreasonable on semantic grounds to claim that tense and negation derive from underlying predicates—that is, that they have in their scope the clauses that contain them in surface structure. Consider the following sentence.

(11) Mary is not here.

Semantically, the proposition *Mary (be) here* is in the scope of *PRESENT*, since the state of affairs represented by this proposition is what is said to be located at the present moment in time. Moreover, *Mary (be) PRESENT here* is in the scope of the predicate *not*, since the present existence of this state of affairs is being denied. If these intuitive judgments are accepted, Figure 3.1–8 can be given as the propositional structure of (11).

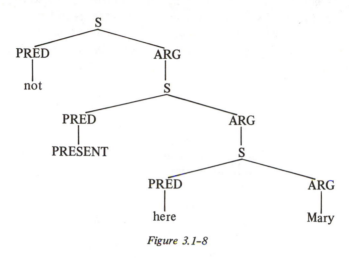

Figure 3.1–8

Finally, let us consider the claim that conjunctions also derive from underlying predicates. If the clauses of a conjoined structure are analyzed as being in the scope of the associated conjunction, (12) must have a semantic representation resembling Figure 3.1–9 (tense is omitted).

(12) Donkeys bray, seals bark, and elephants trumpet.

This analysis may or may not prove to be correct, but since conjunctions are meaningful (there is an important semantic difference between *and* and *or*), the proposal to treat them as predicates is not inherently improbable.

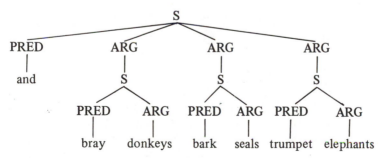

Figure 3.1–9

Diagrams like the ones given above are incomplete and may very well be wrong in certain details. With the limitations of present linguistic knowledge, any attempt at completeness in the description of semantic structures is doomed to inevitable and ignominious failure. Linguists have only begun to deal with the complexities of semantic representations. Needless to say, few problems have been definitively resolved, and many hypotheses concerning semantic structure are subject to continuing controversy. Nevertheless, the little we do at present know about semantic structure is sufficient to provide important insights regarding the operation of syntactic rules.

Further aspects of semantic representations will be discussed in subsequent sections.

Problem 3.1–1   English

The sentences below display a systematic discrepancy between their underlying propositional structure and their surface clause structure. Each sentence is accompanied by a rough sketch of its surface clause structure. Show the propositional structure of each sentence by means of a diagram analogous to these surface structure diagrams. (Show only enough detail to illustrate the point in question; there is no need to depict the internal structure of propositions or to posit separate underlying propositions for such elements as tense, modals, and negation.) Describe the systematic difference between the underlying and surface structures.

(1) Tomorrow he said he would mow the lawn.

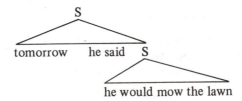

(2) When he gets caught, Gerald is likely to cry.

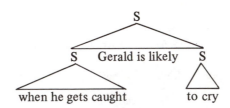

(3) If they resort to violence, I believe the protesters should be shot.

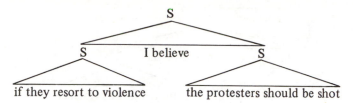

(4) In cases of civil disobedience, I believe a fair trial is not possible.

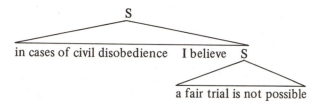

(5) Before she leaves, I think she should clean up her room.

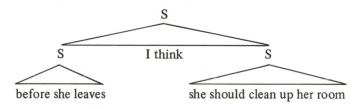

Solution

(1)

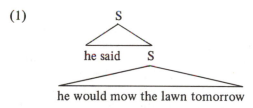

(2)

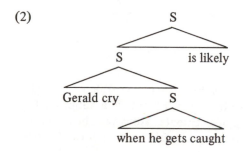

(3)

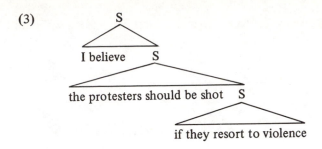

(4)

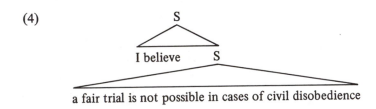

(5)

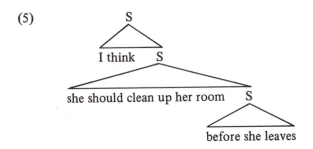

In all these examples an adverbial expression which occurs at the beginning of the sentence belongs semantically to a subordinate clause, even though it is not a constituent of this clause in surface structure. These adverbial elements include the word *tomorrow* in sentence (1), the phrase *in cases of civil diso-bedience* in (4), and the initial subordinate clauses of (2), (3), and (5). In (1), for instance, *tomorrow* does not modify the verb *said* (in fact, *He said . . . tomorrow* is semantically peculiar—*tomorrow* cannot modify a verb in the past tense); rather, it modifies *mow*, specifying when the projected mowing is to take place.

Discussion

On the basis of sentences such as these, we can postulate for English a syntactic rule that moves an adverbial element out of a subordinate clause and transports it to the beginning of a sentence. However, the data is not sufficient to make it apparent precisely how this rule must be formulated.

SYNTACTIC MOTIVATION

The abstract structures postulated to underlie sentences must properly reflect their semantic organization. However, semantic appropriateness is not in itself sufficient to justify a putative underlying representation. Meaning is a slippery thing, and underlying structures postulated on the basis of meaning alone must always be regarded with a certain amount of skepticism. Fortunately, it is often possible to find purely syntactic arguments to justify hypothesized underlying representations. When semantic considerations and syntactic evidence converge to favor a particular underlying representation for a sentence, a convincing case can be made for its essential correctness.

The syntactic regularity involving preposition deletion discussed in Chapter 1 (pp. 7–10) illustrates the use of purely syntactic evidence to motivate an underlying representation. Recall that underlying structures such as (1) below were postulated for sentences such as (2) in order to make it possible to state a certain generalization—namely, that sequences of the form *ADJ P NP* are permitted in English to the exclusion of sequences of the form **ADJ NP*.

(1) *I am certain of that Dick is loyal.
(2) I am certain that Dick is loyal.

This generalization does not hold at the level of surface structure, as (1) and (2) attest, but it does hold for the slightly more abstract level of structure in which the underlying prepositions are still present (before being eliminated by the rule of preposition deletion; see Figure 1.1–4, p. 9). If underlying structures such as (1) were postulated solely to make it possible to state this generalization, their validity might well be questioned. However, abstract syntactic structures like (1) turn out to have strong independent motivation, since they make it possible to account for the otherwise unexplained prepositions that show up in sentences like (3) and in question-answer pairs like (4) and (5).

(3) What I am certain *of* is that Dick is loyal.
(4) (a) What are you certain *of*?
    (b) I am certain that Dick is loyal.
(5) (a) Are you certain that Dick is loyal?
    (b) Yes, I am certain *of* it.

Structure (1) is therefore strongly motivated on the basis of purely syntactic evidence.

In this particular example we are dealing with a rather superficial syntactic phenomenon of English, and there is really no reason to claim that structure (1) reflects the meaning of sentence (2) much more directly than its surface structure does. We are still justified in positing (1) as an underlying representation on syntactic grounds, but (1) is not the most abstract representation that underlies (2) and does not receive any clear positive support from semantic considerations. In many instances, however, hypothesized underlying representations can be motivated by both syntactic and semantic evidence.

Consider the following sentences.

(6) I want Bill to go.   (12) (a) *You want you to go.
(7) Bill wants me to go.   (b) You want to go.
(8) I want you to go.   (13) (a) *I want me to go.
(9) You want me to go.   (b) I want to go.
(10) You want Bill to go.   (14) (a) *Bill wants Bill to go.
(11) Bill wants you to go.   (b) Bill wants to go.

These sentences all consist of two clauses; the main clause has the form *NP want S*, and the subordinate clause has the form *(NP) to go*. On the basis of sentences (6)–(11), it is apparent that *I, you*, and *Bill* (like an indefinite number of other noun phrases) can occur as either the subject of the main clause or the subject of the subordinate clause. However, the (a) expressions seem to vitiate this otherwise valid generalization. Although (12) (a)–(14) (a) contain no main or subordinate clause subject that does not appear in the same role in (6)–(11), these sentences are ungrammatical.

Closer examination reveals this irregularity to be only apparent. The ungrammatical sentences are not randomly distributed in (6)–(14); they are exactly those sentences in which the main and subordinate clause subjects are identical. Moreover, each of these ungrammatical (a) sentences is paralleled by a grammatical sentence—namely, the corresponding (b) sentence—that is identical to it except for the lack of a subordinate clause subject. The (b) sentences fill the gap in an otherwise regular pattern that is created by the ungrammaticality of the (a) sentences.

These facts suggest that a syntactic rule of English requires the deletion of the subject in subordinate clauses marked with *to* when the subject happens to be identical to a noun phrase in the main clause. Thus (12) (a)–(14) (a) can be posited as underlying representations; at the level of underlying representations the generalization is maintained that *I, you, Bill*, and so on can function as either main or subordinate clause subjects. This regularity is obscured somewhat in surface structure by the operation of the subject deletion rule, which derives the (b) sentences from the underlying (a) structures. This derivation is exemplified in Figure 3.1–10.

We see, consequently, that underlying structures such as *I want I/me to go* have a certain amount of syntactic motivation. By positing them as underlying structures we avoid having to mar an otherwise regular pattern by excluding structures in which the two subjects happen to be identical; moreover, such structures provide a source for the (b) sentences. These putative underlying structures also have semantic motivation. In (12) (b) *you* bears the same semantic relation to *go* that it does in (8). In (13) (b) *I* is semantically the subject of *go*, just as it is in (7). Similarly, *Bill* is understood as the person who

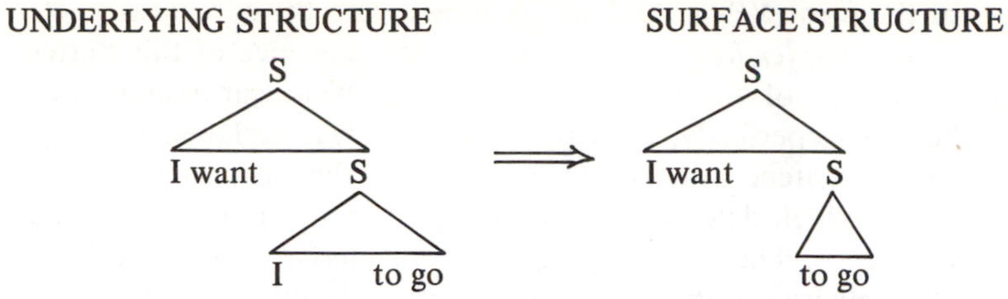

UNDERLYING STRUCTURE   SURFACE STRUCTURE

Figure 3.1-10

does the going in (14) (b). Notice that these semantic observations are accounted for if we claim that the (b) sentences are derived from the (a) structures. In the underlying (a) structures, the *NP* which is understood to be the subject of the subordinate verb is in fact present as its subject. These underlying representations thus have both syntactic and semantic value. This convergence of evidence constitutes a strong argument that such structures are essentially correct.

Problem 3.1–2 English

The sentences that follow are *comparatives*, that is, sentences involving the elements *more/er . . . than, as . . . as,* or *less . . . than.* Postulate underlying representations for the (c) sentences and cite syntactic and semantic evidence in their support.

 (1) (a) Ralph is thinner than Peter is fat.
   (b) *Ralph is thinner than Peter is thin.
   (c) Ralph is thinner than Peter is.
 (2) (a) Margaret is taller than Marianne is short.
   (b) *Margaret is taller than Marianne is tall.
   (c) Margaret is taller than Marianne is.
 (3) (a) José is as handsome as Terry is ugly.
   (b) *José is as handsome as Terry is handsome.
   (c) José is as handsome as Terry is.
 (4) (a) Raymond is as stupid as Joseph is smart.
   (b) *Raymond is as stupid as Joseph is stupid.
   (c) Raymond is as stupid as Joseph is.
 (5) (a) Lynn is less happy than Susan is sad.
   (b) *Lynn is less happy than Susan is happy.
   (c) Lynn is less happy than Susan is.

Solution

The (b) structures can be postulated to underlie the (c) sentences. The (a) sentences indicate the existence of a syntactic pattern of English in which two clauses of the form *NP be ADJ* are combined with the comparative elements *as . . . as* or *more/er/less . . . than*. Given the existence of this pattern, the ungrammaticality of the (b) sentences is somewhat surprising, since they follow the pattern perfectly. This apparent anomaly is explained if we hypothesize that the (c) sentences derive from structures of the form (b) by an obligatory syntactic rule which deletes the second of two identical adjectives in a comparative sentence. These underlying structures derive support from the fact that they eliminate an apparent syntactic irregularity and provide a source for the (c) sentences.

This syntactic evidence converges with semantic evidence. In sentence (1) (c) it is understood that Peter's thinness is under discussion, not his baldness or happiness. In (2) (c) it is clearly Marianne's height that is under consideration, not her ugliness or disposition. In all the (c) sentences the meaning of an adjective figures in the semantic representation of the truncated final clause (*NP is*). Moreover, the adjective in question is in each case the adjective that occurs in the initial clause. The fact that the meaning of the adjective figures in the interpretation of both clauses constitutes semantic evidence in favor of the (b) structures as underlying representations, since the understood adjective is present in the (b) structures.

CONCLUSION

To summarize, structures more abstract than surface structures are posited for either of two reasons. First, underlying representations facilitate syntactic description by making it possible to capture generalizations that are not apparent in terms of surface structures alone. Second, underlying structures reflect semantic properties of sentences that are obscured in surface structure. Since the function of syntactic rules is to state the relationship between semantic and surface structures, considerations of meaning are extremely important in justifying underlying representations.

Syntactic evidence may not always be available to corroborate semantically motivated structures. By the same token, not all syntactically motivated underlying structures are abstract enough to receive support from semantic considerations. Underlying any given surface structure is a semantic representation and a whole series of intermediate structures, each derived from the preceding one by the application of some lexical or syntactic rule; many of these intermediate structures are much more similar to surface than to semantic structures. Nevertheless, it is sometimes possible to invoke both semantic and syntactic evidence in support of an underlying representation. When abstract structures postulated for purely syntactic reasons turn out to have explanatory value with respect to the meanings of the sentences they are said to underlie, this is a strong indication that the analysis is on the right track.

FURTHER PROBLEMS

Problem 3.1–3   Luiseño

The underlying propositions of a sentence frequently outnumber its surface clauses. Derivational affixes often derive from the predicates of propositions that are not retained as separate clauses in surface structure. Reexamine the Luiseño data of Problem 2.3–2 (p. 76). Sketch the propositional structure of sentences (2), (3), and (6) by means of diagrams analogous to Figures 3.1–1 through 3.1–9.

Problem 3.1–4   English

Postulate underlying representations for the (c) sentences below. Cite both syntactic and semantic evidence to motivate these underlying representations.

  (1) (a) I like you.
      (b) *I like me.
      (c) I like myself.
      (d) *I like yourself.
  (2) (a) You like us.
      (b) *You like you.
      (c) You like yourself.
      (d) *You like ourselves.
  (3) (a) We like him.
      (b) *We like us.
      (c) We like ourselves.
      (d) *We like himself.

3.2   Rule Types

Syntactic and lexical rules specify the relationship between the semantic representations of sentences and their surface structures. Among the syntactic rules are those that delete constituents or replace them with reduced forms such as pronouns; those that insert sentence trappings; and those that effect permutations and rearrange constituent structure. Syntactic rules of these three types are called **transformations**. A transformation is a syntactic rule that modifies a tree structure in one of the ways mentioned above, yielding a modified or **derived** structure that more closely resembles the surface structure. Non-transformational syntactic rules will be considered in section 3.8.

REDUCTION RULES

We have already encountered several examples of reduction rules in English, including the rule deleting a preposition before a subordinating particle such as *that*. Other reduction rules apply in the derivation of sentences (1)–(3).

(1) Algernon is as stubborn as our father is.
(2) Penelope hates to wash dishes.
(3) The old hermit who lived in this tree killed himself.

In (1) the truncated clause *our father is* derives from the fuller underlying structure *our father is stubborn* by a transformation that deletes a repeated adjective in a comparative sentence. *Penelope* functions semantically as the subject of both *hates* and *wash* in (2). This is accounted for by postulating an underlying structure containing *Penelope* as the subject of *wash*; this second occurrence of *Penelope* is deleted by a rule that eliminates the subject of a subordinate clause when it is identical to a noun phrase in the main clause (compare *Penelope hates for David to wash dishes*, in which the main and subordinate clause subjects are different). In (3) the understood object of *killed*—namely, *the old hermit who lived in this tree*—is reduced to a reflexive pronoun by virtue of being identical to the subject.

Examples such as these indicate that languages tend to avoid repetition by reducing or deleting one of two identical constituents. However, matters are not nearly so simple as this informal statement might make them appear. For one thing, not all deletions are prompted by repetition; the deletion of a preposition before *that*, for instance, takes place regardless of whether or not an identical preposition occurs elsewhere in the sentence. In addition, the reduction of a repeated constituent can normally be effected only under certain specific conditions, and the discovery of these conditions is not an easy matter. Finally, there are difficulties in determining when two constituents count as being identical.

To illustrate the problem of ascertaining the conditions under which an element can be deleted, let us consider the rule that deletes the subject of an embedded clause, as in the derivation of sentence (2) above. On the basis of (2), it might appear that the rule can apply whenever the subject of the main clause and the subject of the subordinate clause are identical. However, sentences (4)–(6) show that this is not always the case.

(4) Penelope hates washing dishes.
(5) Penelope knows that she must wash dishes.
(6) *Penelope knows that must wash dishes.

In (2) and (4) the underlying subject of *wash* is *Penelope*, which has been deleted in both cases by virtue of being identical to the main clause subject. *Penelope* can also be interpreted as the underlying subject of *wash* in (5), but although this noun can be pronominalized to *she*, it cannot be deleted; sentence (6) is ungrammatical (unless *that* is interpreted as a demonstrative). We must conclude therefore that subject deletion can apply when the subordinate clause is marked by *to* or *ing*, but not when it is marked by *that*.

The following sentences show that the conditions under which subject deletion can apply are still further restricted.

(7) Washing dishes is easy for Penelope.
(8) Algernon told Penelope to wash dishes.
(9) Algernon promised Penelope to wash dishes.
(10) I know that Penelope wants me to wash dishes.

Sentences (7) and (8) demonstrate that it is not always the subject of the main clause that must be identical to the subordinate clause subject in order for subject deletion to take place; the identical noun phrase is a prepositional object in (7) and an indirect object in (8). Moreover, while *Penelope* is understood to be the subject of *wash* in (8), which has *tell* as the main clause verb, *Algernon* is the semantic subject of *wash* in (9), in which *promise* is the main verb. The predicate of the main clause determines which noun phrase in the main clause must be identical to the subordinate clause subject if subject deletion is to take place. The predicate of the main clause is said to **govern** the deletion of the "lower" subject (that is, the subject of the subordinate clause), and governing predicates differ in the conditions under which they allow the rule to apply. Finally, (10) shows that the identical noun phrase must normally be in the next higher clause for subject deletion to be applicable; *I* is two clauses removed from *me* in (10), as shown in Figure 3.2–1, and the subject of *wash* could be deleted in (10) only if it were *Penelope* instead of *me*.

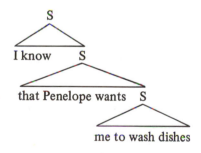

Figure 3.2–1

We have only begun to explore the restrictions on the application of subject deletion, restrictions that linguists have still not fully discovered, despite extensive investigation. Similar problems arise in specifying the applicability of virtually any reduction rule, even though the conditions may seem straightforward enough in simple cases.

Let us turn now to the problem of determining when two constituents count as being identical. There appear to be at least two different kinds of identity relevant to the applicability of reduction rules. One kind is **coreference**. Although the notion of coreference involves many subtle problems, for our purposes it is sufficient to say that two noun phrases are coreferential if they are interpreted as referring to the same object or class of objects. Coreference is the kind of identity required for reflexivization and subject deletion. In (11), for instance, the two occurrences of *Bill* can be taken as referring either to the same person or to two different people who happen to have the same name; only under the former interpretation can the second occurrence of *Bill* be reflexivized to *himself*, as in (12).

> (11) Bill is very fond of Bill.
> (12) Bill is very fond of himself.

Similarly, subject deletion can apply to reduce (13) to (14) only when the two occurrences of *Penelope* are coreferential.

> (13) Penelope wants Penelope to wash dishes.
> (14) Penelope wants to wash dishes.

Since relations of coreference are part of the meaning of a sentence, the semantic representation of a sentence must somehow indicate whether or not two nominals designate the same entity. As an informal and purely notational device, it is customary to indicate coreference by means of identical subscripts, and lack of coreference by means of non-identical subscripts. Thus the nominals *Jones* and *the old man* are marked as coreferential in (15), because they both bear the subscript i. In (16), on the other hand, *Jones* and *the old man* are marked as referring to two different individuals.

> (15) Jones$_i$ may really be sick, but I think the old man$_i$ is pretending.
> (16) Jones$_i$ may really be sick, but I think the old man$_j$ is pretending.

As sentence (15) shows, two noun phrases do not have to be identical in form or even in meaning to be coreferential.

Some reduction rules depend for their applicability, not on coreference, but rather on identity of form and meaning. The rule deleting repeated adjectives in comparative sentences is an example. The two occurrences of *red* in (17), which underlies (18), cannot be regarded as coreferential; in fact, it makes no sense to speak of coreference with respect to such words.

> (17) This apple is as red as that apple is red.
> (18) This apple is as red as that apple is.

The deletion of *swim* from (19) in the derivation of (20) also depends on identity of form and meaning rather than on coreference.

> (19) The dog will swim, and so will the cat swim.
> (20) The dog will swim, and so will the cat.

Problem 3.2–1   French

The sentences which follow illustrate a deletion rule of French. State this rule and ascertain as precisely as possible the conditions under which it can apply.

(1) La femme maigre est intelligente, mais la laide est stupide.
the woman thin is intelligent, but the ugly is stupid
'The thin woman is intelligent, but the ugly one is stupid.'

(2) *La laide est intelligente, mais la femme maigre est stupide.
'The ugly one (= woman) is intelligent, but the thin woman is stupid.'

(3) Pierre adore la maison rouge, mais Henri préfère la blanche.
Peter adores the house red, but Henry prefers the white
'Peter adores the red house, but Henry prefers the white one.'

(4) *Je vois un homme, et Jean voit un aussi.
I see a man, and John sees a also
'I see a man, and John sees one also.'

(5) Voici une femme maigre, et voilà une laide.
here is a woman thin, and there is an ugly
'Here is a thin woman, and there is an ugly one.'

(6) La femme maigre est intelligente, mais la femme laide est stupide.
'The thin woman is intelligent, but the ugly woman is stupid.'

(7) *Je cherche une femme qui soit intelligente, et Pierre aussi cherche une qui soit intelligente.
I look for a woman who be intelligent, and Peter also looks for a who be intelligent
'I am looking for a woman who is intelligent, and Peter also is looking for one who is intelligent.'

Solution

If two identical nouns occur in the same sentence, one of them may optionally be deleted. Coreference is not required. The ungrammaticality of (2) shows that it must be the second of the two identical nouns that is deleted, not the first. Sentence (4) shows that the deletion is not permitted unless the noun is followed by a modifier, and (7) shows that it is not permitted when this modifier is a relative clause. Evidently, the noun to be deleted must be contained in a noun phrase of the form ARTICLE + NOUN + ADJECTIVE.

Problem 3.2–2   *English*

On the basis of the sentences below, describe the formation of imperative sentences in English (imperatives are identified by exclamation marks). Justify the underlying representation of imperative sentences with syntactic and semantic evidence.

    (1) Think about yourself!
    (2) I thought about him.
    (3) *Take care of himself!
    (4) You took care of yourselves.
    (5) *Think about you!
    (6) *You take care of ourselves!
    (7) *Thought about yourself!
    (8) *Take care of myself!
    (9) Take care of yourself!
  (10) You think about yourselves!
  (11) *Think about themselves!
  (12) You take care of yourself!
  (13) *We think about yourself.
  (14) Think about yourselves!
  (15) *Take care of herself!
  (16) *We think about ourselves!

Solution

The verb of an imperative sentence must be inflected for present tense; the imperative sentence (7) is ungrammatical because the verb is marked for past tense rather than present tense. The subject of an imperative must be *you*, singular or plural, and this *you* can optionally be deleted, as in (1), (9), and (14). There is both semantic and syntactic evidence for an underlying subject *you* in these sentences. Semantically, *you* is interpreted as the subject in (1), (9), and (14), just as it is in (4), (10), and (12). There are two kinds of syntactic evidence for *you* as the underlying subject of imperatives. First, *you* can occur overtly as an imperative subject, as in (10) and (12), but no other pronoun can —(16), with *we* as an imperative subject, is ungrammatical. The second kind of evidence is furnished by reflexive objects. Reflexives can normally occur only in place of the second of two coreferential noun phrases in the same sentence. However, (1), (9), and (14) have reflexive objects despite the fact that they contain no other noun phrase in surface structure. Viewed in terms of surface structure, the occurrence of these reflexives is irregular. Given the proposed underlying representations, though, their occurrence is perfectly regular—the subject *you* causes the object *you* to be reflexivized before the former is deleted. The underlying subject must be *you*, and no other pronoun, because only *yourself* and *yourselves* are possible as reflexive objects in imperatives. By restricting the underlying subject to *you*, we explain the ungrammaticality of (3), (8), (11), and (15).

INSERTION RULES

Reduction rules limit the redundancy of sentences by allowing the deletion or simplification of repeated constituents. Other syntactic rules have the opposite effect. They insert into sentences elements that have no independent meaning and that consequently do not appear in the underlying semantic representations. These elements are what we identified in Chapter 2 as sentence trappings.

There are two basic kinds of syntactic rules that introduce sentence trappings. The first type are agreement rules. Agreement rules mark a constituent to agree with another constituent with respect to such categories as gender, number, case, person, and so on. The most common types of agreement rules are no doubt those that induce agreement between a noun and its modifiers and those that mark verbs to agree with their subjects and sometimes their objects. The problems in Chapter 2 contain numerous illustrations of agreement rules. In Problem 2.2–10 (p. 70), for instance, we saw that adjectives in Swahili receive the same prefix as the nouns they modify, while verbs contain prefixes which indicate the person and number (and, in the case of noun subjects, the prefix class) of their subjects and objects.

The second type of syntactic rules that introduce sentence trappings are those that mark the syntactic position or function of a constituent. Rules that mark subjects and objects for case are in this category. In Luiseño, for example, the suffix [i] is added to the object of a verb, as we saw in Problem 2.2–8 (p. 69). A different kind of example is provided by the Papago data of Problem 2.1–3 (p. 43), which shows that the morpheme [g] is prefixed to any noun not in sentence-initial position. In Aztec the word [in] can occur as the first element of any noun phrase; it resembles an article in some respects, but it appears to have no semantic value and might be regarded as a trapping.

Problem 3.2–3   Spanish

State the agreement rule to which the data below attests. Comment on the phonological manifestation of this agreement.

(1)	un caballo blanco	'a white horse'
(2)	las mesas rojas	'the red tables'
(3)	unas casas blancas	'some white houses'
(4)	el palo negro	'the black stick'
(5)	los palos rojos	'the red sticks'

(6) una mesa negra	'a black table'
(7) la mesa blanca	'the white table'
(8) unos caballos negros	'some black horses'
(9) la casa roja	'the red house'
(10) un palo rojo	'a red stick'
(11) las casas negras	'the black houses'
(12) unos palos blancos	'some white sticks'

Solution

The modifiers of a noun (including articles and adjectives) must agree with it in number and gender. On both nouns and adjectives, gender is marked by the endings *o* (masculine) and *a* (feminine). The plural is marked by the ending *s*. The articles follow this pattern for the most part, but the masculine singular articles have special forms. In the masculine singular, the definite article is *el* rather than the anticipated *lo*, and the indefinite article is *un* rather than the anticipated *uno*.

Problem 3.2–4 English

Subordinate clauses are often marked by special trappings. In English the predicate of the main clause governs the ways in which a subordinate clause can be specially marked. Identify the trappings in the subordinate clauses of the sentences below. List the class of main clause predicates that tolerate each type of marking in the subordinate clauses in their scope.

(1) For him to be so stubborn is unusual.
(2) Wilhelm believes that the knuckle-ball is easy to throw.
(3) *For him to have a heart attack is certain.
(4) *Pierre wants my winning the big race.
(5) *That big bully's being a coward at heart is true.
(6) We anticipate that there will be no riot.
(7) For the Canadian government to declare martial law is easy.
(8) *I believe for Susan to be rich.
(9) That cigarettes are good for you is true.
(10) *I anticipate for the alligator to win the wrestling match.
(11) Roderick's being so dense is unusual.
(12) *That the Celtics won the Super Bowl was easy.
(13) She wants for people to leave her alone.
(14) Our having to pay higher taxes is certain.
(15) That Sheila never graduated is unusual.
(16) *They believe his being guilty.
(17) *Harold wants that I come.

(18) *For Herschel to swim is true.
(19) His eating a whole pie is easy.
(20) I anticipate our having to pawn your jewels.
(21) That help is on the way is certain.

Solution

The data illustrates three ways in which subordinate clauses can be marked. One way is by inserting *that* at the beginning of the clause. Main clause predicates that allow this include *believe, anticipate, true, unusual,* and *certain.* A second pattern involves inserting *for* before the subject of the subordinate clause and placing *to* before the verb (in place of the usual inflection for person and tense). Predicates that tolerate the *for . . . to* marking include *want, unusual,* and *easy.* In the third pattern, the subject of the subordinate clause is made into a possessive, and *ing* is suffixed to the verb (again in place of the usual verbal inflection). *Anticipate, certain, unusual,* and *easy* are among the lexical items that permit the *POSSESSIVE . . . ing* pattern.

REARRANGEMENT RULES

In addition to rules that delete and insert elements, languages contain rearrangement rules, rules that change the configuration of tree structures. The simplest type of configurational change involves merely reordering the words of a clause. It is not uncommon for languages to allow the words of a clause to occur in several different orders with at most only minor changes in meaning. We have already encountered numerous examples, including Papago (Problem 2.1–3, p. 43), Luiseño (2.1–6, p. 50), Latin (2.1–10, p. 53), and others.

Other rearrangement rules introduce more radical changes, changes that involve the reorganization of constituent structure. In Problem 3.1–1, for instance, we saw that under certain conditions a syntactic rule of English optionally moves an adverbial constituent from a subordinate clause to the beginning of the main clause of the sentence. The operation of this rule in the derivation of sentence (2) from sentence (1) is illustrated in Figure 3.2–2.

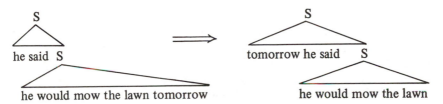

Figure 3.2–2

(1) He said he would mow the lawn tomorrow.
(2) Tomorrow he said he would mow the lawn.

Syntactic rules which rearrange constituent structure are quite common. They are responsible for many of the striking differences between conceptual and surface structures.

Problem 3.2–5 French

The following sentences illustrate the application of an important rearrangement transformation of French syntax. State this rule.

(1)	Il voit Pierre.	'He sees Peter.'
(2)	Il est certain de son innocence.	'He is certain of his innocence.'
(3)	*Il cela voit.	'He sees that.'
(4)	Il est certain de cela.	'He is certain of that.'
(5)	*Il voit le.	'He sees it.'
(6)	*Il un livre voit.	'He sees a book.'
(7)	*Il de cela est certain.	'He is certain of that.'
(8)	Il voit mon ami.	'He sees my friend.'
(9)	Il en est certain.	'He is certain of it.'
(10)	*Il est certain en.	'He is certain of it.'
(11)	Il voit cela.	'He sees that.'
(12)	*Il mon ami voit.	'He sees my friend.'
(13)	*Il de son innocence est certain.	'He is certain of his innocence.'
(14)	*Il est certain de le.	'He is certain of it.'
(15)	Il voit un livre.	'He sees a book.'
(16)	Il le voit.	'He sees it.'
(17)	*Il de le est certain.	'He is certain of it.'
(18)	*Il Pierre voit.	'He sees Peter.'

Discussion

Sentence (5) shows that pronouns cannot occur following *voit* 'sees', even though other kinds of noun phrases can (compare sentences (1), (8), (11), and (15)). On the basis of this observation, it would seem necessary to add to the complexity of the grammar of French by imposing on sentences the restriction that pronouns, unlike other noun phrases, cannot occur after verbs as direct objects. This restriction is an apparent anomaly in an otherwise regular pattern. Sentence (16) reveals another apparent irregularity; the object pronoun *le* occurs before the verb *voit*, but no other object noun phrase is permitted in this position (compare sentences (3), (6), (12), and (18)).

However, these two apparent anomalies are not unrelated. Pronouns are the only kind of object not allowed after the verb, and they are the only kind of object allowed before the verb. Rather than treating this fact as a mere coincidence, we can postulate an obligatory syntactic rule of French that moves object pronouns from post-verbal to pre-verbal position. Sentences like (16), in other words, can be viewed as filling the gap left by the deviance of sentences like (5). At a level of representation slightly more abstract than that of surface structure, all objects will follow the verb, and none will precede the verb. The application of this simple pronoun movement rule accounts simultaneously for both apparent distributional irregularities. Postulating this rule therefore allows us to simplify the analysis and capture generalizations that would not otherwise be valid.

Similar observations can be made with respect to the elements that can precede and follow *est certain* 'is certain'. This predicate can be followed by the preposition *de* plus a noun phrase, as in (2) and (4), except for the combination *de + PRONOUN* (note sentence (14)). (9) shows that *en* 'of it' can precede this predicate, but nothing else can except the subject (compare (7), (13), and (17)). Moreover, *en* cannot follow *est certain*, as shown by (10). The description of French will be simpler and more insightful if the pronoun movement rule is generalized to apply to *de + PRONOUN* when this sequence follows *est certain*. When transported into pre-predicate position, *de + PRONOUN* is manifested phonologically as *en* (this is an example of syncretism).

Solution

If a pronoun, with or without a preceding preposition, follows the predicate of a clause, this sequence is moved into pre-predicate position. When it occurs in this position, the sequence *de + PRONOUN* is manifested phonologically as *en*.

Problem 3.2–6 English

PART A The sentences of each pair in examples (1)–(3) below manifest the same conceptual structure. Determine whether the (a) or (b) sentences are more "basic", in the sense that they reflect more directly the underlying propositional structure. State the syntactic rule that applies to the more divergent sentences to obscure this propositional structure at the surface level. Using a format analogous to Figure 3.2–2, diagram the application of this rule in the derivation of the less basic sentences of (1) and (2).

    (1) (a) That the blonde will win is likely.
        (b) The blonde is likely to win.

(2) (a) That soccer will catch on here eventually is certain.
  (b) Soccer is certain to catch on here eventually.
(3) (a) *That David needs more money appears.
  (b) David appears to need more money.

Solution

The (a) structures are more basic. In example (1), for instance, *the blonde will win* is a proposition that is semantically in the scope of *likely*; (1) (a) reflects this semantic organization in the arrangement of its surface clauses, but (1) (b) does not even contain a clause of the form *the blonde* (*will*) *win*.

The rearrangement rule that applies in the derivation of the (b) sentences can be stated as follows:

> If a subordinate clause functions as the subject of a predicate, the subject of this subordinate clause can replace it as the main clause subject; the remainder of the subordinate clause is positioned at the end of the sentence.

This rule applies to sentences (1) (b) and (2) (b) as follows:

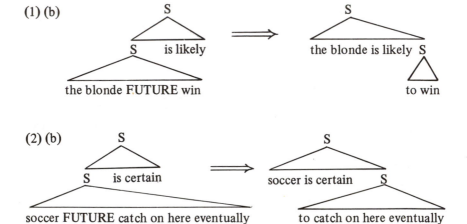

Discussion

This rule is usually called subject raising, because it raises the subject of a subordinate clause into the main clause. Subject raising is permitted with certain main clause predicates, such as the ones in (1)–(3), but not all. *Probable*, for example, does not permit subject raising to apply: *That the blonde will win is probable* but **The blonde is probable to win*. The main clause predicate therefore governs subject raising. Moreover, some predicates require that subject raising apply obligatorily, even though its application is normally optional. One of these predicates is *appear*. In (3) (b) *David needs more money* is semantically in the scope of *appears*, just as *the blonde* (*will*) *win* is semantically in the scope of *likely* in (1) (b). The ungrammaticality of (3) (a) indicates that subject raising must apply obligatorily when the governing predicate is *appear*.

When subject raising applies, *to* occurs in the subordinate clause in place of the usual marking for tense. This is the same *to* that occurs in the *for . . . to* combination discussed in Problem 3.2–4. However, *for* does not appear in the (b) sentences; it appears only when the subordinate clause has a subject in surface structure.

PART B   Subject raising is actually more general than is indicated in Part A. There are grounds for believing that a properly reformulated version of this rule also applies in the derivation of sentences like (4) (b)–(6) (b).

> (4) (a) I believe that Edward is honest.
>   (b) I believe Edward to be honest.
> (5) (a) Felicita expects that her husband will come home late.
>   (b) Felicita expects her husband to come home late.
> (6) (a) I judge that he is a fool.
>   (b) I judge him to be a fool.

Specifically, it is claimed that the (a) and (b) sentences have the same underlying structure; that subject raising derives the (b) sentences from the structures that underlie the (a) sentences; and that in the (b) sentences the underlying subordinate clause subject (*Edward, her husband*, and *him*) functions as the direct object of the main clause in surface structure.

Arguments to support this analysis can be formulated on the basis of sentences like (7)–(9).

> (7) (a) I believe him.
>   (b) I believe him to be honest.
>   (c) *I believe that him is honest.
> (8) (a) Harry believes Alice.
>   (b) Alice is believed by Harry.
>   (c) Harry believes Alice to be a virgin.
>   (d) Alice is believed by Harry to be a virgin.
>   (e) Harry believes that Alice is a virgin.
>   (f) *Alice is believed by Harry that is a virgin.
> (9) (a) Harry believes himself.
>   (b) Harry believes himself to be honest.
>   (c) *Himself is honest.
>   (d) *Harry believes that himself is honest.

Formulate the appropriate arguments. Restate the rule of subject raising in a more general form so that it will apply properly in the derivations of (4) (b)–(6) (b) as well as (1) (b)–(3) (b). Diagram the derivation of (4) (b).

Solution

Sentences (7) (a) and (7) (c) show that at the level of surface structure *him* can function as the object of a verb but not as the subject of a verb. The fact that *him* rather than *he* occurs in (7) (b) is evidence that this pronoun functions as the surface object of *believe*, not as the surface subject of *to be honest*.

The object of a verb can become its subject in a passive sentence. Thus *Alice* is the object of *believe* in (8) (a), but it is the derived subject of the passive sentence (8) (b). Sentences (8) (e) and (8) (f) show that the subject of a subordinate clause cannot become the subject of the main clause by passivization; for this reason (8) (f) is ungrammatical. The fact that (8) (d) is grammatical therefore constitutes syntactic evidence that subject raising has made *Alice* the object of *believe* in (8) (c); once it has been made the object of the main clause, it can be made a passive subject, just as in (8) (b).

Sentences (9) (a), (9) (c), and (9) (d) show that a reflexive pronoun can occur as an object but not as a subject in surface structure. The grammaticalness of (9) (b) thus constitutes syntactic evidence that *himself* is the surface object of *believes* rather than the surface subject of *to be honest*.

The generalized version of subject raising can be stated as follows:

> If a subordinate clause functions as the subject or object of a predicate, the subject of this subordinate clause can replace it as the main clause subject or object; the remainder of the subordinate clause is positioned at the end of the sentence.

Here is the derivation of (4) (b):

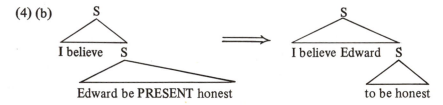

Discussion

When subject raising applies, *to* is inserted in the subordinate clause even when the main clause predicate normally does not tolerate subordinate clauses marked by *for . . . to*. Thus *to* appears in (4) (b) even though **I believe for Edward to be honest* is ungrammatical.

CONCLUSION

To summarize, both lexical and syntactic rules function in connecting semantic representations and surface structures. Among the syntactic rules of a language are some that modify tree structures. These rules are called transformations. Transformations apply sequentially in the derivation of surface structures, with each rule application making a tree structure less abstract and more like its ultimate surface form.

Transformations fall into three major classes: reduction rules, rules that insert trappings, and rearrangement rules. Some reduction rules depend on coreference, but others require only identity of form and meaning. Insertion rules include agreement rules and rules that mark constituents in accordance with their syntactic function. Rearrangement rules sometimes affect only word order, but often they effect much greater configurational changes on tree structures. Some syntactic rules apply obligatorily when appropriate, others only optionally. The application of some rules is governed by lexical items, in that certain lexical items permit the application of the rule in question but others do not.

FURTHER PROBLEMS

Problem 3.2–7   Japanese

The following sentences are from Japanese (see Dingwall, 1969, and Koutsoudas, 1971). Formulate a reduction rule for Japanese on the basis of this data. Comment on the function of the particles *ga* and *o*.

(1) watasi ga sakana o tabeta, biru ga gohan o tabeta
I fish ate, Bill rice ate
'I ate fish, and Bill ate rice.'

(2) taroo ga inu o, biru ga ki o mita
Taro dog, Bill tree saw
'Taro saw a dog, and Bill saw a tree.'

(3) watasi ga inu o taita, taroo ga ki o taita
I dog hit, Taro tree hit
'I hit a dog, and Taro hit a tree.'

(4) biru ga sakana o, watasi ga gohan o tabeta
Bill fish, I rice ate
'Bill ate fish, and I ate rice.'

(5) taroo ga inu o, biru ga ki o taita

Taro dog, Bill tree hit
'Taro hit a dog, and Bill hit a tree.'

(6) watasi ga gohan o, taroo ga sakana o tabeta

I rice, Taro fish ate
'I ate rice, and Taro ate fish.'

(7) taroo ga inu o mita, biru ga ki o mita

Taro dog saw, Bill tree saw
'Taro saw a dog, and Bill saw a tree.'

Problem 3.2–8   English

In the previous section (3.1), arguments were given for the existence in English of a rule of subject deletion. This rule deletes the subject of a subordinate clause (under certain conditions) when it is coreferential to a noun phrase in the main clause, as in the diagram below.

Examine the sentences below. Construct an argument, based on reflexivization, to justify underlying representations such as the one to the left of the arrow in the diagram above.

(1) I want you to examine yourself.
(2) *I respect any doctor who examines myself.
(3) He dislikes himself.
(4) He knows that I dislike myself.
(5) I want to examine myself.
(6) *I want you to examine myself.
(7) He doesn't want to dislike himself.
(8) *He knows that I dislike himself.
(9) I examined myself.

Problem 3.2–9   Lebanese Arabic

The sentences below (Koutsoudas, 1968) illustrate deletion, rearrangement, and the insertion of trappings in Lebanese Arabic. Isolate the independently

meaningful morphemes and give their meanings. State the syntactic rules
required by the data.

(1)	huwwe šaafha la l bint	'He saw the girl.'
(2)	l walid hiyye šaafitu	'She saw the boy.'
(3)	l bint šaafitu la l walid	'The girl saw the boy.'
(4)	samiir ḍarabha la l bint	'Samir hit the girl.'
(5)	šaaf l bint	'He saw the girl.'
(6)	l bint šaafit l walid	'The girl saw the boy.'
(7)	l bint samiir ḍarabha	'Samir hit the girl.'
(8)	ḍarabu la l walid	'He hit the boy.'
(9)	hiyye šaafitha la l bint	'She saw the girl.'
(10)	ḍarab l walid	'He hit the boy.'

Problem 3.2–10 *Hungarian*

Deletion, insertion, and rearrangement rules are all needed to describe the
following Hungarian data (Jones, 1970). State these rules. Assume that objects
follow the verb in underlying representations. Also assume that two conjoined
noun phrases constitute a single, more complex noun phrase. In an expression
like *the onions and the leeks*, for example, *the onions* and *the leeks* are both
simple noun phrases, and the entire expression *the onions and the leeks* is also
a noun phrase.

(1) a tanar latja a fiut, es a szabo lat egy leanyt
    'The teacher sees the boy, and the uncle sees a girl.'

(2) a fiu lat egy leanyt
    'The boy sees a girl.'

(3) a tanar a fiut, es a szabo a leanyt latja
    'The teacher sees the boy, and the uncle sees the girl.'

(4) a tanar egy fiut lat es a leanyt
    'The teacher sees a boy and the girl.'

(5) a tanar latja a fiut es egy leanyt
    'The teacher sees the boy and a girl.'

(6) *a tanar a fiut es lat egy leanyt
    'The teacher sees the boy and a girl.'

(7) a tanar latja a fiut, es a szabo a leanyt
    'The teacher sees the boy, and the uncle sees the girl.'

(8) a fiu a leanyt latja
    'The boy sees the girl.'

(9) a fiu egy leanyt lat
'The boy sees a girl.'

(10) a tanar a fiut latja es egy leanyt
'The teacher sees the boy and a girl.'

(11) a tanar lat egy fiut es a leanyt
'The teacher sees a boy and the girl.'

(12) a fiu latja a leanyt
'The boy sees the girl.'

(13) *a tanar a fiut lat es egy leanyt
'The teacher sees the boy and a girl.'

(14) a tanar a fiut latja, es a szabo a leanyt
'The teacher sees the boy, and the uncle sees the girl.'

(15) a tanar a fiut es egy leanyt lat
'The teacher sees the boy and a girl.'

(16) a tanar egy fiut es a leanyt latja
'The teacher sees a boy and the girl.'

Problem 3.2–11   *Spanish*

The sentences below (see Rivero, 1970) provide evidence for a rearrangement transformation of Spanish. Describe this rule and diagram its application in the derivation of sentence (8). Provide syntactic and semantic justification for the analysis. (Subject pronouns in Spanish can optionally be deleted.)

(1) No prueba gota de vino.
not he touches drop of wine
'He doesn't touch (a drop of) wine.'

(2) *Prueba gota de vino.
'He touches (a drop of) wine.'

(3) No mencionó palabra del asunto.
not he mentioned word about the matter
'He didn't say a word about the matter.'

(4) *Mencionó palabra del asunto.
'He said a word about the matter.'

(5) *No me gusta el hombre que prueba gota de vino.
not me pleases the man who touches drop of wine
'I don't like the man who touches (a drop of) wine.'

(6) *No me gusta el hombre que mencionó palabra del asunto.
'I don't like the man who said a word about the matter.'

(7) Quiero que no pruebes gota de vino.

I want that not you touch drop of wine
'I don't want you to touch (a drop of) wine.'

(8) No quiero que pruebes gota de vino.
'I don't want you to touch (a drop of) wine.'

(9) Creo que no mencionó palabra del asunto.

I believe that not he mentioned word about the matter
'I don't believe he said a word about the matter.'

(10) No creo que mencionara palabra del asunto.
'I don't believe he said a word about the matter.'

Problem 3.2–12 *Luiseño*

PART A   Rules of insertion, deletion, and permutation are all illustrated in the Luiseño sentences below. State these rules. (Ignore subject-verb agreement and the difference between subject and object pronouns.)

(1) noo paapaviš miyq	'I am thirsty.'
(2) poloovup wunaal	'He is good.'
(3) noon ʔowoʔaq	'I am working.'
(4) wunaalup ney maʔmaq	'He likes me.'
(5) *wunaal poloovup	'He is good.'
(6) wunaal paapaviš	'He is thirsty.'
(7) noo paapaviš miyquṣ	'I was thirsty.'
(8) pellaqup wunaal	'He is dancing.'
(9) noon paapaviš	'I am thirsty.'
(10) noon poy maʔmaq	'I like him.'
(11) *nooup poy maʔmaq	'I like him.'
(12) wunaalup paapaviš	'He is thirsty.'
(13) noo ʔowoʔaq	'I am working.'
(14) wunaal paapaviš miyquṣ	'He was thirsty.'
(15) wunaalup pellaq	'He is dancing.'
(16) *wunaaln ney maʔmaq	'He likes me.'
(17) noo paapaviš	'I am thirsty.'
(18) wunaalup poloov	'He is good.'

PART B   Examine sentences (19)–(23) and describe how possession is marked in Luiseño. On the basis of (24)–(27), describe how subordinate clauses are marked when they function as the subject of a sentence. Diagram the surface clause structure of (25) and (26).

(19) noki poloov	'My house is good.'
(20) pokaamay paapaviš	'His son is thirsty.'
(21) nokaamay poloov	'My son is good.'
(22) nokaamayup paapaviš	'My son is thirsty.'
(23) poloov poki	'His house is good.'
(24) noo noʔowoʔax poy wultuniq	'My working makes him angry.'
(25) wunaal popellax yawaywiš	'His dancing is beautiful.'
(26) noo noʔowoʔax miyquṣ	'I had worked.' (literally: my working was)
(27) wunaalup popellax miyquṣ	'He had danced.' (literally: his dancing was)

PART C Consider sentence (28) in terms of the analysis worked out in Parts A and B. Notice in particular that suffixing [up] to [noo] does not make (28) ungrammatical in Luiseño, although (11) is ungrammatical because it contains this combination. Can you explain this discrepancy? Sketch the underlying structure of (28) and show its derivation. *No, it's not an error.*

    (28) nooup poy nomaʔmax   'I like him.'

3.3 Rule Ordering

INTERMEDIATE STRUCTURES

Various problems in section 3.2 have made it apparent that the derivation of a surface structure involves the application of a series of distinct syntactic rules, each of which can be motivated independently of the others and can apply in sentences where the others do not. In Problem 3.2–10, for instance, it was found that rules (A), (B), and (C) must be posited for Hungarian.

    (A) A noun which functions as a direct object receives the suffix *t*.
    (B) A noun phrase which directly follows the verb can be moved in front of the verb.
    (C) A verb receives the suffix *ja* if its object is definite (and if certain other conditions are met).

All three rules apply in the derivation of sentence (1), which is sketched in Figure 3.3–1.

    (1) a tanar a fiut latja   'The teacher sees the boy.'

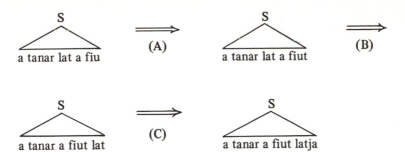

Figure 3.3-1

(A), (B), and (C) are distinct rules, not a single complex rule, since they can apply separately. In some sentences (A) applies but not (B) or (C). Similarly, (B) can apply without the application of (C), and conversely. Consequently, the derivation of (1) from its underlying representation proceeds in several stages.

The claim that syntactic rules apply sequentially in the derivation of a sentence, producing along the way structures intermediate between conceptual and surface structures, does not rest solely on the observation that numerous distinct rules apply in the derivation of a given sentence. By postulating these intermediate structures, it is often possible to capture generalizations that could not be expressed in terms of semantic or surface representations alone.

Consider sentence (2).

(2) I want to believe myself to be blasé.

Semantically, (2) involves at least three propositions, as shown in Figure 3.3–2.

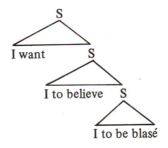

Figure 3.3-2

The noun phrase *I* figures in all three clauses, but there is only one occurrence of *I* in each clause. In terms of this underlying representation, therefore, there is no reason to anticipate the reflexive *myself* in sentence (2), since reflexives normally result only when a single clause contains two coreferential nominals (see Problem 3.2–8). Nor can the occurrence of the reflexive be accounted for in terms of the surface structure of (2), shown in Figure 3.3–3, since *I* and *myself* belong to different surface clauses. From the standpoint of conceptual and surface structures alone, then, the occurrence of *myself* in (2) appears to be irregular.

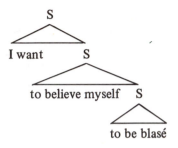

Figure 3.3-3

This apparent irregularity vanishes if we trace the derivation of (2) through intermediate stages produced by the application of syntactic rules. The relevant rules are subject raising, reflexivization, and subject deletion, all well-established rules of English discussed in sections 3.1 and 3.2. As we have seen, *believe* is one of the verbs that allow the application of subject raising; when this rule is applied to Figure 3.3–2, the subject *I* of the lowest clause is raised and becomes the derived object of *believe* in the middle clause, yielding Figure 3.3–4.

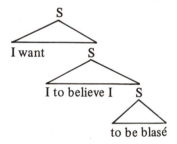

Figure 3.3-4

Figure 3.3–4 is an intermediate structure, a structure that is produced by the application of one rule and will subsequently undergo other transformations in the derivation of the ultimate surface structure. It is in this intermediate structure that the conditions for reflexivization are met; the middle clause of Figure 3.3–4 contains two occurrences of *I*. The regular rule of reflexivization, which must be restricted to single clauses on the basis of a variety of independent evidence, can be applied to this structure to yield Figure 3.3–5.

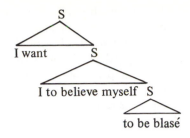

Figure 3.3–5

Finally, the rule of subject deletion deletes the subject of *believe* in the middle clause of Figure 3.3–5, resulting in the surface structure of (2) (Figure 3.3–3). Only in the intermediate structure (Figure 3.3–4) are the conditions for reflexivization met, and only by positing this abstract structure can the occurrence of *myself* in (2) be accounted for by the regular and quite general rule of reflexivization in English.

Many other examples could be given of generalizations that can be captured only by positing underlying structures more abstract than surface structures but not sufficiently abstract to be regarded as semantic representations. The evidence for intermediate structures in a derivation, and hence for the sequential application of syntactic rules, is therefore quite compelling.

ORDERING

There is considerable evidence to suggest that the mode of syntactic rule application is still more complex. Specifically, the rules that derive a surface structure from an underlying semantic representation must in many instances apply in a fixed order. Unless some rules were assumed to apply prior to the application of others, the rules of a grammar would in many cases have to be made more complex.

It is often the case that one rule must apply before another simply because conditions for the application of the second rule never arise except through the application of the first. For example, *that* insertion must precede preposition deletion in the derivation of sentences like (1).

(1) I am disturbed that Ted is so stubborn.

That has no semantic value in such sentences and thus cannot be posited as part of their semantic representation. A syntactic rule must therefore be responsible for inserting *that* as a subordinate clause trapping, which results in intermediate structures such as (2).

(2) I am disturbed at that Ted is so stubborn.

The rule of preposition deletion, which erases *at* to yield sentence (1), must apply after *that* insertion, because the rule deletes a preposition only when it directly precedes a subordinating particle. It would not do to reformulate preposition deletion so that it simply deleted a preposition before a subordinate clause. Sentence (3) shows that the preposition remains before a subordinate clause if the first element of the clause is not a subordinating particle (it also motivates the claim that the preposition *at* follows *disturbed* in the underlying representation of (1)).

(3) I am disturbed at Ted's being so stubborn.

Consequently, preposition deletion must apply after the insertion of subordinating particles, because only after they have been inserted are the conditions for the application of this rule satisfied.

In other cases, one rule must be ordered to apply before another because failure to order the rules in such a way would lead to incorrect results (or else to the need to complicate the rules unnecessarily). Consider the following sentences from Navaho (compare Problem 2.2–12, p. 72).

(4) ší naašbé   'I swim about.'
(5) naašbé   'I swim about.'
(6) ni nanibé   'You swim about.'
(7) nanibé   'You swim about.'
(8) *naabé   'I swim about.'

The verbs in (4)–(7) contain markers that agree with the subject pronoun; [š] agrees with the subject [ší] 'I', and [ni] agrees with the subject [ni] 'you'. An agreement rule of Navaho must therefore mark verbs to agree with their subjects; the ungrammaticality of (8) as a variant of (4) and (5) demonstrates that this rule must be obligatory. Sentences (5) and (7) result from the application of a second syntactic rule of Navaho, one that optionally deletes a subject pronoun. The simplest and hence most desirable formulation of these two rules is (A) and (B).

(A) A verb must agree with its subject.
(B) A subject pronoun can optionally be deleted.

Now consider the ordering of rules (A) and (B). If (A) is ordered so that it always applies before (B), no incorrect results will be obtained, and (A) and (B) can be maintained in the simple form in which they are given. Sentence (5), for instance, has the following derivation:

$$\text{ší naabé} \Rightarrow \text{ší naašbé} \Rightarrow \text{naašbé}$$
$$\quad\quad\quad\quad\;\;(A)\quad\quad\quad\;\;(B)$$

With (A) ordered before (B), the subject pronoun is guaranteed to be present when the agreement rule that must refer to it applies. Suppose, however, that (B) were ordered before (A), or that the two rules could apply in either order.

If this were the case, (B) could delete the subject pronoun before (A) applied. But (A) makes reference to the subject; if the subject were deleted prior to the application of (A), agreement could not correctly be imposed, and ungrammatical sentences like (8) would erroneously be allowed by the grammar. The situation could be remedied only by complicating the rules in some way, perhaps by letting (B) apply only to sentences whose verb contains a subject marker. This needless complexity can be avoided if the rules are strictly ordered.

In the remainder of this book no distinction will be made between the two kinds of rule ordering. Two rules, (A) and (B), will be described as ordered with respect to each other when either: (1) the conditions for the application of (B) never arise except through the prior application of (A); or (2) the application of (B) before the application of (A) would yield incorrect outputs (unless one or both of the rules were complicated in some ad hoc fashion).

Problem 3.3–1 *Luiseño*

In Problem 3.2–12 sentences like (1)–(5) below led to the postulation of an insertion rule and a permutation rule of Luiseño. These two rules are restated here as (A) and (B). Assuming that (A) and (B) must be ordered with respect to each other, give an argument for ordering them in one particular way rather than the other.

(A) A predicate can optionally be advanced to the beginning of a sentence.

(B) A suffix that agrees with the subject of a sentence can optionally be added to the first word. The suffix is [n] if the subject is first person singular, and [up] if it is third person singular.

(1) noon pellaq   'I am dancing.'
(2) wunaalup pellaq   'He is dancing.'
(3) wunaalup poloov   'He is good.'
(4) pellaqup wunaal   'He is dancing.'
(5) poloovup wunaal   'He is good.'

Solution

Rule (A) must apply before rule (B). If the suffix were added before (A) optionally advanced the predicate to sentence-initial position, it would always go on the subject, never on the predicate. (A) must therefore precede (B), not conversely, unless pointless complications are to be introduced in the rules. (For example, (B) could precede (A) if (B) were reformulated so as to add a suffix to either the subject or the predicate and if (A) were complicated so that it applied obligatorily to a predicate to which [n] or [up] had been added.)

Problem 3.3–2   English

In addition to *that* insertion and preposition deletion, the following sentences illustrate the application of a third syntactic rule of English having to do with subordinate clauses. State this rule and comment on its ordering with respect to the others. Show the application of all three rules in the derivation of sentence (2).

(1) I know that he is well educated.
(2) My mother is disturbed I let my hair grow.
(3) Everyone is certain that professional wrestling is phoney.
(4) My mother is disturbed that I let my hair grow.
(5) I know he is well educated.
(6) Everyone is certain professional wrestling is phoney.

Solution

The subordinating particle *that* may optionally be deleted. We saw earlier that preposition deletion must follow *that* insertion. However, preposition deletion must precede *that* deletion, because it refers to the subordinating particle. If *that* were deleted before preposition deletion applied, ungrammatical sentences such as the following would be allowed in surface structure: **My mother is disturbed at I let my hair grow*. The derivation of (2) must proceed in this way:

my mother is disturbed at I let my hair grow   ⇒
        (*that* insertion)
my mother is disturbed at that I let my hair grow   ⇒
        (preposition deletion)
my mother is disturbed that I let my hair grow   ⇒
        (*that* deletion)
my mother is disturbed I let my hair grow

Discussion

It might seem suspicious to insert *that* by means of one rule only to delete it by another; an alternative would be to make *that* insertion optional. It is conceivable that this alternative could prove correct, but it is nonetheless true that there is syntactic evidence to motivate inserting *that* and later optionally deleting it. This evidence is provided by sentences like (2) and (6), which lack the prepositions *at* and *of* normally associated with *disturbed* and *certain* respectively. Evidence was put forth earlier (p. 132) that preposition deletion must be formulated so as to delete a preposition before a subordinating particle (not simply before a subordinate clause). If this formulation is correct, *that* must be present at one stage in the derivation of (2) and (6), since their prepositions have been deleted. Since *that* is a meaningless particle, it cannot exist in the semantic representations of these sentences; nor does it exist in their surface structures. Consequently, it must be present in some intermediate structure. It follows that the derivation of (2) and (6) requires *that* insertion, preposition deletion, and subsequently *that* deletion.

CONCLUSION

In summary, the syntactic derivation of a sentence involves the sequential application of a series of rules. The output of each rule application is an intermediate structure that serves as input to the next rule. Not only must the rules apply sequentially; in many instances they must apply in a certain order. The ordering of rules and the postulation of intermediate structures make it possible to capture significant linguistic generalizations that could not otherwise be expressed.

To claim that rules apply sequentially in a particular order is not to suggest that a speaker runs through these rules in chronological sequence as he constructs a sentence. The grammar of a language is a description of an abstract set of principles, not a description of the process of sentence production and recognition. Grammatical rules are ordered in an abstract, logical sense, not in a temporal sense. By way of analogy, the two ends of a chain are connected by a series of links. It is appropriate to speak of these links as forming an ordered sequence, but it is not appropriate to speak of the relationship among these links as a temporal one, each preceding the other in time. The sequential relationship is purely structural.

The analogy can be extended a bit further. If the two ends of a chain are labeled A and B, we can speak of the links as "leading from" or "going from" A to B. In speaking this way, we do not attribute any motion to the links or the chain; it is only a metaphorical way of referring to the structure of the chain. By the same token, we are using a metaphor when we say that a surface structure is "derived from" a semantic representation. Such a metaphor is useful in describing the relationship between semantic and surface structures, but it should not be taken as implying any physical or psychological movement from one to the other. Nor should it be taken as implying that special emphasis is being given to speaking as opposed to hearing—the principles relating conceptual and surface structures are presumably used in both enterprises. The directionality implicit in such expressions as "derive from", "underlie", and "precede" must be recognized for what it is—namely, a convenient way of conceptualizing and talking about linguistic phenomena. Any further significance remains to be established.

The ordering of rules is a complicated matter that is at best only partially understood, and many aspects of the problem are unclear and controversial. However, the somewhat oversimplified picture of rule ordering presented in this section is sufficient for present purposes.

FURTHER PROBLEMS

Problem 3.3–3   English

On the basis of sentences like the ones below, argue for an ordering relation between the deletion of *you* in imperatives (see Problem 3.2–2) and reflexivization in English. Give the derivation of (1).

(1) Take care of yourself!
(2) *Think about you!
(3) Think about yourselves!
(4) *Take care of you!

Problem 3.3–4   English

On the basis of sentences like the ones below, argue for an ordering relation between subject raising (see Problem 3.2–6) and subject-verb agreement in English. Give the derivation of (2).

(1) That he will lose his whole wad in Las Vegas is certain.
(2) They are likely to disobey orders.
(3) *They is likely to disobey orders.
(4) *He are certain to lose his whole wad in Las Vegas.
(5) *That they will disobey orders are certain.
(6) He is likely to disobey orders.
(7) They are certain to disobey orders.
(8) He is certain to lose his whole wad in Las Vegas.

Problem 3.3–5   Luiseño

Problem 3.2–12 established the need for the following three rules of Luiseño:

(A) When a subordinate clause functions as the subject of a sentence, the subordinate clause verb is marked with a prefix and a suffix. The prefix is the possessive prefix that corresponds to the subject of the subordinate clause. The suffix is [x].

(B) A suffix that agrees with the subject can optionally be added to the first word of a sentence.

(C) The present tense form of the verb meaning 'be', [miyq], can optionally be deleted.

These rules function in the derivation of sentences like (1)–(3). Determine how, if at all, these three rules must be ordered with respect to one another.

(1) wunaalup popellax miyquş   'He had danced.'
(2) nooup poy noma?max   'I like him.'
(3) wunaalup popellax   'He dances.'

Problem 3.3–6   Hungarian

Problem 3.2–10 established the need for several syntactic rules of Hungarian. One is a permutation rule that allows the direct object of a verb to be moved in front of it. Another is an insertion rule that suffixes *ja* to a verb whose object is definite, that is, whose object contains the definite article *a* 'the'. Reexamine the data of Problem 3.2–10, particularly the sentences with conjoined objects, and argue for an ordering relation between these two rules.

3.4   Complex Sentences

The definition of a **complex sentence** can be made relative to either surface structures or underlying representations. In terms of surface structure, a complex sentence is one consisting of more than one **clause**. A clause (usually labeled *S* in tree diagrams) can in turn be defined as a constituent consisting of a predicate together with its assorted adjuncts, such as its subject, its object, adverbs, and so on. Many sentences are non-complex in surface structure. In terms of underlying representations, a complex sentence is one that consists of more than one proposition. A proposition (also labeled *S* in tree diagrams) consists of a predicate and its arguments. At the level of underlying representations, it is perhaps true that all sentences are complex.

The clauses of a complex sentence may be connected in different ways. When one clause functions as a constituent of another, as shown in Figure 3.4–1, the relation between them is referred to as **subordination**. The "lower" or **subordinate clause** of such a structure is said to be **embedded** in the "upper" or **main clause**. The relation between two connected clauses is referred to as **coordination** when neither clause is a constituent of the other. Coordination will be our immediate concern. We will return shortly to the topic of subordination.

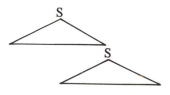

Figure 3.4–1

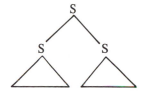

Figure 3.4–2

COORDINATION

The clauses of a coordinate structure are said to be **conjoined**, and each conjoined constituent is said to be a **conjunct**. Figure 3.4–2 depicts a coordinate structure. Each conjunct is a clause, and the two conjuncts taken together constitute a complex sentence, indicated by the uppermost node *S*. Figure 3.4–2, of course, is only illustrative. Constituents other than clauses can be conjoined, and a conjoined structure may have indefinitely many conjuncts. Consider the following sentences.

> (1) The Huns sacked and burned the city.
> (2) I want to go either to Detroit or to Oakland.
> (3) For Christmas I want a boat, and a car, and a whistle, and an erector set, and a cap pistol . . . .

In (1) the verbs *sacked* and *burned* are conjoined. The conjoined constituents are prepositional phrases in (2), and in (3) the direct object is a conjoined noun phrase (one that potentially contains indefinitely many conjuncts).

Several types of syntactic rules affect conjoined structures. One type consists of rules that specify the surface position of **conjunctions**, the morphemes that accompany conjoined constituents. In English the basic conjunctions are *and* and *or*, and we will confine our attention to these forms and their equivalents in other languages.

Conjunctions can occupy various positions in surface structures. In some languages conjunctions precede the conjuncts. Consider the French sentences (4) and (5).

> (4) Et Jean et Pierre et Henri sont venus.
> 'John and Peter and Henry came.'

> (5) Ou il neige, ou il ne neige pas.
> 'Either it's snowing or it isn't snowing.'

The conjunctions *et* 'and' and *ou* 'or' can occur before each conjunct of a conjoined structure. The same is true of English, as shown in sentence (3) above, except that *and* and *or* cannot precede the first conjunct. However, the conjunction combinations *both . . . and* and *either . . . or* are more similar to the French conjunctions.

> (6) Both Rodney and Tristan need help.
> (7) Either the Vikings or the Raiders or the Colts will win the Super Bowl.

In some languages conjunctions follow the conjuncts. Consider the following example from Tarahumara, a Uto-Aztecan language of Mexico.

> (8) akiua to bawi sunu napega
> here bring water corn and
> 'Bring water and corn here!'

Conjunctions are often attached, phonologically at least, to one of the conjuncts. In sentence (3) above, for instance, each occurrence of *and* is associated phonologically with the immediately following noun phrase; it is possible to pause slightly after each noun phrase (where the commas are), but it is much less natural to pause directly after an *and* in an uninterrupted articulation of the sentence. In some languages conjunctions even appear as affixes inside one or both of the conjuncts. This is true, for example, of the Japanese conjunction *to* 'and', used to conjoin noun phrases. *To* occurs as a suffix on each conjunct:

> (9) taroo-to biru-to ga sakana o tabeta
> 'Taro and Bill ate fish.'

Various kinds of reduction rules also affect the surface manifestation of conjoined structures. It is often possible to delete one or more occurrences of a repeated conjunction. In English and French, for example, all but the last conjunction in a series may be deleted; thus sentence (10) is grammatical as well as (7), and (11) is a variant of (4).

> (10) The Vikings, the Raiders, or the Colts will win the Super Bowl.
> (11) Jean, Pierre, et Henri sont venus.
> 'John, Peter, and Henry came.'

In Japanese, the last occurrence of *to* in a conjoined structure can be deleted; sentence (12) is thus an acceptable variant of (9).

> (12) taroo-to biru ga sakana o tabeta
> 'Taro and Bill ate fish.'

Sometimes it is possible to delete all occurrences of a conjunction, particularly one meaning 'and', so that the conjoining is indicated merely by the juxtaposition of two or more constituents. This is marginally possible with English *and*; the resulting sentences, like (13) below, are on the borderline of acceptability, and they have special stylistic import.

> (13) We will not relent in our pursuit of freedom, happiness, justice.

A similar deletion derives (15) as a variant of the Japanese sentence (14); *sosite* 'and' is used instead of *to* when the conjuncts are clauses.

> (14) watasi ga sakana o tabeta, sosite biru ga gohan o tabeta
> 'I ate fish, and Bill ate rice.'
> (15) watasi ga sakana o tabeta, biru ga gohan o tabeta
> 'I ate fish, and Bill ate rice.'

When conjoined constituents (especially clauses) are similar in certain ways, special reduction rules are often applicable. In Problem 3.2–7 we saw that the verb of the first of two conjoined clauses can be deleted in Japanese if it is identical to the verb of the second clause; sentence (16) is thus an acceptable variant of (15).

> (16) watasi ga sakana o, biru ga gohan o tabeta
> 'I ate fish, and Bill ate rice.'

Problem 3.2–10 established the existence of a similar rule in Hungarian, illustrated in sentences (17) and (18); here it is the verb of the second conjunct that is deleted.

> (17) a tanar latja a fiut, es a szabo latja a leanyt
> 'The teacher sees the boy, and the uncle sees the girl.'
> (18) a tanar latja a fiut, es a szabo a leanyt
> 'The teacher sees the boy, and the uncle sees the girl.'

Rules that delete a repeated verb in conjoined clauses are found in many languages. This phenomenon is called "gapping", because it leaves a gap in the truncated clause (Ross, 1970).

More radical in its effects is the rule of conjunction reduction. This rule is posited to account for the fact that some sentences containing conjoined constituents are semantically equivalent to conjoined clauses. Consider the following.

> (19) Felix likes radishes and Robespierre likes radishes.
> (20) Felix and Robespierre like radishes.

In sentence (19) two clauses are conjoined to form a complex sentence. Sentence (20), with a conjoined subject, is non-complex in surface structure, but semantically it involves two propositions, one concerning Felix's liking of radishes and the other Robespierre's. Sentences (19) and (20) are semantically equivalent and have the same underlying representation. (19) reflects this common underlying representation fairly directly in surface structure; conjunction reduction applies in the derivation of (20), however, serving to collapse the underlying conjoined clauses into a single surface clause with a conjoined subject. This derivation is sketched in Figure 3.4–3. (Verb inflection is omitted to simplify matters.)

Conjunction reduction can optionally apply whenever the conjoined clauses are identical in all but one corresponding constituent; in (19), for instance, the two clauses are identical except for their subject noun phrases. The effect of the rule is to collapse the clauses into a single clause and to conjoin the non-identical constituents. The new conjoined elements are not always noun phrases. The conjoined verb phrases in (21) and the conjoined prepositional phrases in (22) exemplify the derivation of other conjoined constituents by the rule of conjunction reduction.

> (21) The president is believed by everyone to be untrustworthy and is likely to lose in the next election.

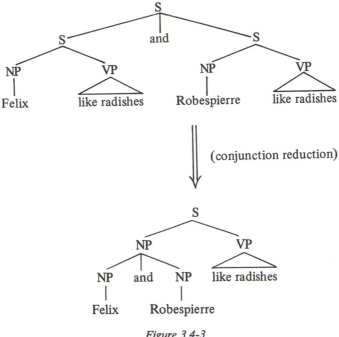

Figure 3.4-3

(22) She has lived in Dallas and in Seattle.

Conjunction reduction is a controversial rule. However, it seems necessary to assume that some conjoined constituents result from the reduction of underlying conjoined clauses, because constituents conjoined in surface structure are not always semantic units and hence could hardly have been coordinated entities at the semantic level. The underlying representation of (21), for example, is sketched in Figure 3.4–4. The surface structure of (21) contains the conjoined verb phrases *is believed by everyone to be untrustworthy* and *is likely to lose in the next election*, but neither of these verb phrases is a constituent in Figure 3.4–4. Only after certain syntactic rules have applied, resulting in the intermediate structure (23), do these surface constituents arise.

(23) The president is believed by everyone to be untrustworthy, and the president is likely to lose in the next election.

To grant the existence of conjunction reduction, however, is not to claim that all conjoined constituents derive from underlying conjoined clauses. Many sentences with conjoined elements are not semantically equivalent to conjoined clauses, and for these an analysis involving conjunction reduction would be inappropriate. In (24)–(26), for instance, the (a) sentences are not semantically equivalent to the (b) sentences.

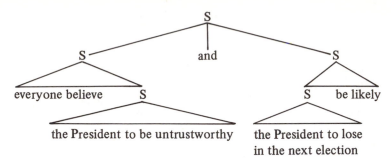

Figure 3.4-4

(24) (a) Line MN and line PQ are parallel.
    (b) Line MN is parallel and line PQ is parallel.
(25) (a) Felix and Robespierre met last week.
    (b) *Felix met last week and Robespierre met last week.
(26) (a) My arm is black and blue.
    (b) My arm is black and my arm is blue.

The constituents connected by *and* in (24) (a)–(26) (a) are presumably conjoined at the level of underlying representations, as they are in surface structure.

Problem 3.4–1 English

Formulate a reduction rule of English to account for the conjoined sentences below, and determine as precisely as possible from the data the conditions under which the rule can apply. Identical subscripts indicate coreference.

(1) Tom plays the trombone, Joy plays the flute, George plays the drums, and Abernathy plays the baritone.
(2) *Tom plays the trombone, and Joy the trombone.
(3) Tom plays the trombone, Joy the flute, George the drums, and Abernathy the baritone.
(4) *Tom the trombone, Joy the flute, George the drums, and Abernathy plays the baritone.
(5) *Tom$_i$ plays the trombone, and Tom$_i$ the flute.
(6) Tom plays the trombone, Joy plays the flute, George the drums, and Abernathy the baritone.
(7) *Tom plays the trombone, Joy the flute, George the drums, and Abernathy plays the baritone.
(8) Tom plays the trombone, Joy plays the flute, George plays the drums, and Abernathy the baritone.

Solution

The rule is gapping. If the verbs of all the conjuncts in a conjoined structure are identical, one or more of these verbs can be deleted. (4) shows that the English gapping rule (unlike the Japanese one) does not allow the verb of the first clause to be deleted. Sentences (3), (6), and (8) show that gapping can apply to more than one clause, so long as the verb of the first clause is retained. From (7) it appears that if gapping applies to one conjoined clause, it must apply to all the following clauses of the conjoined structure for the sentence to be grammatical. The ungrammaticality of (2) and (5) indicates that gapping cannot apply if the subjects or objects of the conjoined clauses are identical. Finally, (1) shows that gapping is optional.

Problem 3.4–2   Papago

Examine the following sentences (Saxton, 1969, and Hale, 1969) and describe the marking of conjoined clauses in Papago. A hyphen marks a morpheme boundary inside a word.

(1) mįḍ Ɂo g-pančo, č Ɂo-ki čikpan

   run(ning) is Pancho, and is-evidently work(ing)
   'Pancho is running, and he is evidently working.'

(2) t-wo i mɨɨ g-pančo, k wo i gɨi

   will run Pancho, and will fall
   'Pancho will run, and he will fall.'

(3) mua Ɂat g-pančo g-wisilo, ku-t g-husi g-kooǰi mua

   kill PAST Pancho calf, and-PAST José pig kill
   'Pancho killed the calf, and José killed the pig.'

(4) husi Ɂo čɨm si Ɂɨ-hasčud, č pi huu g-muuñ

   José is try(ing) INTENSIVE himself-aggrandize, and not ate beans
   'José is trying to act big, and (so) he didn't eat beans.'

(5) Ɂam Ɂat hu hii g-pančo, ku-t g-husi pi hii

   there PAST away go Pancho, and-PAST José not go
   'Pancho went over there, and José didn't go.'

(6) haiwañ Ɂant hɨma wuḍ-k, gn hu biha g-ñ-wiǰina siil-moɁo Ɂan

   cow I PAST one rope-and, there away wrapped my-rope saddle-horn on
   'I roped a cow, and I wrapped my rope around the saddle horn.'

Solution

Three different forms can be used with the meaning 'and': [ku], [k], and [č]. In the data presented, [k] or [č] is used when the two subjects are identical, and [ku] is used when the subjects of the two clauses are different. The choice between [k] and [č] apparently relates to tense or aspect. In the two sentences in which [č] appears, (1) and (4), the first clause describes ongoing activity (as indicated by 'be . . . ing' in the English gloss); this is true of neither (2) nor (6), the two sentences with [k]. The morpheme [ku] is attached to the past tense marker of the second clause in the two sentences in which it occurs, (3) and (5). In (6) [k] is suffixed to the verb of the first clause, but [č] and [k] are unattached in the other examples. Finally, in those sentences in which the subjects of the two clauses are the same, the subject is unexpressed in the second clause.

Discussion

In Problem 2.1–3 we found that [g] is prefixed to any Papago noun that is not in sentence-initial position. In (6), however, [siil-moʔo] 'saddle-horn' does not have the [g] prefix. This may have something to do with its being a compound, or it may have to do with the following postposition [ʔan] 'on', of which it is the object.

SUBORDINATION

Of the various kinds of subordinate clauses to be found in human languages, we will focus our attention on two that are of fundamental importance, **complement clauses** and **relative clauses**. Complement clauses are those that function by themselves as subjects or objects. In (1), for instance, the subject is the complement clause *that Fred is a fink*.

(1) That Fred is a fink is obvious.

The surface structure of (1) is quite analogous to that of (2), except that the subject nominal in the former is a clause rather than a noun with a modifier.

(2) The defect is obvious.

The surface structures of (1) and (2) are depicted in Figures 3.4–5 and 3.4–6 respectively.

Relative clauses do not function by themselves as subjects or objects. Rather they function as modifiers of noun phrases. In (3), for example, *that I read* is a relative clause that modifies *the story*.

(3) The story that I read was sad.

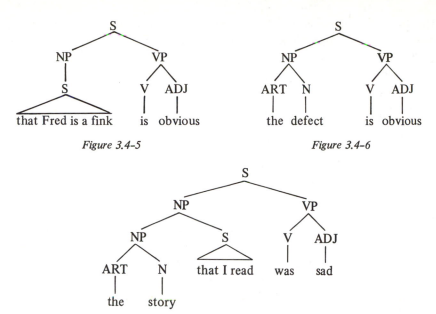

Figure 3.4-5   Figure 3.4-6

Figure 3.4-7

Compare Figure 3.4–7, the surface structure of (3), with Figure 3.4–5. As Figure 3.4–5 shows, the subordinate clause of (1) is itself the subject noun phrase. Figure 3.4–7 indicates, on the other hand, that the subordinate clause of (3) combines with the noun phrase *the story* to form a complex noun phrase, and the entire complex noun phrase is the main clause subject.

On the basis of meaning and other properties, a distinction is normally made between **restrictive** and **non-restrictive** (or **appositive**) relative clauses. The relative clause in (3) is restrictive, but the one in (4) is non-restrictive (appositive).

(4) Sally, who I have known for years, is a good sport.

In English restrictive and non-restrictive clauses are distinguished on the basis of intonation; specifically, non-restrictive clauses are bounded by slight but noticeable pauses (indicated typographically by commas), whereas no pauses occur around restrictive clauses. The semantic difference between these two types of relative clauses is that restrictive relatives serve to specify or "narrow down" the class of entities designated by the modified noun phrase; appositive clauses lack this specifying function and introduce essentially extraneous information about the modified noun. Thus in (3) the relative clause *that I read* helps to identify the story that is under discussion; *the story that I read* is a more precise specification than *the story* alone. The appositive clause in (4), *who I have known for years*, does nothing to identify the modified noun, *Sally*; it merely provides additional information about her. It has been suggested that non-restrictive relatives derive from conjoined clauses—(4), for instance, may derive from (5) through the intermediate structure (6)—but we will not pursue this hypothesis here.

> (5) Sally is a good sport, and I have known her for years.
> (6) Sally, and I have known her for years, is a good sport.

In the following discussion we will be primarily concerned with restrictive relatives.

RELATIVIZATION

The noun which a relative clause modifies is called the **head noun**. (This term is also used more generally to designate the principal noun of any noun phrase, whether or not it contains a modifying clause.) For example, *story* is the head noun of the nominal *the story that I read*. Because the function of a relative clause is to characterize the head noun, this noun must somehow figure in the semantic representation of the clause. The underlying representation of a relative clause must therefore contain a noun that is coreferential to the head. In *the story that I read*, for instance, *story* is understood as the semantic object of the verb *read*, although the relative does not contain *story* in surface structure. Figure 3.4–8 thus approximates an underlying representation (not the most abstract one that could be posited) of (1); coreference is indicated by identical subscripts.

> (1) The story that I read was sad.

As we might expect, one of the two coreferential noun phrases in a relative clause construction is virtually always reduced in some way. More often than not, the head noun is retained intact and the coreferential noun inside the relative clause is reduced. Thus the second occurrence of *story* in Figure 3.4–8

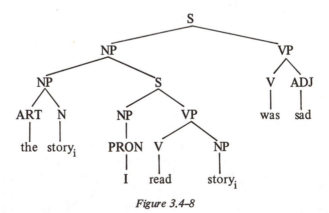

Figure 3.4–8

is reduced to *that* in surface structure. In many languages, however, the head noun can or must be the one that undergoes reduction. In the following example from Navaho (courtesy of Kenneth Hale) the head noun has been deleted, while the coreferential noun inside the relative clause has been retained in surface structure. Subordinate clauses will sometimes be enclosed in brackets in order to facilitate discussion.

> (2) [šižéʔé Łííʔ yikʔidahʔaznil-ę́ę́] yóóʔ ʔeelwod
>
> my father horse saddled-REL away ran
> 'The horse my father saddled ran away.'

In (2) the noun [Łííʔ] 'horse' has been retained inside the relative clause, but the coreferential head noun in the main clause has been deleted. The verb suffix [ę́ę́] marks the clause containing it as a relative clause; elements with this function will be symbolized as *REL*.

The repeated nominal can be reduced in several ways. In some languages it is simply deleted. This is true of Japanese, for example, as well as Classical Aztec. Sentence (3) is an Aztec example. The word [kinamaka] by itself constitutes a relative clause; the repeated noun phrase has been deleted, as well as the subject pronoun (subject pronouns are always optional in Aztec).

> (3) tisaλ [kinamaka] pošawak
> chalk sells soft
> 'The chalk which he sells is soft.'

In other languages the repeated noun phrase undergoes regular pronominalization. This is possible in some dialects of Arabic, for instance, and also in certain non-standard varieties of English and French. (4) is a French example.

> (4) l'homme [que je lui ai dit de venir]
>
> the man REL I him told to come
> 'the man that I told to come'

Still a third possibility is for the repeated noun phrase to be reduced to a special pronominal form called a ***relative pronoun***. In English *who*, *which*, and *that* are the major relative pronouns. *Who* substitutes for human nouns, *which* for non-human nouns, and *that* for either:

> (5) the girl [who I kissed]
> (6) the table [which I repaired]
> (7) the girls and tables [that I painted]

The formation of relative clauses frequently involves more than just reducing the repeated noun phrase. For example, relative pronouns are commonly moved to the beginning of the clause, adjacent to the head noun. This is the case in English, as (5)–(7) show, since the relative pronouns are in clause-initial position despite the fact that they substitute for the direct object. Moreover, if the relative pronoun is part of a prepositional phrase or complex noun phrase, it is sometimes possible to transport the entire constituent containing the pronoun into clause-initial position:

(8) the spy [to whom I sent the microdot]
(9) the table [the bottom of the leg of which I painted]

Another common marking device for relatives is the insertion of a special particle, usually at the beginning of the clause. In Aztec this relativizing particle is [in]; it is optional, appearing in (10) but not in (3):

(10) yewaλ [in aškan nemi]
it REL now lives
'that which now remains'

The particle *jang* marks relative clauses in Indonesian (Kwee, 1965):

(11) itulah ruman [jang kita tyari]
that house REL we look for
'That is the house we are looking for.'

Often the verb of the relative clause bears special trappings. As we saw in example (2), the verb suffix [ę̄ę̄] marks relatives in Navaho. In Swahili a relativizing affix is inserted between the tense prefix and the verb root, as in (12) (Perrott, 1951).

(12) chakula [ki-li-cho-tosha]
food NOUN PREFIX-PAST-REL-enough
'the food which sufficed'

Turkish (Lewis, 1953) is interesting because it shows that relative clause formation sometimes differs depending on whether the subject or the object of the embedded clause is relativized, and it also illustrates the not uncommon connection between relativization and possessives. When the subject is relativized, [en] is suffixed to the subordinate verb, as in (13).

(13) [bunu bil-en] adam-lar
this know-REL man-PLURAL
'men who know this'

On the other hand, when a nominal other than the subject is relativized, the verb takes the suffix [dik], which translates roughly as 'pertaining to', followed by the possessive suffix that corresponds to the subject.

(14) [gel-dik-leri] tren
come-REL-their train
'the train on which they came'

Gumbaiŋgar, an aboriginal language of Australia, also forms relatives differently depending on whether a subject or non-subject is relativized (Dixon, 1969). For sentences with both a subject and an object, a case distinction is made in Gumbaiŋgar between an "ergative" case (*ERG*), the case taken by the subject, and a "nominative" case (*NOM*), associated with the object. In a relative clause, the noun coreferential to the head is deleted. If the deleted noun is the subject of the relative clause, two suffixes are added to the verb, the relative marker *andi* and the case ending of the head noun in the main clause (the nominative ending is often zero).

> (15) [juraal bjeinb-aŋ-andi-u] niigad-u gugaamgan bua-aŋ
>
> food NOM eat-PAST-REL-ERG man-ERG emu NOM kill-PAST
>
> 'The man who had eaten the food killed an emu.'

Since the head noun *niigadu* 'man' is in the ergative case, the verb of the subordinate clause also receives the ergative ending, *u: bjeinbaŋandiu*. Suppose now that the object is relativized. In this event, the relative marker and the case inflection of the head noun are added to the subject of the relative clause, following its own case inflection:

> (16) ŋiinda duuwa maaniei [niigad-u-ndi giiṛi-ŋ]
>
> you ERG boomerang NOM hold man-ERG-REL NOM make-PAST
>
> 'Do you have the boomerang which the man made?'

Since the head noun *duuwa* 'boomerang' is in the nominative case, the nominative inflection (which happens to be zero) follows the relative marker on the embedded subject: *niigadundi*.

The preceding examples make it clear that relative clauses can occur in several different positions with respect to the noun they modify. In some languages, including Japanese, Turkish, and many others, relative clauses precede the head noun. In English, French, Indonesian, and Swahili, among many others, the modifying clause follows the head noun. Both orders are permitted in Aztec; alongside (3) and (10), in which the relative follows the head noun, we find expressions like (17), in which it precedes.

> (17) in [kinamaka] ičkaλ
>
> the sells cotton
>
> 'the cotton which he sells'

Similar variation is found in Palauan (see Problem 2.1–8, p. 52); notice that [el], the relative clause marker, occurs before or after the head noun but always adjacent to it.

(18) a malk [el merros]
the chicken REL crows
'the chicken that crows'

(19) a [merros el] malk
the crows REL chicken
'the chicken that crows'

It should be noted that a relative clause need not always occur directly adjacent to the noun it modifies in surface structure. This is illustrated by the two examples from Gumbaiŋgar above. In (15) the clause modifying *niigadu* 'man' directly precedes it, but the clause modifying *duuwa* 'boomerang' in (16) is separated from it by the main clause verb. In English too it is sometimes possible to move a relative clause to the end of the sentence, separating it from the head noun in surface structure, particularly when very little would follow the clause otherwise.

(20) Many diseases [for which medicine has found no cure] exist.

(21) Many diseases exist [for which medicine has found no cure].

Stylistically, (21) is to be preferred over (20).

Problem 3.4–3   Papago

Examine the data below and describe the formation of relative clauses in Papago.

(1) hɨgay čioǰ ʔo giʔɨǰ
that man PRESENT big
'That man is big.'

(2) gogs ʔo huhuʔid hɨgay wisilo
dog PRESENT chase that calf
'The dog is chasing that calf.'

(3) čioǰ ʔat hačičpos g-wipsilo
man PAST brand calves
'The man branded the calves.'

(4) ʔaañi ʔant wuu g-wisilo
I I PAST rope calf
'I roped the calf.'

(5) ʔaačim ʔatt čipos g-wisilo
we we PAST brand calf
'We branded the calf.'

(6) husi ʔo ñiid g-čioǰ

José PRESENT see man
'José sees the man.'

(7) higay čioǰ mat hačičpos g-wipsilo ʔo giʔij
'The man who branded the calves is big.'

(8) higay wisilo mant ʔaañi wuu ʔo giʔij
'The calf that I roped is big.'

(9) gogs ʔo huhuʔid higay wisilo matt ʔaačim čipos
'The dog is chasing the calf that we branded.'

(10) higay mo g-husi ñiid čioǰ ʔo giʔij
'The man that José sees is big.'

Solution

Relative clauses in Papago evidently require that the head noun be preceded by the demonstrative [higay] 'that'. However, [higay] does not have its usual demonstrative force in the relative construction; it translates simply as 'the' rather than as 'that'.

Papago sentences typically contain a word that marks tense and agrees with the subject; exemplified in (1)–(6) are [ʔo] 'PRESENT', [ʔat] 'PAST', [ʔant] 'I PAST', and [ʔatt] 'we PAST'. When a sentence is embedded as a relative clause, this tense-agreement marker is affected in two ways. First, the prefix [m] is substituted for the initial [ʔ]. Second, the tense-agreement marker is advanced to the beginning of the clause (in non-embedded clauses, it does not occur initially). The relative clause follows the head noun in (7)–(9), but (10) shows that it can also precede, coming between [higay] and the head noun. The noun coreferential to the head is deleted.

Discussion

In Problem 2.2–4 (p. 61) [higay] was translated as 'he', while in this problem it functions as the demonstrative 'that'. This duality is not at all uncommon. Many languages lack a special pronoun for the third person, and the demonstrative is frequently used in its place.

The data for this problem allows us to further refine the rule specifying the occurrence of [g]. [g] does not occur before a pronoun: *[gʔaañi], *[gʔaačim]. Moreover, it does not occur before a noun modified by the demonstrative [higay]: *[higay gčioǰ]. Apparently, then, it is restricted to unmodified nouns that are not in clause-initial position. (However, it can occur before a possessive prefix—see example (6) of Problem 3.4–2.)

Problem 3.4–4 Mandarin Chinese

The following Mandarin expressions (Annear, 1965) are all noun phrases containing relative clauses. The relatives are enclosed in brackets. The diacritics [′ ` ˇ ¯] stand for tone (rising, falling, low falling-rising, and high).

Isolate the morphemes in (1)–(10) and state their meanings. Describe the formation of relative clauses in Mandarin.

(1)	[máo xiěde] nèibĕn shū	'the book Mao wrote'
(2)	yíjian [wǒ xǐhuānde] yīfu	'a dress I like'
(3)	nèijian [wǒ xǐhuānde] yīfu	'that dress I like'
(4)	[wǒ xǐhuānde] nèijian yīfu	'the dress I like'
(5)	[wǒ bùxǐhuānde] nèijian yīfu	'the dress I don't like'
(6)	nèibĕn [hòude] shū	'that thick book'
(7)	[hòude] nèibĕn shū	'the thick book'
(8)	yìbĕn [máo xiěde] shū	'a book Mao wrote'
(9)	[báode] nèibĕn shū	'the thin book'
(10)	[wǒ xǐhuānde] yīfu	'the dress I like'

Solution

'Mao' = máo	'wrote' = xiě	'not' = bù
'book' = shū	'like' = xǐhuān	'a' = yíjian, yìbĕn
'dress' = yīfu	'thick' = hòu	'the, that' = nèibĕn, nèijian
'I' = wǒ	'thin' = báo	

De functions as a relative marker.

The articles can be further segmented into two morphemes each. *Nèi* is evidently the form for 'the, that', and *yí* or *yì* the form for 'a' (the tone difference is unexplained in terms of the data given). *Jian* is attached to either article whenever it modifies *yīfu* 'dress', and *bĕn* is added to the article when it modifies *shū* 'book'. The nature of this "agreement" is not clear from the limited data. The forms with *nèi* translate as 'that' when they precede the relative clause, and they translate as 'the' when they follow the relative. Expressions (4) and (10) show that the *nèi* form is optional; when it is not present, the translation is 'the' rather than 'that'.

A relative clause precedes the noun it modifies in Mandarin. The noun coreferential to the head noun is deleted, and the relative marker *de* is suffixed to the predicate of the relative.

COMPLEMENTATION

As mentioned earlier, embedded clauses that function as subjects or objects are referred to as complement clauses. *That Fred is a fink* is a complement clause in (1)–(3).

(1) That Fred is a fink is obvious.
(2) I know that Fred is a fink.
(3) We are certain that Fred is a fink.

It functions as the subject in (1) and as the direct object of *know* in (2). In (3) the *that* clause is a prepositional object, although this is obscured in surface structure by the rule of preposition deletion.

Complement clauses are very often accompanied by special trappings to mark their subordinate status. The use of a special subordinating particle similar to *that* is not at all uncommon, and such particles often come at the beginning of a clause. The Aztec particle [in] is another example.

(4) akin ƛamama-s [in tona-s]
who take charge of-FUTURE SUBORDINATOR sun rise-
    FUTURE
'Who will see to it that the sun rises?'

Not infrequently, the trappings of a complement clause include a possessive element. The complement clause in (5), for example, is marked by the *POS-SESSIVE . . . ing* combination, and (6) illustrates a similar construction of Luiseño (compare Problem 3.3–5).

(5) [The governor's being so stubborn] is scandalous.
(6) [wunaal po-pellax] miyquṣ
    he his-dance was
    'He had danced.'

Turkish provides another example (Lees, 1965).

(7) [adam-in vergi ver-diy-i] belli
    man-his tax pay-ing-his known
    'That the man pays his taxes is obvious.'

In sentences (5)–(7) the syntax treats the subordinate verb as if it were possessed by its subject. The subordinate status of a verb may also be marked in other ways. In English the non-possessive elements *to* and *ing* can accompany a complement verb, as in (5) and (8).

(8) I hesitate [to commit myself].

In Luiseño the suffix [pi] is sometimes added to a complement verb that describes a future action or one that is not yet accomplished.

(9) noo maʔma-q [po-ŋee-pi]
    I want-PRESENT his-leave-UNACCOMPLISHED
    'I want him to leave.'

In addition to rules that insert trappings, complement clauses are also subject to reduction and rearrangement rules. We saw earlier that the complement subject may be deleted in English when it is identical to some nominal in the main clause; *I* is the underlying complement subject in (8) and is deleted by this rule. Another rule affecting complement clauses in English applies optionally to clauses marked with *that* or *for . . . to* and transports them to sentence-final position. The pronoun *it* (lacking its usual meaning) replaces them in surface structure. Sentences (11) and (13) are thus optional variants of (10) and (12) respectively.

    (10) [For the mayor to accept the money] would be improper.
    (11) It would be improper [for the mayor to accept the money].
    (12) [That I don't like him] bothers Harvey.
    (13) It bothers Harvey [that I don't like him].

Comparable rules are to be found in many other languages.

    Particularly interesting are those rearrangement rules that transport a constituent out of a complement clause and insert it as a surface constituent of the main clause. One such rule, discussed in Problem 3.1–1, raises an adverbial element from the complement and places it at the beginning of the main clause. Thus (15) is an optional variant of (14).

    (14) He said [he would mow the lawn tomorrow].
    (15) Tomorrow he said [he would mow the lawn].

Another such rule is subject raising (see Problem 3.2–6), which optionally replaces a complement clause with its subject and moves the remainder of the embedded clause to the end, as in the derivation of (17) from (16).

    (16) [That Egbert will bungle the job] is certain.
    (17) Egbert is certain [to bungle the job].

In Problem 3.2–11 evidence was found for a rule of Spanish that raises the negative element *no* from a complement clause to the main clause. This optional rule accounts for the synonomy of (18) with (19), which is derived from (18).

    (18) Quiero [que no pruebes gota de vino].
    (19) No quiero [que pruebes gota de vino].
         'I don't want you to touch (a drop of) wine.'

THE SURFACE REALIZATION OF SEMANTIC PREDICATES

Many semantic predicates have only minor status in surface structure. By definition, every predicate is the core of a separate proposition at the semantic level. In surface structure, however, it is not uncommon for a single clause to contain several elements each of which manifests a semantic predicate.

It follows that some syntactic rules (other than reduction rules) have the effect of reducing the number of clauses in the structure of a sentence. Complement clauses figure prominently in this picture.

Many derivational affixes are most reasonably analyzed as underlying predicates. Consider the Luiseño suffix [viču] 'want', illustrated in (1), which has been discussed extensively in previous problems.

> (1) noo paaʔi-viču-q
>   I drink-want-PRESENT
>   'I want to drink.'

Semantically, [noo paaʔi] 'I drink' is in the scope of [viču] in (1). Consequently, the semantic representation of (1) involves at least two propositions (excluding tense), as sketched in Figure 3.4–9 (compare Problem 2.3–6, p. 81). The proposition [noo paaʔi] 'I drink' functions as an argument of the predicate [viču] 'want'.

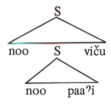

Figure 3.4–9

However, the surface structure of (1) contains only one clause. Two basic rules function in the derivation of this surface structure from Figure 3.4–9. One rule, which we have called subject deletion, elides the lower occurrence of [noo] 'I', since this nominal is coreferential to the subject of the main clause. A second rule combines [paaʔi] and [viču] into the complex verb [paaʔiviču] 'want to drink'. This rule of Luiseño was stated as derivational rule (A) in Problem 2.3–2 (p. 76).

> (A) The meaning 'want to *V*' can be expressed by a complex verb consisting of *V* plus the suffix [viču].

Since the two underlying predicates are combined into a single complex verb by this rule, the surface structures it derives have only one clause, not two.

Causative affixes, such as Luiseño [ni] 'cause, make', provide another example. Like [viču], [ni] functions semantically as a predicate, as in example (2). The underlying representation of (2) is sketched in Figure 3.4–10.

> (2) noo po-y paaʔi-ni-q
>   I he-OBJECT drink-cause-PRESENT
>   'I am making him drink.'

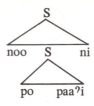

Figure 3.4–10

Two rules function in the derivation of (2) from this underlying representation. First, [po] 'he', which is the subordinate clause subject in underlying structure, becomes the main clause object in surface structure by virtue of a rearrangement transformation analogous to the English rule of subject raising (see Problem 3.2–6). Thus [po] appears in surface structure with the object marker [y]. Second, the separate predicates [paaʔi] and [ni] are combined into the single complex verb [paaʔini], which entails that (2) has only one surface clause, not two. This rule of Luiseño was stated as derivational rule (B) in Problem 2.3–2.

> (B) The meaning 'make . . . V' can be expressed by a complex verb consisting of V plus the suffix [ni].

Rules (A) and (B) are very similar. Both have the effect of combining two predicates to form a complex verb in such a way that the predicate of the original main clause is manifested as a derivational suffix on the predicate of the original subordinate clause. Indeed, it may be correct to combine these (and other) rules into a single, more general syntactic rule that reduces semantic predicates to the surface status of derivational suffixes. Analogous transformations could be posited to account for the introduction of other derivational affixes that appear to reflect semantic predicates. However, the proposal to treat derivational rules like those discussed in section 2.3 as ordinary syntactic transformations is a controversial one. It is simply not known whether all productive derivational patterns are best handled by syntactic rearrangement transformations, nor has a comprehensive theory along these lines been worked out.

Nonetheless, it should be noted that causative affixes like Luiseño [ni] represent a universal linguistic tendency; they are extremely common, and they tend to occur as suffixes rather than prefixes. The English suffix *en* is another example, though it is restricted to relatively few predicates:

> (3) The smoke blackened the walls.

In Turkish [dür] (or its phonetic variant [dir]) is a causative suffix (Lewis, 1953); sentence (4) is quite similar in structure to the Luiseño sentence (2).

> (4) ben fare-yi öl-dür-dü-m
> I mouse-the die-cause-PAST-I
> 'I killed the mouse.'

The causative suffix is [ri] in Tyapukay, a language of Australia (data from Kenneth Hale).

    (5) pama-lu tʸulpin wanta-ri-lna
         man-ERG tree fall-cause-FUTURE
         'The man will fell the tree.'

Problem 2.3–7 (p. 81) illustrated the causative suffix [a] of Urdu. Many other examples could be cited.

It should be noted that not all semantic predicates without predicate status in surface structure wind up as derivational affixes. For example, there are semantic grounds for maintaining that English *not* derives from an underlying predicate (see section 3.1), yet *not* is a separate word in surface structure.

    (6) The bomb will not explode.

The analysis of *not* as an underlying predicate is supported by the fact that negation occurs overtly as a predicate in some languages. Diegueño is an example (Stenson, 1970). In (7) the suffix [x] on the subordinate verb indicates an action not yet accomplished, much like the Luiseño suffix [pi] in (8).

    (7) [ñaa uuyaw-x] maaw
         I know-UNACCOMPLISHED not
         'I don't know.'
    (8) noo maʔma-q [po-ŋee-pi]
         I want-PRESENT his-leave-UNACCOMPLISHED
         'I want him to leave.'

Of course, if negation is correctly analyzed as a predicate in underlying representations, it is necessary to posit a syntactic rule that lowers it into the clause it negates for those languages, like English, in which it does not surface as a predicate.

From examples such as these, it is apparent that the number and arrangement of clauses in surface structure may differ radically from the number and arrangement of propositions in underlying representations. The extent of these differences cannot as yet be accurately assessed, for much too little is known about the details of semantic representations. However, the general tendency is definitely for surface clauses to be fewer in number than underlying propositions. An element that seems to have only minor status in surface structure may derive from an underlying predicate that forms the core of a separate proposition at the semantic level. This is apparently true of negation and certain derivational affixes; other possible candidates include modals (such as *can*, *must*, and *will*), tense, modifiers, conjunctions, and quantifiers (such as *all*, *some*, and *several*). No definitive list can be given at present. Nevertheless, it does not seem unreasonable to conjecture, on the basis of present evidence, that all sentences are complex at the level of semantic representation.

Problem 3.4–5 French

In Problem 3.2–5 it was shown that a syntactic rule of French moves the sequence *de* + *PRONOUN* from its position after the predicate into pre-predicate position; in this position, *de* + *PRONOUN* is manifested phonologically as *en*. When a pronoun is substituted for *cela* 'that' in (1), therefore, the result is not (2) but (3).

> (1) Je suis certain de cela. 'I am certain of that.'
> (2) *Je suis certain de le. 'I am certain of it.'
> (3) J'en suis certain. 'I am certain of it.'

This rule is actually more general, since it also affects modifiers of the subject when they have the form *de* + *PRONOUN*. Thus when *ce livre* 'this book' is replaced by a pronoun in (4), the result is (6) rather than (5).

> (4) La préface de ce livre est trop flatteuse.
>   'The preface of this book is too flattering.'
> (5) *La préface de le est trop flatteuse.
>   'Its preface is too flattering.'
> (6) La préface en est trop flatteuse.
>   'Its preface is too flattering.'

It may not appear that any movement has taken place in the derivation of (6), but in fact the modifier has been detached from the subject nominal and attached as the first member of the verb group; this is apparent from the position of *en* with respect to the negative element *ne* in (7), the negative version of (6); *ne* occurs only as part of the verb group.

> (7) La préface n'en est pas trop flatteuse.
>   'Its preface is not too flattering.'

Sentences like (8) and (9) show that *de* + *PRONOUN*, when it derives from a modifier of the subject, can normally be attached only to the immediately adjacent verb—if it is moved over the adjacent verb and attached to a subordinate verb, the resulting sentence is ungrammatical.

> (8) L'auteur en a oublié de venir me voir.
>   'Its author forgot to come see me.'
> (9) *L'auteur a oublié d'en venir me voir.
>   'Its author forgot to come see me.'

With these facts in mind, consider (10)–(12) (Ruwet, 1970).

> (10) (a) L'auteur de ce livre va devenir célèbre.
>   'The author of this book will become famous.'
>   (b) *L'auteur en va devenir célèbre.
>   'Its author will become famous.'

       (c) L'auteur va en devenir célèbre.
          'Its author will become famous.'
(11) (a) La porte de la cathédrale semble être fermée.
          'The door of the cathedral seems to be closed.'
       (b) *La porte en semble être fermée.
          'Its door seems to be closed.'
       (c) La porte semble en être fermée.
          'Its door seems to be closed.'
(12) (a) La solution de ce problème doit être simple.
          'The solution to this problem must be simple.'
       (b) *La solution en doit être simple.
          'Its solution must be simple.'
       (c) La solution doit en être simple.
          'Its solution must be simple.'

In light of the preceding discussion, it is surprising that the (b) sentences are not grammatical; these are the sentences that should be obtained when the object of *de* is replaced by a pronoun in the modifier of the subject in the (a) sentences. Furthermore, the (c) sentences are grammatical instead of the (b) sentences, even though *de* + *PRONOUN* appears to have been moved over the adjacent verb into a subordinate clause.

Propose an analysis that explains this apparent anomaly.

Solution

In surface structure *l'auteur de PRONOUN* is the subject of *va* 'will, is going to' in (10). Similarly, *la porte de PRONOUN* is the surface subject of *semble* 'seems' in (11), and *la solution de PRONOUN* is the surface subject of *doit* 'must' in (12). However, this surface configuration does not necessarily reflect the underlying propositional structure. On semantic grounds, it might be argued that the subjects of *va*, *semble*, and *doit* are really propositions. In (10), for example, the proposition 'its author become famous' can be regarded as an argument of the predicate *va* 'will', since (10) (c) asserts the futurity of the state of affairs described by this proposition. (11) (c) states that the proposition 'its door is closed' seems to be true; semantically, this proposition is in the scope of *semble* 'seems'. By the same token, 'its solution is simple' can be viewed as an argument of *doit* 'must' in (12) (c).

The underlying representations given on the following page can therefore be proposed for the (c) sentences on the basis of semantic considerations. The essential correctness of these underlying representations is strongly supported by syntactic evidence, since they explain the position of *en* in the (c) sentences. Two syntactic rules serve to derive the (c) sentences from the proposed underlying structures: the rule that detaches *de* + *PRONOUN* from the subject noun phrase and adjoins it to the immediately following

(10) (c)

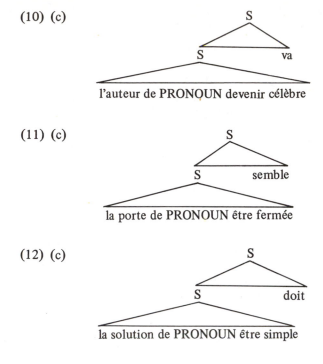

(11) (c)

(12) (c)

verb, and the rule of subject raising, discussed (for English) in Problem 3.2–6 and elsewhere. If the two rules apply in this order, the (c) sentences are correctly derived from the structures given above and the position of *en* is explained in terms of independently motivated rules and structures.

The derivation of (10) (c) proceeds as follows. First, *de + PRONOUN* is detached from the subject and attached to the following verb, *devenir* 'become', where it is manifested phonologically as *en*.

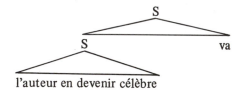

Second, the rule of subject raising applies to the subject of the complement clause, which now consists of *l'auteur* alone, and makes it the subject of the higher clause, moving the remainder of the complement clause to the end of the sentence. The resulting structure is depicted at the top of the next page. This is the surface structure of (10) (c). Sentences (11) (c) and (12) (c) have analogous derivations.

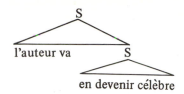

It is evident, then, that *en* has not been moved over a verb into the subordinate clause in sentences like (10) (c)–(12) (c). It was attached to the immediately adjacent verb at a stage in the derivation of these sentences when the noun it modifies was still the subject of the subordinate verb. The fact that underlying structures of the sort proposed and the rule of subject raising account for the apparent anomaly in the location of *en* constitutes strong evidence in their support.

Problem 3.4–6   English

In Chapter 1, sentences like (2) were used to support the contention that sentences like (1) contain prepositions in their underlying structure.

(1) ⌐I am certain¬ ⌐that Dick is loyal.¬

(2) What ⌐I am certain of¬ is ⌐that Dick is loyal.¬

The occurrence of *of* in (2) is explained if (1) contains *of* in underlying structure, but its occurrence is irregular otherwise. *Of* does not surface in (1) because of the rule of preposition deletion.

A similar argument can be used to motivate fairly abstract underlying representations for certain sentences, representations that involve the verb *do*. Consider (3)–(6).

(3) ⌐Alvin¬ ⌐stole a car.¬

(4) What ⌐Alvin did¬ was ⌐steal a car.¬

(5) ⌐Melvin¬ ⌐heard a shot.¬

(6) *What ⌐Melvin did¬ was ⌐hear a shot.¬

When a verb phrase such as *stole a car* is put into the position of "focus" (that is, the position after *be* in sentences like (2)), a form of the verb *do* unexpectedly appears, just as *of* unexpectedly appears in (2); this is illustrated in (4). However, the ungrammaticality of (6) shows that not all verb phrases can be put into focus position with the concomitant appearance of *do*. Roughly speaking, this construction involving *do* is possible only with predicates that describe volitional activities, such as *steal, run, coax, think*, and so on; it is not possible with predicates like *hear, exist, be tall*—predicates that describe states or non-volitional activities—except in special uses of these forms. We will call the former ***active predicates*** and the latter ***stative predicates***.

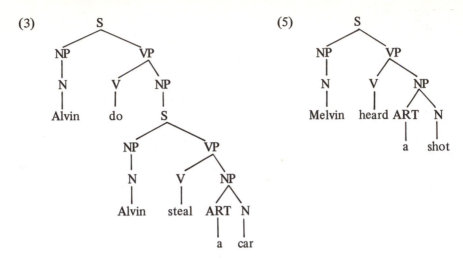

To account for this difference, we might hypothesize that clauses with active predicates, but not stative predicates, are embedded in underlying structure as complements to the predicate *do*. The hypothesized underlying representations of (3) and (5) are given above (tense will not be considered). The underlying structure proposed for (5) is the same as its surface structure. To derive the surface structure of (3), two rules are needed. One is subject deletion; the subject of *steal* is deleted under coreference to the subject of the main clause. Subject deletion produces an intermediate structure of the form *Alvin do [steal a car]*. The second rule that is needed deletes *do* when it directly precedes another verb which is subordinate to it. Applied to the intermediate structure just given, *do* deletion derives the surface structure of (3).

However sentences like (4) are to be derived, it is clear that the derivation of (4) will be simplified by the availability of the intermediate structure *Alvin do [steal a car]*, which contains the verb *do* that shows up in this sentence. On the other hand, the derivation of (5) does not involve any underlying or intermediate structure containing the verb *do*. Consequently, the proposed analysis correctly predicts that (6) is ungrammatical.

Two additional arguments can be given in support of this proposed analysis on the basis of the data below. Formulate these arguments.

 (7) (a) What did he buy?
   (b) He bought a car.
 (8) (a) What did he do?
   (b) He stole a car.
 (9) (a) He said Joe was stupid because I told him to say Joe was
     stupid.
   (b) He said Joe was stupid because I told him to say it.
 (10) (a) He stole a car because I told him to steal a car.
    (b) He stole a car because I told him to do it.

Solution

To answer a question that begins with a question word, it is necessary to replace the question word with a constituent that responds to it. Thus (7) (b), in which *a car* has replaced *what*, is one possible answer to (7) (a). The relation between (8) (a) and (8) (b) will be exactly parallel to the relation between (7) (a) and (7) (b) if (8) (b) is derived from an underlying structure containing *do*. If *what* in (8) (a) is replaced by a noun phrase consisting of the complement clause *he steal a car*, the underlying structure *he do [he steal a car]* is obtained for (8) (b). Subject deletion and *do* deletion derive the surface structure of (8) (b). Underlying structures with *do* are thus motivated by the fact that they bring question-answer pairs like (8), in which *do* unexpectedly appears in the question, in line with the more general pattern illustrated in (7).

Examples (9) and (10) provide an additional argument in favor of underlying structures containing *do* for sentences with active verbs. (9) illustrates the application of a rule that pronominalizes a complement clause to *it* when it repeats an identical clause that occurs earlier in the sentence; (9) (b) is derived from (9) (a) by reducing the second occurrence of *Joe was stupid* to *it*. The same rule appears to have applied in the derivation of (10) (b) from (10) (a). However, in terms of surface structure, the occurrence of *do* in (10) (b) is surprising, since there is no occurrence of *do* in (10) (a).

The occurrence of *do* in (10) (b) is explained by the proposed analysis. Both (10) (a) and (10) (b) have the following underlying structure (tense is omitted).

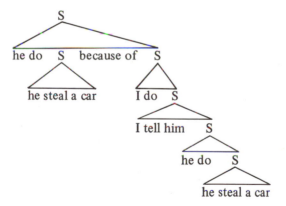

(10) (a) is derived from this underlying structure by rules previously discussed, including subject deletion, *do* deletion, *to* insertion, and preposition deletion. (10) (b) carries the derivation one step further: The second occurrence of *he steal a car* is reduced to *it* by the same rule that derives (9) (b) from (9) (a). *Do* deletion then cannot apply in the lowest clause, since *do*

is followed by *it*, not by a verb, and *do* deletion applies only when another verb directly follows. Consequently, the occurrence of *do* in (10) (b) is explained, with no additional rules, in terms of the proposed analysis.

CONCLUSION

We have made a sharp distinction between conjunction, relativization, and complementation, and the distinction is clearly a valid one. Nevertheless, these three ways of combining simple sentences to form complex ones often have properties in common, and in practice it is not always an easy matter to maintain the distinction in all instances. For example, the embedded clause in (1) is like a relative clause in some ways (it combines with a noun phrase to form a complex noun phrase subject), but it is like a complement clause in other ways (*that* cannot be replaced by *who* or *which*).

    (1) The fact [that the Arabs are outraged] is not surprising.

Moreover, if the proposal (mentioned on p. 146) to derive non-restrictive relative clauses from underlying conjoined structures proves correct, the distinction between conjunction and relativization will become very tenuous.

    The trappings of different kinds of complex sentences and the rules that apply to them are often very similar. In English *that* can head a complement clause and can also serve as a relative pronoun. In addition, both complement and relative clauses can sometimes be moved to the end of a sentence, as (2) and (3) show.

    (2) It is not surprising [that the Arabs are outraged].
    (3) Several men came in [who had been drinking heavily].

We have seen that the Aztec particle [in] can occur at the beginning of both relative and complement clauses. We have also seen that both relative and complement clauses can be marked in Turkish by suffixing [dik] (or its phonetic variant [diy]) to the subordinate verb followed by the possessive that corresponds to its subject. In Problem 3.4–2 we saw that conjunction is marked differently in Papago depending on whether or not the subjects of the two conjoined clauses are coreferential. Certain kinds of subordinate clauses are also marked differently in Papago depending on sameness or difference of subject (Hale, 1969). This list of similarities could be extended.

    The syntax of complex sentences has tremendous linguistic significance. We have been able to give this grammatical domain only cursory examination, and many kinds of complex sentences have not been dealt with at all. Some of these types of complex sentences may just be special cases of conjunction, relativization, or complementation. To take just one example, *when* clauses in English are probably best analyzed as relative clauses; (5) and (6), in other words, might be regarded as optional variants of (4).

(4) I'll talk to him at the time at which he comes home.
(5) I'll talk to him at the time when he comes home.
(6) I'll talk to him when he comes home.

Other kinds of complex sentences may similarly reduce to conjunction, relativization, or complementation.

FURTHER PROBLEMS

Problem 3.4–7 English

The rule of conjunction reduction reduces conjoined clauses to single clauses containing a conjoined constituent. The rule of reflexivization (see Problems 3.1–4 and 3.2–8) reduces the second of two coreferential noun phrases in the same sentence to a reflexive pronoun. On the basis of the sentences below, determine the order in which these two rules must apply.

(1) I saw myself.
(2) I told Peter to help me.
(3) *I told Peter to help myself.
(4) Peter saw me and he yelled at me.
(5) *Peter saw me and he yelled at myself.
(6) Peter saw me and yelled at me.
(7) *Peter saw me and yelled at myself.

Problem 3.4–8 French

In Problem 3.4–6 evidence was given for positing an underlying structure with the verb *do*, together with a rule that deletes *do* when it directly precedes another verb, for English sentences containing active predicates. The same analysis can be proposed for French on the basis of similar evidence. The French verb for 'do' is *faire*, and 'only' is expressed by *ne . . . que*. On the basis of the data that follows, construct an argument to justify underlying representations containing *faire* for sentences with active verbs in which *faire* does not appear in surface structure.

(1) Il a deux amis.   'He has two friends.'
(2) Il n'a que deux amis.   'He has only two friends.'
(3) Je vois un arbre.   'I see a tree.'
(4) Je ne vois qu'un arbre.   'I see only a tree.'
(5) Il travaille.   'He works.'
(6) Il ne fait que travailler.   'He only works.'
(7) *Je ne fais que voir un arbre.   'I only see a tree.'
(8) Il court.   'He runs.'
(9) Il ne fait que courir.   'He only runs.'

Problem 3.4–9 *Lardil*

The expressions that follow (data from Kenneth Hale) are from Lardil, a language of Australia. They exemplify relative clauses in which the subject is identical to the head noun. Isolate the morphemes in these expressions and state their meanings. Describe the formation of relative clauses in Lardil (relatives are overtly marked). Diagram the surface structure of (8).

     (1) weṇe kepeen ṭaŋka
        'man that gathers food'

     (2) kentapal ketmen ṭaŋka
        'man that catches sea turtles'

     (3) ṭaŋka ṇeyin pinŋen
        'woman that kills men'

     (4) ṭaŋka ṇeyitʸar waŋal
        'boomerang that doesn't kill men'

     (5) waŋal kelen ṭaŋka
        'man that cuts boomerangs'

     (6) waŋal wiin ṭaŋka
        'man that trims boomerangs'

     (7) weṇe pantʸiin ŋawa
        'dog that sniffs food'

     (8) ṭaŋka ṇeyin waŋal kaparin ṭaŋka
        'man that makes boomerangs that kill men'

     (9) weṇe ḷaan ṭaŋka
        'man that spears food'

    (10) ṭaŋka peen ŋawa
        'dog that bites men'

    (11) ṭaŋka ṇeyin waŋal
        'boomerang that kills men'

Problem 3.4–10 *English*

In Problem 3.2–11 evidence was presented for a syntactic rule of Spanish that optionally raises a negative from a subordinate clause into the main clause under certain conditions. A similar rule can be posited for English. Examine the sentences below and construct two arguments to support the putative rule of negative raising.

(1) *The bomb will explode until 5 P.M.
(2) The bomb will not explode until 5 P.M.
(3) *The sheriff heard a shot until midnight.
(4) The sheriff did not hear a shot until midnight.
(5) *I did not plant a bomb [that will explode until 5 P.M.].
(6) I believe [the bomb will not explode until 5 P.M.].
(7) I do not believe [the bomb will explode until 5 P.M.].
(8) I think [the sheriff did not hear a shot until midnight].
(9) I do not think [the sheriff heard a shot until midnight].
(10) The bomb will explode, won't it?
(11) The bomb will not explode, will it?
(12) The sheriff heard a shot, didn't he?
(13) The sheriff did not hear a shot, did he?
(14) *I believe the bomb will explode, will it?
(15) I do not believe the bomb will explode, will it?
(16) *I think the sheriff heard a shot, did he?
(17) I do not think the sheriff heard a shot, did he?

Problem 3.4–11   *Japanese*

Isolate the independently meaningful morphemes in the Japanese sentences below (Kuroda, 1965) and state their meanings. Diagram the surface structure of (9) as well as its propositional structure (exclusive of tense). Describe the formation of Japanese sentences that express causation.

(1) john ga kodomo ni hon o yomaseru
    'John makes a child read a book.'

(2) kodomo ga neru
    'A child sleeps.'

(3) tom ga john o utawaseru
    'Tom makes John sing.'

(4) john ga kodomo ni tegami o kakaseru
    'John makes a child write a letter.'

(5) isya ga kusuri o tukurru
    'A doctor prepares medicine.'

(6) kodomo ga okasi o taberu
    'A child eats cake.'

(7) john ga kodomo o tabesaseru
    'John makes a child eat.'

(8) kodomo ga hon o yomru
    'A child reads a book.'

(9) john ga kodomo ni okasi o tabesaseru
'John makes a child eat cake.'

(10) watasi ga isya ni kosaseru
'I make a doctor come.'

(11) john ga kodomo o nesaseru
'John makes a child sleep.'

(12) kodomo ga taberu
'A child eats.'

(13) john ga kodomo ni tabesaseru
'John makes a child eat.'

(14) kodomo ga tomodati ni tegami o kakru
'A child writes a letter to a friend.'

(15) watasi ga isya ni kusuri o tukuraseru
'I make a doctor prepare medicine.'

(16) watasi ga isya o kosaseru
'I make a doctor come.'

(17) john ga utawru
'John sings.'

Problem 3.4–12   Diegueño

In this problem from Diegueño (Neufeld, 1970), we will be concerned not with grammatical elements smaller than words but rather with more global aspects of complex sentence formation. On the basis of the sentences below, formulate the reduction and rearrangement rules that account for the formation of relative and complement clauses in Diegueño. Assume that the verb is the last member of a clause in underlying structure. Diagram the derivation of (7) and (10).

(1) ñaač siñ kupaa uuyaaw
I lady came know
'I know the lady who came.'

(2) ñaač iipač paam ʔaarap
I man came hit
'I hit the man who came.'

(3) ñaač siñ xəkwal uuyaaw čəmxan
I lady child know like
'I like the lady who knows the child.'

(4) ñaač siñ xaṭ xənuu aarap ʔəwuu
I lady dog sick hit saw
'I saw the lady who hit the dog that was sick.'

(5) ñaač siñ xəkwal xənuum uuyaaw čəmxan
I lady child sick know like
'I like the lady who knows the child is sick.'

(6) ñaač siñbo uuyaw iipačəč məxan
I lady know man like
'I know the lady who the man likes.'

(7) ñaač siñ ʔəwuu xaṭ xənuu aarap
I lady saw dog sick hit
'I saw the lady who hit the dog that was sick.'

(8) ñaač siñ xwič xəčañ wəpisəm uuyaaw
I lady hate girl (I) kiss know
'I hate the lady who knows I kissed the girl.'

(9) ñaač čəwaayp čəmxan
I talk like
'I like to talk.'

(10) ñaač iipač aaLuuxəm aarapč ʔaṛ
I man snore hit want
'I want to hit the man who is snoring.'

(11) siñ waṛ ñaač šawii saaw
lady want I mush eat
'The lady wants me to eat the mush.'

Problem 3.4–13 *Dyirbal*

PART A The data for this problem (Dixon, 1969) is from Dyirbal, an aboriginal language of Australia. As in Gumbaiŋgar, two cases can be distinguished, ergative (*ERG*) and nominative (*NOM*). In sentences with both a subject and an object, the subject typically is marked for ergative case, and the object for nominative case. The nominative case ending is usually zero.

Examine the sentences below and describe the use of the "passive" suffix *ŋa* as well as the way in which possession is expressed in Dyirbal.

(1) njalŋga yaṛa-ŋgu djilwa-n

child NOM man-ERG kick-PAST
'The man kicked the child.'

(2) yaṛa njalŋga-ŋgu djilwal-ŋa-nju

man NOM child-ERG kick-PASSIVE-PAST
'The child was kicked by the man.'

(3) guda njalŋga-ŋgu djilwa-n

dog NOM child-ERG kick-PAST
'The child kicked the dog.'

(4) njalŋga guda-ŋgu djilwal-ŋa-nju

child NOM dog-ERG kick-PASSIVE-PAST
'The dog was kicked by the child.'

(5) guda yaṛa-ŋgu

dog NOM man-ERG
'The dog is the man's.'

(6) njalŋga badibadi-ŋgu

child NOM Badibadi-ERG
'The child is Badibadi's.'

PART B Examine the sentences below and describe the formation of relative clauses in Dyirbal. Can you explain why some nouns have two case endings?

(7) yibi [njalŋga-ŋgu djilwal-ŋa-ŋu] yaṛa-ŋgu buṛa-n

woman NOM child-ERG kick-PASSIVE-REL NOM man-
ERG see-PAST
'The man saw the woman by whom the child had been kicked.'

(8) yibi [njalŋga-ŋgu djilwa-ŋu] yaṛa-ŋgu buṛa-n

woman NOM child-ERG kick-REL NOM man-ERG see-
PAST
'The man saw the woman who the child had kicked.'

(9) yibi yaṛa-ŋgu [njalŋga-ŋgu djilwal-ŋa-ŋu-ru] buṛa-n

woman NOM man-ERG child-ERG kick-PASSIVE-REL-
ERG see-PAST
'The man by whom the child had been kicked saw the woman.'

(10) yibi yaṛa-ŋgu [njalŋga-ŋgu djilwa-ŋu-ru] buṛa-n

woman NOM man-ERG child-ERG kick-REL-ERG see-
PAST
'The man who the child had kicked saw the woman.'

(11) njalŋga guda-ŋgu [yaṛa-ŋu-ndjin-du] badja-n

child NOM dog-ERG man-REL-ERG-ERG bite-PAST
'The man's dog bit the child.'

(12) yibi [yaṛa-ŋu-ndjin-du] guda-ŋgu badja-n

woman NOM man-REL-ERG-ERG dog-ERG bite-PAST
'The man's dog bit the woman.'

(13) [badibadi-ŋu-ndjin] yabu yaṛa-ŋgu djilwa-n

Badibadi-REL-ERG NOM mother NOM man-ERG kick-
   PAST
'The man kicked Badibadi's mother.'

Problem 3.4–14 Modern Greek

PART A Examine the sentences below (Drachman, 1970) and describe the
form and use of articles (words meaning 'the' and 'a') in modern Greek.

(1) o kinigos skotose ton liko
'The hunter killed the wolf.'

(2) o periklis ipye to nero
'Pericles drank the water.'

(3) to [oti ilthe arga] ksafniase ton petro
'That he came late startled Peter.'

(4) ego edosa tu pavlu mia lira
'I gave Paul a gold sovereign.'

(5) o thanasis edose to sitari tu ftoxu
'Thanasis gave the corn to the poor man.'

(6) o agrotis skotose ton liko
'The farmer killed the wolf.'

(7) o periklis ipye tin bira
'Pericles drank the beer.'

(8) ego vrika to pigadi
'I found the well.'

(9) edosa tu pavlu mia drachme
'I gave Paul a drachma.'

(10) ego perimeno [oti o thanasis tha kerdisi to laxio]
'I expect that Thanasis will win the lottery.'

PART B Sentences (11)–(16) illustrate the application of a rule that inserts sentence trappings. State this rule.

(11) o kinigos ton skotose ton liko
'The hunter killed the wolf.'

(12) o thanasis tu edose to sitari tu ftoxu
'Thanasis gave the corn to the poor man.'

(13) ego to perimeno to [oti tha yirisi o petros]
'I expect that Peter will return.'

(14) o periklis tin ipye tin bira
'Pericles drank the beer.'

(15) to perimeno to [na yirisi o petros]
'I expect Peter to return.'

(16) to [oti ilthe arga] ton ksafniase ton petro
'That he came late startled Peter.'

PART C Subject raising is a rule of modern Greek. As in English, its application is possible only with certain main clause predicates, among them the verb meaning 'expect'. On the basis of sentences (17)–(23), construct a syntactic argument to show that the underlying subject of a subordinate clause may function as the object of the main clause in surface structure. Give the derivation of (22) and comment on rule ordering.

(17) ego perimeno o thanasis na kerdisi to laxio
'I expect Thanasis to win the lottery.'

(18) perimeno ton thanasi na kerdisi to laxio
'I expect Thanasis to win the lottery.'

(19) o petros ton perimeni ton perikli na figi
'Peter expects Pericles to go.'

(20) perimeno ton kosta na elthi
'I expect Kostas to come.'

(21) ton perimeno ton thanasi na kerdisi to laxio
'I expect Thanasis to win the lottery.'

(22) ton perimeno ton kosta na elthi
'I expect Kostas to come.'

(23) o petros perimeni ton perikli na figi
'Peter expects Pericles to go.'

PART D On the basis of (24)–(31), formulate a deletion rule that affects conjoined clauses. Comment on the ordering of this rule with respect to subject raising. Diagram the derivation of (28).

(24) o petros perimeni ton perikli na figi, ke o kostas perimeni ton thanasi na elthi

'Peter expects Pericles to go, and Kostas expects Thanasis to come.'

(25) ego edosa tu pavlu mia lira, ke o kostas tis ketis mia drachme

'I gave Paul a gold sovereign, and Kostas gave Kathy a drachma.'

(26) o periklis tin bira ipye, o sokratis tin lemonada ipye, ke o manolis to nero ipye

'Pericles drank the beer, Socrates drank the lemonade, and Manolis drank the water.'

(27) *o periklis tin bira, o sokratis tin lemonada, ke o manolis ipye to nero

'Pericles drank the beer, Socrates drank the lemonade, and Manolis drank the water.'

(28) o petros ton perimeni ton perikli na figi, ke o kostas ton thanasi na elthi

'Peter expects Pericles to go, and Kostas expects Thanasis to come.'

(29) o periklis ipye tin bira, o sokratis tin lemonada, ke o manolis to nero

'Pericles drank the beer, Socrates drank the lemonade, and Manolis drank the water.'

(30) o periklis tin bira, o sokratis tin lemonada, ke o manolis to nero ipye

'Pericles drank the beer, Socrates drank the lemonade, and Manolis drank the water.'

(31) o periklis ipye tin bira, o sokratis ipye tin lemonada, ke o manolis ipye to nero

'Pericles drank the beer, Socrates drank the lemonade, and Manolis drank the water.'

Problem 3.4–15 Samoan

PART A In Samoan a noun phrase is preceded by a "case" particle that expresses the semantic relationship between the noun phrase and the verb. These particles are analogous to prepositions in English and to case inflections in languages like Latin and Russian, but their semantic value tends to be more regular than for prepositions and case inflections, and there is no special case for subjects or direct objects. Examine the data below (Pizzini, 1969). Isolate the morphemes and state their meanings. Describe as precisely as possible the semantic values of the case particles. Samoan orthography is used.

    (1) e sogi e le tama le ufi i le to'i
        'The boy cuts the yam with the axe.'

    (2) sa sogi e le teine le ufi
        'The girl cut the yam.'

    (3) sa fa'apa'ū e ioane le to'i
        'John dropped the axe.'

    (4) e fa'apa'ū e le teine le peni
        'The girl drops the pen.'

    (5) sa pa'ū le ufi
        'The yam fell.'

    (6) e pa'ū le to'i
        'The axe falls.'

    (7) e mana'o le tama i le teine
        'The boy wants the girl.'

    (8) sa sogi e ioane le ufi i le peni
        'John cut the yam with the pen.'

PART B On the basis of (9)–(15), describe the formation of complement clauses in Samoan. Construct a syntactic argument to show that subject raising applies in the derivation of (11) and (14).

    (9) e mana'o le tama ina ia pa'ū le peni
        'The boy wants the pen to fall.'

    (10) e fa'amoemoe le tama ia mana'o le teine ia fa'apa'ū e ioane le
         peni
        'The boy hopes the girl wants John to drop the pen.'

    (11) e mana'o le tama i le to'i ia pa'ū
        'The boy wants the axe to fall.'

    (12) e mana'o le tama ia pa'ū le peni
        'The boy wants the pen to fall.'

    (13) e fa'amalosi e le teine ia alu le tama
        'The girl forces the boy to go.'

(14) e mana'o le teine i le peni ina ia pa'ū
'The girl wants the pen to fall.'

(15) e fa'amalosi e le teine ina ia alu le tama
'The girl forces the boy to go.'

PART C   Sentences (16)–(21) illustrate the application of a rule that can be called "topicalization". Describe the effects of this rule. Can you explain why both (20) and (21) are possible variants of (19)?

(16) o le tama e sogi le ufi i le to'i
'The boy cuts the yam with the axe.'

(17) o le ufi sa sogi e le tama i le to'i
'The boy cut the yam with the axe.'

(18) ou te mana'o i le teine sa fa'apa'ū le peni
'l want the girl that dropped the pen.'

(19) ou te fa'amalosi ina ia alu le tama
'I force the boy to go.'

(20) ou te fa'amalosi o le tama ina ia alu
'I force the boy to go.'

(21) o le tama ou te fa'amalosi ina ia alu
'I force the boy to go.'

Problem 3.4–16   *Luiseño*

The following Luiseño nominals all contain relative clauses. Some nominals are given in the form they have as subjects, and others in the form they have as objects. On the basis of this data, describe the principles for constructing relative clauses in Luiseño.

(1) ṣuŋaali poneeyi ʔaamomokwiči
'the woman that was hunting' (object)

(2) ʔataaxumi poneemi ʔaamoqatumi
'the people that are hunting' (object)

(3) ʔawaali poneeyi noo nokoʔivoy
'the dog that I bit' (object)

(4) ʔataaxum pomom noo noyiʔyipi
'the people that I will play with' (subject)

(5) ṣuŋaali poneeyi ʔaamoluti
'the woman that will hunt' (object)

(6) Pawaalum pomom waʔimokwičum
'the dogs that were barking' (subject)

(7) Pataaxumi poneemi ṣuŋaal poyiʔyiqati
'the people that the woman is playing with' (object)

(8) ṣuŋaal po Pawaal pokoʔivo
'the woman that the dog bit' (subject)

(9) ṣuŋaal po paaʔiqat
'the woman that is drinking' (subject)

(10) Pawaalum pomom waʔikutum
'the dogs that will bark' (subject)

(11) Pawaalumi poneemi waʔikutumi
'the dogs that will bark' (object)

(12) Pataaxumi poneemi Paamomokwičumi
'the people that were hunting' (object)

(13) Pawaalum pomom waʔiqatum
'the dogs that are barking' (subject)

(14) Pataaxumi poneemi ṣuŋaal poyiʔyipiy
'the people that the woman will play with' (object)

(15) Pawaal po waʔimokwiš
'the dog that was barking' (subject)

(16) Pawaal po waʔiqat
'the dog that is barking' (subject)

(17) Pawaali poneeyi paaʔiluti
'the dog that will drink' (object)

(18) Pataaxum pomom noo noyiʔyiqat
'the people that I am playing with' (subject)

(19) ṣuŋaali poneeyi Paamoqati
'the woman that is hunting' (object)

(20) ṣuŋaal po Pawaal pokoʔipi
'the woman that the dog will bite' (subject)

(21) Pawaalumi poneemi waʔimokwičumi
'the dogs that were barking' (object)

(22) Pawaal po waʔilut
'the dog that will bark' (subject)

(23) Pawaalum pomom paaʔikutum
'the dogs that will drink' (subject)

(24) ʔataaxumi poneemi ṣuŋaal poyiʔyivoy
'the people that the woman played with' (object)

(25) ʔawaali poneeyi noo nokoʔiqati
'the dog that I am biting' (object)

(26) ṣuŋaal po paaʔimokwiš
'the woman that was drinking' (subject)

(27) ʔawaalumi poneemi waʔiqatumi
'the dogs that are barking' (object)

(28) ṣuŋaal po ʔawaal pokoʔiqat
'the woman that the dog is biting' (subject)

(29) ʔawaali poneeyi paaʔimokwiči
'the dog that was drinking' (object)

(30) ʔataaxumi poneemi ʔaamokutumi
'the people that will hunt' (object)

(31) ʔawaalum pomom paaʔiqatum
'the dogs that are drinking' (subject)

(32) ʔawaali poneeyi noo nokoʔipiy
'the dog that I will bite' (object)

(33) ʔawaali poneeyi paaʔiqati
'the dog that is drinking' (object)

(34) ṣuŋaal po paaʔilut
'the woman that will drink' (subject)

(35) ʔataaxum pomom noo noyiʔyivo
'the people that I played with' (subject)

(36) ʔawaalum pomom paaʔimokwičum
'the dogs that were drinking' (subject)

3.5 Sentence Types

Sentences can be used in various ways. Most of the sentences we have examined so far have been the kind used in making statements or assertions, but sentences can also be used to request information, give orders, issue warnings, make promises, and so on. The way a sentence is used is referred to as its ***illocutionary force***. For example, the illocutionary force of sentence (1) is assertion, that of (2) is interrogation or questioning, and that of (3) is ordering.

(1) Figs are very expensive this year.
(2) How many angels can dance on the head of a pin?
(3) Gag the defendant!

Sentences like the above are known respectively as *declarative*, *interrogative*, and *imperative* sentences. In the following discussion we will restrict our attention to these three sentence types.

The illocutionary force of a sentence is clearly part of its meaning. This force is sometimes made explicit by means of a special clause in surface structure, as in sentences (4)–(6), but usually it must be deduced from the form of the sentence or from the context in which the sentence is uttered.

> (4) I say to you that figs are very expensive this year.
> (5) I ask you how many angels can dance on the head of a pin.
> (6) I order you to gag the defendant.

It can reasonably be maintained that (4)–(6) approximate the respective conceptual structures of (1)–(3), at least insofar as illocutionary force is concerned, but the specifics of the relationship are not very clear to linguists at present. Notice that the clause expressing the illocutionary force of a sentence can sometimes be modified even when the clause is not present in surface structure. In (7), for instance, the clause *since you are an expert on theology* modifies *I ask you*; the same semantic relation seems to hold in (8), even though (8) contains no equivalent of *I ask you* at the surface level.

> (7) Since you are an expert on theology, I ask you how many angels can dance on the head of a pin.
> (8) Since you are an expert on theology, how many angels can dance on the head of a pin?

Declarative sentences are usually accorded special prominence in linguistic analysis. One reason is that they are intuitively less "special" than interrogatives or imperatives and are no doubt employed more frequently. There are also structural grounds for according declarative sentences special prominence. Interrogatives and imperatives often bear special markings not borne by declarative sentences, as we will see, and their surface form can usually be simply described in terms of modifications of the corresponding declaratives. For example, the surface form of an English imperative is obtained by deleting the subject *you* from the corresponding declarative structure. It is with declaratives that our examination of sentence types will begin.

DECLARATIVE SENTENCES

The syntax of declarative sentences is a vast topic, and we can do little more than touch briefly on certain of its fundamental aspects. The most basic elements of a simple declarative sentence are a predicate and zero or more noun phrase adjuncts. It will not be possible to pay systematic attention here to all the other entities that can appear in declarative sentences, such as adverbials (including words, phrases, and modifying clauses), modals, auxiliary verbs, negation, and so on.

In most if not all languages there are grounds for recognizing **subjects**, **direct objects**, and **oblique objects** among the nominal adjuncts of predicates. In (1), for instance, *I* is the subject of *bought*, *a watch* is the direct object, and *Harvey* and *three clam shells* are oblique objects.

(1) I bought a watch from Harvey for three clam shells.

Subjects, direct objects, and oblique objects have special grammatical properties that distinguish them from one another. In English, for example, the subject nominal is the one that the predicate agrees with; the direct object differs from oblique objects in that it typically occurs immediately after the verb and is the only object not preceded by a preposition. The distinguishing properties of subjects and objects of course vary from language to language.

To some degree, the semantic relation that a nominal bears to its predicate is correlated with its function as a subject, direct object, or oblique object. For instance, English verbs describing physical activities usually have as their subject the nominal designating the individual that carries out the action in question; (2) and (3) are examples.

(2) Ann bit her mother.
(3) Ann washed her mother with cold water.

For these same verbs, the direct object is typically the nominal designating the recipient of the action, as in the case of *her mother* in (2) and (3). Prepositions and other markings identifying oblique objects often have fairly consistent meanings which specify the semantic relations these objects bear to the predicate (though there are naturally many irregularities). For example, *for* and *from* are intrinsically meaningful in (1) above, and so is *with* in (3) and (4).

(4) I stirred the soup with a fly swatter.

However, there is no consistent semantic value associated with being a subject or direct object. For example, the semantic relation between the subject *Ann* and the following verb is very different in (2), (5), and (6).

(5) Ann likes her mother.
(6) Ann preoccupies her mother.

In (2) *Ann* is the agent of a volitional activity. Sentence (5), on the other hand, describes a mental disposition on her part rather than an act, and (6) attributes to her neither physical nor mental activity. Similarly, the direct object *her mother* is said to receive or undergo a physical action in (2) and (3), but this semantic relation between object and verb does not obtain in (5). In (6), moreover, the object *her mother* is attributed mental activity, just as the subject *Ann* is in (7).

(7) Ann thinks about her mother.

The semantic relation between the subject *Ann* and *preoccupies* in (6) is quite similar to that between *thinks* and the oblique object *her mother* in (7). In (8) no specific physical or mental activity is posited of either the subject or the object.

> (8) Ann complements her mother.

Finally, consider (9)–(11).

> (9) Ann opened the door with the key.
> (10) The key opened the door.
> (11) The door opened.

The semantic relation between *the door* and *opened* remains constant in these three sentences, despite the fact that *the door* is the direct object in (9) and (10) but the subject in (11). The semantic relation between *the key* and *opened* is the same in (9) and (10), although this nominal is an oblique object in one sentence and the subject in the other. Notice also that the semantic relation between the subject and verb is different in all three sentences.

The point of these examples is that predicates differ considerably in the semantic relations they bear to their noun phrase adjuncts. The semantic relations between nominals and predicates must be made explicit in any comprehensive description of underlying representations, but at the surface level these relations are obscured, being manifested in a highly inconsistent way. The notions subject and object are not primarily semantic in character (though some correlations can be observed, such as the tendency noted above for the nominal designating the agent of a physical activity to occur as a subject). What it means semantically for a noun phrase to be a subject or direct object (and to some degree, an oblique object) depends on the properties of the associated predicate. For this reason, nominal adjuncts are described as arguments, rather than as subjects and objects, in discussing semantic representations.

Languages employ various devices to mark nominals as subjects, direct objects, and oblique objects. Often nominals are identified by position. In most English declarative sentences, the noun phrase that precedes the verb is the subject, and one that immediately follows the verb is a direct object. Many languages use overt markings to flag subjects and objects. The syntactic function of a nominal may be indicated by a special particle that precedes or follows it. In Japanese, for instance, the particle *ga* follows the subject, and *o* follows the object; in addition, the subject consistently precedes the object in Japanese, as in (12).

> (12) kodomo ga hon o yomru
> 'A child reads a book.'

Affixation or case inflection is also commonly used to specify the syntactic function of nominals. Finally, agreement often makes it possible to determine which nominal in a sentence is the subject or direct object; we have seen numerous examples of languages in which predicates are marked to agree with their nominal adjuncts. When overt markings indicate the syntactic function of nominals, there is a tendency for subjects and (to a lesser degree) direct objects to bear the simplest marking. Often, as in English, this marking is zero.

In languages with case inflection, such as German, Russian, and Latin, subjects are often marked with one special case, the ***nominative***, and objects with another, the ***accusative***. The subject and object in Latin sentences like (13) and (14) can thus be identified despite variability in word order. (A bar above a vowel indicates length.)

(13) Puer rēgīnam amat.

boy NOM queen ACC loves
'The boy loves the queen.'

(14) Rēgīnam amat puer.

queen ACC loves boy NOM
'The boy loves the queen.'

A slightly different pattern, not at all uncommon, is illustrated by Australian languages such as Gumbaingar (Dixon, 1969). One case, the ***ergative***, is used only with the subject of sentences that also have an object. Another case, the ***nominative***, is used both with objects and with the subject of sentences that have no object. This pattern is illustrated in (15) and (16).

(15) jaraŋ duuwaŋ

he NOM cried
'He cried.'

(16) ŋaidja gugaamgan njaawaŋ

I ERG emu NOM saw
'I saw the emu.'

The word order of subject, verb, and object tends to be relatively free in languages that mark subjects and objects by inflection.

The notion subject is related to another important notion, that of ***topic***, which is not nearly so well understood. Roughly speaking, the topic of a sentence is the element that the sentence is "about". The rest of the sentence, called the ***comment***, contributes new information about the topic. The constituent that occurs in sentence-initial position is normally interpreted to be the topic. In English the subject is usually interpreted as the topic, because the subject is usually sentence-initial. However, there are also devices for marking some other element as the topic. In (18) and (19) the direct object of (17), *Elwood*, is topicalized by being moved to the beginning of the sentence; the coreferential pronoun *him* is left behind in its place.

(17) I saw Elwood last night.
(18) Elwood, I saw him last night.
(19) As for Elwood, I saw him last night.

The Samoan topicalization process was illustrated in Problem 3.4–15. (20) contains no topic, but in sentence (21) the noun phrase *le tama* 'the boy' has been moved to sentence-initial position, the topic position, and marked with the particle *o*, which substitutes for the usual "case" particle.

(20) e sogi e le tama le ufi i le to'i
     PRESENT cut CASE the boy the yam with the axe
     'The boy cuts the yam with the axe.'

(21) o le tama e sogi le ufi i le to'i
     TOPIC the boy PRESENT cut the yam with the axe
     'The boy cuts the yam with the axe.'

In similar fashion, the particle *wa* marks a nominal as a topic in Japanese. *Wa* substitutes for *ga*, *o*, or *ni*, the particles that accompany subjects, direct objects, and indirect objects (see Problem 3.4–11), and the topicalized nominal advances to sentence-initial position.

The passive construction in English, illustrated in (22), is closely connected with topicalization, since it allows in subject (and hence topic) position a nominal that would normally figure as an object.

(22) The window was shattered by the sonic boom.

A similar construction in Dyirbal, also involving interchange of subject and object as well as modification of the verb, was treated in Problem 3.4–13.

In addition to topicalization, languages have syntactic devices that allow one or more of the nominal adjuncts of a verb to remain unexpressed. With some verbs in English, for example, it is possible simply to omit a direct or oblique object; thus we find sentences like (23) and (25) alongside fuller sentences like (24) and (26).

(23) He ate.
(24) He ate clams.
(25) Martha talked.
(26) Martha talked to my sister about space suits.

By resorting to the passive in English, one can omit the nominal that would otherwise be the subject, since the *by* phrase of a passive is optional; compare (22) and (27).

(27) The window was shattered.

In French the expected subject of a sentence can sometimes be omitted by means of a special use of the reflexive, as in (28).

> (28) Cela se dit toujours.
> that itself says always
> 'That is always said.'

Semantically, *cela* bears the same relation to *dit* in (28) that it does in (29), in which it is the direct object.

> (29) Pierre dit cela toujours.
> 'Peter always says that.'

In Aztec, to take just one more example, the subject can be omitted if a special suffix, [lo], is added to the verb; (30) contains no nominal in surface structure.

> (30) koči-lo 'One sleeps.'

Moreover, it is quite possible that some sentences contain no nominal either in surface structure or in underlying representations. The Spanish sentence (31) is a likely example.

> (31) Llueve. 'It's raining.'

More surprising, perhaps, is the fact that some sentences have no verb or adjective in surface structure, while others have a verb whose sense is so general or vague that one might argue it has no meaning at all. The verbs in question are those that translate as 'have' and 'be'. In languages all over the world sentences involving 'have' and 'be' have distinctive and sometimes perplexing grammatical properties. Among the notions commonly expressed by these predicates are existence, identity, possession, and location, as well as notions of tense and aspect. However, the way these and related notions are manifested varies widely from language to language; a given notion may be expressed with 'have' in one language, with 'be' in another, and with no verb at all in another. To take just one example, possession can be expressed in English by either *have* or *be*.

> (32) I have a new car.
> (33) That new car is mine.

In Russian possession is expressed by means of the preposition *u*, which means 'at' or 'near'; (34) contains no surface verb.

> (34) u menya kniga
> at me book
> 'I have a book.'

There is little point in proliferating examples. Suffice it to say that the syntax of 'have' and 'be' involves many peculiarities, and that there is some important but as yet only dimly understood linguistic relationship holding among such notions as existence, identity, possession, location, and tense. The elucidation of these relationships will have profound consequences for our understanding of the semantic structure of human language.

Problem 3.5–1   Swahili

Both passive and active (that is, non-passive) sentences are included in the data given below (Perrott, 1951). On the basis of this data, describe the formation of passive sentences in Swahili.

(1) mtoto alivunja kikombe
'The child broke the cup.'

(2) kikombe kilivunjwa na mtoto
'The cup was broken by the child.'

(3) barua ilisomwa na mwalimu
'The letter was read by the teacher.'

(4) baba alipiga mtoto
'The father beat the child.'

(5) mwalimu alisoma barua
'The teacher read the letter.'

(6) mtoto alipigwa na baba
'The child was beaten by the father.'

Solution

In forming the passive, *w* is inserted before the final *a* of the verb. The subject of the corresponding active sentence follows the verb, being preceded by the particle *na*. The object of the corresponding active sentence functions as the subject in the passive. Consequently it precedes the verb, and the initial prefix of the verb agrees with it.

Problem 3.5–2   English

It has been suggested that *have*, in some of its uses, is the semantic equivalent of *be with* (in one of the senses of *with*) and may even derive from an underlying representation containing *be with* (see Fillmore, 1969). The following noun phrases with relative clauses provide evidence for this analysis. Construct an argument to support the hypothesis.

(1) (a) a woman who is from Chicago
    (b) a woman from Chicago
(2) (a) a rabbit that has a harelip
    (b) a rabbit with a harelip
(3) (a) the doll that is under the bed
    (b) the doll under the bed
(4) (a) the table that has a scratch on it
    (b) the table with a scratch on it
(5) (a) the boy who has a crewcut
    (b) the boy with a crewcut
(6) (a) the little old man who is in the corner
    (b) the little old man in the corner

Solution

Examples (1), (3), and (6) point to the existence of a reduction rule that affects relative clauses in English. The (b) expressions can be regarded as reduced versions of the (a) expressions. Evidently, the reduction rule optionally deletes a relative pronoun plus a form of the verb *be* when this sequence directly precedes a preposition.

A second reduction rule is apparently needed for examples (2), (4), and (5). If the (b) expressions are taken to be reduced versions of the (a) expressions, which is quite reasonable on the basis of form and meaning, some rule must have the effect of deleting a relative pronoun plus a form of the verb *have* and replacing this sequence with *with*. Unlike the rule mentioned above, this one is not restricted to applying when a preposition follows.

On the face of it, the two rules are quite different. One deletes *be*, and the other *have*. One applies before prepositions, the other before noun phrases. One inserts *with*, and the other inserts nothing. However, the two rules are also similar in certain ways; both apply optionally to relative clauses and delete a relative pronoun plus some particular verb. It would be desirable for an analysis to express this generalization, but it cannot be expressed if two separate rules are posited.

However, the generalization can be captured if *have* is regarded as a variant of *be with*. In terms of this proposal, (5) (a) has a derivation roughly like this:

the boy who is with a crewcut $\Rightarrow$ the boy who has a crewcut

Expressions (2) (a) and (4) (a) have analogous derivations. Now, given underlying representations containing *be with* instead of *have*, the reduction that operates in the derivation of (2) (b), (4) (b), and (5) (b) is seen to be exactly the same reduction that derives (1) (b), (3) (b), and (6) (b). For example, the underlying structure of (5) (b) is *the boy who is with a crewcut*. In this underlying representation, a relative pronoun plus a form of *be* precedes the preposition *with*. The first reduction rule discussed above is therefore applicable, and its effect is to delete *who is*, resulting in (5) (b). The reduction rule is optional, and if it does not apply, (5) (a) results when *be with* is replaced by *have*.

The analysis of *have* as deriving from *be with* therefore receives a certain measure of syntactic support. It allows us to capture a significant generalization concerning the truncation of relative clauses, and it simplifies the description in that only one reduction rule is required rather than two.

IMPERATIVE SENTENCES

Imperative sentences can be formed only with relatively few of the many different sentence types characteristic of declaratives. Although languages differ somewhat in details, imperatives tend to be restricted to sentences with (underlying) second person subjects and active verbs that describe actions over which a person has some voluntary control. They are also restricted in tense. Sentences like the following are thus ungrammatical or at least semantically peculiar.

(1) *He leave right away!
(2) *Be a web-footed mammal!
(3) *Got out of here!

Sentences similar to imperatives can often be found which have non-second person subjects.

(4) Let's go!
(5) Let him come!

However, these sentences commonly have special syntactic properties, such as the initial *let* in (4) and (5), and might best be considered a separate sentence type. English also contains sentences that have the form of imperatives but whose predicates do not describe actions subject to voluntary control.

(6) Be tall and everyone will consider you a great lover.

Semantically, however, such sentences are equivalent to conditional sentences. (6), in other words, is apparently a variant of (7).

(7) If you are tall, everyone will consider you a great lover.

When the illocutionary force of an imperative sentence is not marked by means of an explicit verb like *order* or *request*, special marking devices are often employed. The second person subject is commonly deleted, as in (8).

(8) Bring me more whisky!

It is also quite common for a special form of the verb to be used in imperative sentences. The imperative form of a verb is frequently the simplest form, lacking the usual verbal inflection. The simplest form of the verb is used with imperatives in English, as (8) shows, and the same is true in Swahili (Perrott, 1951); in the imperative sentence (9), the usual subject prefix and tense marker are lacking.

> (9) soma   'Read!'

The imperative marker [ši] replaces the usual subject marker in Aztec imperatives (compare Problem 2.3–5, p. 81).

> (10) ši-k-poowa-kaan
>   IMPERATIVE-it-count-PLURAL
>   'You (PLURAL) count it!'

In Urdu *o* is suffixed to the verb in imperatives addressed to social inferiors, and *ie* in imperatives addressed to superiors (Bailey, 1956). Special verb forms used in Maltese imperatives were illustrated in Problem 2.4–5 (p. 90). In negative imperatives, the use of a special marker, similar to English *don't*, is a common syntactic device. For example, the Indonesian negative imperative marker is *djangan* (Kwee, 1965).

> (11) djangan lari   'Don't run!'

Problem 3.5–3   Luiseño

Analyze the following sentences and describe the formation of imperative sentences in Luiseño. The designation 'PLURAL' refers to the plurality of the understood subject.

(1)	noo nečiq	'I buy.'
(2)	paaʔiyam	'Drink (PLURAL)!'
(3)	pellax	'Dance!'
(4)	tuşu heelax	'Don't sing!'
(5)	noo hatiʔaq	'I go.'
(6)	hatiʔax	'Go!'
(7)	noo pellaq	'I dance.'
(8)	paaʔi	'Drink!'
(9)	tuşu hatiʔax	'Don't go!'
(10)	tuşum nečiyam	'Don't pay (PLURAL)!'
(11)	wunaal heelaq	'He sings.'
(12)	wunaal paaʔiq	'He drinks.'
(13)	neči	'Pay!'
(14)	hatiʔaxam	'Go (PLURAL)!'
(15)	wunaal toonavq	'He makes baskets.'
(16)	tuşu paaʔi	'Don't drink!'

(17) tuşum pellaxam	'Don't dance (PLURAL)!'
(18) toonav	'Make baskets!'
(19) heelaxam	'Sing (PLURAL)!'
(20) pellaxam	'Dance (PLURAL)!'
(21) tuşum toonavyam	'Don't make baskets (PLURAL)!'
(22) nečiyam	'Pay (PLURAL)!'
(23) toonavyam	'Make baskets (PLURAL)!'
(24) heelax	'Sing!'

Solution

The subject 'you' does not appear in the surface structure of Luiseño imperatives. For positive imperatives, the verb stem is used without the present tense
ending, and [x] is suffixed if the verb ends in [a]. If the underlying subject is
plural, [xam] is suffixed to verbs ending in [a], and [yam] to other verbs.
Negative imperatives are formed in the same way, except that the negative
imperative marker [tuşu] is inserted before the verb. If the underlying subject
is plural, [m] is added to [tuşu] as a suffix.

INTERROGATIVE SENTENCES

Unlike imperatives, interrogatives can be formed that correspond to any of
the many types of declarative sentences. There are two basic kinds of question
sentences, those that ask which of two or more alternative propositions is
true and those that ask for the further specification of some constituent. Let
us call the former *alternative questions* and the latter, for lack of a better
term, *specification questions*.

Alternative questions are closely related to sentences conjoined with 'or'.
(1), for instance, is the interrogative counterpart of (2); in uttering (1), a
speaker assumes or *presupposes* the truth of (2).

> (1) Did you buy the wallet, or did you steal it, or did you find it on
> the street?
> (2) Either you bought the wallet, or you stole it, or you found it on
> the street.

To answer an alternative question, it is necessary to indicate which of the
conjuncts of the corresponding declarative sentence is the correct one. Questions
answerable by 'yes' or 'no' are a special case of alternative questions. (5), for
example, is a reduced form of the alternative question (3); (4) represents an
intermediate stage in the derivation.

> (3) Is it raining, or isn't it raining?
> (4) Is it raining, or not?
> (5) Is it raining?

A yes-no question results when an alternative question has exactly two clauses, the second of which is the negation of the first.

Just as alternative questions bear a special relation to 'or', specification questions bear a special relation to the indefinite 'some'. For example, (6) and (8) are the interrogative counterparts of (7) and (9) respectively; (6) presupposes the truth of (7), and (8) presupposes the truth of (9).

(6) Who stole my wallet?
(7) Someone stole my wallet.
(8) Why did he steal my wallet?
(9) He stole my wallet for some reason.

To answer a specification question, it is necessary to replace the indefinite in the corresponding declarative sentence with a constituent having greater semantic content.

The syntax of interrogative sentences differs considerably in detail from language to language, but several devices for marking questions recur in languages all over the world. One device is intonation. Yes-no questions very often have a rising intonation that sets them apart from the corresponding statements (though this is by no means true of every language). In French, for instance, yes-no questions can be marked by rising intonation alone.

(10) Pierre est là.
     'Peter is there.'

(11) Pierre est là?
     'Is Peter there?'

This is also the usual way of forming yes-no questions in Maltese (Aquilina, 1965). A second common way of marking interrogation is by a change in word order. English, for example, uses a change in word order combined with rising intonation to indicate yes-no questions. Specifically, the subject of the corresponding declarative is permuted with the first element of the verb group (or with a specially inserted *do* if only the main verb is present).

(12) Can Johnny come out and play?
(13) Has the little boy finished his supper?
(14) Did she find her mother?

A third common device for marking yes-no questions is the insertion of a special question marker, often but not always at the beginning of the sentence. In Diegueño questions are marked by suffixing [a] to the last element of the predicate (Langdon, 1970).

(15) maač maayp-a
     you talk-INTERROGATIVE
     'Do you talk?'

Specification questions may be marked with the same devices, though rising intonation is less frequently associated with them than with yes-no questions. In addition, of course, specification questions can normally be identified by the presence of a special question word, like *who* or *why* in English. Example (16), from Lebanese Arabic (Koutsoudas, 1968), contains two question words.

(16) miin bihib miin 'Who likes whom?'

There is a tendency—a rule in many languages—for these question words to be moved to the beginning of the sentence. Thus *what* is sentence-initial in (17) even though it is the direct object of *say*.

(17) What did he say?

Further illustration of interrogative marking devices is provided by Indonesian (Kwee, 1965). Yes-no questions can be marked either by intonation alone or by the initial question particle *apa*. In addition, specification questions use special question words, some related in form to *apa*; these question words do not have to occur initially.

(18) kamu berenang
     you swim
     'Do you swim?'

(19) apa kamu gila
     INTERROGATIVE you crazy
     'Are you crazy?'

(20) kamu siapa
     you who
     'Who are you?'

Problem 3.5–4 Lushai

The following data (courtesy of William Bright) is from Lushai, a Tibeto-Burman language spoken in northeastern India. The diacritics [′ ‵ ˇ] mark tone (high, mid, and rising), and [ʔà] is a third person pronoun. On the basis of this data, describe the formation of yes-no questions in Lushai.

(1) ʔàkál	'He goes.'	(6) ʔàkálěm	'Does he go?'
(2) ʔàhláa	'It's far.'	(7) ʔàbéyěm	'Does it stick?'
(3) ʔàʔíněm	'Does he drink?'	(8) ʔàthíi	'He's dead.'
(4) ʔàthíiʔěm	'Is he dead?'	(9) ʔàhláaʔěm	'Is it far?'
(5) ʔàʔín	'He drinks.'	(10) ʔàbéy	'It sticks.'

Solution

Yes-no questions are formed by adding [ěm] or [ʔěm] as a suffix to the verb. The former is used when the verb ends in a consonant, and the latter when it ends in a vowel.

FURTHER PROBLEMS

Problem 3.5–5 Spanish

We have seen that one use of the passive in English is to make possible the omission of the nominal that would normally be the subject of a sentence; *Valuable jewels were stolen* is an example. A different way of avoiding the specification of the subject in Spanish is illustrated in the sentences below. Describe this syntactic device.

(1)	Se mató el hombre.	'The man killed himself.'
(2)	Se vió la mujer.	'The woman saw herself.'
(3)	Se mataron las mujeres.	'The women killed themselves.'
(4)	Se vieron los hombres.	'The men saw themselves.'
(5)	El hombre rompió la ventana.	'The man broke the window.'
(6)	La mujer rompió las ventanas.	'The woman broke the windows.'
(7)	La mujer tocó el timbre.	'The woman rang the bell.'
(8)	Los hombres tocaron el timbre.	'The men rang the bell.'
(9)	Se rompieron las ventanas.	'The windows were broken.'
(10)	Se rompió la ventana.	'The window was broken.'
(11)	*Se rompieron la ventana.	'The window were broken.'
(12)	Se tocó el timbre.	'The bell was rung.'
(13)	Se tocaron los timbres.	'The bells were rung.'
(14)	*Se tocaron el timbre.	'The bell were rung.'

Problem 3.5–6 Luiseño

Analyze the following sentences and describe the formation of questions in Luiseño.

(1)	hax ṣu ʔowoʔaq	'Who is working?'
(2)	hax ṣu ney naqmaq	'Who is listening to me?'
(3)	wunaalum hiš naqmawun	'They are listening to something.'
(4)	yaʔaš ṣu ney toowq	'Does the man see me?'
(5)	noo ʔowoʔaq	'I am working.'
(6)	hax ʔowoʔaq	'Someone is working.'
(7)	wunaal ṣu ʔaxiyi naqmaq	'Who is he listening to?'
(8)	wunaalum ṣum xaariwun	'Are they growling?'
(9)	noo ṣu ʔowoʔaq	'Am I working?'
(10)	hiiča ṣu xaariq	'What is growling?'
(11)	wunaal ʔaxiyi naqmaq	'He is listening to someone.'
(12)	yaʔaš ney toowq	'The man sees me.'
(13)	yaʔayčum ṣum ʔaxiyi toowwun	'Who do the men see?'
(14)	wunaalum xaariwun	'They are growling.'
(15)	wunaalum ṣum hiš naqmawun	'What are they listening to?'

(16) wunaal ṣu hiš toowq — 'What does he see?'
(17) hiiča xaariq — 'Something is growling.'
(18) hax ney naqmaq — 'Someone is listening to me.'
(19) yaʔayčum ʔaxiyi toowwun — 'The men see someone.'
(20) wunaal hiš toowq — 'He sees something.'

Problem 3.5–7   French

In Problem 3.2–5 we saw that a rearrangement rule of French transports an object pronoun, with or without a preposition, from its original position after the verb into pre-verbal position. The following data illustrates the interaction of this rule with a rule that specifies the surface form of imperatives. Describe these two rules and determine the order in which they must apply.

(1) Vous travaillez. — 'You are working.'
(2) Regardez-le! — 'Look at him!'
(3) Parlez de cela! — 'Talk about that!'
(4) Vous parlerez de cela. — 'You will talk about that.'
(5) Je regarde Pierre. — 'I am looking at Peter.'
(6) Vous travaillerez. — 'You will work.'
(7) Parlez-en! — 'Talk about it!'
(8) Ne travaillez pas! — 'Don't work!'
(9) Vous le regardez. — 'You are looking at him.'
(10) Ne regardez pas Pierre! — 'Don't look at Peter!'
(11) *Le regardez! — 'Look at him!'
(12) Vous ne parlez pas de cela. — 'You are not talking about that.'
(13) Vous regarderez Pierre. — 'You will look at Peter.'
(14) Je travaille. — 'I am working.'
(15) Travaillez! — 'Work!'
(16) Vous ne regardez pas Pierre. — 'You are not looking at Peter.'
(17) *En parlez! — 'Talk about it!'
(18) Je parle de cela. — 'I am talking about that.'
(19) Vous en parlez. — 'You are talking about it.'
(20) Ne le regardez pas! — 'Don't look at him!'
(21) Regardez Pierre! — 'Look at Peter!'
(22) N'en parlez pas! — 'Don't talk about it!'
(23) Vous ne travaillez pas. — 'You are not working.'
(24) Ne parlez pas de cela! — 'Don't talk about that!'

Problem 3.5–8   Mandarin Chinese

Examine the following sentences (Elliott, 1965, and Wang, 1965). Isolate the morphemes and state their meanings. Describe the formation of alternative questions and yes-no questions (a special case of alternative questions) in Mandarin.

(1) nǐ bù qù
'You are not going.'

(2) nǐ hǎo
'You are well.'

(3) nǐ qù kàn diànyǐng háishi qù mǎi dōngxi
'Are you going to see the movie or going to buy things?'

(4) nǐ máng bu máng
'Are you busy (or not)?'

(5) tā kàn wǒde shū bu kàn wǒde shū
'Is he reading (= seeing) my book (or not)?'

(6) nǐ hǎo ma
'Are you well?'

(7) tā lái le ma
'Did he come?'

(8) tā míngtian kàn shū ma
'Will he read (= see) the book tomorrow?'

(9) nǐ dào túshūguǎn qù háishi bù qù
'Are you going to the library (or not)?'

(10) tā mǎi shū bu mǎi shū
'Does he buy books (or not)?'

(11) nǐ kàn shū háishi kàn bào
'Are you reading (= seeing) the book or reading (= seeing)
  the newspaper?'

(12) nǐ lái bu lái
'Are you coming (or not)?'

(13) nǐ lèi ma
'Are you tired?'

(14) tā bu mǎi shū
'He doesn't buy books.'

(15) nǐ kàn shū kàn bào
'Are you reading (= seeing) the book or reading (= seeing)
  the newspaper?'

(16) nǐ gēn wǒ lái ma
'Are you coming with me?'

(17) tā lái bu lái
'Is he coming (or not)?'

(18) nǐ lái háishi bu lái
'Are you coming (or not)?'

(19) tā kàn shū le ma
'Did he read (= see) the book?'

(20) nǐ qù kàn diànyǐng ma
'Are you going to see the movie?'

(21) nǐ lèi bu lèi
'Are you tired (or not)?'

(22) tā mǎi shū bu mǎi
'Does he buy books (or not)?'

(23) tā kàn bu kàn wǒde shū
'Is he reading (= seeing) my book (or not)?'

(24) tā lái ma
'Is he coming?'

(25) tā kàn wǒde shū bu kàn
'Is he reading (= seeing) my book (or not)?'

(26) tā mǎi shū
'He buys books.'

(27) tā mǎi bu mǎi shū
'Does he buy books (or not)?'

3.6 Nominal Elements

The terms *nominal* and *noun phrase* are used more or less interchangeably in modern linguistics. The latter is an unfortunate term, since it is used to designate clauses and single words as well as phrases; in fact, some noun phrases do not even contain nouns (for example, *the rich*). The defining properties of a nominal or noun phrase pertain to syntactic function rather than internal structure. The most important of these properties is perhaps the ability to function as a subject or object. The existence of syntactic rules that can apply to any of the elements referred to as nominals, but to no other constituents, can sometimes be adduced as further justification for grouping together disparate elements under this rubric.

The internal composition of noun phrases shows considerable variety. Some noun phrases, such as *I* or *him*, consist of only a pronoun. More typically, a nominal consists of a head noun flanked by modifiers of various sorts; examples are *Ralph's house in the country* and *seven towering old oaks that had been ravaged by the elements, woodpeckers, and time itself*. In section 3.4 we saw that some nominals—for example, *that Henry forgot his pajamas*—lack a head noun and consist of only a clause. There are also nominals that seem to combine properties of the last two types. For instance, *Ralph's construction of the dam* is quite parallel in terms of surface structure to *Ralph's house in the country*. They both contain a head noun (*house* or *construction*) preceded by a possessive modifier and followed by a prepositional phrase modifier. At the same time, *Ralph's construction of the dam* is very similar semantically, and to some degree syntactically, to the clause *(that) Ralph construct(ed) the dam*. One controversial analysis of such nominals holds that they derive by transformation from underlying clauses. *Ralph's construction of the dam* would thus be considered a **nominalization** of the underlying clause *(that) Ralph construct(ed) the dam*.

NOMINAL MODIFIERS

In the following discussion we will be primarily concerned with noun phrases that consist of a head noun and various sorts of modifiers. Let us first consider **determiners**, a class of modifiers that includes **articles** (for example, *a* and *the*), **demonstratives** (*this, that*), and **quantifiers** (*many, seven*). A fundamental distinction can be made between **definite** and **indefinite** determiners (or between definite and indefinite nominals). Roughly speaking, a definite determiner is appropriate when the speaker presupposes (that is, takes for granted) that the identity of the object or individual being referred to is apparent both to him and to the hearer. For example, *the* is definite and *a* is indefinite. Sentence (1) would be appropriate if both the speaker and the hearer had a particular elephant in mind.

> (1) The elephant is tied up out back.

(If the speaker were wrong in this presupposition, the hearer might reply *What elephant?*) On the other hand, (2) does not presuppose any previous knowledge by the speaker or hearer of the identity or existence of the elephant (rather this sentence asserts its existence).

> (2) An elephant is tied up out back.

The semantic distinction between definite and indefinite nominals is probably valid for all languages, though the distinction is not always marked overtly in any obvious way, as it is in English by the contrasting articles *a* and *the*. Indeed, many languages lack articles entirely. Luiseño, for example, has no articles, and a noun phrase consisting of just a noun may be translated with either 'a' or 'the' in English; thus [yaʔaš] can mean either 'a man' or 'the man'. In languages that do have articles, the article is sometimes an affix on the head noun rather than a separate word. Turkish is an interesting example (Lewis, 1953). The indefinite article [bir] is the same as the word for 'one' (this is true in many languages) and precedes the head noun: [bir adam] can thus mean either 'a man' or 'one man'. As we might expect, this article is not used with plural nouns. Hence the form for 'men' is [adamlar], with no overt article ([lar] is the plural morpheme). The definite article in Turkish is [i] or [ɨ], depending on vowel harmony (see Problem 2.1–4, p. 45), but it occurs only with direct objects, where it shows up as a suffix. The plural form [adamlar] can therefore be translated as 'the men' as well as 'men' if it functions as a subject. The direct object form [adamɨ] means 'the man', while [adamlarɨ] means 'the men'.

Many languages lack overt articles, but it is perhaps true that no language lacks demonstratives or quantifiers. Demonstratives are modifiers that can be used in pointing things out, such as *this* and *that* in English. Because of their meaning, demonstratives are always definite. Quantifiers, as the name implies, are modifiers that pertain to quantity in some way. Representative examples from English are *some, all, many, several, one, three, much,* and *few.* Quantifiers can sometimes occur with definite determiners, as in *the few books that I managed to read last winter,* but they themselves are indefinite. Nominals that have no determiner other than a quantifier (for example, *several crocodiles*) are therefore indefinite as well. Some quantifiers can occur in surface structure as predicates, as in sentence (4) below, which has approximately the same meaning as (3).

(3) I read many books last winter.
(4) The books that I read last winter are many.

It has been suggested that all quantifiers originate as predicates in under-lying structure—that is, that (4) or some similar structure underlies (3)—but this proposal is highly controversial.

In addition to determiners, noun modifiers include phrases, relative clauses, and single-word modifiers such as possessives and adjectives. Relative clauses were discussed extensively in section 3.4, and we will not deal with them separately here. However, relative clauses are believed by many linguists to be the source of many (if not all) modifying phrases and words. In Problem 3.5–2, for instance, we found reason to believe that (5) is a reduced form of (6), just as (7) is a reduced form of (8); (5) and (7) have modifying phrases, while (6) and (8) are modified by relative clauses.

(5) the girl with a green sweater on
(6) the girl who has a green sweater on
(7) the meadowlark in the attic
(8) the meadowlark that is in the attic

Similarly, adjectival modifiers can be viewed as reduced relative clauses, as in the following derivations.

those men who are anxious for work ⇒ those men anxious for work

a girl who is homely ⇒ a girl homely ⇒ a homely girl

As these derivations show, a simple adjective is moved before the noun in English, but an adjectival phrase usually remains after the noun.

Possessives too may derive from modifying clauses. For example, expression (9) or something similar might be proposed as the source of (10).

    (9) the car that is mine
   (10) my car

It is not known whether all modifiers such as these are correctly regarded as reduced modifying clauses.

Problem 3.6–1   Igbo

The expressions below (Welmers, 1969) are from Igbo (also spelled Ibo), a Niger-Congo language spoken in Nigeria. The diacritics [′ `] stand for high and low tone respectively. Determine the meaning of each form. Describe the types of noun modifiers present in the data and their position with respect to one another and to the head noun.

  (1) úgbó óhúrú   'a new car'
  (2) ŋwáànyì áhù   'that woman'
  (3) éwú átó   'three goats'
  (4) m̀mánú áhù dúm̀ 'all that oil'
  (5) úló à   'this house'
  (6) ócé ŋké átó   'the third chair'
  (7) ùwé dí ójí   'a suit which is black'
  (8) ósísí dí ógólógó 'a tree which is tall'
  (9) éféré úkwú   'a large plate'
 (10) ócé átó   'three chairs'
 (11) ótútú íkó   'a lot of cups'
 (12) éféré ócá   'a white plate'
 (13) ńrí dí ókú   'food which is hot'
 (14) m̀mádù níílé   'every person'
 (15) úgbó dí óhúrú 'a car which is new'
 (16) úlò ŋké átó   'the third house'
 (17) ùfódú úlò   'some houses'
 (18) ńrí dí útó   'food which is delicious'
 (19) ócé átó áhù   'those three chairs'
 (20) íkó úkwú   'a large cup'
 (21) m̀mádù dúm̀   'all the people'

Solution

'goat' = éwú	'three' = átő
'chair' = ócé	'a lot' = őtűtű
'house' = űlǒ, űló	'some' = ùfődű
'cup' = íkó	'this' = à
'person' = m̀mádǔ	'that' = áhǔ
'oil' = m̀mánű	'all' = dúm̀
'woman' = ŋwáànyì	'every' = níílé
'tree' = ósísí	'which is' = dí
'food' = ńrí	'tall' = ógólógó
'car' = űgbő	'hot' = őkű
'plate' = éféré	'delicious' = űtő
'suit' = ùwé	'large' = úkwú
'new' = őhűrű	'white' = őcá
'black' = ójí	'ORDINAL' = ŋ̀ké

The singular-plural distinction is not marked in the data, nor is any article represented. Of the noun modifiers illustrated, only the quantifiers [őtűtű] 'a lot' and [ùfődű] 'some' precede the head noun; all the others follow. Besides modifying clauses consisting of [dí] plus an adjective, the post-nominal modifiers include the following: simple adjectives; the demonstratives [à] 'this' and [áhǔ] 'that'; and the quantifiers [dúm̀] 'all', [níílé] 'every', and [átő] 'three'. When [ŋ̀ké] is inserted between the head noun and a numeral, the numeral has the semantic value of an ordinal rather than a cardinal number ('the third' rather than 'three'). From expressions (4) and (19), it appears that demonstratives follow numerals but precede other quantifiers.

Problem 3.6–2 English

Examine the possessive expressions below. Propose a source for the (f) expressions and motivate it with syntactic and semantic evidence.

(1) (a) a book of John's
    (b) that book of John's
    (c) this book of John's
    (d) some book of John's
    (e) *the book of John's
    (f) John's book
(2) (a) a dream of his
    (b) that dream of his
    (c) this dream of his
    (d) some dream of his
    (e) *the dream of his
    (f) his dream

(3) (a) a doll of Sue's
    (b) that doll of Sue's
    (c) this doll of Sue's
    (d) some doll of Sue's
    (e) *the doll of Sue's
    (f) Sue's doll

Solution

The ungrammatical (e) expressions can be postulated as the source for the possessive expressions in (f). If an obligatory rule converts (e) to (f), the ungrammaticality of the former in surface structure is explained. This analysis is syntactically advantageous, for the ungrammaticality of the (e) expressions is otherwise quite surprising. The nominals in (a)–(d) show that a determiner, whether definite or indefinite, can precede sequences of the form *N of NP's*. The ungrammaticality of the (e) expressions thus constitutes a gap in an otherwise regular pattern, and this irregularity is eliminated if the nominals in (f) are analyzed as the surface manifestations of the (e) structures. The analysis is tenable on semantic grounds as well, since the (e) and (f) expressions are semantically equivalent. In particular, the (f) expressions share the presupposition normally associated with the definite article *the*. For instance, when someone uses the phrase *John's book*, he is taking it for granted that he and the hearer have a particular book of John's in mind.

NOMINAL TRAPPINGS

— *do not have semantic values in themself*
∴ *are inserted by transformation.*

Nominals are involved in several different ways with syntactic rules that insert sentence trappings. As we have seen in various problems, it is extremely common for the predicate of a sentence to agree with its subject and objects in regard to number, person, gender, and other categories. By the same token, it is common for the nominals of a clause to bear markings that indicate their syntactic function with respect to the predicate. Inflections, affixes, and special particles such as prepositions indicate whether a nominal functions as a subject, a direct object, or an oblique object. To some extent, these markings are independent of the particular predicate of the clause containing the nominal in question. In English, for example, the third person singular masculine pronoun is always *he* (never *him*) when it functions as a subject in surface structure, regardless of what predicate follows. However, the trappings induced on a nominal are sometimes determined idiosyncratically by the predicate, particularly in regard to object nominals. The fact that we say *hopes for rain* but not **wants for rain* reflects essentially arbitrary syntactic properties of the verbs *hope* and *want*, not any general principle.

External / internal — shows relationship in reference to something else in sentence

The trappings described in the previous paragraph pertain to external relations between a nominal and the clause in which it functions. Rules that insert trappings on nominals on the basis of their internal relations are also quite common. Some of these rules are agreement rules. The modifiers of a noun, especially articles, demonstratives, and adjectives, often agree with it in number, gender, case, or other categories. We saw in Problem 2.2–10 (p. 70) that an adjective in Swahili takes the same prefix as the noun it modifies. Spanish articles and adjectives agree with their head noun in gender and number, as illustrated in Problem 3.2–3. Problem 3.4–14 shows that articles are inflected for case to agree with their head nouns in modern Greek. Examples like these could easily be multiplied.

Not all the trappings induced on nominals on the basis of internal relations are inserted by agreement rules. In Aztec, for example, the particle [in] can optionally be inserted as the first element of virtually any nominal; [in] can be regarded as an article, but it occurs with both definite and indefinite nominals and is probably a meaningless trapping. A syntactic rule of English inserts *of* between the head noun of a nominal and a modifying noun phrase that immediately follows it, as in Figure 3.6–1. This rule accounts for the *of* that appears in nominalizations such as (1) and (2).

(1) the construction of a new office building
(2) his refusal of the offer

Figure 3.6–1

It also accounts for the *of* which appears in possessive expressions of the sort discussed in Problem 3.6–2 above. *A book of John's*, for instance, has the derivation shown below; the two rules involved in this derivation are the reduction of relative clauses (see Problem 3.5–2) and the insertion of *of*.

a book which is John's ⇒ a book John's ⇒ a book of John's

John's book carries the derivation one step further, as argued in Problem 3.6–2.

the book which is John's ⇒ the book John's ⇒ the book of John's ⇒ John's book

Rules analogous to *of* insertion are perhaps responsible for marking possessor noun phrases with a special **genitive** case in those languages that express possession by means of case inflection.

Problem 3.6–3 Russian

On the basis of the sentences below, describe the marking of nominals in Russian with respect to their syntactic function.

(1) gosty znaet ženščinu   'The guest knows the woman.'
(2) doktor znaet babušku   'The doctor knows the grandmother.'
(3) ženščina vidyit doktora   'The woman sees the doctor.'
(4) babuška vidyit doktora   'The grandmother sees the doctor.'
(5) doktor vidyit gostya   'The doctor sees the guest.'
(6) ženščina znaet gostya   'The woman knows the guest.'
(7) gosty vidyit babušku   'The guest sees the grandmother.'
(8) babuška znaet ženščinu   'The grandmother knows the woman.'

Solution

The nominals illustrated in the data fall into two classes in regard to their marking for case. One class is represented by the forms for 'guest' and 'doctor'. In the subject (or nominative) case, these forms end in a consonant. In the direct object (or accusative) case, the ending [a] is added. The other class is represented by the forms for 'woman' and 'grandmother'. These forms end in [a] in the nominative case. In the accusative case, [a] is replaced by [u].

		Nominative	*Accusative*
Class I	'guest'	gosty	gostya
	'doctor'	doktor	doktora
Class II	'woman'	ženščina	ženščinu
	'grandmother'	babuška	babušku

Problem 3.6–4 Luiseño

Describe the agreement exhibited by the Luiseño nominals listed below. Included are direct objects (labeled "object") and various kinds of oblique objects.

(1) kiik xwaayaanik   'to the white house'
(2) muuta paapaviš   'the thirsty owl'
(3) ʔawaali xwaayaanti   'the white dog' (object)
(4) tooŋay yawaywiŋay   'from the pretty rock'
(5) kičam yawaywičum   'the pretty houses'
(6) muutam paapavičum   'the thirsty owls'
(7) toota yawaywiš   'the pretty rock'

(8) Pawaalumi paapavičumi	'the thirsty dogs' (object)
(9) tootal xwaayaantal	'with the white rock'
(10) kiča yawaywiš	'the pretty house'
(11) muutami yawaywičumi	'the pretty owls' (object)
(12) kiŋa yawaywiŋa	'in the pretty house'
(13) Pawaal paapaviš	'the thirsty dog'
(14) tootam yawaywičum	'the pretty rocks'
(15) kiŋay yawaywiŋay	'from the pretty house'
(16) Pawaalum yawaywičum	'the pretty dogs'

Solution

Adjectives agree with the nouns they modify in regard to number and object case. On both nouns and adjectives, plurality is indicated by the suffix [um], which has the variant [m] after vowels. Object case is marked by the suffix [i], which follows the plural ending if both are present.

Adjectives also agree with the nouns they modify in regard to the postpositions [ik] 'to', [ŋa] 'in', [ŋay] 'from', and [tal] 'with'; these postpositions occur as suffixes on nouns and adjectives.

Discussion

When the suffix [um] or [i] is added to an adjective that ends in [š], this [š] is replaced by [č]. In the data presented, [š] appears only in word-final position and [č] appears only before a vowel. The alternation between [š] and [č] may therefore reflect the operation of a general phonological principle.

In addition to this phonological alternation, a certain amount of morphological variation attends the addition of suffixes to noun and adjective stems. Four stems have special short forms that are used with postpositions: [yawaywiš] 'pretty', [kiča] 'house', [toota] 'rock', and [xwaayaant] 'white' shorten to [yawaywi], [ki], [too], and [xwaayaan] respectively when a postposition is added. The other stems are not exemplified with postpositions.

The suffix [ŋay] 'from' should possibly be analyzed as a complex postposition consisting of [ŋa] 'in' plus a second postposition [y] (compare Problem 2.2–9, Turkish, p. 69); the data is insufficient to determine whether this analysis is correct. In (9) [al] rather than [tal] could be analyzed as the postposition meaning 'with'. However, this would entail a complication of the rule that specifies the short forms of noun and adjective stems. It would require a special statement to the effect that [xwaayaant] does not shorten to [xwaayaan] when the postposition to be added is 'with'. It would also require a special statement that [toota] shortens to [toot] (rather than [too]) before this postposition. These irregularities are avoided if [tal] rather than [al] is posited as the postposition meaning 'with'.

FURTHER PROBLEMS

Problem 3.6–5   French

Examine the data from French below. Propose an analysis for the (c) and (d) expressions. The (e) sentences illustrate the use of the (d) expressions in full sentences (compare Problem 3.2–1).

(1) (a) le livre qui est sur la table
'the book that is on the table'

    (b) le livre sur la table
'the book on the table'

(2) (a) la maison qui est à côté du lac
'the house that is beside the lake'

    (b) la maison à côté du lac
'the house beside the lake'

(3) (a) Le livre rouge est plus joli que le livre vert.
'The red book is prettier than the green book.'

    (b) Le livre rouge est plus joli que le vert.
'The red book is prettier than the green one.'

(4) (a) La maison rouge est plus jolie que la maison verte.
'The red house is prettier than the green house.'

    (b) La maison rouge est plus jolie que la verte.
'The red house is prettier than the green one.'

(5) (a) un livre qui est à moi
'a book that is mine'

    (b) un livre à moi
'a book of mine'

(6) (a) le livre qui est à moi
'the book that is mine'

    (b) *le livre à moi
'the book of mine'

    (c) mon livre
'my book'

    (d) le mien
'mine'

    (e) Ce livre est plus joli que le mien.
'This book is prettier than mine.'

(7) (a) une maison qui est à moi
'a house that is mine'

    (b) une maison à moi
'a house of mine'

(8) (a) la maison qui est à moi
'the house that is mine'
(b) *la maison à moi
'the house of mine'
(c) ma maison
'my house'
(d) la mienne
'mine'
(e) Cette maison est plus jolie que la mienne.
'This house is prettier than mine.'

Problem 3.6–6   Luiseño

Examine the expressions below and describe the formation of Luiseño possessives.

(1)	čamʔaačum ʔanom	'our coyotes'
(2)	yaʔayčum pomki	'the men's house'
(3)	čamyu	'our hair'
(4)	poki	'his house'
(5)	kiča	'the house'
(6)	yaʔaš pokaamayum pomkaytu poʔaačum ʔawaalum	'the man's sons' enemy's dogs'
(7)	yaʔaš pokaytum pomki	'the man's enemies' house'
(8)	noʔaačum ʔawaalum	'my dogs'
(9)	pomyu	'their hair'
(10)	noki	'my house'
(11)	yula	'the hair'
(12)	yaʔaš poki	'the man's house'
(13)	šuṣṇalum pomkaamayum pomki	'the women's sons' house'
(14)	noʔaaš ʔawaal	'my dog'
(15)	yaʔaš pokaytu poyu	'the man's enemy's hair'
(16)	čamʔaaš ʔano	'our coyote'
(17)	noyu	'my hair'
(18)	pomki	'their house'
(19)	šuṇaal pokaamay poyu	'the woman's son's hair'
(20)	šuṇaal pokaytum pomʔaaš ʔawaal	'the woman's enemies' dog'
(21)	poyu	'his hair'
(22)	čamki	'our house'

Problem 3.6–7   Latin

In sentences containing a subject, a verb, and one object, most Latin verbs require that the object be marked for accusative case. However, some verbs govern instead another case called the "dative", among them the verb meaning 'please'. Examine the sentences below and state the rules that determine nominal and verbal inflection. Summarize the inflectional endings in a table analogous to the one in Problem 3.6–3.

(1) Amīcus bonus puellae beātae placet.
    'The good friend pleases the happy girl.'

(2) Dominī beātī rēgīnam bonam audiunt.
    'The happy masters hear the good queen.'

(3) Puellae beātae rēgīnīs bonīs placent.
    'The happy girls please the good queens.'

(4) Dominus beātus rēgīnās bonās audit.
    'The happy master hears the good queens.'

(5) Rēgīna beāta amīcōs bonōs audit.
    'The happy queen hears the good friends.'

(6) Amīcī bonī dominīs beātīs placent.
    'The good friends please the happy masters.'

(7) Rēgīnae bonae dominō beātō placent.
    'The good queens please the happy master.'

(8) Puella bona amīcum bonum audit.
    'The good girl hears the good friend.'

(9) Dominī beātī amīcō bonō placent.
    'The happy masters please the good friend.'

(10) Amīcus beātus puellam beātam audit.
    'The happy friend hears the happy girl.'

(11) Rēgīnae beātae dominōs beātōs audiunt.
    'The happy queens hear the happy masters.'

(12) Dominus bonus puellīs beātīs placet.
    'The good master pleases the happy girls.'

(13) Puella beāta amīcīs bonīs placet.
    'The happy girl pleases the good friends.'

(14) Rēgīna bona puellās beātās audit.
    'The good queen hears the happy girls.'

(15) Puellae bonae dominum beātum audiunt.
    'The good girls hear the happy master.'

(16) Amīcī bonī rēgīnae bonae placent.
    'The good friends please the good queen.'

Problem 3.6–8   *Classical Aztec*

PART A Describe the syntax of noun modifiers in Classical Aztec as exemplified below. In addition to the rule that inserts [in], one transformation is needed.

(1)	nonakayo	'my body'
(2)	inin siwaλ	'this woman'
(3)	in siwaλ	'the woman'
(4)	inin paλi	'this medicine'
(5)	siwaλ	'the woman'
(6)	yewantin	'they'
(7)	in yewaλ	'he, she'
(8)	ipepeč	'his, her bed'
(9)	inon siwaλ	'that woman'
(10)	inakayo	'his, her body'
(11)	in paλi in	'this medicine'
(12)	yewaλ	'he, she'
(13)	in newaλ	'I'
(14)	siwaλ on	'that woman'
(15)	nopepeč	'my bed'
(16)	inin aλ	'this water'
(17)	newaλ	'I'

PART B Expressions (18)–(25) point to the existence of two further syntactic rules of Aztec. Formulate these two rules.

(18)	ipan	'on him, her, it'
(19)	apan	'on the water'
(20)	nopan	'on me'
(21)	in tolteka yewantin λayakana	'The Toltecs took the lead.'
(22)	in yewantin tolteka λayakana	'The Toltecs took the lead.'
(23)	aλ ipan	'on the water'
(24)	in tolteka λayakana	'The Toltecs took the lead.'
(25)	ipan aλ	'on the water'

PART C The five nominals in (26) are paraphrases, as are the five nominals in (27). Presumably the members of each set all reflect the same underlying structure. Can you explain the surface variation? What new rules are needed to account for the data? Comment on rule ordering. Show the derivations of (26) (b) and (27) (d).

(26)	(a)	inin siwaλ inakayo	
	(b)	in siwaλ in inakayo	
	(c)	siwaλ in inakayo	'this woman's body'
	(d)	in inakayo in siwaλ	
	(e)	inakayo in siwaλ	

(27) (a) inin okičλi ipepeč
    (b) in okičλi in ipepeč
    (c) okičλi in ipepeč   } 'this man's bed'
    (d) in ipepeč in okičλi
    (e) ipepeč in okičλi

3.7 Verbal Elements

Most clauses in surface structure contain more than one element that can reasonably be regarded as deriving from a semantic predicate. One of these elements can typically be designated on semantic or structural grounds as the principal verb (or adjective) of the clause. Such an element will be referred to here as the **main verb** (or adjective). (In this use of the term, a main verb is not necessarily non-subordinate—both subordinate and non-subordinate clauses have main verbs.) The remaining semantic predicates often mark tense, aspect, or modality, and they have varying surface manifestations within the clause. Sometimes they are realized as separate verb-like entities, called **auxiliary verbs**, that accompany the main verb. They can also appear as separate words or particles of a non-verbal character. Finally, they can be included among the many markings often borne by the main verb of a clause.

TENSE, ASPECT, AND MODALITY

The distinction between **tense** and **aspect** is subtle, and in practice it is sometimes quite difficult to make. Basically, tense refers to the time of an event, while aspect refers to the inception, duration, or completion of an event. Tense is often expressed by means of a verbal affix, but it can also be expressed as a separate word. In Problem 3.4–15, for example, we saw that tense can be expressed as a separate word in Samoan.

The names traditionally associated with tenses are fairly descriptive of their meanings—present, past, future, remote past, remote future, and so on. However, these names can sometimes be misleading. The English "present" tense, for instance, generally describes usual, habitual, or "generic" activities rather than activities concurrent with the utterance of the sentence; (1) is an example.

    (1) The owner of this tenement sings in the shower.

To describe an action taking place at the time of the utterance, the English "present" tense is used in combination with the aspect marker *be...ing*, as in (2).

    (2) The owner of this tenement is singing in the shower.

Furthermore, languages do not always neatly categorize tenses into past, present, and future, as we might expect. Many languages distinguish only between past and non-past, or between future and non-future. In fact, it might be argued that English distinguishes only between past and non-past tense. The present tense inflection is not restricted to indicating present activity, as we have seen, and it might best be labeled non-past; moreover, the future marker *will* might best be regarded as a modal rather than a tense marker. Notice that the English "present" tense can describe future events, and that the "future" *will* does not necessarily express future time.

(3) She leaves tomorrow.
(4) Zinc will dissolve in hydrochloric acid.

As mentioned above, aspect refers to the inception, duration, or completion of an event. The English auxiliary verbs *have* and *be* function as aspect markers, as do their counterparts in many other languages (compare Problem 2.4–2, p. 88). *Have*, which indicates the completion of an action or the achievement of a state, induces a past participial ending (usually *ed* or *en*) on the verb that follows, as in sentences (5) and (6).

(5) So they have finally succeeded!
(6) Sally has been pregnant before.

Be, on the other hand, combines with *ing* to indicate ongoing activity, as in sentence (2) above. Other aspectual notions are marked by main verbs in English, among them *start, finish, continue, keep,* and *stop*. A wide array of aspectual notions similar to these are specially marked in various languages of the world.

Modality pertains to truth, possibility, probability, necessity, and kindred notions. The modality of a proposition is often expressed by a main verb or an adjective, with the proposition functioning as its subject. Sentences (7)–(9) are typical examples.

(7) That he tried to bribe me is true.
(8) That we will all fail this course is likely.
(9) For anyone to solve this problem in only seven hours is impossible.

Negation pertains to truth and hence qualifies as a modal element on semantic grounds, although the particle *not* is non-verbal in surface structure. In addition, English has a special set of modal auxiliaries that precede both the main verb of a clause and the aspectual verbs *have* and *be*. These include *can, shall, will, may,* and *must*; all but *must* have a "past tense" form (*could, should, would, might*). Sentences (10)–(12), which consist of one clause each in surface structure, are examples.

(10) We must get there before closing time.

(11) Shelley could have been singing in the shower.
(12) They may have left already.

In English, as in many other languages, modals are notorious for the multiplicity, variability, and subtlety of their meanings.

On the basis of their semantic relationship to the rest of the sentence, tense, aspect, and modality are most plausibly analyzed as separate predicates at the level of propositional structure. Sentence (13), for example, may have a semantic representation analogous to Figure 3.7–1.

(13) They can be working.

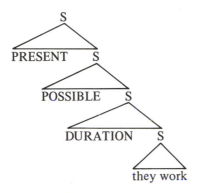

Figure 3.7–1

The predicate *PRESENT* surfaces as present tense inflection (zero in (13)); *POSSIBLE* is realized as the modal *can;* and *DURATION* is manifested as the aspect marker *be...ing*. As we see from this example, it is possible for an apparently simple sentence, one having only a single clause in surface structure, to derive from a complex underlying representation involving numerous propositions.

Underlying representations such as Figure 3.7–1 seem to reflect properly the semantic relation between tense, aspect, and modality and the propositions they qualify. If so, structures analogous to it are probably appropriate for the description of all languages. However, the surface manifestation of tense, aspect, and modality is subject to considerable variation. As we have seen, these elements may be expressed as main verbs, as verbal affixes, or as auxiliary verbs. Thus in English, tense (past versus non-past) surfaces as verbal inflection, while aspect and modality are realized either as auxiliary verbs (such as *have, be, must, can,* and *will*) or as main verbs or adjectives (such as *start, keep,* and *possible*).

The verbal character of auxiliary verbs is usually quite clear, but at the same time they tend to have very special syntactic properties and can normally be used only under the aegis of an accompanying main verb. In many languages the auxiliary verb rather than the main verb is inflected for tense and for agreement with the subject or object. In English, for instance, the first auxiliary verb in the verb group is inflected for tense and subject agreement; the main verb is inflected only if no auxiliary verb is present (compare (1), (2), (6), and (11) above).

There is also a tendency for tense and subject agreement to be marked on the first or second constituent of a clause. Thus the inflected auxiliary verb normally appears directly after the subject noun phrase in English; moreover, when some other constituent is advanced to the beginning of a clause, the subject is often permuted with the inflected auxiliary so that the latter remains in second position.

(14) He is working.
(15) Why is he working?

In Papago (see Problems 2.2–4, p. 6$\bar{1}$, and 3.4–3), a special auxiliary constituent marks tense and subject agreement; this constituent is normally the second in a clause, despite other fluctuations in word order.

(16) Ɂaañi Ɂañ čikpan

I I PRESENT work
'I am working.'

(17) čikpan Ɂañ

work I PRESENT
'I am working.'

As we saw in Problem 3.4–15, tense is marked in Samoan by a special particle that occurs in clause-initial position or in second position (after a topicalized nominal). In the latter case, this marker sometimes has a special form that "agrees with" the topicalized noun phrase:

(18) e mana'o le tama i le teine
PRESENT want the boy CASE the girl
'The boy wants the girl.'

(19) ou te mana'o i le teine
I PRESENT want CASE the girl
'I want the girl.'

The special importance of second position in a clause is further illustrated by Luiseño (see Problem 3.2–12), in which an affix that marks subject agreement may be suffixed to the first word in a sentence. Tense and modality are marked in a similar way in Luiseño.

Problem 3.7–1   German

Discuss the syntax of verbal elements in German, as revealed in the data that follows.

(1)	(a)	Ich sehe den Mann.	'I see the man.'
	(b)	Er sieht den Mann.	'He sees the man.'
(2)	(a)	Ich sah den Mann.	'I saw the man.'
	(b)	Er sah den Mann.	'He saw the man.'
(3)	(a)	Ich habe den Mann gesehen.	'I have seen the man.'
	(b)	Er hat den Mann gesehen.	'He has seen the man.'
(4)	(a)	Ich hatte den Mann gesehen.	'I had seen the man.'
	(b)	Er hatte den Mann gesehen.	'He had seen the man.'
(5)	(a)	Ich werde den Mann sehen.	'I will see the man.'
	(b)	Er wird den Mann sehen.	'He will see the man.'
(6)	(a)	Ich will den Mann sehen.	'I want to see the man.'
	(b)	Er will den Mann sehen.	'He wants to see the man.'
(7)	(a)	Ich wollte den Mann sehen.	'I wanted to see the man.'
	(b)	Er wollte den Mann sehen.	'He wanted to see the man.'
(8)	(a)	Ich kann den Mann sehen.	'I can see the man.'
	(b)	Er kann den Mann sehen.	'He can see the man.'
(9)	(a)	Ich konnte den Mann sehen.	'I could see the man.'
	(b)	Er konnte den Mann sehen.	'He could see the man.'
(10)	(a)	Ich habe den Mann sehen wollen.	'I have wanted to see the man.'
	(b)	Er hat den Mann sehen wollen.	'He has wanted to see the man.'
(11)	(a)	Ich habe den Mann sehen können.	'I have been able to see the man.'
	(b)	Er hat den Mann sehen können.	'He has been able to see the man.'
(12)	(a)	Ich hatte den Mann sehen wollen.	'I had wanted to see the man.'
	(b)	Er hatte den Mann sehen wollen.	'He had wanted to see the man.'

Solution

A clause contains a main verb with or without accompanying auxiliary verbs. In (1) and (2), which have no auxiliary verbs, the main verb is inflected for tense and subject agreement, and it occurs in second position. The distinction between first and third person singular is marked in the present tense (*sehe* versus *sieht*), but there is no overt distinction in the past (*sah* for both).

In the data presented, one or two auxiliary verbs can optionally accompany the main verb. With one of these auxiliaries, the aspect marker 'have', the main verb appears as *gesehen* (the past participial form). With the others, the main verb appears as *sehen* (the infinitival form). Having the meanings 'will', 'want', and 'can', this class of auxiliary verbs can reasonably be regarded as modals.

When one auxiliary verb is present, it is inflected for tense and subject agreement and occurs in second position, with the main verb transposed to the end of the clause. As with the main verb, the distinction between first and third person singular is not marked overtly in the past tense form of the auxiliary; it is not marked at all for the modals 'can' and 'want'.

The only combinations of auxiliary verbs illustrated in the data are the aspect marker 'have' plus the modals 'want' and 'can'. When these combinations occur, 'have' is inflected for tense and subject agreement and occurs in second position. 'Want' and 'can' assume the respective forms *wollen* and *können* (the infinitival forms) and are moved to the end of the clause, where they follow the main verb.

Problem 3.7–2   Diegueño

A wide array of predicates appear as auxiliary verbs in the languages of the world. Among these predicates are a number of verbs that function as the main verb in clauses. When used as an auxiliary, such a verb does not always retain the meaning it has when it functions as a main verb, or it may retain this meaning only by metaphorical extension. (In English, for instance, the verb *have* as an aspect marker does not literally imply possession.) Consequently, a sentence containing an auxiliary verb may have a less specific or less vivid meaning than a literal, morpheme-by-morpheme translation might make it appear.

Among the auxiliary elements of Diegueño are the following (with literal translations): [yiiw] 'come', [ʔaa] 'go', [yak] 'lie', [yuu] 'stand', [waa] 'sit', [kwaa] 'make noise', and [paa] 'be there'. Their use is illustrated in the sentences below (Baker, 1970). Isolate the other morphemes and state their meanings. Discuss the markings that pertain to tense and aspect.

(1)	ñaa ʔyiiw tiyiiw	'I came.'
(2)	ñaa ʔamx tipaa	'I was going to go.'
(3)	ñaa ʔšmaa tiyak	'I was sleeping.'
(4)	xkwañ wəmii təkwaa	'The baby was crying.'
(5)	iipač wəwaawx	'The man will holler.'

(6) ñaa saawx tipaa ‘I was going to eat.’
(7) iipač wǝwaaw tǝkwaa ‘The man was hollering.’
(8) ñaa Ɂaa tiɁaa ‘I went.’
(9) xkwañ wǝmiix ‘The baby will cry.’
(10) ñaa tǝnay Ɂimaa tipaa ‘I was dancing yesterday.’
(11) ñaa piyii Ɂnak tiwaa ‘I was sitting here.’
(12) xkwañ wǝmii tǝkwaax ‘The baby will cry.’
(13) ñaa ñǝpilʸ Ɂimaa pipaa ‘I am dancing now.’
(14) iipač wǝwaawx mǝšiyay ‘The man is afraid to holler.’
(15) iipač wǝwaawx tǝkwaa ‘The man was going to holler.’
(16) ñaa piyii pǝškwii tiyuu ‘I was standing here.’
(17) iipač wǝwaawx waṛ ‘The man wants to holler.’
(18) ñaa Ɂimaax ‘I will dance.’
(19) iipač wǝwaaw ‘The man is hollering.’
(20) iipač wǝnuu pǝɁaa ‘The man is running.’
(21) iipač wǝwaawx pǝkwaa ‘The man is going to holler.’
(22) maač tǝmpaa ‘You were there.’

Solution

‘I’ = ñaa	‘sit’ = Ɂnak	‘stand’ = pǝškwii
‘you’ = maač	‘holler’ = wǝwaaw	‘want’ = waṛ
‘come’ = Ɂyiiw	‘baby’ = xkwañ	‘be afraid’ = mǝšiyay
‘go’ = Ɂaa, Ɂam	‘cry’ = wǝmii	‘eat’ = saaw
‘man’ = iipač	‘yesterday’ = tǝnay	‘PRESENT’ = pi, pǝ
‘run’ = wǝnuu	‘dance’ = Ɂimaa	‘NON-PRESENT’ = ti, tǝ
‘sleep’ = Ɂšmaa	‘now’ = ñǝpilʸ	‘UNACCOMPLISHED’ = x
‘here’ = piyii		

The auxiliary word appears in final position in all the sentences in which it is illustrated. In most instances, it consists of the auxiliary verb stem preceded by the prefix [ti] or [pi]. (These affixes have the variant shapes [tǝ] and [pǝ] before certain stems.) The prefix [pi] always marks a sentence for present tense. Sentences containing [ti] are sometimes past and sometimes future.

The verbal suffix [x] is a crucial element in the Diegueño tense-aspect system. When suffixed to a main verb that lacks an auxiliary, it signals future tense, as it does when suffixed to an auxiliary; examples are (9) and (12). When suffixed to a main verb that is followed by an auxiliary, it adds the meaning ‘is/was going to’, as in (15) and (21). Finally, it occurs on the verb subordinate to ‘be afraid’ and ‘want’ in (14) and (17), apparently adding no special meaning to these sentences. The element of meaning shared by “future” actions—those that ‘will’, ‘are going to’, or ‘were going to’ take place—and by actions that one is ‘afraid of’ or ‘wants’ is that the action in question is unaccomplished. Consequently, [x] can be analyzed as an aspect marker and can be glossed as 'UNACCOMPLISHED'.

Once the semantic value of [x] is established, the tense-aspect system of Diegueño begins to make sense. A verb that is accompanied by no special marking at all, neither an auxiliary nor [x], is interpreted as being in the present tense. A verb is also interpreted as present tense if it is followed by an auxiliary with [pi]. The prefix [ti] does not have the meaning 'PAST' or 'FUTURE'; rather it means 'NON-PRESENT'. If an auxiliary with [ti] occurs without a suffix, it is interpreted as marking past tense. However, if [x] is suffixed, it is interpreted as marking future. In other words, a non-present event that is unaccomplished must be future rather than past. Moreover, an unaccomplished event must also be future as opposed to present. Thus a main verb with the suffix [x] is interpreted as future—literally 'UNACCOM-PLISHED'—when there is no following auxiliary. When the main verb has the suffix [x] and an auxiliary follows, the sentence is glossed as 'is/was going to', depending on the tense of the auxiliary. An event that is at present unaccomplished 'is going to' occur; an event that was unaccomplished at some point in the past 'was going to' occur.

Finally, (22) contains an auxiliary but no main verb. The auxiliary stem [paa] 'be there' contributes the locational sense of the sentence, and [tə] marks it as past tense.

Discussion

The prefix [m] in (22) cannot be identified conclusively by means of the data for this problem alone; it marks agreement with the subject [maač] 'you'. Notice that English shares with Diegueño the peculiarity of using an auxiliary verb, *be*, as the surface main verb in sentences expressing location.

VERB MARKINGS

The internal complexity of English verbs tends to be fairly restricted; auxiliary elements occur as separate words, inflection is quite limited, and derivational affixes are not exploited nearly so heavily as they are in many languages. Languages vary greatly in this regard, and verbs, being the central and defining elements of clauses, often have highly complex internal structure. The load of syntactic and semantic markers borne by a verb can reach far greater proportions than it does in English.

Although the markings that occur on verbs resist neat categorization, for expository purposes they can be divided into three types: derivational elements, in a fairly broad sense of the term; "adverbial" elements, including tense, aspect, and modality in particular; and nominal elements, of which markings for subject and object agreement are the most familiar exponents.

In addition, markers of coordination and subordination often appear on verbs, as we saw in section 3.4.

Verbs may contain several kinds of derivational affixes. One type consists of affixes that derive verbs from members of other lexical classes. The suffix *ize*, for instance, derives the verb *stylize* from the noun *style*. Derivational affixes with such meanings as 'cause' and 'want' have been abundantly illustrated in previous problems and discussion (see, for example, Problem 2.3–2, p. 76). Typically these affixes are attached to verbs to form derived verbs, but there are other possibilities as well. In Aztec, for example, the causative ending [tia] can make an intransitive verb (one without an object) into a transitive verb (one that takes an object), but it can also make a noun into an intransitive verb.

(1) nemi-tia
    live-cause
    'cause to live, vivify'

(2) te-tia
    rock-cause
    'petrify, become rock'

Passive markers, imperative markers, and other morphemes that indicate sentence types (see section 3.5) might also be counted as derivational affixes, using the term somewhat broadly. By and large, derivational morphemes combine with a root to form a verb stem, to which other elements are attached, but the division into root, stem, and word is not always clear, and derivational affixes cannot always be assigned to the stem. For instance, the Aztec imperative marker [ši] is separated from the stem by the inflectional morpheme [k] in (3).

(3) ši-k-poowa-kaan
    IMPERATIVE-it-count-PLURAL
    'You (PLURAL) count it!'

We saw earlier that tense, aspect, and modality are often marked by auxiliary verbs or by separate main verbs. However, in many languages these adverbial notions, and others as well, are indicated by verbal affixes. In Problem 3.7–2, for example, we saw that the Diegueño aspect marker [x] 'UNACCOMPLISHED' can occur as a suffix on either an auxiliary verb or the main verb.

(4) xkwañ wəmii tə-kwaa-x

    baby cry NON-PRESENT-make noise-UNACCOMPLISHED
    'The baby will cry.'

(5) xkwañ wəmii-x
    baby cry-UNACCOMPLISHED
    'The baby will cry.'

Tense, aspect, and modality are all marked by affixes on the main verb in the following sentence from Luiseño; the modal suffix [vota] 'can' requires the possessive prefix that corresponds to the subject ([čam] 'our' in this example).

(6) čaam ʔo-y qay čam-ʔohoʔvan-vota-quṣ

we you-OBJECT not our-believe-can-PAST DURATION
'We couldn't believe you.'

Negation, which is marked by a main verb in Diegueño and by separate particles in English and Luiseño, is frequently marked as an affix on the main verb, as in the following Turkish example.

(7) iste-me-di-m
want-not-PAST-I
'I did not want'

In Swahili, negation is marked by the verbal prefix *ha;* in the present tense, the usual present tense marker *na* is dropped and the final vowel of the verb stem is changed from *a* to *i.*

(8) tu-na-soma
we-PRESENT-read
'we are reading'

(9) ha-tu-somi
not-we-read
'we are not reading'

Numerous other adverbial notions can be marked on the verb, including notions of direction, location, manner, time, intensity, and so on. In Classical Aztec, for example, the verb prefixes [on] and [wal] impart the respective notions of 'going' and 'coming' (sometimes only metaphorically).

(10) on-pewa
go-begin
'it begins'

(11) an-ki-wal-toka-keʔ

you (PLURAL)-him-come-follow-PLURAL
'you (PLURAL) follow him (here)'

Example (12) is from Mono, a Uto-Aztecan language spoken in California (Lamb, 1958). This verb form contains prefixes indicating manner and intensity.

(12) ʔa-h-wɨh-tapo-hti

it-hard-with whip-like motion-strike-PAST
'struck it hard with a whip-like motion'

Tarascan, a language spoken in Mexico, displays an elaborate system of verbal affixes referring to shape, space, direction, and location (Friedrich, 1969). For instance, [nči] glosses as 'upward' or 'above'; [ci] as 'downward' or 'near the ground'; and [nska] as 'on the ground'. The use of these affixes is exemplified in (13)–(15) ([ni] is the infinitive ending, equivalent to English *to*).

(13) kʰuani-nči-ni   'to throw upward'
(14) šuru-ci-ni   'to extend along the ground'
(15) amba-nska-ni   'to clean up the floor'

Verbs can be marked to agree with their subject or objects in regard to numerous categories. For instance, Problem 3.2–9 illustrated agreement in gender between a verb and its subject and direct object in Lebanese Arabic. In Problem 3.2–10 we saw that Hungarian verbs agree with their objects in definiteness. However, nominal-verb agreement most commonly involves number and person, as we have seen many times. Examples include the Turkish subject marker [m] 'I' in (7) above, the Swahili subject marker *tu* 'we' in (8) and (9), the Aztec subject marker [an] 'you (PLURAL)' and plural marker [keʔ] in (11), and the Mono object marker [ʔa] 'it' in (12).

Number distinctions are sometimes finer than the division into *singular* versus *plural* (one versus more than one) encountered in English and many other languages. A frequent alternative to the singular-plural dichotomy is the division into singular, *dual*, and plural; in such a system, dual refers to just two individuals and plural to more than two. Singular, dual, and plural variants of a Navaho suppletive verb were given in Problem 2.2–12, (p. 72). This distinction is also marked on the verb in Onondaga, an American Indian language of the Iroquoian family (Chafe, 1970).

(16) ciha kahnyaahaʔ   'The dog is barking.'
(17) ciha knihnyaahaʔ   'The dogs (DUAL) are barking.'
(18) ciha kõtihnyaahaʔ   'The dogs (PLURAL) are barking.'

Number distinctions can also be made between one, a small number, and a large number of objects; between objects gathered together and objects scattered about; and so on.

Person distinctions pertain to the participants of the communication situation. A nominal referring to the speaker(s) is *first person*; one referring to the hearer(s) is *second person*; and one designating neither is *third person*. In the plural finer distinctions are possible. The form for 'we' often differs depending on whether or not 'we' includes the hearer. Similarly, the form for 'you (PLURAL)' may differ depending on whether it includes the hearers alone or other individuals as well. Additional person distinctions are also possible (see Problem 3.7–5).

Viewed in the most general terms, nominal-verb agreement involves the copying of a nominal, or certain features of a nominal, on the verb. To the extent that features of a nominal are incorporated in the verb, they can often be deleted from the nominal itself. Thus in the Onondaga sentences (16)–(18), number is not marked on the subject but it is marked on the verb. Since the main semantic value of a pronoun consists in an indication of person and number, a pronoun can very often be deleted when a verb agrees with it in regard to these categories. The following Navaho sentences (see Problem 2.2–12, p. 72) are among the many examples we have seen.

(19) ší naa-š-niš
I about-I-work
'I work about.'

(20) naa-š-niš
about-I-work
'I work about.'

Nominal elements incorporated in the verb are sometimes quite similar in form to their independent or possessive form, especially in the case of pronouns. Thus the Navaho subject pronouns [ší] 'I' and [ni] 'you' are closely matched by the verbal subject markers [š] and [ni]. In sentence (6) above the Luiseño subject pronoun [čaam] 'we' is very similar phonologically to the possessive prefix [čam] attached to the verb. In Eskimo the same suffixes used as possessives on nouns are used as subject and object markers on the verb (Mey, 1970): [a] signifies a singular object or singular possession, and [i] a plural object or plural possession; [t], which follows [a] or [i] when it occurs, marks a plural subject or possessor.

(21) (a) tiguva-a   'he holds it'
     (b) tiguva-i   'he holds them'
     (c) tiguva-a-t 'they hold it'
     (d) tiguva-i-t 'they hold them'

(22) (a) nuna-a   'his land'
     (b) nuna-i   'his lands'
     (c) nuna-a-t 'their land'
     (d) nuna-i-t 'their lands'

Nominal incorporation is not restricted to pronouns. In Mohawk, an Iroquoian language, the entire direct object noun, even if it is quite complex, can be incorporated in the verb, with the original object optionally being deleted (Postal, 1964).

(23) kaksaʔa kanuhweʔs nekaʔsreht
girl likes car
'The girl likes the car.'

(24) kaksaʔa kaʔsreht-nuhweʔs
girl car-likes
'The girl likes the car.'

Moreover, it is quite common for verbs to incorporate nouns that name the instrument with which an action is performed, including nouns that name body parts. Among the instrumental prefixes of Mono, for instance, are [puh] 'with the eyes', [mah] 'with the hands', [tɨh] 'with a rock', [pa] 'with water', and [kuh] 'with fire', all very similar in form to the corresponding nouns (Lamb, 1958).

Problem 3.7–3 *Cupeño*

Cupeño is a Uto-Aztecan language closely related to Luiseño. The verb stems of Cupeño fall into three main classes. Some consist of the verb root alone; others consist of the verb root followed by the derivational suffix [inə]; still others consist of the root followed by the derivational suffix [yaxə]. Some verb roots can form stems in two or even all three classes. To a considerable degree, membership in each of the three stem classes is correlated with certain semantic properties. Examine the verb forms below (Hill, 1969) and ascertain, as precisely as possible, the semantic properties characteristic of each class.

(1) (a) xəə 'be windy'
    (b) xəə-inə 'blow (wind)' (transitive)
    (c) xəə-yaxə 'blow (wind)'
(2) (a) ————
    (b) mələkʷə-inə 'twist'
    (c) mələkʷə-yaxə 'be twisted, wound up'
(3) (a) ————
    (b) čayəwə-inə 'climb up'
    (c) čayəwə-yaxə 'rise (as in elevator)'
(4) (a) yuyə 'snow'
    (b) ————
    (c) ————
(5) (a) ————
    (b) wəčaʔə-inə 'throw down'
    (c) wəčaxə-yaxə 'drop (accidentally)'
(6) (a) ————
    (b) maqə-inə 'gather'
    (c) maqə-yaxə 'be gathered together'

(7) (a) wəwə 'rain'
    (b) ————
    (c) ————
(8) (a) təwə 'grow (plants)'
    (b) ————
    (c) ————
(9) (a) ničə 'grow old (women)'
    (b) ————
    (c) ————
(10) (a) ————
    (b) silʸə-inə 'pour out'
    (c) silʸə-yaxə 'spill'
(11) (a) ————
    (b) čaşə-inə 'polish'
    (c) čaşə-yaxə 'shine' (intransitive)
(12) (a) pisaʔə 'rot'
    (b) ————
    (c) ————
(13) (a) hučə 'skin'
    (b) hučə-inə 'take off'
    (c) hučə-yaxə 'be undone, untied'

(14) (a) ʔaṣəqətu 'menstruate'
    (b) ———
    (c) ———
(15) (a) ———
    (b) čawələ-inə 'shake' (transitive)
    (c) čawələ-yaxə 'shake' (intransitive)
(16) (a) ———
    (b) čipilə-inə 'break' (transitive)
    (c) čipilə-yaxə 'break' (intransitive)
(17) (a) havəčə 'be morning'
    (b) havəčə-inə 'pass (night)'
    (c) havəčə-yaxə 'get light, dawn'
(18) (a) ———
    (b) kʷatə-inə 'wake up' (transitive)
    (c) kʷatə-yaxə 'awaken'
(19) (a) ṣəʔə 'bloom'
    (b) ———
    (c) ———
(20) (a) ———
    (b) piqə-inə 'touch'
    (c) piqə-yaxə 'bump into (accidentally)'

Solution

For the most part, verb stems with [inə] designate volitional acts (acts willfully undertaken), while stems with [yaxə] designate events undergone passively or inadvertently. Stems with no suffix designate "natural" events, such as meteorological developments, bodily functions, or stages in the development of plant life. However, not all stems fit neatly into this semantic scheme; for instance, the verb [hučə] 'skin' can be considered a "natural" event only by metaphorical extension.

Problem 3.7–4 Tamil

Tamil is a Dravidian language spoken in southern India. Isolate the morphemes in the verbs below (Schiffman, 1969) and state their meanings. Comment on the nature of the verbal affixes.

(1)	varalaam	'may come'
(2)	muṭiyaatu	'(is) not possible'
(3)	eṭukkalaam	'may take'
(4)	ceyyamaaṭṭ	'will not do'
(5)	varakuuṭaatu	'should not come'
(6)	pookalaam	'may go'
(7)	muṭiyalaam	'may be possible'
(8)	paakkamuṭiyaatu	'can not see'
(9)	pookakuuṭaatu	'should not go'
(10)	pookamaṭṭa	'will not go'
(11)	ceyyaveeṇṭaam	'ought not do'
(12)	paṭimuṭiyum	'can study'
(13)	pookaṇum	'must go'

Solution

'come' = vara	'may' = laam
'go' = pooka	'ought not' = veeṇṭaam
'do' = ceyya	'must' = ṇum
'study' = paṭi	'will' = m
'see' = paakka	'possible' = muṭiy, muṭiyum, muṭiya
'take' = eṭukka	'should' = kuuṭ
	'not' = aatu, aaṭṭ, aṭṭa

Since the morpheme meaning 'not' varies in shape, it may be possible to segment [veeṇṭaam] 'ought not' into [veeṇṭ] 'ought' and [aam] 'not'.

The verbal suffixes all express modality. Two modals can occur on a verb if the second modal is one meaning 'not'. The modal [muṭiy], which expresses possibility and translates as either 'possible' or 'can', can function as either a suffix of modality or a verb root. As a verb root, it can itself be followed by other modals.

Problem 3.7–5 *Potawatomi*

It was observed earlier that the person distinctions made in languages are sometimes more subtle than a simple trichotomy into first, second, and third person. This is illustrated by Potawatomi, an American Indian language of the Algonquian family. The data below (Hockett, 1966) contains independent pronoun forms and verbs that are marked for nominal-verb agreement. Divide the pronouns of (1)–(7) into morphemes and state the meaning or function of each. The initial consonant of each verb form is a prefix that marks agreement with nominals. There are three such prefixes. What determines which prefix is used? (Verb suffixes can be ignored for purposes of this problem.)

(1)	nin	'I'
(2)	kin	'you'
(3)	win	'he'
(4)	ninan	'we (HEARER EXCLUDED)'
(5)	kinan	'we (HEARER INCLUDED)'
(6)	kinwa	'you (PLURAL)'
(7)	winwa	'they'
(8)	nwapma	'I see him.'
(9)	kwapma	'You see him.'
(10)	wwapman	'He sees him.'
(11)	nwapmamun	'We (HEARER EXCLUDED) see him.'
(12)	kwapmamun	'We (HEARER INCLUDED) see him.'
(13)	kwapmawa	'You (PLURAL) see him.'

(14)	wwapmawan	'They see them.'
(15)	nwapmuk	'He sees me.'
(16)	kwapmuk	'He sees you.'
(17)	nwapmuknan	'He sees us (HEARER EXCLUDED).'
(18)	kwapmuknan	'He sees us (HEARER INCLUDED).'
(19)	nwapmukok	'They see me.'
(20)	kwapmukok	'They see you.'
(21)	nwapmuknanuk	'They see us (HEARER EXCLUDED).'
(22)	kwapmuknanuk	'They see us (HEARER INCLUDED).'
(23)	kwapmukwak	'They see you (PLURAL).'
(24)	kwapmun	'I see you.'
(25)	kwapmunmun	'We see you.'
(26)	kwapum	'You see me.'
(27)	kwapmuymun	'You see us.'

Solution

The pronoun forms (1)–(7) are all built around the pronoun base [in]. In both the singular and the plural one of three prefixes is attached—[n], [k], or [w]. In the plural the suffix [an] or [wa] is also present. The suffix [an] is used only for the 'we' forms—that is, with the pronouns that designate a group that includes the speaker; [wa] is used otherwise. The ending [an] can therefore be glossed as 'PLURAL, SPEAKER INCLUDED', while [wa] can be glossed as 'PLURAL, SPEAKER EXCLUDED'. With regard to the prefixes, the fact that [k] occurs in both (5) and (6) shows that the division into first, second, and third person is not sufficient. [k] is used when the group designated by the pronoun includes the hearer; [n] is used when this group includes the speaker but not the hearer; and [w] is used when the group includes neither.

The same three prefixes occur on verb forms, with parallel meaning: [k] is prefixed to the verb when the subject or object includes the hearer; [n] is used when the speaker, but not the hearer, is included in the subject or object; and [w] is used when neither the speaker nor the hearer is included in the subject or the object.

FURTHER PROBLEMS

Problem 3.7–6 French

To express simple past tense in French, the present tense of the auxiliary verb *avoir* 'have' is used, together with a form of the main verb called the past participle. The auxiliary verb is the one marked to agree in person and number with the subject, but under certain circumstances the participle also agrees with a nominal. Describe this agreement and the conditions under which it occurs. (*Que* is a relative pronoun that substitutes for the noun of the relative clause that is coreferential to the head noun.)

(1)	Vous avez surpris le garçon.	'You surprised the boy.'
(2)	Vous avez surpris la femme.	'You surprised the woman.'
(3)	Vous avez trouvé la mère.	'You found the mother.'
(4)	Vous avez trouvé le père.	'You found the father.'
(5)	Vous l'avez surpris.	'You surprised him.'
(6)	Vous l'avez surprise.	'You surprised her.'
(7)	Vous l'avez trouvé.	'You found him.'
(8)	Vous l'avez trouvée.	'You found her.'
(9)	Voilà le garçon que vous avez surpris.	'There is the boy that you surprised.'
(10)	Voilà la femme que vous avez trouvée.	'There is the woman that you found.'
(11)	Voilà le père que vous avez trouvé.	'There is the father that you found.'
(12)	Voilà la mère que vous avez surprise.	'There is the mother that you surprised.'
(13)	Quel garçon avez-vous trouvé?	'Which boy did you find?'
(14)	Quelle mère avez-vous trouvée?	'Which mother did you find?'
(15)	Quelle femme avez-vous surprise?	'Which woman did you surprise?'
(16)	Quel père avez-vous surpris?	'Which father did you surprise?'
(17)	*Vous avez surprise la femme.	'You surprised the woman.'
(18)	*Vous avez trouvée la mère.	'You found the woman.'
(19)	*Vous l'avez surpris.	'You surprised her.'
(20)	*Vous l'avez trouvée.	'You found him.'

Problem 3.7–7   Classical Aztec

In section 3.5 we saw that the subject of an Aztec sentence can be omitted when a special suffix, [lo], is added to the verb. Aztec also permits direct objects to remain unspecified. Analyze the sentences below and state the principles that determine verb affixation pertaining to objects.

(1)	kinamaka in siwaλ	'He sells the woman.'
(2)	kiλalia	'He builds it.'
(3)	kimati in siwaλ	'He knows the woman.'
(4)	temiktia	'He kills (someone).'
(5)	kiλalia in kalli	'He builds the house.'
(6)	kinamaka	'He sells her.'
(7)	λamati	'He knows (something).'
(8)	kimiktia	'He kills her.'

(9) kimati in sasanillatolli	'He knows the fable.'
(10) kinamaka in ickaλ	'He sells cotton.'
(11) λaλalia	'He builds (something).'
(12) tenamaka	'He sells (someone).'
(13) kimiktia in siwaλ	'He kills the woman.'
(14) λanamaka	'He sells (something).'
(15) temati	'He knows (someone).'
(16) kimati	'He knows her.'

Problem 3.7–8   Luiseño

The first word of a Luiseño sentence sometimes bears a special suffix that agrees with the subject, as shown in Problem 3.2–12. These suffixes are further illustrated in the sentences below. Analyze these suffixes in regard to their form and meaning.

(1) wunaalupil ?owo?aquṣ	'He was working.'
(2) pitoon noo ?owo?aq	'I am working today.'
(3) waxaam ?aamoquṣ ?omom	'You (PLURAL) were working yesterday.'
(4) noo poy wotiq	'I am hitting him.'
(5) wunaalummil ?aamoquṣ	'They were hunting.'
(6) ?omomum ?owo?aan	'You (PLURAL) are working.'
(7) ?omup poy wotiq	'You are hitting him.'
(8) noonil ?aamoquṣ	'I was hunting.'
(9) wunaalum ?owo?aquṣ waxaam	'They were working yesterday.'
(10) ?om pellaquṣ	'You were dancing.'
(11) waxaamčamil čaam pellaquṣ	'We were dancing yesterday.'
(12) pellaqup wunaal pitoo	'He is dancing today.'
(13) poyupil ?omom wotiquṣ	'You (PLURAL) were hitting him.'
(14) pitoo wunaal ?aamoq	'He is hunting today.'
(15) pitoopum wunaalum pellaan	'They are dancing today.'
(16) čaam ?owo?aan	'We are working.'
(17) waxaamupil ?om poy wotiquṣ	'You were hitting him yesterday.'
(18) čaamča ?aamowun	'We are hunting.'

Problem 3.7–9   Indonesian

We saw in Problem 2.3–9 (p. 83) that many noun stems in Indonesian consist of a root plus a derivational prefix, a derivational suffix, or both.

The same is true of verb stems. Analyze the data below (Kwee, 1965) and describe the formation of passive sentences in Indonesian. Assume that a transformational rule derives passive sentences from underlying active structures.

(1) (a) dokter memeriksa saja   'The doctor examined me.'
    (b) saja diperiksa oleh dokter   'I was examined by the doctor.'
(2) (a) tino menulis surat itu   'Tino wrote the letter.'
    (b) surat itu ditulis oleh tino   'The letter was written by Tino.'
(3) (a) ia mendjual kuda itu   'He sold the horse.'
    (b) kuda itu didjual olehnja   'The horse was sold by him.'
    (c) kuda itu didjualnja   'The horse was sold by him.'
(4) (a) saja membatja pengumuman itu   'I read the announcement.'
    (b) pengumuman itu saja batja   'The announcement was read by me.'
    (c) *pengumuman itu dibatja oleh saja   'The announcement was read by me.'
(5) (a) kamu mentjurigai orang itu   'You suspected that man.'
    (b) orang itu kamu tjurigai   'That man was suspected by you.'
    (c) orang itu kautjurigai   'That man was suspected by you.'
    (d) *orang itu ditjurigai oleh kamu   'That man was suspected by you.'
(6) (a) kami mentjontoh pekerdjaannja   'We copied her work.'
    (b) pekerdjaannja kami tjontoh   'Her work was copied by us.'
    (c) *pekerdjaannja ditjontoh oleh kami   'Her work was copied by us.'
(7) (a) mereka mendorong kereta itu   'They pushed the cart.'
    (b) kereta itu mereka dorong   'The cart was pushed by them.'
    (c) *kereta itu didorong oleh mereka   'The cart was pushed by them.'
(8) (a) ia menawari saja pekerdjaan   'He offered me a job.'
    (b) saja ditawari pekerdjaan   'I was offered a job.'
    (c) pekerdjaan ditawarkan kepada saja   'A job was offered to me.'
(9) (a) ia memberi kusin hadiah   'He gave Kusin a gift.'
    (b) kusin diberi hadiah   'Kusin was given a gift.'
    (c) hadiah diberikan kepada kusin   'A gift was given to Kusin.'

Problem 3.7–10   *Maori*

Maori is a Malayo-Polynesian language spoken in New Zealand. Examine the sentences below (Hohepa, 1967) and state the meaning or function of each word, particularly those related to tense and aspect. Describe the formation of passive sentences in Maori. State the principles that determine word order for the sentences included in the data.

(1)	kua haere te waka	'The canoe has gone.'
(2)	kua mutu te taŋata	'The man has finished.'
(3)	kua haere te tamaiti	'The boy has gone.'
(4)	kua mate te hoiho	'The horse has died.'
(5)	kua taŋata te tamaiti	'The boy has become a man.'
(6)	i oma te tamaiti ki te toa	'The boy ran to the store.'
(7)	i kite te taŋata i te maŋoo	'The man saw the shark.'
(8)	i kite au i te pukapuka	'I saw the book.'
(9)	i haere au ki te kura	'I went to the school.'
(10)	e haere ana au ki te paa	'I was going to the village.'
(11)	kua taria te taŋata e te pirihimana	'The man has been taken by the policeman.'
(12)	kua patua te kurii e te taŋata	'The dog has been hit by the man.'
(13)	kua rewa te waka	'The canoe is afloat.'
(14)	ko poomare te taŋata	'The man is Poomare.'
(15)	kua pakaru te wati	'The watch is broken.'
(16)	e rere ana te manu	'The bird is flying.'
(17)	e kimi ana te faaea i tamaiti	'The mother is searching for the boy.'
(18)	kei te fare au	'I am at the house.'
(19)	i oma ŋaa taataŋata	'The men ran.'
(20)	i piri ŋaa teeina	'The brothers hid.'
(21)	kei te kaaiŋa ŋaa tuaakana	'The sisters are at home.'
(22)	i patua te kurii e hemi	'The dog was hit by Jim.'
(23)	i te fare au	'I was at the house.'
(24)	i haere te taŋata ki te toa	'The man went to the store.'
(25)	i kitea te tamaiti e te pirihimana	'The boy was found (= seen) by the policeman.'
(26)	ko pita teenei	'This is Peter.'
(27)	ko hemi teenei tamaiti	'This boy is Jim.'
(28)	ko hooni teenei taŋata	'This man is John.'
(29)	kei hea te fare	'Where is the house?'
(30)	ko te raŋatira teenei	'This is the chief.'
(31)	i patua te kurii e te taŋata	'The dog was hit by the man.'

Problem 3.7–11   Atayal

The following data (Egerod, 1966) is from Atayal, a language spoken in northern Taiwan. Listed below are the subject and possessive forms of the pronouns illustrated in the data:

Subject Pronouns		*Possessive Pronouns*	
sakuʔ, kuʔ	'I'	mamu	'your'
suʔ	'you'	niaʔ	'his'
taʔ	'we'	mian, taʔ	'our'
simu	'you (PLURAL)'		

Hyphens are used to mark the morpheme boundaries in the main verbs. The words for 'this' and 'here' are identical. Finally, 'sister' and 'ancestor' are each expressed by two non-adjacent words—'sister' by [ssueʔ] 'sibling' and [kneril] 'female', and 'ancestor' by [mrhuu] 'forefather' and [raral] 'ancient'.

Isolate the remaining morphemes in the sentences below and state their meanings. Describe the syntax of these sentences as precisely as possible, paying particular attention to verbal elements. What are the rules that determine what elements appear in first and second position in a sentence?

(1)	m-uŋiʔ sakuʔ	'I forget.'
(2)	kta-n sakuʔ niaʔ	'I am seen by him.'
(3)	squliq sakuʔ	'I am a man.'
(4)	m-itaʔ sakuʔ squliq	'I see the man.'
(5)	kta-n sakuʔ naʔ squliq	'I am seen by the man.'
(6)	kiopu-n squliq bliŋ qani	'Men are placed (in) this jail.'
(7)	ual niaʔ pso-n stunux rumaʔ	'Some were sent by him (to) Stunux.'
(8)	niux taʔ sia-n laqiʔ ssueʔ niaʔ kneril	'His sister is pregnant by (one of) us.' (literally: a child has been put (in) his sister by (one of) us)
(9)	p-iuŋiʔ suʔ	'You will forget.'
(10)	iiat taʔ mn-kitaʔ	'We have not seen (each other).'
(11)	sŋŋua-n sakuʔ naʔ squliq	'I am frightened by the man.'
(12)	kialu-n taʔ niaʔ	'We are talked to by him.'
(13)	ʔtaial sakuʔ	'I am an Atayal.'
(14)	iiat suʔ taial balai	'You are not a true Atayal.'
(15)	niux kuʔ mamu qlaŋu-n	'I am neglected by you.'
(16)	niux mian uaha-n qani	'We have arrived here.' (literally: this (place) has been reached by us)
(17)	ual niaʔ pso-n stunux mrhuu mamu raral	'Your ancestor was sent by him (to) Stunux.'
(18)	niux sakuʔ nbuʔ	'I am ill.'
(19)	iiat simu p-ʔagal	'You (PLURAL) will not get (anything).'
(20)	biqu-n sakuʔ lukus naʔ squliq	'I am given the man's clothes.'
(21)	m-itaʔ taʔ puniq	'We see a fire.'

3.8   Patterns and Constraints

In this chapter we have been primarily concerned with the class of syntactic rules called transformations. These rules modify tree structures to produce derived trees that more closely resemble surface structures. However, not all syntactic regularities can be captured by transformational rules. Some regularities are best stated as constraints on the patterns of elements permitted in surface structure. Others pertain to the operation of numerous syntactic rules, not individual rules, and are best stated as general constraints on rule application.

SURFACE STRUCTURE CONSTRAINTS

Constraints on the patterns of elements permitted in surface structure are of at least two types. Some constraints are best described as positive in nature. Positive surface structure constraints require that the elements of a surface structure occur in a certain configuration in order for a sentence to be grammatical, and they can be viewed as imposing this configuration on sentences. Constraints on the order of affixes in complex lexical items are prime examples. In Problem 2.3–5 (p. 81), for instance, we saw that the internal structure of a verb in Classical Aztec can be summarized by the formula *PAST + SUBJECT MARKER + OBJECT MARKER + ROOT + TENSE + PLURAL.* If these elements are combined in any other order, the resulting verb is ill formed. This formula is a syntactic rule that specifies the conditions a verb must meet in order for a sentence containing it to be grammatical.

Another surface structure constraint most easily stated in positive terms is the requirement that a (non-imperative) sentence contain a subject in surface structure. This requirement is part of the grammar of English, French, and many other languages. However, there are also many languages, of which Spanish and Aztec are only two examples, that do not have such a requirement. Because of this surface constraint, subject pronouns cannot be deleted in English and French, while they can be deleted in Spanish and Aztec. Thus if sentences (1)–(4) are all interpreted to mean 'I die', only the Spanish and Aztec sentences, (3) and (4), are grammatical.

> (1) *Die.
> (2) *Meurs.
> (3) Muero.
> (4) ni-miki

Moreover, because of this requirement, English and French sentences which have no semantic subject require the insertion of a "dummy" subject, one with no semantic value. The *it* (French *il*) that occurs with "weather" verbs is the most obvious example; contrast the English sentences (5) and (6) with their Spanish counterparts (7) and (8).

(5) It is raining.
(6) It is hot.
(7) Llueve.
(8) Hace calor. (literally: makes heat)

Yet another ramification of this requirement in English is the need to insert *it* in subject position when a subject complement clause is moved to the end of the sentence. Contrast (9) with (10), which derives from (9).

(9) To photograph hummingbirds requires considerable patience.
(10) It requires considerable patience to photograph hummingbirds.

Other constraints on the surface structure of sentences are best stated in negative terms. Negative surface structure constraints specify configurations of elements that make a sentence ungrammatical. For example, a negative surface structure constraint of French precludes the pronoun sequence *y y* before the verb. *Y* translates as 'of it' in (11) and as 'there' in the homophonous (12).

(11) Il y pense.   'He thinks of it.'
(12) Il y pense.   'He thinks there.'

Thus we might expect 'He thinks of it there' to be expressed with two consecutive occurrences of *y*, but the resulting sentence is in fact ungrammatical:

(13) *Il y y pense.   'He thinks of it there.'

The deviance of (13) is not semantic in character, since the intended meaning of (13) is perfectly clear and non-anomalous; nor is it easy to state in terms of constraints on the operation of transformational rules. The simplest way to state the generalization is by means of a negative surface structure constraint which stipulates that a sentence is ungrammatical if it contains the sequence *y y* in the surface structure.

Surface structure constraints are important, but as yet they are only poorly understood. Moreover, the distinction between positive and negative constraints is not always a clear one, and it should not be taken too seriously. For present purposes, the important point is simply that certain syntactic regularities are more easily stated as constraints on the configuration of elements permitted in surface structure rather than as transformational rules or constraints on their application.

Problem 3.8–1   Spanish

Formulate a surface structure constraint that accounts for the ungrammaticality of the sentences marked by an asterisk in the data below (Rivero, 1970). Assume for purposes of this problem that the rule of complement subject deletion, which erases the subject of a complement clause when it is coreferential to the main clause subject, has the effect in Spanish of collapsing two clauses into one, so that the complement ceases to count as a separate clause once complement subject deletion has applied. For example, *Yo quiero salir* 'I want to leave', which is derived by subject deletion from *Yo quiero* [*yo salir*], is assumed to contain only one clause in surface structure.

(1) Muchos aviones no se estrellan.
    'Many airplanes do not crash.'

(2) No muchos aviones se estrellan.
    'Not many airplanes crash.'

(3) *No muchos aviones no se estrellan.
    'Not many airplanes do not crash.'

(4) Muchos chicos se preocupan de esos asuntos, pero no muchas chicas se preocupan de esos asuntos.
    'Many boys care about those matters, but not many girls care about those matters.'

(5) Muchos chicos se preocupan de esos asuntos, pero no muchas chicas.
    'Many boys care about those matters, but not many girls.'

(6) *Muchos chicos no se preocupan de esos asuntos, pero no muchas chicas no se preocupan de esos asuntos.
    'Many boys do not care about those matters, but not many girls do not care about those matters.'

(7) Muchos chicos no se preocupan de esos asuntos, pero no muchas chicas.
    'Many boys do not care about those matters, but not many girls (do not).'

(8) No creo que yo lo haga bien.
    'I do not believe that I do it well.'

(9) No creo hacerlo bien.
    'I do not believe that I do it well.'

(10) No creo que yo no lo haga bien.
    'I do not believe that I do not do it well.'

(11) *No creo no hacerlo bien.
    'I do not believe that I do not do it well.'

Solution

The required surface structure constraint is a negative one. It states that a sentence is ungrammatical if it contains two occurrences of *no* 'not' in the same clause.

Discussion

Sentences (1) and (2) show that *no* can occur either before the verb group (*se estrellan* 'crash') or before the quantifier *muchos* 'many', with different semantic effects. Sentence (3) contains *no* in both positions. The deviance of (3) is not semantic in character, since its meaning is perfectly clear and non-anomalous. Apparently, the syntax of Spanish simply does not tolerate the simultaneous occurrence of *no* in both positions. The surface structure constraint stated above accounts for this.

Sentences (4) and (5) point to the existence of a rule that optionally deletes everything but *no* and the subject of a clause initiated by *pero* 'but', provided that the deleted elements are repeated elsewhere in the sentence. (7), which is grammatical, derives from the ungrammatical (6) by the application of this rule. The deleted material is *no se preocupan de esos asuntos* 'do not care about those matters'. (6) is ungrammatical because it contains two occurrences of *no* in the clause after *pero*, but (7) is well formed because the deletion rule has eliminated one occurrence of *no*. Despite its ungrammaticality, (6) must be postulated as an underlying structure, for otherwise there would be no source for (7). This constitutes evidence that the constraint that disallows (6) must be a surface structure constraint rather than a semantic one or a constraint on the syntactic rules that derive sentence structures like (4) and (6).

The rule of complement subject deletion derives (9) from (8) and (11) from (10); by assumption, it has the effect of collapsing two underlying clauses into one surface clause. The surface structure constraint therefore predicts correctly that (11), with two occurrences of *no* in a single surface clause, is ungrammatical. If it were not for this independently motivated constraint, the deviance of (11) would be unexplained, since (11) and (10) are related in exactly the same way that (9) and (8) are related.

GENERAL CONSTRAINTS ON RULE APPLICATION

All transformational rules are subject to fairly strict constraints on their application. The rule of subject-verb agreement, for instance, must mark a verb to agree only with its own subject, never with the subject of some other clause. In Papago [g] can be inserted before a noun only when certain conditions are met: The noun must not be preceded by a demonstrative; it must not be the first element of the sentence; and so on.

Some of these constraints, such as the restrictions on [g] insertion in Papago, are peculiar to individual rules. Others hold for all rules of a language, or for all rules of a particular type, and cannot be taken as idiosyncrasies of individual rules. Consequently, they are best regarded as general constraints on rule application, constraints that govern the application of numerous individual rules. Consider examples (1)–(4).

(1) (a) Mike$_i$ works hard, and he$_i$ is sure to get ahead.
    (b) *He$_i$ works hard, and Mike$_i$ is sure to get ahead.
(2) (a) Gatsby likes pecans, and Zelda walnuts.
    (b) *Gatsby pecans, and Zelda likes walnuts.
(3) (a) Herman broke a window, and his sister did too.
    (b) *Herman did too, and his sister broke a window.
(4) (a) Wilt is tall, and so is Lew.
    (b) *So is Wilt, and Lew is tall.

All these examples are conjoined sentences in which an element in one conjunct has undergone reduction by virtue of being identical to a corresponding element in the other conjunct. In (1) one of two coreferential occurrences of *Mike* is pronominalized to *he*. The rule of gapping deletes the repeated verb *likes* in (2). In (3) the repeated verb phrase *broke a window* reduces to *did too*. And in (4) a change of word order accompanies the replacement of *tall* by *so*. The (a) sentences are uniformly grammatical, and the (b) sentences ungrammatical, despite the fact that exactly the same reduction occurs in the derivation of both. The difference is that the second conjunct undergoes reduction in the (a) sentences, whereas the first conjunct is reduced in the (b) sentences. The following thus appears to be a general principle of English syntax:

> When a syntactic rule reduces elements in one conjunct of a conjoined structure by virtue of identity to the corresponding elements of another conjunct, reduction must take place in the second of these conjuncts, never the first.

This regularity cannot be captured if the restriction is simply stated over and over with each separate reduction rule of English. The restriction must be considered a general constraint that governs the application of all reduction rules. As such, it is not a transformational rule but rather a constraint on the application of transformations.

Problem 3.8–2   English

Formulate a general constraint on transformations that will account for the ungrammaticality of the sentences marked by an asterisk below.

    (1) (a) You saw someone.
        (b) Whom did you see?
        (c) You saw someone and your mother.
        (d) *Whom did you see and your mother?

(2) (a) She accepted the money.
　　(b) This is the money that she accepted.
　　(c) She accepted the diamonds and the money.
　　(d) *This is the money that she accepted the diamonds and.
(3) (a) She seeks happiness.
　　(b) It's happiness that she seeks.
　　(c) She seeks wealth and happiness.
　　(d) *It's happiness that she seeks wealth and.
(4) (a) I have no time for women.
　　(b) Women I have no time for.
　　(c) I have no time for women and song.
　　(d) *Women I have no time for and song.

Solution

A rule that moves a noun phrase may not break up a conjoined noun phrase by moving only one of its conjuncts.

Problem 3.8–3　French

General constraints on transformations differ somewhat from language to language, although there are many similarities. The constraint illustrated in the data below is characteristic of French but not English. Formulate a general constraint that will account for the deviance of the (c) sentences.

(1) (a) Il parle à quelqu'un.　　'He speaks to someone.'
　　(b) À qui parle-t-il?　　'To whom does he speak?'
　　(c) *Qui parle-t-il à?　　'Who does he speak to?'
(2) (a) Il parle à cette femme.　　'He speaks to that woman.'
　　(b) Voilà la femme à qui il parle.　　'There is the woman to whom he speaks.'
　　(c) *Voilà la femme qu'il parle à.　　'There is the woman that he speaks to.'
(3) (a) Il parle à la femme.　　'He speaks to the woman.'
　　(b) C'est à la femme qu'il parle.　　'It's to the woman that he speaks.'
　　(c) *C'est la femme qu'il parle à.　　'It's the woman that he speaks to.'

Solution

No transformation may separate a noun phrase from the preposition of which it is the object.

FURTHER PROBLEMS

Problem 3.8–4   English

Formulate a surface structure constraint that will correctly predict the ungrammaticality of the sentences marked by an asterisk below (McCawley, 1969).

(1) (a) Not many of the boys didn't consult John.
    (b) *John wasn't consulted by not many of the boys.
    (c) *The doctor didn't examine not many of the students.
    (d) Not many of the students weren't examined by the doctor.
(2) (a) John doesn't like Brahms, and neither does Harry; but not Max—Max loves Brahms.
    (b) *John doesn't like Brahms, and neither does Harry; but Max doesn't not like Brahms—Max loves Brahms.
(3) (a) Who didn't say anything? Not Max.
    (b) *Who didn't say anything? Max didn't not say anything.

Problem 3.8–5   French

An obligatory syntactic rule of French transports an object pronoun (under certain conditions) into pre-verbal position (see Problem 3.5–7). When more than one pronominal object follows a verb, all the objects can be transported if the proper conditions are fulfilled. The pronominal objects occurring before a verb must appear in a rigidly prescribed order. Examine the sentences below and formulate a positive surface structure constraint that will correctly impose the proper ordering on pre-verbal object pronouns.

(1) Je le vois.	'I see him.'
(2) Je la vois.	'I see her.'
(3) Je les vois.	'I see them.'
(4) Je lui parle.	'I speak to her.'
(5) Je leur parle.	'I speak to them.'
(6) Je lui en parle.	'I speak to him about it.'
(7) Je leur en parle.	'I speak to them about it.'
(8) Il me voit.	'He sees me.'
(9) Il me parle.	'He speaks to me.'
(10) Il m'en parle.	'He speaks to me about it.'
(11) Il se voit.	'He sees himself.'
(12) Il se parle.	'He speaks to himself.'
(13) Il s'en parle.	'He speaks to himself about it.'
(14) Il me le donne.	'He gives it to me.'
(15) Il me les donne.	'He gives them to me.'

(16) Il se la donne.   'He gives it to himself.'
(17) Il se les donne.   'He gives them to himself.'
(18) Je la leur donne.   'I give it to them.'
(19) Je les lui donne.   'I give them to him.'
(20) Je le leur donne.   'I give it to them.'

Problem 3.8–6   English

Formulate a general constraint on rule application that will correctly account for the deviance of the (d) expressions below. In each set of examples, (d) bears to (c) the same structural relation that (b) bears to (a).

(1) (a) The sinister man beat the girl.
    (b) It's the girl that the sinister man beat (not the boy).
    (c) I know the sinister man who beat the girl.
    (d) *It's the girl that I know the sinister man who beat.
(2) (a) The woman bought something there.
    (b) What did the woman buy there?
    (c) You met the woman who bought something there.
    (d) *What did you meet the woman who bought there?
(3) (a) The child broke a toy.
    (b) I liked the child that broke a toy.
    (c) This is the toy that the child broke.
    (d) *I liked the child that this is the toy that broke.

4
Phonological Analysis

If the syntactic regularities of a language are to be understood, the surface structures of sentences must be viewed in relation to the much more abstract structures that underlie them—namely, their semantic representations. The situation is quite analogous in the domain of phonology. Underlying the "surface" or *phonetic* representation of a sentence or lexical item is a more abstract entity referred to as its *phonological* representation. The goal of phonological analysis is to determine the nature of these underlying phonological representations and to discover the general principles that relate them to their phonetic manifestations.

Every lexical item consists in part of an underlying phonological representation. This representation includes precisely those phonological properties that are peculiar to the lexical item and not predictable by general rules. Phonological rules derive the phonetic representation of a lexical item from its phonological representation.

The phonological representation of a sentence consists of the various underlying representations of its component lexical items, together with a characterization of the way in which these lexical items combine syntactically. By and large, then, the phonological representation of a sentence can be equated with its surface structure. (For certain phonological phenomena, semantic information is also relevant and must be included in the phonological representation of a sentence; see section 4.4.)

The phonological representations of sentences (that is, their surface structures) are the "input" to the phonological component. This component consists in a series of rules which derive the phonetic manifestations of sentences from their underlying phonological representations. Phonological rules apply to sentences sequentially; often they must apply in a particular order. Each rule application modifies the phonological representation of the sentence in some way, making it more like the ultimate phonetic representation.

We will begin our discussion of phonological analysis with an examination of the phonological representations of lexical items and the grounds for positing them.

4.1   Underlying Representations

Some morphemes lack phonological substance of their own and are manifested through the modification of other morphemes. In Diegueño, for instance, plurality is marked on some verbs by a change in the length of the final vowel (from long to short or from short to long; see Problems 2.2–5 and 2.4–7, pp. 66 and 91). Morphemes such as these are called process morphemes.

More typically, the phonological representation of a morpheme consists of a sequence of sound segments. Some morphemes have different segmental representations depending on the environment in which they appear, and this variation (when not predictable) is also part of a morpheme's phonological representation. For example, the phonological representation of the Luiseño verb meaning 'run' must specify that its phonological shape is [pokwa] when it has a singular subject, but [ŋoora] when the subject is plural (see Problem 2.2–8, p. 69). Finally, the phonological representation of a morpheme must indicate how it interacts with phonological rules. It must specify whether the morpheme is an exception to any general phonological rules; whether it undergoes any rules that are restricted in application to only a small subclass of lexical items; and so on.

By definition, the phonological representation of a lexical item comprises only those properties that are idiosyncratic to it and that cannot be predicted by rules of a more general character. It is precisely these properties that are distinctive and have contrastive value. Since the traits determined by a phonological rule are common to an entire class of lexical items, they cannot serve to distinguish the members of the class from one another.

DISTINCTIVENESS

Let us begin our discussion of distinctiveness with a concrete example. Stress in Classical Aztec regularly falls on the second vowel from the end of a word (see Problem 2.1–9, p. 52). Since the placement of stress in Aztec is predictable by this general rule, it is not distinctive and cannot serve to differentiate lexical items. Therefore stress is not marked in the underlying representations of Aztec morphemes. Rather, it is inserted by a phonological rule that can be stated roughly as follows:

    (A) The second vowel from the end of a word is stressed.

The word [némi] 'live', for instance, has the derivation shown in Figure 4.1–1. On the other hand, there is no general rule of Aztec that will allow us to predict that the first segment of the verb for 'live' will be [n] rather than [m], [t], or some other sound. The information that the first segment of 'live' is [n] must therefore be specified in the underlying phonological representation of this morpheme.

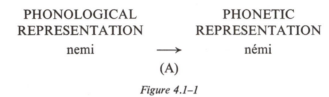

PHONOLOGICAL   PHONETIC
REPRESENTATION   REPRESENTATION
nemi   ⟶   némi
(A)

Figure 4.1–1

Strictly speaking, phonetic segments are not fully comparable to the corresponding phonological segments, even when the same symbol is used for both. Phonetically, the [n] of [némi] is voiced, unrounded, non-glottalized, and so on, but these properties are predictable by general rules and hence are not contrastive. At the phonological level, the first segment of [némi] does not contain all the phonetic features normally subsumed under the symbol [n], but only the distinctive ones; it is probably sufficient to specify that the segment is a dental nasal. Rules such as (B) and (C) then serve to introduce the redundant or predictable features.

    (B) All nasals are voiced.
    (C) All segments are non-glottalized.

Because every phonetic segment consists in part of properties that are predictable by general rules, the phonetic and phonological representations of a segment are never fully congruent.

    Underlying segments are traditionally called **phonemes**, and underlying representations can therefore be referred to as **phonemic** representations. Phonemic and phonetic segments are usually represented with the same inventory of symbols; when it is necessary to avoid possible confusion, phonemic representations are enclosed in slanted lines while phonetic representations are enclosed in brackets. The underlying or phonemic representation of the Aztec word for 'live' would thus be written /nemi/; phonetically, it is written [némi].

Many phonemes have more than one possible manifestation at the phonetic level. (In physical terms, no two sounds are ever precisely alike; consequently, every phoneme has an indefinite number of possible phonetic manifestations. However, most of the phonetic differences are minute or infinitesimal and are irrelevant for purposes of linguistic analysis. We will restrict our attention to variation that is substantial enough to be considered linguistically significant.) When the differences among the various phonetic shapes of a phoneme are slight and depend largely on the surrounding phonetic environment, the different phonetic manifestations are referred to as the ***allophones*** of the phoneme. For instance, the phoneme /ʔ/ has the two allophones [ʔ] and [ʔʸ] in Maxakalí, a language of Brazil (Gudschinsky and Popovich, 1970). The palatalized glottal stop [ʔʸ] occurs after plain or nasalized [i] or a palatal consonant and [ʔ] occurs in all other environments. Thus /piʔa/ 'where' is manifested phonetically as [piʔʸa], and /kaʔok/ 'strong' is manifested as [kaʔox].

Usually, it is reasonable to designate one of the allophones of a phoneme as the ***basic allophone***. This is the allophone that will occur unless the segment happens to be in a specified environment that demands some other allophone. The basic allophone of a phoneme is written with the same symbol used for the phoneme itself; it is so chosen that the rules which derive the non-basic allophones are as simple and general as possible. Thus [ʔ] is the basic allophone of /ʔ/ in Maxakalí, and the rules that connect /ʔ/ and [ʔ] will be taken for granted. [ʔʸ], on the other hand, is a special allophone that occurs only in a specified environment; [ʔʸ] derives from /ʔ/ by a simple and general phonological rule that palatalizes a glottal stop when it follows a palatal segment (that is, a high front vowel or a palatal consonant).

The first step in finding the phonological representations of lexical items consists in determining which phonological traits have contrastive value; traits predictable by rule, such as the palatalization of [ʔ] in Maxakalí, have no contrastive value and are excluded from phonological representations. Languages vary significantly in this regard. In English, for example, the difference between [t] and [č] is distinctive. Both sounds can occur in the same phonological environment, as in *tip* versus *chip*, and the difference between them serves to differentiate morphemes. The distinction between alveolar and palatal obstruents must therefore be marked in the phonological representations of English morphemes, for no general rule can be given that will correctly predict when [t] will occur as opposed to [č]. In Papago, on the other hand, [t] and [č] do not contrast, as we saw in Chapter 1 (p. 12). The segment [č] occurs only before the vowels [i ɨ u], and [t] never occurs in this environment; the two sounds are in ***complementary distribution***. Consequently, the difference between [t] and [č] can never be the only trait that distinguishes two morphemes in Papago, and this difference cannot be regarded as contrastive. The two sounds are allophones of the phoneme /t/, and [t] is the basic allophone. The variant [č] can be predicted by a rule that palatalizes /t/

before a high vowel. (If [č] were chosen as the basic allophone, the rule predicting the variant [t] would not be quite so simple.) Since the difference between [t] and [č] in Papago is not contrastive, it does not have to be incorporated in the phonemic representations of lexical items.

As this example shows, sounds which are in complementary distribution do not contrast and may be allophones of the same phoneme. Two sounds may also be allophonic variants if they occur in the same environment but do not contrast. For example, aspirated and unaspirated stops both occur optionally in word-final position in Luiseño, but the difference between them is not distinctive; [kut] and [kutʰ] both mean 'fire'. [t] and [tʰ] are thus allophonic variants of the phoneme /t/; [t] is the basic allophone, and [tʰ] is derived by an optional rule that aspirates word-final stops. The two sounds are said to be in *free variation*, since the choice between them has no consequences in determining the identity of morphemes and is not dictated one way or the other by phonological rules.

Sounds that contrast in one environment will not necessarily contrast in all environments. When a contrast is suspended in some environment, it is said to be *neutralized*. For example, voiced and voiceless stops are contrastive in most environments in English (as in *pit* versus *bit*, *lip* versus *lib*), but this contrast is neutralized after initial [s]. Only voiceless stops can appear in this position (*spit*, *stick*, *skid*, but not **sbit*, **sdig*, **sgim*). The voicelessness of these stops can be predicted by rule and hence is not phonemic. To take another example, there are five distinctive vowels in Luiseño stressed syllables: /i e a o u/. (Length is also distinctive.) In unstressed syllables, on the other hand, there is only a three-way contrast: /i a u/. Thus [i] and [e], as well as [u] and [o], are in contrast in stressed syllables, but in unstressed syllables they are in free variation.

Problem 4.1–1   English

In some dialects of American English the "complex" vowels [ay] and [ʌy] bear a special relationship to each other. Examine the forms below and determine the nature of this phonological relationship.

bite	bʌyt	*time*	taym	*rice*	rʌys
tie	tay	*rise*	rayz	*type*	tʌyp
ride	rayd	*write*	rʌyt	*ninth*	naynθ
file	fayl	*fight*	fʌyt	*fire*	fayr
life	lʌyf	*buy*	bay	*bike*	bʌyk

Solution

[ay] and [ʌy] are in complementary distribution: [ay] does not occur directly before voiceless segments, and [ʌy] occurs only in this environment. Therefore the two sounds do not contrast. [ʌy] can be regarded as the variant of [ay]

that occurs before voiceless sounds. *Bite*, for instance, has /bayt/ as its phonemic representation; the phonetic representation [bʌyt] is derived by a rule that changes [ay] to [ʌy] directly before voiceless segments.

Discussion

The vowels [a] and [ʌ] contrast in English, as shown by the difference between *slot* and *slut*, but the distinction is neutralized when the vowels combine with the glide [y] to form a **diphthong**. /a/ rather than /ʌ/ is chosen as the underlying vowel because this choice allows a simpler statement of the rule that predicts the variant. It is simpler to specify that [ay] changes to [ʌy] before a voiceless segment than to specify that [ʌy] changes to [ay] before a voiced segment (as in *ride*) or when no segment at all follows (as in *tie*).

This rule has two important exceptions for many speakers of English; *nice* is [nays] rather than [nʌys] phonetically, and *like* is [layk] rather than [lʌyk]. For such speakers, the fact that these two morphemes do not undergo the otherwise quite general rule [ay] → [ʌy] must be marked as part of their phonological representations.

Problem 4.1–2   Araucanian

The forms below (Echeverría and Contreras, 1965) are from Araucanian, a language spoken in Chile and Argentina. Determine the phonological status of stress in Araucanian as exemplified in the data. The symbol ['] marks primary stress and [ˋ] a stress of secondary intensity.

ṭipánto	'year'	akúle	'if he comes'
wulé	'tomorrow'	ináy	'he scratches himself'
elúmuyù	'give us'	iḷmén	'rich, noble'
elúaènew	'he will give me'	eḷwáfimì	'you will give him'
kimúfalùwulày	'he pretended	ñuké	'mother'
	not to know'		

Solution

Stress is predictable by rule. Consequently, it is not distinctive and is not part of the underlying phonological representations of lexical items. The second vowel of a word bears primary stress. Every even-numbered vowel (after the second) bears secondary stress.

Problem 4.1–3   Mohawk

The following data (Postal, 1969) is from Mohawk, an American Indian language of the Iroquoian family. Examine the forms below and determine the status of vowel length in Mohawk. A segmental symbol is written twice to indicate that the segment is long. In the case of stressed long vowels, stress is written only on the first symbol.

ranahéezʌs	'he trusts her'	wahrehyáaraʔneʔ	'he remembered'
ragéedas	'he scrapes'	ɔwadunizaʔáshegeʔ	'it will be ripening
rayʌ́thos	'he plants'		repeatedly'
waháagedeʔ	'he scraped'	yékreks	'I push it'
wísk	'five'	royóʔdeʔ	'he works'
rehyáaraʔs	'he remembers'		

Solution

Vowel length is predictable by rule and is therefore not distinctive. All vowels are short except stressed vowels followed by only one consonant. The phonological component of Mohawk apparently contains a rule that lengthens a stressed vowel if only a single consonant follows.

Problem 4.1–4   Alabaman

The forms below (Rand, 1968) are from Alabaman, an American Indian language of the Muskogean family. Determine what vowel phonemes must be posited for this language and list the allophones of each. Do the same for the voiceless stops. State the rules that determine which allophone of a segment will be used in a given environment. A stop marked with the diacritic [ˀ] is *unreleased*; that is, the stop closure is maintained until the articulation of the following segment has been initiated. [.] indicates that the closure is farther back in the mouth than usual. Give the phonemic representation of the form for 'three' and describe the derivation of its phonetic manifestation by the rules you have posited.

ĩnkʰaa	'give'	itʰospʰaa	'knee'
pʰosnoo	'we'	tʰaatʰaa	'father'
hipˀloo	'snow'	tʰãnkʰaa	'dark'
okˀkʰiitʰaṭˀkʰaa	'see'	sloṭˀkʰaa	'full'
kʰolbii	'basket'	hoomaa	'bitter'
tʰoṭˀčĩnnaa	'three'	pʰiičii	'mother'
haṭˀkʰaa	'white'	ĩmpʰiičii	'breast'
tʰĩnnaa	'dull'	solotˀlii	'smooth'
hõmmaa	'red'	kʰanoo	'good'
čafaakʰaa	'one'	itˀtʰoo	'tree'
kʰopˀlii	'water glass'	akʰostʰĩnnii	'think'
pʰaanii	'creek'	itˀtʰabii	'leg'
okˀčakˀkʰoo	'green, blue'	ikˀbaa	'hot'
ikˀfii	'belly'		

Solution

The vowels /i a o/ are distinctive. Vowel length is also distinctive, but not in all environments. For most environments, rules can be given to predict vowel length: Word-final vowels are always long; word-initial vowels are always short; and a vowel is always short when it is followed by a cluster of two consonants. Consequently, vowel length is distinctive only for medial vowels followed by just one consonant. For instance, there is no apparent way to predict that the first vowel of 'father' is long while the first vowel of 'good' is short. Vowel nasalization is not distinctive since it can be predicted by a general rule: A vowel is nasalized if it is followed by a consonant cluster of which the first member is nasal. Thus the first vowel of 'dark' is nasalized because it is followed by the consonant cluster [nk^h], the first member of which is nasal; but the first vowel of 'good' is non-nasal because it is followed by only one consonant.

The distinctive voiceless stops are /p t k/. The phonetic manifestation of these phonemes is determined by the following principles: A voiceless stop is aspirated if it precedes a vowel, and it is unreleased if it precedes a consonant. In addition, /t/ is articulated farther back than usual when it occurs before /č/ or /k/.

The allophones of the vowels and voiceless stops are summarized below.

/i/	[i ĩ ii]	/ii/	[ii]	/p/	[p^h p⁷]
/a/	[a ã aa]	/aa/	[aa]	/t/	[t^h t⁷ ṭ⁷]
/o/	[o õ oo]	/oo/	[oo]	/k/	[k^h k⁷]

The phonemic representation of 'three' is /totčinna/; vowel length is fully predictable and need not be specified. The phonetic manifestation of this form is [t^{h}oṭ⁷čĩnnaa]. The first two vowels are short because they are followed by consonant clusters. The third vowel is long because it is in word-final position. /i/ is nasalized because it is followed by the consonant cluster /nn/, the first member of which is a nasal. The initial /t/ appears in the aspirated form [t^h] because it precedes a vowel. The second occurrence of /t/ is unreleased, since a consonant follows, and it is retracted to [ṭ⁷] because the following segment is [č].

ABSTRACT PHONOLOGICAL REPRESENTATIONS

Morphemes commonly have different phonetic shapes depending on the environment in which they occur. Sometimes this variation is idiosyncratic and must be listed as part of a morpheme's phonological representation. For example, there is no way to predict on the basis of general rules that the English plural morpheme has the form *en* when suffixed to the noun *ox*. Quite often, however, the different phonetic shapes of a morpheme can be predicted by general rules. When this is the case, a morpheme can be attributed a single underlying representation despite its phonetic variation. The hypothesis that morphemes have uniform underlying representations whose divergent phonetic shapes can be accounted for by general rules constitutes a powerful tool of phonological investigation.

Consider, for example, the infinitive and present tense forms of the Spanish verb *poder* 'be able to'.

poder	poðér	'to be able to'
puedo	pwéðo	'I am able to'
puedes	pwéðes	'you are able to'
puede	pwéðe	'he is able to'
podemos	poðémos	'we are able to'
podéis	poðéys	'you (PLURAL) are able to'
pueden	pwéðen	'they are able to'

The segmental phonetic shape of the root varies from form to form; in some cases it is [poð], and in others it is [pweð]. [o] and [we] are said to be in **alternation**. However, this alternation is anything but sporadic and irregular. Whenever the root is stressed, [we] appears; the root vowel is [o] whenever the root is unstressed. The alternation is completely regular, therefore, and depends on the placement of stress (stress in Spanish can itself be predicted by a general rule; see Problem 4.4–4 below).

We can account for this alternation by means of a phonological rule that changes stressed [o] to [we]: [ó] → [wé]. 'Be able to' thus has the uniform underlying representation /pod/. When the root vowel happens to be stressed, the rule changing [ó] to [wé] derives [pwéd] from [pód], and the ultimate phonetic manifestation [pwéð] results from the application of another general rule of Spanish (see Problem 4.1–8 below). The rule changing [ó] to [wé] proves to have considerable generality. Compare *morir* [morír] 'to die' and *muero* [mwéro] 'I die'; *cuerpo* [kwérpo] 'body' and *corpiño* [korpíño] 'little body'. (Not every occurrence of [ó] in Spanish changes to [wé], however; the rule must be refined in terms of a distinction between tense and lax vowels. Further discussion would carry us too far afield.)

We see from this example that the discrepancies between phonemic and phonetic representations are sometimes considerable. The phonemic segment /o/ is manifested phonetically as the sequence of segments [wé], each of which also occurs separately in Spanish as the manifestation of another phoneme. Moreover, neither [w] nor [e] shares all the features that characterize the underlying phoneme /o/ (for instance, [w] is not a vowel and [e] is not back or rounded). The regularity and predictability of the alternation precludes any real doubt that the rule changing [ó] to [wé] is a valid structural principle of Spanish—consider the consequences of claiming that it was not. First, it would be necessary to attribute to 'be able to' (and many other morphemes) two different underlying representations, one with /o/ and one with /we/, instead of a single, uniform representation. Second, one would have to list those uses of 'be able to' requiring the phonological representation with /o/ and those requiring the representation with /we/. Finally, one would be claiming that the correlation between the [o]-[we] alternation and the placement of stress was merely an elaborate coincidence devoid of structural significance. Such an analysis would be both uninsightful and more complex than the one proposed. Thus by any reasonable criteria the rule changing [ó] to [wé], as well as phonological representations with /o/, must be judged to be strongly motivated. We may conclude, then, that the phonemic representations posited to account for regular alternations in the phonetic shape of morphemes are sometimes quite abstract. These abstract representations are justified by the significant generalizations they allow.

Clearly it is desirable to be able to postulate a single phonological representation to underlie the various phonetic shapes of a morpheme; by listing several different phonological representations for a morpheme, we do no more than describe the lack of a generalization. However, there is little point in positing an abstract but uniform phonemic representation unless its alternative phonetic shapes can be derived from it by general rules. For example, the underlying representation of the English plural morpheme is /z/ for most nouns, but it must be different, perhaps /en/, for the plural of *ox*. It would be possible to eliminate the special form /en/ by positing a rule that changes /z/ to [en] after *ox* (the ultimate phonetic shape [ŋ]—syllabic [n]—would be derived by general rules beyond the scope of this discussion). But this analysis is quite unsatisfactory. The rule changing /z/ to [en] is totally ad hoc, since it accounts for only one form and has no independent justification. The analysis serves only to obscure a lexical irregularity by disguising it as a phonological one and is thus devoid of significance; we must simply face up to the fact that the English plural morpheme has more than one underlying segmental representation. By way of contrast, the rule changing [ó] to [wé] in Spanish is quite general and accounts for variations in the manifestation of many different morphemes. It can be justified independently of any consideration of *poder*.

In justifying abstract phonemic representations, consequently, the simplicity, generality, and naturalness of the requisite phonological rules are important considerations. If the postulation of a particular underlying representation permits the derivation of its divergent phonetic manifestations by means of simple and natural phonological rules that can be motivated on independent grounds, this is evidence of the strongest kind that the hypothesized phonological representation is correct in its essentials. Other factors relevant to the justification of underlying representations include the desirability of minimizing the number of different phonemes that must be postulated; the tendency for the segmental inventories of languages to fall into symmetrical patterns of certain kinds; and most important, the possibility of capturing significant generalizations that could not be captured with alternative analyses.

Consider the following forms from Classical Mongolian (Lightner, 1965); [ɣ] stands for a voiced velar fricative, a sound like [g] except that it is a fricative rather than a stop.

uɣuta	'bag'
köbegün	'son, boy'
qubilʲan	'transformation'
kötelbüri	'instruction'

Classical Mongolian displays a system of vowel harmony very similar to the one described for Turkish in Problem 2.1–4, (p. 45). All the vowels in a word must be front vowels, or else they must all be back vowels. The one exception to this generalization is that [i] can appear with either front or back vowels in a word, though phonetically it is front. Thus [i] occurs with the back vowels [u a] in the word for 'transformation', and with the front vowels [ö e ü] in the word for 'instruction'. The vowel system of Classical Mongolian is also very much like that of Turkish, except that there are only seven vowels; the high back unrounded [ɨ] of Turkish does not occur phonetically in Mongolian.

FRONT		BACK	
i	ü		u
e	ö	a	o

The vowel system is slightly skewed; if there were an [ɨ] in Classical Mongolian, the system would be perfectly symmetrical.

Given these facts, it is not unreasonable to posit an eighth underlying vowel for Classical Mongolian, the vowel /ɨ/. This eighth vowel is rendered phonetically as [i] by virtue of a rule that changes [ɨ] to /i/ in all environments. Thus /ɨ/, not /i/, occurs in the underlying representation of the word for 'transformation', but /i/ appears in the underlying representation of the form for 'instruction'. At this abstract level, consequently, the rule of vowel harmony has no exceptions; the vowels of a word must all be front vowels or they must all be back vowels, and /i/ occurs only with the former (/ɨ/ with the latter). The postulation of abstract representations with /ɨ/ thus has two simultaneous advantages: it regularizes the rule of vowel harmony, and it leads to a more symmetrical system of underlying vowels. There is a concomitant disadvantage, namely, that one extra underlying segment must be posited, as well as an extra phonological rule. Further evidence is therefore needed before the analysis can be established conclusively. Some additional support for the analysis is provided by the fact that [ɨ] occurred phonetically at an earlier stage in the history of Mongolian, eventually merging with [i].

For a second illustration of the kinds of evidence that bear on the postulation of abstract phonemic representations, let us consider restrictions on word-initial consonant clusters in English. The alveolar fricative [s] can occur before a number of consonants as the first member of an initial consonant cluster: *smack, snare, spike, stick, skill, slip.* Some combinations involving [s] are excluded for independent reasons extraneous to the point at hand (for example, [s] cannot be followed by a voiced consonant because the members of an English obstruent cluster must agree in voicing), but the non-occurrence of one particular combination, *[sr], lacks apparent explanation. There are no forms like *srack* or *srip*, and there would seem to be no principled reason for this gap. With the palatal fricative [š] the facts are very different. Leaving aside words like *Schlitz, schnook,* and *schlemiel*—words that were borrowed from German or Yiddish or that are modeled after words borrowed from these languages—[š] does not occur at all as the first member of word-initial consonant clusters. However, there is one notable exception; [š] does occur in the cluster [šr]: *shrimp, shrill, shrink, shroud.*

We thus seem to be faced with two irregularities, the occurrence of [šr] and the non-occurrence of *[sr].

sp	st	sk	sm	sn	sl	*sr
*šp	*št	*šk	*šm	*šn	*šl	šr

However, it is apparent that both irregularities can be eliminated by positing phonemic representations beginning in /sr/ for words that begin phonetically in [šr]. These abstract representations are partially justified by the generalizations they allow us to capture in regard to the distribution of /s/ and /š/. The price that must be paid for these generalizations is the postulation of an additional phonological rule, one that changes /s/ to [š] before [r].

Because the regularization of the distributional patterns of [s] and [š] is at least partially offset by the need for a special phonological rule, further evidence would be desirable. As indirect corroboration of the analysis one might cite dialects of English in which [sr] occurs instead of initial [šr]; in these dialects, for instance, *shrimp* is pronounced [srɪmp] rather than [šrɪmp]. The existence of such dialects is readily explained in terms of the proposed analysis, since phonetic sequences such as [srɪmp] coincide exactly with the hypothesized phonological representations. *Shrimp* has the phonemic representation /srɪmp/ in all dialects, but not all dialects happen to share the rule that converts this underlying representation to [šrɪmp]. (Anecdotal evidence can also be cited. A speaker of the dialect with [šr], when making a Spoonerism of the expression *Freudian slip*, spontaneously produced *Shreudian flip* instead of the expected *Sreudian flip*. The putative rule [s] → [š] is evidently responsible.) All things considered, then, a strong (though hardly conclusive) case can be made for abstract representations with /sr/.

A final example of the justification of abstract phonemic representations is provided by Nupe, a language spoken in Nigeria (compare Hyman, 1970).

The surface vowels of Nupe include [i e a o u]. There are three distinctive tones, high, mid, and low, marked by the respective diacritics [' ^ ']. Before the front vowels [i e], consonants are regularly palatalized. Consonants are regularly labialized before the rounded vowels [o u]. The following examples illustrate the palatalization and labialization rules:

/êgî/ ⟶ êgʸî 'child'

/êgê/ ⟶ êgʸê 'beer'

/êgû/ ⟶ êgʷû 'mud'

/êgó/ ⟶ êgʷó 'grass'

The rules seem to break down for consonants before [a], however. In some forms, consonants palatalize before [a]; in others, they labialize; and in still others, they undergo neither modification:

    êgʸà 'blood'   êgʷâ 'hand'   êgâ 'stranger'

The difference between plain, palatalized, and labialized consonants appears to be distinctive before [a], therefore, although their distribution is predictable in other environments.

However, an alternative analysis is possible, one in which palatalized and labialized consonants can be eliminated from the inventory of phonemes. Two additional underlying vowels can be postulated, the front vowel /ɛ/ and the back rounded vowel /ɔ/. /ɛ/ rather than /a/ is posited in the underlying representations of those forms in which palatalization occurs, and /ɔ/ in those in which labialization occurs. Phonemic /a/ is posited only for those forms to which neither rule applies. In addition, a phonological rule must be postulated that changes /ɛ/ and /ɔ/ to [a]. Under this alternative analysis, palatalization and labialization are fully predictable, the former applying only before front vowels and the latter only before rounded vowels; /a/, of course, is neither front nor rounded. The derivations of 'blood', 'hand', and 'stranger' are sketched in Figure 4.1–2.

PHONOLOGICAL   PHONETIC
REPRESENTATION   REPRESENTATION

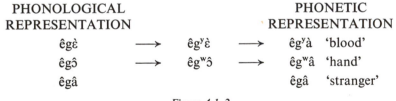

    êgὲ   ⟶   êgʸὲ   ⟶   êgʸà 'blood'

    êgɔ̂   ⟶   êgʷɔ̂   ⟶   êgʷâ 'hand'

    êgâ   êgâ 'stranger'

Figure 4.1–2

This alternative analysis requires two new vowels and one new rule, but on balance its advantages are more impressive. For one thing, it makes palatalization and labialization fully regular and general processes in Nupe, whereas they appeared sporadic in the former analysis. Second, it eliminates palatalized and labialized consonants from the inventory of underlying segments, since their occurrence is always predictable—this saving more than compensates for the need to posit two new vowel phonemes. Further motivation for the analysis is provided by the treatment of loan words in Nupe. For example, when the Yoruba word [tɔ̂rɛ̂] 'give a gift' was borrowed into Nupe, it assumed the phonetic shape [tʷârʸâ]; this is exactly the shape predicted by the rules of palatalization and labialization, as well as the rule changing /ɛ ɔ/ to [a].

This example from Nupe also illustrates the ordering of phonological rules. Clearly, palatalization and labialization must apply prior to the rule changing /ɛ ɔ/ to [a]. If the latter applied first, there would be no way to ensure that palatalization and labialization would occur in the correct forms.

Problem 4.1–5   Nupe

In the preceding discussion, evidence was advanced to support the hypothesis that certain underlying representations in Nupe contain the vowels /ɛ ɔ/, both of which are manifested phonetically as [a]. The pairs of words below (Hyman, 1970) illustrate a process of Nupe by means of which nouns are derived from verbs. State the rule that determines the phonological shape of a derived noun in relation to the shape of the underlying verb. On the basis of this data, construct a further argument for positing the underlying vowels /ɛ ɔ/ in Nupe. The diacritics [' ^ '] stand for high, mid, and low tone respectively.

Verbs		*Nouns*	
gʸí	'eat'	gʸîgʸí	'eating'
gʸê	'be good'	gʸîgʸê	'goodness'
gʷú	'puncture'	gʷûgʷú	'puncturing'
gʷò	'receive'	gʷûgʷò	'receiving'
tá	'tell'	tʸîtá	'telling'
tʷá	'trim'	tʷûtʷá	'trimming'
tʸá	'be mild'	tʸîtʸá	'mildness'

Solution

The nouns are derived phonologically from the verbs by inserting before the verb stem a syllable consisting of a consonant plus a vowel. The consonant is the same as the consonant of the verb stem. The vowel is always [î] or [û], and its quality depends on the nature of the stem vowel. Based on the first five pairs, the generalization seems to be that the added vowel is [û] if the stem vowel is rounded, but [î] otherwise.

The forms for 'trimming' and 'mildness' seem to violate this generalization, since the added vowels are [û] and [î] respectively, despite the fact that the stem vowel in both words is the unrounded vowel [á]. However, the discrepancy is cleared up if the analysis involving underlying /ɛ ɔ/ for words with [a] is adopted. The underlying stem vowel of 'trim' must be /ɔ/, since the initial /t/ of 'trim' is labialized. If the underlying stem vowel is /ɔ/, the occurrence of [û] in the derived noun is regular, because /ɔ/ is a rounded vowel. Similarly, the underlying stem vowel of 'be mild' must be /ɛ/, which is unrounded, because the initial /t/ of 'be mild' is palatalized. Thus the form for 'mildness' has [î], in accordance with the general rule. 'Trimming' and 'mildness' have the following derivations:

$$/tɔ́/ \longrightarrow tûtɔ́ \longrightarrow t^wût^wɔ́ \longrightarrow t^wût^wá$$
$$/tɛ́/ \longrightarrow tîtɛ́ \longrightarrow t^yît^yɛ́ \longrightarrow t^yît^yá$$

Discussion

Rule ordering is crucial if the significant generalizations in the data are to be captured. The formation of derived nouns by the addition of an initial syllable to the verb stem must precede palatalization and labialization, because the added consonant undergoes these rules. Noun formation must also precede the change of /ɛ ɔ/ to [a], since it must distinguish between /ɛ/ and /ɔ/, which are no longer distinct once they both become [a]. We saw earlier that palatalization and labialization must also apply before /ɛ ɔ/ change to [a].

Problem 4.1–6   Classical Aztec

Several morphemes in the data below have more than one phonetic shape. Posit uniform underlying representations for these morphemes and justify your choice. Formulate a general phonological rule that will account for the phonetic variation. The morpheme [ƛi] or [li] is called an **absolutive** ending (*ABS*). On the basis of the data, state the syntactic conditions that determine whether or not the absolutive ending is used.

kal-li	taʔ-ƛi	teš-ƛi
house-ABS	father-ABS	flour-ABS
'house'	'father'	'flour'
no-kal	no-taʔ	no-teš
my-house	my-father	my-flour
'my house'	'my father'	'my flour'
akal-li	akal-lan	mo-ƛan
boat-ABS	boat-near	your-near
'boat'	'near a boat'	'near you'
ƛal-li	ƛaokoya	ni-wal-laokoya
land-ABS	sad	I-come-sad
'land'	'he is sad'	'I am sad'

Solution

The absolute suffix and the morphemes for 'near' and 'sad' vary in their phonetic manifestations. *ABS* appears as either [ƛi] or [li], 'near' as either [ƛan] or [lan], and 'sad' as either [ƛaokoya] or [laokoya]. In all these forms there is an alternation between [ƛ] and [l]. This alternation is governed by the phonological environment; [l] is used when the preceding segment is [l], and [ƛ] is used when the preceding segment is another consonant or a vowel, or when no segment at all precedes. Consequently, /ƛi/, /ƛan/, and /ƛaokoya/ can be posited as the underlying representations of these morphemes. The phonetic variants in [l] are derived by a rule that changes /ƛ/ to [l] immediately after another occurrence of [l]. 'House', for instance, has the derivation /kal-ƛi/ → [kal-li].

/ƛ/ rather than /l/ is posited as the underlying consonant in those morphemes that show the alternation because a simple rule can be given that specifies the conditions under which /ƛ/ changes to [l]. If [l] were chosen as the underlying consonant, the rule changing [l] to [ƛ] would be more complex, since the rule would have to be able to apply in any of three environments: after a vowel, after any consonant other than [l], or in word-initial position. Moreover, such a rule would have many exceptions (for example, [no-kal] 'my house'). The change of /ƛ/ to [l] is predictable, but the converse would not be.

The absolutive ending /ƛi/ occurs on nouns to which no other affix is attached; it apparently has no meaning. When a possessive prefix or a postposition is added to a noun, the absolutive does not appear.

Problem 4.1–7 English

In Problem 4.1–1 a rule was formulated that changes [ay] to [ʌy] directly before a voiceless segment in English. This problem concerns the interaction between this rule and a rule affecting alveolar stops.

In the words transcribed below, certain morphemes have more than one phonetic shape. Posit uniform phonemic representations for these morphemes and justify your choice. Formulate a phonological rule that accounts for the phonetic variation and state how this rule is ordered with respect to the rule [ay] → [ʌy]. Show the derivations of *sights* and *sighted*. [D] stands for a voiced alveolar flap, a sound much like [d] produced by flapping the tongue rapidly against the alveolar ridge. [ɹ̩] represents a *syllabic* [r]. Syllabic elements are those that stand as the "nucleus" of a syllable; most vowels are therefore syllabic, but consonants normally are not.

write	rʌyt	lighter	lʌyDɹ̩	sighted	sʌyDəd
writer	rʌyDɹ̩	lightest	lʌyDəst	sightless	sʌytləs
writing	rʌyDɪŋ	lighting	lʌyDɪŋ	tight	tʌyt
night	nʌyt	lightning	lʌytnɪŋ	tightly	tʌytli
nightly	nʌytli	sight	sʌyt	tighter	tʌyDɹ̩
light	lʌyt	sights	sʌyts	tightness	tʌytnəs

Solution

Some root morphemes have two alternate phonetic shapes, one ending in [t] and the other ending in [D]. The distribution of these variants is predictable by rule: [D] is used when the following segment is syllabic, and [t] otherwise. Underlying representations with /t/ can therefore be postulated, and [D] is derived by a rule that changes /t/ to [D] when it occurs between two syllabic elements (the diphthong [ʌy] is a syllable nucleus and can thus be counted as a syllable element). *Sights* and *sighted*, for instance, have the following derivations:

/sayt-s/ ⟶ sʌyt-s

/sayt-əd/ ⟶ sʌyt-əd ⟶ sʌyD-əd

/t/ rather than /D/ must be posited in the underlying representations. One reason is that it is simpler to state the environment of the rule /t/ → [D] than that of its converse. A second reason is that [ʌy] appears in the phonetic representations of all these forms; the rule changing /ay/ to [ʌy] applies only before a voiceless consonant, and if /D/ were posited, the rule could never apply in the derivation of words like *writer* and *sighted*. For the same reason, /ay/ → [ʌy] must precede the voicing of /t/ to [D]. The former requires a following voiceless segment, but the following segment will be voiced once /t/ → [D] applies.

CONCLUSION

To summarize, underlying phonological representations list those phonological properties of a lexical item that are idiosyncratic to it and not predictable by rules of any generality. The phonological representation of most morphemes includes a sequence of distinctive phonological segments, or phonemes. Phonemes typically have alternate phonetic manifestations that are predictable by rules, usually on the basis of the surrounding phonological environment.

The phonemic representations of lexical items are sometimes very abstract. Deriving the phonetic manifestation of a lexical item from its phonological representation often involves the application of many ordered rules, and in many instances it is impossible to tell from the phonetic properties of a segment alone what underlying segment it represents. Abstract representations are posited in phonology for the same basic reason that they are posited in syntax; namely, they make it possible to reveal structural regularities and to capture significant linguistic generalizations that could not otherwise be expressed. It is in these terms that a putative underlying representation can be most strongly motivated.

FURTHER PROBLEMS

Problem 4.1–8   Spanish

Phonetically, the voiced obstruents of Spanish include a series of voiced stops, [b d g], and a series of voiced fricatives, [β ð γ]; the first member of each series is bilabial, the second dental, and the third velar. On the basis of the forms below, determine the phonological relationship of these two series of obstruents.

usted	usteð	'you'	*miga*	miγa	'bit'
libertad	liβertað	'liberty'	*gobernar*	goβernar	'govern'
boga	boγa	'vogue'	*gato*	gato	'cat'
ambos	ambos	'both'	*hago*	aγo	'I do'
lobo	loβo	'wolf'	*dormido*	dormiðo	'slept'
cubo	kuβo	'cube'	*boda*	boða	'wedding'
dado	daðo	'given'	*donde*	donde	'where'
falda	falda	'skirt'			

Problem 4.1–9   Klamath

The data below (Kisseberth, *to appear*) is from Klamath, an American Indian language spoken in Oregon. All the forms consist of a verb stem followed by a suffix or a series of suffixes; the boundary between the stem and suffixes is marked by a hyphen. Phonetically, the stems in column I differ from the corresponding stems in column II. Determine which set of stems are best regarded as being most similar to the underlying phonological representations, and formulate a rule that will derive the other set of stems from them. The superscript [ʔ] indicates that the preceding segment is glottalized.

I		II	
somʔalwʔ-a	'writes'	somʔaloo-yeega	'starts to write'
čoLy-oola	'takes off a shirt'	čoLii-bli	'puts a shirt back on'
nidw-alla	'guesses someone's plot'	nidoo-s	'guessing'
mbotyʔ-a	'wrinkles'	mbotii-tk	'wrinkled up'
saǰaqw-a	'washes the hands'	saǰaqoo-ča	'goes to wash the hands'
smʔoqʔy-a	'has a mouthful'	smʔoqʔii-tk	'having a mouthful'
čonw-a	'vomits'	čonoo-nʔapga	'feels like vomiting'

Problem 4.1–10   Luiseño

Luiseño has a set of absolutive suffixes that function much like the Aztec absolutive ending /ƛi/ discussed in Problem 4.1–6 (compare also Problem 3.6–4, p. 201). Three of these suffixes are illustrated in the list of nouns below. Isolate the non-stem morphemes in the data and discuss the character of their phonological representations. Describe the derivation of the object form of 'river'.

kutapiš	'bow'	waniča	'river'
kutapičum	'bows'	waničam	'rivers'
nokutapi	'my bow'	waniš	'river' (object)
nokutapim	'my bows'	huula	'arrow'
huukapiš	'pipe'	huulam	'arrows'
huukapičum	'pipes'	nohuu	'my arrow'
nohuukapi	'my pipe'	huul	'arrow' (object)
nohuukapim	'my pipes'	yula	'hair'
kiča	'house'	noyu	'my hair'
kičam	'houses'	yul	'hair' (object)
noki	'my house'	paala	'water'
nokim	'my houses'	paal	'water' (object)
kiš	'house' (object)		

Problem 4.1–11   Yawelmani

The verb forms below (Kuroda, 1967) are from the Yawelmani dialect of Yokuts, an American Indian language of the California Penutian family. Each form consists of a verb stem and an affix that indicates either the "aorist" tense (in the first column) or the passive aorist tense (in the second column). Isolate the morphemes and posit, where possible, a single underlying representation for each. State the rule or rules responsible for the variation in their phonetic manifestation. Give the derivation of [panat] 'arrive (PASSIVE AORIST)'.

Aorist	*Passive Aorist*	
xathin	xatit	'eat'
gophin	gopit	'take care of infant'
giyʔhin	giyʔit	'touch'
ṣaphin	ṣaapit	'burn'
gobhin	goobit	'take in'
mekʔhin	meekʔit	'swallow'
panaahin	panat	'arrive'
hoyoohin	hoyot	'name'
ʔileehin	ʔilet	'fan'
pʔaxatʔhin	pʔaxaatʔit	'mourn'
ʔopothin	ʔopootit	'arise from bed'
hibeyhin	hibeeyit	'bring water'

Problem 4.1–12   *French*

Despite phonetic variation, each of the French morphemes in the data below can be attributed a single phonological representation. Their phonetic manifestations are derived by two phonological rules. Posit a phonemic representation for each morpheme and state the required rules. Show the derivations of *fin* and *un*. [ü] stands for a high front rounded vowel (the rounded counterpart of [i]), and [ö] stands for a mid front rounded vowel (the rounded counterpart of [ɛ]).

noir	nwar	'black' (masculine)	*noire*	nwarə	'black' (feminine)
clair	klɛr	'bright' (masculine)	*claire*	klɛrə	'bright' (feminine)
certain	sɛrtɛ̃	'certain' (masculine)	*certaine*	sɛrtɛnə	'certain' (feminine)
fin	fɛ̃	'fine' (masculine)	*fine*	finə	'fine' (feminine)
vain	vɛ̃	'vain' (masculine)	*vaine*	vɛnə	'vain' (feminine)
un	ɔ̃	'one' (masculine)	*une*	ünə	'one' (feminine)
Jean	žã	'John'	*Jeanne*	žanə	'Jean'
bon	bɔ̃	'good' (masculine)	*bonne*	bɔnə	'good' (feminine)
bonté	bɔ̃te	'goodness'	*santé*	sãte	'health'
parfum	parfɔ̃	'perfume'	*parfumer*	parfüme	'to perfume'
don	dɔ̃	'gift'	*donner*	dɔne	'to give'
visible	viziblə	'visible'	*invisible*	ɛ̃viziblə	'invisible'
égal	egal	'equal'	*inégal*	inegal	'unequal'

Problem 4.1–13   *Tulu*

Tulu (data from William Bright) is a Dravidian language spoken in southern India. Isolate the morphemes in the data and posit a uniform underlying representation for each one. Formulate two rules that will account for the variation in their phonetic manifestations. Determine how these two rules must be ordered.

koru	'give!'	tini	'eat!'
korle	'give (PLURAL)!'	tinle	'eat (PLURAL)!'
korka	'let's give!'	tinka	'let's eat!'
korpæ	'I give'	tinpæ	'I eat'
korpa	'you give'	tinpa	'you eat'
korpe	'he gives'	tinpe	'he eats'
korpolu	'she gives'	tinpolu	'she eats'
korpa	'we give'	tinpa	'we eat'
korpari	'you (PLURAL) give'	tinpari	'you (PLURAL) eat'
korperi	'they give'	tinperi	'they eat'

kalpu	'learn!'	kullu	'sit!'
kalpule	'learn (PLURAL)!'	kullule	'sit (PLURAL)!'
kalpuga	'let's learn!'	kulluga	'let's sit!'
kalpuvæ	'I learn'	kulluvæ	'I sit'
kalpuva	'you learn'	kulluva	'you sit'
kalpuve	'he learns'	kulluve	'he sits'
kalpuvolu	'she learns'	kulluvolu	'she sits'
kalpuva	'we learn'	kulluva	'we sit'
kalpuvarɨ	'you (PLURAL) learn'	kulluvarɨ	'you (PLURAL) sit'
kalpuverɨ	'they learn'	kulluverɨ	'they sit'

4.2 Phonological Features

Speech sounds can be analyzed from several different points of view. One approach is to study the physical properties of sound waves being transmitted through the air. Another is to analyze sounds from the standpoint of speech perception. A third approach is to analyze sounds in terms of their production; such studies may pertain either to the covert neurological and physiological factors determining speech production or to the more readily observable movements of the organs by means of which speech sounds are articulated. This last approach, called **articulatory phonetics**, is by far the most firmly established and has been the basis for most advances in phonological analysis.

MOTIVATION OF FEATURES

Phonetically, a sound segment can be viewed as a simultaneously occurring bundle of articulatory properties. For instance, the English sound [s] is characterized phonetically as being simultaneously a fricative, alveolar, voiceless, non-nasal, non-labialized, non-glottalized, and so on. The sound [ɛ] is phonetically a vowel, front, mid, lax, non-nasal, voiced, unrounded, non-pharyngealized, and so forth. Phonemes also consist in bundles of properties, but at the phonemic level the bundles contain only distinctive properties. The phoneme /s/, for example, is fully characterized as a voiceless alveolar fricative, and /ɛ/ as mid, front, and lax. Other properties of [s] and [ɛ] are excluded at the phonemic level because they are predictable.

The properties in terms of which segments are characterized are referred to as **phonological features**. Choosing and justifying a set of features adequate to the analysis of the varied phonological systems of human languages is one of the primary theoretical concerns of modern linguistics. It is important to note that the choice and justification of a set of phonological features is empirical in nature, not a matter of personal preference or flipping a coin.

The fundamental decision to analyze segments as bundles of phonological features, rather than treating them as unanalyzable units, is also empirical in nature. A feature analysis is motivated by virtue of its efficacy in allowing us to capture significant linguistic generalizations that could not otherwise be expressed.

Consider, for example, the rule of English phonology that changes [ay] to [ʌy] (see Problem 4.1–1). The applicability of this rule depends on the following segment. The rule applies before such segments as [p t k f θ s], but it fails to apply before such segments as [b d g m n v z r l]. The class of segments before which the rule can apply is not an arbitrary one—all these segments are voiceless, and no voiced segment allows its application. The class is a phonetically natural one, therefore, since it consists of exactly those segments that share a certain phonetic property. This is a significant linguistic generalization, and it can be captured by formulating the rule in terms of the voicing feature: [ay] changes to [ʌy] before a voiceless segment. Notice, however, that this generalization can be captured only if segments are assumed to be properly analyzed as bundles of phonological features, so that it makes sense to speak of the class of segments that share the feature of voicelessness. If, instead, segments were treated as unanalyzable units, the rule could not refer to this specific feature but only to the segments as wholes. Such an analysis would be undesirable because the generalization could not be expressed. The rule changing [ay] to [ʌy] would have to list all those segments before which the change is permitted, as if these segments had no common defining property. The analysis would further be undesirable because of its needless complexity. A rule that merely listed each member of the phonetically natural class of voiceless segments would be no less complex than a rule specifying some fully arbitrary class of segments, such as [b o h y š l]. Consequently, the rule [ay] → [ʌy] provides empirical evidence for the decision to analyze segments as bundles of features, and also for the decision to include among these features the voiced-voiceless distinction.

Any phonological feature imposes a classification on the sound segments of a language. For instance, the voicing feature divides the segments of a language into two classes, those that are voiced and those that are voiceless. Of the myriad of features that could conceivably be proposed on the basis of purely phonetic properties, only relatively few prove to have phonological significance, in the sense that the classes of segments they define function alike with respect to phonological rules. Voicing is one such feature; the class of voiceless segments function alike with respect to the rule changing [ay] to [ʌy] in English. Many other examples could be cited of phonological rules whose most insightful formulation depends on the distinction between voiced and voiceless segments. Another feature crucial to the statement of general phonological rules in many languages is front versus back. For instance, the Turkish rule of vowel harmony requires that all the vowels in a word agree in their value for the front-back feature (see Problem 2.1–4,

p. 45). Phonological rules thus provide an empirical basis for choosing a set of features to be employed in the analysis of phonological systems. A particular set of features is motivated to the extent that it permits the simple expression of phonological regularities.

Many phonological rules must refer to individual segments rather than to classes of segments, but such rules are less general than rules formulable for entire classes of elements, and an analysis which minimizes the number of such rules is therefore desirable. Clearly the choice of features determines the classes of segments that can be referred to as a unit by means of a feature specification. Thus the front-back feature enables us to refer to the Turkish segment class [ɨ a u o] simply by specifying the feature value "back". The specification "voiced fricative" designates the segment class [v ð z ž] in English. On the other hand, no system of features seriously contemplated allows us to specify the class [b o h y š l], excluding all other segments of English, by means of one or a small number of feature values. In terms of features, it is simpler to refer to the class [v ð z ž] than to any individual member of this class. The entire class is designated by the two-feature specification "voiced fricative", but more than two features are needed to describe any individual segment; to uniquely indicate [z], for example, the three-feature specification "voiced alveolar fricative" is required. The segments [v ð z ž] are said to be a *natural class* in English, since in terms of features it is simpler to refer to the entire class than to any individual member of it; [b o h y š l] is not a natural class given any reasonable set of features.

A properly chosen set of features will therefore maximize the number of phonological rules that operate in terms of natural classes. If the present conception of phonological features is even remotely correct, it should prove possible to find many rules that affect the class of voiceless segments of a language, the class of back vowels, or the class of voiced fricatives, but few if any rules should operate on the class [b o h y š l] to the exclusion of all other segments. Not all rules apply only to natural classes of segments, but a great many certainly do—the concept of feature analysis has received an overwhelming amount of empirical support. However, the optimal inventory of features for describing the possible phonological systems of human languages has yet to be determined. This aspect of linguistic investigation is very much alive and involves many uncertainties, although a great deal has already been learned.

Problem 4.2–1   Maxakalí

The following data (Gudschinsky and Popovich, 1970) is from Maxakalí, a language spoken in Brazil. The forms in column I are underlying representations for the phonetic forms in column II (phonetic detail irrelevant to the point at hand has been omitted). State the rules necessary to relate the phonemic and phonetic representations of these words, treating segments as unanalyzable units. Restate the rules in terms of phonological features. These features should be such that they divide segments into natural classes that are motivated by virtue of their interaction with the phonological rules.

I	II	
/mep/	mbep, bep	'fox'
/nač/	ndač, dač	'pot'
/ñokoma/	ñǰokoma, ǰokoma	'below'
/ŋahap/	ŋgahap, gahap	'bottle'

Solution

If segments are treated as unanalyzable units, the following rules are required:

    (A) [b] is inserted after word-initial /m/.

    (B) [d] is inserted after word-initial /n/.

    (C) [ǰ] is inserted after word-initial /ñ/.

    (D) [g] is inserted after word-initial /ŋ/.

    (E) Before [b d ǰ g], [m n ñ ŋ] are optionally deleted in word-initial position.

   It is apparent that rules (A)–(E) do not express the generalizations implicit in the data. (A)–(D) are clearly special cases of a single general phenomenon, and in (E) it has been necessary to resort to lists of segments, as if the segments involved had no common defining property. The generalizations can be captured in terms of features such as "nasal", "voicing", "stop", and "place of articulation", with this last feature having the alternative values "labial", "alveolar", "palatal", and "velar". The general rules (F) and (G) then relate the forms in column I to those in column II:

    (F) After a word-initial nasal, a voiced stop is inserted that has the same value as the nasal with respect to place of articulation.

    (G) A word-initial nasal is optionally deleted before a voiced stop.

The segments [b d ǰ g] are grouped as a natural class by means of the two-feature specification "voiced stop", and [m n ñ ŋ] by means of the specification "nasal".

Discussion

The segment [ǰ] is not quite parallel to [b d g], since it is a voiced affricate rather than a voiced stop. However, affricates are closely related to stops, since they involve a stop closure that is released with the turbulence characteristic of fricatives. The occurrence of [ǰ] rather than a simple palatal stop after /ñ/ is not unexpected in terms of universal phonological tendencies. While palatal stops do occur, they are much less common than palatal affricates. There is a universal tendency for (oral) palatal consonants formed with stop closure to be realized as affricates rather than simple stops, and for non-palatal consonants to be realized as simple stops rather than affricates. The apparent non-parallelism between [j] and [b d g] thus results from the interaction of (F), a rule of Maxakalí, with a phonological universal.

TYPES OF FEATURES

A definitive inventory of features to be employed in the description of phonological systems has yet to be established. It would be inappropriate to discuss the advantages and disadvantages of competing systems in a book of this sort. We will concern ourselves instead with a brief survey of the kinds of features that have proved relevant in phonological description, primarily from the point of view of articulatory phonetics.

The features which divide the segments of a language into the largest subclasses are referred to as *major class features*. The most important of these features is the consonant-vowel distinction. Many phonological generalizations require reference to consonants or vowels in their statement, the nature of the consonants or vowels being irrelevant. In Mohawk, for instance, a stressed vowel is lengthened if at most one consonant follows (see Problem 4.1–3). In Yawelmani a vowel is shortened when it is followed by two consonants or a single consonant and a word boundary (Problem 4.1–11).

A second major class feature is the distinction between obstruents and sonorants (also called resonants). Obstruents include stops, fricatives, and affricates, sounds whose articulation involves an obstruction in the vocal tract. Sonorants include vowels, liquids, glides, and nasals. Nasals sometimes pattern like obstruents, since they are articulated with an oral stop closure; however, air continues to flow (through the nasal cavity) throughout their articulation, and in this respect they are like the other sonorants. The obstruent-sonorant feature functions in the statement of a constraint on possible consonant clusters in English. All the obstruents in a cluster must agree in voicing. Voiceless clusters like [čt] are therefore possible (for example, *reached*), as are voiced clusters such as [zd] (*raised*), but mixed clusters such as [čd] or [sd] are not permitted. Mixed consonant clusters are possible, however, when one consonant is a sonorant (*art, lamp*).

Within the class of consonants, segments are further divided according to their *manner of articulation*. Nasals, stops, fricatives, affricates, glides, and liquids embody the major manners of consonant articulation. It is not clear precisely what features are optimal for the characterization of consonant classes, but it is clear that many rules must refer to these classes. We will continue to refer to nasals, stops, fricatives, affricates, glides, and liquids as natural classes without speculating as to exactly what features should be postulated. In Alabaman, for example, a vowel is nasalized if it precedes two consonants, the first of which is a nasal (Problem 4.1–4). A voiced stop in Spanish becomes a fricative after a vowel (Problem 4.1–8). In Klamath a stem-final glide becomes a long vowel before a consonant (Problem 4.1–9). The members of each class of consonants can be further divided with respect to what might be called secondary-manner-of-articulation features. Among these features are voiced versus voiceless, tense versus lax, aspirated versus unaspirated, labialized (that is, rounded) versus non-labialized, palatalized versus non-palatalized, and so on.

Unlike consonants, vowels are relatively uniform as to their manner of articulation. They are produced by the passage of air through the oral or nasal cavity without significant obstruction or turbulence. Vowels are virtually always voiced, though voiceless vowels do exist at the phonetic level in some languages (such as Japanese and Comanche). Secondary-manner-of-articulation features most pertinent to the classification of vowels include tenseness, nasalization, and rounding; others, such as glottalization, are much more important for consonants than for vowels.

Both consonants and vowels can be further classified on the basis of their *place of articulation*. For the consonants, the major places of articulation are labial, dental, alveolar, palatal, velar, and glottal. Of course, there are intermediate possibilities as well, and it is sometimes pertinent to take into account the portion of the tongue involved in a consonant articulation (the tip, blade, or dorsum) as well as the point along the vocal tract at which the articulation is made. For some purposes, it is useful to regard labial, dental, alveolar, palatal, velar, and perhaps glottal as alternate values of a single "place of articulation" feature; this feature allowed us to make a simple statement of rule (F) for Maxakalí in Problem 4.2–1. However, some of these places of articulation behave alike with respect to phonological rules and should perhaps be grouped together by means of additional features. For example, in Alabaman palatals and velars function alike as opposed to other consonants; /t/ is retracted to [ṭ] when the following segment is /č/ or /k/, but not before vowels or other consonants (Problem 4.1–4). Similarly, labials and velars sometimes display properties not shared by other consonants, as do dentals, alveolars, and palatals. Features that determine natural classes with respect to place of articulation must take such affinities into account. Two segments that have the same place of articulation are said to be *homorganic*. [m] and [p], for instance, are homorganic, since both are bilabial. By making use of this traditional concept (which is not easily expressed in terms of most feature systems in current use), we can simplify the statement of rule (F) in Problem 4.2–1 still further: After a word-initial nasal, a homorganic voiced stop is inserted.

For vowels, place of articulation is discussed in reference to a "horizontal" and a "vertical" dimension. During the articulation of a vowel, the tongue is arched toward some point along the roof of the mouth, from the alveolar ridge to the velar region. Vowels are characterized as front, central, or back according to their place of articulation along this dimension. They are characterized as high, mid, or low depending on the degree to which the tongue approaches the roof of the mouth. Naturally, finer distinctions can be made along both of these dimensions when necessary. It is not clear whether high, mid, and low should be regarded as alternate values of a single height feature or whether vowel height should be categorized by means of two-valued features such as high versus non-high and low versus non-low.

Although different features are normally used to characterize vowels and consonants, certain vowels and consonants bear special relationships to one another due to proximity in their place of articulation or to the sharing of secondary-manner-of-articulation features. For example, there is a tendency for palatal or fronted velar consonants to appear in contiguity with high vowels, particularly high front vowels, since the tongue approaches the palatal region during the articulation of these vowels. Thus /ʔ/ has the palatalized allophone [ʔʸ] after [i] in Maxakalí, as mentioned earlier. The palatalization of consonants before front vowels in Nupe is phonetically natural, as is the rounding or labialization of consonants before rounded vowels. The glide [y] is intimately related to the high front vowel [i], and the rounded glide [w] to the rounded back vowels [u] and [o], as the Klamath data of Problem 4.1–9 clearly shows. The tendency for vowels to be nasalized when adjacent to a nasal consonant is another example (see Problem 4.1–12, French).

Problem 4.2–2   Kitsai

According to the analysis of Bucca and Lesser (1969), Kitsai, an American Indian language of the Caddoan family, has the following inventory of distinctive segments: /t k ʔ s h n r y w i u e a/. The forms in column I below are the underlying representations for the forms in column II. Determine which segments function alike with respect to the rule that derives the forms in II from their phonemic representations, and state the rule in terms of a feature that groups these segments in a natural class.

I	*II*	
/kukuhunantsakya/	kukuhunahtsakya	'stuck in the ground'
/ahunanki/	ahunahki	'hoes'
/kusanʔatsiu/	kusahʔatsiu	'house grass'
/warasnyuk/	warasnyuk	'he is bad'

Solution

/n/ changes to [h] when the following segment is [t], [k], or [ʔ]. These segments can be distinguished from all the others and grouped as a natural class by means of the "stop" feature. The rule that derives the forms in II from their underlying representations in I can be stated as follows: /n/ changes to [h] before a stop.

Problem 4.2–3   *English*

Certain English vowels always occur in combination with a following glide that is not present at the phonemic level. Describe these vowels by means of a feature specification that groups them as a natural class. State the glide insertion rule. Irrelevant phonetic detail is omitted.

cat	kæt	*seen*	sin	*pool*	pul	*often*	ɔfn̩
bid	bɪd	*ball*	bɔl	*fame*	feym	*bowl*	bowl
moat	mowt	*trade*	treyd	*put*	pʊt	*tonic*	tanɪk
set	sɛt	*float*	flowt	*send*	sɛnd	*waste*	weyst

Solution

Phonetically, [e] is always followed by [y], and [o] by [w]. [e o] can be distinguished from the other vowels by means of the two-feature specification "mid tense". The feature "mid" distinguishes them from the high vowels [i ɪ u ʊ] and the low vowels [æ a]. The specification "tense" distinguishes them from the mid lax vowels [ɛ ɔ]. The glide insertion rule can be stated as follows: After a mid tense vowel, a glide is inserted that agrees with the vowel in rounding.

FURTHER PROBLEMS

Problem 4.2–4   *Kitsai*

Column I contains the underlying representations of the Kitsai forms in column II (Bucca and Lesser, 1969; compare Problem 4.2–2). Determine which segments function alike with respect to the major rule that derives the forms in II from those in I, and state the required rules in terms of feature specifications that group the proper segments as natural classes. Comment on rule ordering. Give the derivation of the first form.

I	*II*	
/atrihku/	anihku	'I tell'
/atakrihku/	ataknihku	'I tell them'
/asrikuku/	asnikuku	'you are sensible'
/atarakrikuku/	ataraknikuku	'we are sensible'
/nutrahikahu/	nunahikahu	'he is telling a story'
/asrakrihku/	asnaknihku	'you (PLURAL) tell him'
/nikayrat/	nikayrat	'he sates himself'

Problem 4.2–5   Klamath

The simple and complex verb stems below (Kisseberth, *to appear*) illustrate four kinds of prefixation in Klamath. Determine the character of the phonological representations of these prefixes; their phonological representations should be uniform despite phonetic variation. State the phonological rules required by the data. Major class features are pertinent, and there is one rule that applies in the derivation of all the stems containing prefixes.

nooga	'is cooked'	smookʔa	'tans a hide'
nonooga	'are cooked'	smosmookʔa	'tan a hide'
hosnooga	'causes to be cooked'	twaaqʔa	'paints'
peewa	'bathes'	satwaaqʔa	'paints oneself'
pepeewa	'bathe'	lmeelʔga	'sink'
hespeewa	'causes to bathe'	snelmeelʔga	'makes sink'
geejiga	'is tired'	pʔlooqʔa	'smears with pitch (on head)'
gegeejiga	'are tired'		
snegeejiga	'makes tired'	sopʔlooqʔa	'smears oneself with pitch (on head)'
čaantgi	'admires'		
hasčaantgi	'causes to admire'		
sačaantgi	'admires oneself'		

Problem 4.2–6   English

Certain English consonants have syllabic allophones (marked with the diacritic [̩]); their occurrence is predictable by rule. Formulate a rule that accounts for the syllabic consonants in the data below.

center	sɛntṛ	*baffle*	bæfl̩	*bottom*	baDm̩
central	sɛntr̩l	*baffling*	bæflɪŋ	*children*	čɪldr̩n
centrality	sɛntrælɪDi	*baffled*	bæfl̩d	*helm*	hɛlm
winter	wɪntṛ	*baffler*	bæflṛ	*darn*	darn
wintry	wɪntri	*kindle*	kɪndl̩	*fission*	fɪšn̩
shovel	šʌvl̩	*kindling*	kɪndlɪŋ	*vision*	vɪžn̩
shoveling	šʌvlɪŋ	*lime*	laym	*buxom*	bʌksm̩
shoveled	šʌvl̩d	*man*	mæn	*vixen*	vɪksn̩
shoveler	šʌvlṛ	*rail*	reyl	*tunnel*	tʌnl̩
shovels	šʌvl̩z	*near*	nir	*swimmer*	swɪmṛ

4.3   Segmental Phonology

In this section we will be primarily concerned with phonological processes that pertain to sequences of segments. Suprasegmental phenomena are the subject of section 4.4.

RULE TYPES

Of the several kinds of phonological rules that apply to sequences of segments, rules that change the value of a segment for some phonological feature are no doubt the most common. Numerous feature-changing rules were discussed in sections 4.1 and 4.2. Examples from English include the change from [ay] to [ʌy] before a voiceless segment (see Problem 4.1–1), the change from /s/ to [š] before [r], and the voicing of /t/ to [D] between two syllabic elements (Problem 4.1–7). We saw that in Spanish a voiced stop becomes a fricative directly after a vowel (Problem 4.1–8). In Alabaman (Problem 4.1–4) a stop is unreleased when it precedes a consonant. An *intervocalic* consonant—that is, a consonant occurring between two vowels— is voiced in Tulu (Problem 4.1–13). Feature-changing rules in Kitsai include the manifestation of /n/ as [h] before a stop (Problem 4.2–2) and the change of /r/ to [n] after an obstruent (Problem 4.2–4). Examples of rules that change the feature values of segments in particular phonological environments could be multiplied almost indefinitely.

Other phonological rules have the effect of altering the order or number of segments in an expression. A change in the order of a sequence of segments is called *metathesis*. Metathesis rules are not nearly so common as other rule types, but they do occur. For example, in Koasati, a Muskogean language, the plural prefix is [uh] before vowels; before consonants it is [hu], indicating the existence of a rule that metathesizes [u] and [h] in the proper environment (Thompson, 1969). Additional examples of metathesis rules are given in the problems for this section.

Several types of phonological rules have the effect of changing the number of segments in an expression. Among these are rules that merge two separate segments into a single phonetic segment, and the converse of this, rules that split a single segment into a segment sequence at the phonetic level. One example of a merger rule is French vowel nasalization, which derives nasal vowels from an underlying segment sequence consisting of an oral vowel plus a nasal consonant before a consonant or word boundary (Problem 4.1–12). The merger of the diphthongs [ay] and [aw] to mid vowels such as [e] and [o] respectively is extremely common.

Rules that break up a segment into a segment sequence are somewhat less common than merger rules. One example, discussed in section 4.1, is the Spanish rule that changes [ó] to [wé]. In the phonetic sequence [wé], the glide [w] preserves the rounding of the underlying [ó], while [é] preserves its property of being a mid vowel; the frontness of [é] is no doubt related to the fact that Spanish has no non-low back vowels which are unrounded.

It is not always possible to make a sharp distinction between rules that merge and split segments on the one hand and rules that insert and delete segments (sometimes with concomitant modification of adjacent segments) on the other. The insertion of the respective glides [y] and [w] after [e] and [o] in English was illustrated in Problem 4.2–3. In Maxakalí a homorganic obstruent is inserted after an initial nasal consonant, as we saw in Problem 4.2–1. Moreover, once the homorganic obstruent has been inserted, the nasal can be deleted. Problem 4.1–13 demonstrated that the final vowel of a stem is deleted in Tulu when an ending is added and a consonant cluster does not precede; the underlying representation /tini-ka/ 'let's eat!' reduces to [tin-ka] by the application of this rule. The deletion of unstressed vowels is extremely common, particularly when the unstressed vowel is not the first or last vowel in the word and its deletion does not result in a cluster of more than two consonants.

One class of insertion rules deserve special mention. These are rules of *reduplication*. Reduplication rules have the effect of copying a root, syllable, or segment and attaching it to the original. Normally a reduplicated element is added at the beginning of a form, but it may also be added at the end or, less commonly, somewhere in the middle. Problem 4.1–5 provided an example from Nupe. Nouns can be derived from certain verbs by prefixing to the verb root a syllable consisting of the initial consonant of the verb root plus a vowel; the added vowel is [û] if the root vowel is rounded and [î] otherwise. In the derivation of 'eating' from 'eat', for instance, the initial consonant and vowel of /gí/ 'eat' are reduplicated as [gî] to form the sequence [gîgí] 'eating' (which is phonetically [gʸîgʸí] due to palatalization). In Problem 4.2–5 we saw that the plural form of a verb in Klamath is derived from the singular form by reduplicating the initial *CV*, that is, the initial consonant and vowel. (More precisely, the initial consonant is reduplicated and prefixed to the stem along with a vowel whose quality is made to agree with that of the first stem vowel by another, more general rule.) As these examples indicate, reduplication frequently has grammatical or semantic significance. Most commonly, it has the semantic value of plurality, intensity, repetition, or duration. Opposed to reduplication is simple *epenthesis*, the insertion of a segment not necessarily identical to any adjacent segment; epenthesis is usually triggered by phonological factors alone.

Problem 4.3–1   Papago

Listed below are singular and plural noun forms from Papago (Hale, 1970). Formulate rules to account for the derivation of the plural forms from the corresponding singulars. Show the derivation of 'tails'. To simplify matters, the forms are not given phonetically; the representations below are fairly abstract, and several phonological rules (including the one that palatalizes [t] to [č] before high vowels) must apply in the derivation of their phonetic shapes.

Singular	Plural	
bana	baabana	'coyote'
kuna	kuukuna	'husband'
tɨho	tiithɨo	'cave'
sona	soosona	'base'
naaka	naanaka	'ear'
toona	tootona	'knee'
piha	piiphia	'penis'
tini	tiitini	'mouth'
bahi	baabhai	'tail'
paga	paapaga	'hole'
tɨɨma	tɨɨtɨma	'heel'

Solution

The plural of these nouns is a process morpheme that reduplicates the initial *CV* before the noun stem. In the plural the reduplicated vowel is always long and the initial vowel of the stem is short, even if it was originally long.

In a reduplicated plural an intervocalic [h] is metathesized with the preceding vowel. Reduplication and metathesis are both illustrated in the derivation of the form for 'tails':

/bahi/ ⟶ baabahi ⟶ baabhai

Problem 4.3–2   Kasem

PART A   This problem (compare Chomsky and Halle, 1968) concerns the marking of singular and plural for one class of nouns and adjectives in Kasem, a Niger-Congo language spoken in Ghana and Upper Volta. Examine the forms below and determine how number is regularly marked for nouns and adjectives in this class.

Singular	Plural	
bakada	bakadi	'boy'
mimina	mimini	'thin'
fala	fali	'white man'
kukuda	kukudi	'dog'
fana	fani	'knife'
čana	čani	'shoulder'

Solution

A singular form is marked by the suffixation of /a/ to the stem, and a plural form by the suffixation of /i/.

PART B Assume that the principle for marking number discovered in Part A is fully regular for the following class of nouns at the level of underlying representation. Formulate four rules that will derive the phonetic forms below from the expected underlying representations. Determine how these rules must be ordered. Give the derivations of the forms for 'rivers', 'rooms', and 'legs'.

Singular	*Plural*	
kambia	kambi	'cooking pot'
pia	pi	'yam'
buga	bwi	'river'
diga	di	'room'
laŋa	læ	'song'
naga	næ	'leg'

Solution

Since the singular form 'cooking pot' is [kambia], the stem for this noun must be /kambi/. The underlying representation of the plural should therefore be /kambi-i/, but phonetically it is [kambi] rather than [kambi-i]. Similarly, 'yams' is [pi] rather than [pi-i], though its underlying representation must be /pi-i/. To account for these discrepancies, rule (A) can be postulated; it can be formulated as either a merger rule or a deletion rule.

      (A) Two adjacent occurrences of the vowel /i/ are merged into a single, short vowel.

The other four plural forms have the following underlying representations: /bug-i/ 'rivers', /dig-i/ 'rooms', /laŋ-i/ 'songs', and /nag-i/ 'legs'. In all four cases, the final velar consonant of the stem fails to appear in the phonetic representation of the plural. To account for this, rule (B) can be posited.

      (B) A velar consonant is deleted before /i/.

The application of rule (B) to the four underlying representations yields the respective forms [bu-i], [di-i], [la-i], and [na-i].

    Rule (A) is applicable to [di-i] 'rooms', and it correctly derives the phonetic representation [di]. However, two additional rules are needed to complete the derivations of the other plurals.

      (C) A rounded vowel becomes a glide (that is, [u] changes to [w]) before another vowel.

      (D) The sequence [ai] merges to [æ].

Rules (A)–(D) are illustrated in these derivations:

$$\text{/bug-i/ 'rivers'} \longrightarrow \underset{(B)}{bu\text{-}i} \longrightarrow \underset{(C)}{bw\text{-}i}$$

$$\text{/dig-i/ 'rooms'} \longrightarrow \underset{(B)}{di\text{-}i} \longrightarrow \underset{(A)}{di}$$

$$\text{/nag-i/ 'legs'} \longrightarrow \underset{(B)}{na\text{-}i} \longrightarrow \underset{(D)}{næ}$$

Rule (B) must precede the other three rules; only after the velar consonant is deleted are the pairs of vowels that undergo rules (A), (C), and (D) adjacent to one another. There is no evidence for any particular ordering relation among (A), (C), and (D).

PART C Revise one of the rules postulated above and formulate one additional rule to account for the forms that follow. Discuss rule ordering. Give the derivations of the plural forms.

Singular	*Plural*	
pia	pæ	'sheep'
babia	babæ	'brave'

Solution

If the singular forms directly reflect their phonological representations, the underlying representations of the two plural forms must be /pi-i/ and /babi-i/. However, the plurals end phonetically in [æ], which derives from [ai] by means of rule (D); the occurrence of this final [æ] will therefore be most easily explained if the sequence [ai] occurs at an abstract level of representation; however, it does not occur in /babi-i/ or /pi-i/. This suggests that some other choice of phonological representations might be more insightful.

Suppose the stems for 'sheep' and 'brave' are taken to be /pia/ and /babia/ respectively. The phonological representations for the singular and plural forms will then be the following:

Singular	*Plural*	
/pia-a/	/pia-i/	'sheep'
/babia-a/	/babia-i/	'brave'

A slightly modified version of rule (A) will now serve to derive the singular forms from their underlying representations.

(A′) Two adjacent occurrences of the same vowel are merged into a single, short vowel.

(A′) is simpler and more general than (A), since it can apply to any identical vowels, not just high front vowels. When applied to /pia-a/ 'sheep', and /babia-a/ 'brave', (A′) correctly merges /aa/ to [a] to derive [pia] and [babia] respectively.

As for the plurals, the final vowel sequence /ai/ will correctly yield [æ] by rule (D), but the first occurrence of /i/ in each underlying form must somehow be deleted. It would not suffice to add a rule that deletes /i/ before /a/, since [ia] occurs overtly in the singular. Another possibility would be to delete /i/ before [æ] after the latter is derived from /ai/. However, there is still another possibility, one which has the advantage of relating the deletion of /i/ to the more general vowel deletion rule (A'). This is to posit a rule that metathesizes /ia/ when /i/ follows.

(E) /ia/ is metathesized to [ai] before /i/.

Here are the hypothesized derivations of the plural forms:

/pia-i/   'sheep' ⟶ pai-i   ⟶ pai   ⟶ pæ
                  (E)   (A')   (D)

/babia-i/   'brave' ⟶ babai-i ⟶ babai ⟶ babæ
                (E)   (A')   (D)

Rule (E) must be ordered before (A'), since the two occurrences of [i] are adjacent and eligible for simplification only after metathesis has taken place. (A') must precede (D); one occurrence of [i] must be deleted, and (A') can accomplish this if it applies to the sequence [ii], but this sequence would no longer be available if (D) applied first to merge [ai] to [æ]. The ordering of the five rules is diagramed below; the arrow is to be read "precedes".

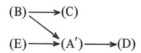

ASSIMILATION

Many phonological rules have the effect of modifying segments in such a way that they more closely resemble contiguous segments. The modification of sounds in the direction of greater similarity to the surrounding phonological environment is called **assimilation**. Assimilation is a pervasive and ubiquitous feature of the phonological systems of human languages, and we have already encountered numerous examples of this process. In Problem 4.1–6, for instance, we saw that the phonemic sequence /lλ/ is realized in Aztec as the phonetic sequence [ll]. /λ/ is assimilated to the preceding /l/ by means of a general rule. This assimilation process is said to be **progressive**, since the first segment influences the manifestation of the second. **Regressive** assimilation, in which one segment influences another that precedes it, is somewhat more common than progressive assimilation. The rule that backs /t/ to [ṭ] before [č] and [k] in Alabaman (Problem 4.1–4) is an example; [ṭ] is closer to [č k] than [t] is in point of articulation.

Among the many varieties of assimilation are some that occur so commonly in human languages that they merit special discussion. One such process is a weakening or **lenition** in the articulation of obstruents in certain environments, particularly intervocalically or between a vowel and a resonant. The lenition may take the form of a change from tense to lax, or from voiceless to voiced, or from a stop to a fricative. Problem 4.1–7 established the existence of an assimilation rule in English that voices /t/ to [D] intervocalically or between a vowel and a syllabic resonant. In Problem 4.1–8 we saw that voiced stops become fricatives in Spanish when they follow a vowel. In Tulu voiceless stops become voiced stops or voiced fricatives intervocalically (Problem 4.1–13). These changes constitute assimilations because vowels and other resonants are typically voiced, articulated without full obstruction of the outflowing air, and more lax in articulation than obstruents.

Another common type of assimilation is the agreement in voicing of consonant clusters, particularly obstruent clusters. The Aztec rule /lλ/ → [11] conforms to this tendency, since [l] is voiced while [λ] is voiceless. The Maxakalí rule that inserts a homorganic stop after an initial nasal consonant also conforms, because the epenthetic stop, like the nasal, must be voiced (Problem 4.2–1). In Kitsai /n/ is manifested as [h] before a stop (Problem 4.2–2); this change can be viewed in part as an assimilation in voicing, since the Kitsai stops are all voiceless. In English all the segments in an obstruent cluster must agree in voicing, as noted earlier. Moreover, there is a tendency for English sonorants to be at least partially devoiced before or after a voiceless obstruent; thus *prime*, *stilt*, and *snip* may be realized phonetically as [pr̥aym], [stɪl̥t], and [sn̥ɪp] ([ˌ] beneath the symbol for a voiced segment indicates partial or complete devoicing).

Vowels frequently assimilate to an adjacent nasal consonant, particularly one that follows the vowel and occurs in the same syllable. For instance, we saw in Problem 4.1–4 that vowel nasalization in Alabaman derives [tãnka] from the phonemic representation /tanka/ (other rules eventually yield [tʰãnkʰaa]). Sometimes vowel nasalization occurs with concomitant loss of the original nasal consonant. French vowel nasalization, illustrated by the derivation of [bõte] 'goodness' from /bɔnte/, is one of the best known examples (Problem 4.1–12). Vowel nasalization occurs sporadically in English, with a great deal of variation from speaker to speaker and from form to form; for some speakers, vowel nasalization is the primary phonetic difference between *can* ([kæn]) and *can't* ([kæ̃(t)]).

The tendency for adjacent segments to agree in palatalization and rounding also illustrates assimilation. It is especially common for consonants to assimilate to vowels with respect to these features, and the assimilation is typically regressive, but vowels can assimilate as well, and progressive assimilation in palatalization and rounding also occurs. As we have seen, dental stops are palatalized in Papago before high vowels, and in Nupe consonants are palatalized before front vowels and labialized before rounded vowels. The manifestation of [ʔ] as [ʔʸ] after palatal segments in Maxakalí exemplifies progressive assimilation with respect to palatal articulation. The English glide insertion rule discussed in Problem 4.2–3 must be so formulated that the inserted glide agrees in rounding with the preceding vowel.

Harmony can be regarded as a special kind of assimilation. Harmony rules most commonly affect vowels, but consonant harmony also occurs, and sometimes harmony rules affect both vowels and consonants. We saw in Problem 2.1–4 (p. 45) that the vowels in a Turkish word (with certain exceptions) must all be front vowels or all be back vowels. Actually, Turkish vowel harmony is somewhat more complex and involves rounding as well (Lewis, 1953). Unrounded vowels must be followed by unrounded vowels, as in [salɨnǰak] 'swing', while rounded vowels may be followed by low unrounded vowels or high rounded vowels, as in [olmak] 'to become' and [oldum] 'I became'. Harmony in Classical Mongolian also requires that the vowels of a word agree with respect to the front-back feature, and this harmony extends to the velar consonants as well (Lightner, 1965). The front velars [k g] occur in words with front vowels, such as [köbegün] 'son' while the back velars [q γ] are restricted to words with back vowels, like [qubilγan] 'transformation'. Another example of consonant harmony was cited in Chapter 2 (p. 42); in Chumash more than one [s] can appear in a single word, and more than one [š], but [s] and [š] cannot both occur in the same word. Finally, affixes often harmonize in some way with the stem to which they are attached, even though this harmony is not required for segments within the same stem. For example, Problem 4.2–5 indicated the existence of a rule in Klamath that harmonizes the vowel of a verb prefix with the first vowel of the stem.

Despite the strong tendency for contiguous segments to assimilate to one another, the opposite phenomenon, ***dissimilation***, also occurs in many languages. The Kitsai rule that changes /n/ to [h] before a stop is in part a dissimilation rule (Problem 4.2–2); [n], unlike [h], resembles stops in that its articulation involves an oral closure. A famous phonological rule of Sanskrit and ancient Greek known as Grassmann's law is another example. The effect of this rule is to deaspirate the first of two aspirated stops occurring in the same stem. Thus the present tense form of the Sanskrit verb 'burst' is [pʰalati], but the perfect form, whose derivation involves reduplication of the initial syllable, is [papʰala] rather than [pʰapʰala].

Problem 4.3–3   Maxakalí

Examine the following Maxakalí expressions (Gudschinsky and Popovich, 1970) and formulate a rule that accounts for the phonetic variation in the shape of morphemes. Phonetic detail irrelevant to the point at hand has been omitted.

nõʔõm	'that'	kõnnɨ̃ŋ n̥õʔõm	'that macaw'
ŋãñ	'angry'	kõmãn ŋ̥ãñ	'angry co-godmother'
ñɨ̃čɨč	'yellow'	mãhãm ñɨ̃čɨč	'yellow fish'
mɨ̃nnɨ̃	'black'	kõnnɨ̃ŋ m̥ɨ̃nnɨ̃	'black macaw'
		mattɨk mɨ̃nnɨ̃	'black toad'

Solution

A non-palatal nasal is devoiced in word-initial position when the preceding word ends in a nasal. This devoicing is a form of dissimilation.

Problem 4.3–4 *Walbiri*

Walbiri is a language spoken in central Australia. The words below (Hale, *to appear*, b) illustrate two suffixes meaning 'to' and 'hither', each of which has two phonetic manifestations. Posit uniform phonemic representations for these two suffixes together with a phonological rule that accounts for their phonetic variation.

kaṇṭaku	'to the woman'	yantaṇi	'come hither!'
waḷuku	'to the fire'	yaniṇi	'to come hither'
kaḷiki	'to the boomerang'	yanuṇu	'came hither'
katiki	'to the man'	paṇkat ʸaṇi	'ran hither'
kaṇuku	'to the boy'	wil ʸpipaḍit ʸaṇi	'emerged hither'
ŋapaku	'to the water'	t ʸuulpuŋuṇu	'jumped hither'

Solution

The phonological representation of 'to' is /ku/, and that of 'hither' is /ṇi/. Both suffixes show a phonetic alternation between [u] and [i]. The variants [ki] and [ṇu] can be accounted for by the following rule. The vowel of a suffix harmonizes (that is, agrees in frontness and roundness) with the final vowel of the stem if the stem vowel is high.

Problem 4.3–5 *English*

Examine the forms below and state the principles that determine the allophonic variants of word-initial /k/. The symbol [ʷ] indicates rounding of the lips during the articulation of the preceding segment; [̪] beneath a consonant symbol indicates a point of articulation farther toward the front than usual. It is pertinent to note that English [r] is phonetically rounded in many environments. (Aspiration is omitted from consideration.)

kin	ḵɪn	*keel*	ḵil
crisis	kʷrʌysɪs	*kettle*	ḵɛDl̩
cut	kʌt	*cot*	kat
clip	klɪp	*quit*	kʷwɪt
came	ḵeym	*cool*	kʷul
cope	kʷowp	*caught*	kʷɔt
cat	ḵæt	*crisp*	kʷrɪsp

Solution

Word-initial /k/ assimilates to the following segment. Specifically, /k/ is fronted to [ḵ] before a front vowel, and it is rounded to [kʷ] before a rounded segment. /k/ is manifested as the basic allophone [k] when neither of these conditions is met.

PHONOTACTIC RULES

The phonological representations permitted for the lexical items of a language never include all the possible segment sequences that can be formed from the language's segment inventory. Restrictions on the possible combinations of segments are an important part of the phonological component of a language. These restrictions are known as **phonotactic rules**. Unlike other phonological rules, phonotactic rules do not modify, insert, delete, or rearrange segments. Rather they constitute the "ground rules" in terms of which the phonological system of a language must operate. The phonological representations of individual lexical items must be constructed in accordance with these ground rules, and the application of phonological rules must often be so constrained as to avoid violations of the ground rules in the course of a derivation.

Restrictions on permissible consonant clusters are good examples of phonotactic rules. Some languages permit few if any consonant clusters, while others permit clusters of great complexity. English is perhaps average in this regard, allowing consonant clusters, but only when they follow certain restricted patterns. In word-initial position, for instance, English does not permit consonant clusters beginning with a sonorant; there are no words like **mlit*, **lpang*, or **wmelt*. Clusters beginning with obstruents are possible in English, but the restrictions on them are severe. Only /s/ can occur before nasals and obstruents (*snap*, *stamp*, *sphere*, but not **fmap*, **pvart*, **hselt*, or **jnace*); some obstruent-sonorant combinations are not allowed (*price* and *quip*, but not **pwart* or **tlop*); and so on. For medial and final clusters, the restrictions are somewhat different. In particular, many clusters occur medially and finally that cannot occur at the beginning of a word: *actor*, *film*, *butler*, *aunt*, *lengths*, but not **ctar*, **lmeat*, **tlown*, **ntip*, **ngthsir*.

In describing the phonotactic patterns of a language, the notion of the **syllable** quite often proves important. Like the word, the syllable is a difficult entity to define. Informally and impressionistically, a syllable can be said to consist of a vocalic **nucleus** together with the consonants on either side that cohere to it. The vocalic nucleus, in turn, consists of either a simple vowel, long or short; a diphthong, or sequence of two vocalic segments, one of which is normally articulated fully or partially as a glide; or a syllabic consonant. In words with only one vocalic nucleus there can be only one syllable, and all the consonants in the word must be assigned to that syllable. The English word *striped*, for instance, consists of the diphthong [ʌy] preceded by the cluster [str] and followed by the cluster [pt]; [str] is referred to as the syllable **onset**, and [pt] as the **coda**. In words of more than one syllable, it is not always so easy to decide which syllable a given consonant belongs to, though it is usually possible to bring phonetic, structural, or intuitive evidence to bear on the matter. Medial consonant clusters are typically, though not invariably, divided between the preceding and following syllables. In the word *Aztec*, for example, [z] is the coda of the initial syllable [æz], while [t] is the onset of the final syllable [tɛk]; the fact that [z] and [t] do not assimilate in voicing, as English obstruent clusters normally do, may be taken as phonetic evidence that the two segments belong to different syllables. *Aztec* can thus be transcribed [æz.tɛk], where a period symbolizes a syllable boundary.

Many phonological rules, both phonotactic and otherwise, receive their most general and natural formulation in terms of syllable structure. Consider French vowel nasalization, which was discussed in Problem 4.1–12. If the rule is formulated without reference to syllables, vowel nasalization must be stated as in (A).

> (A) A vowel and following nasal consonant merge to form a nasal vowel before another consonant or a word boundary.

The reference to another consonant accounts for the nasalization in words like *bonté* [bɔ̃te] 'goodness', from /bɔnte/, while the reference to a word boundary accounts for *bon* [bɔ̃] 'good', from /bɔn/; (A) cannot apply to words like *bonne* [bɔnə] 'good (FEMININE)', in which [ɔn] is followed by a vowel. Although this rule accounts for the facts, it fails to achieve maximum generality, since two separate environments are mentioned, that before a consonant and that before a word boundary. Because a single intervocalic consonant normally coheres to the following vowel, reference to syllabic structure will permit a simpler, more general statement of French vowel nasalization. The respective underlying representations of *bonté*, *bon*, and *bonne* are /bɔn.te/, /bɔn/, and /bɔ.nə/. In the first two forms /ɔ/ and /n/ are in the same syllable, and in both cases vowel nasalization occurs. Vowel nasalization does not occur in the third form, since /ɔ/ and /n/ belong to separate syllables. Rule (B), which expresses this generalization, can therefore be adopted in lieu of (A).

> (B) Within a syllable, a vowel and following nasal consonant merge to form a nasal vowel.

There is a general tendency for phonological systems to avoid consonant clusters in the onset or coda of syllables. Many languages allow no consonant clusters at all within a syllable, and in languages where such clusters do occur, there are usually fairly severe restrictions on the allowable combinations. In Maxakalí, for example, syllables have the form $(C)V(C)$, where parentheses stand for optionality. Except for some clusters introduced by rules that specify fine phonetic detail (compare Problem 4.2–1), consonant clusters arise in Maxakalí only through the juxtaposition of the coda of one syllable and the onset of the next, as in /pat.kip/ 'rib' (Gudschinsky and Popovich, 1970). Similarly, at the level of phonological representation Papago forms are quite uniform in having the structure $CV.CV.CV$.... This is not true at the phonetic level, however, since the deletion of unstressed vowels under certain conditions has the effect of creating phonetic consonant clusters (Hale, 1965).

It was observed earlier that the phonotactic rules of a language constitute the ground rules in accordance with which the phonological representations of lexical items must be constructed and phonological rules must operate. The above example from Papago demonstrates that the phonotactic constraints of a language may be somewhat different at the phonological and phonetic levels. Phonotactic patterns may also differ depending on the style of speech. For instance, the initial cluster [kn] does not occur at all in careful, deliberate English speech, but in rapid informal speech this and many other special clusters may arise through omission of unstressed vowels; depending on style, *kinetic* may be pronounced [kɪnɛDɪk] or [knɛDək], and there are other possible variants as well.

Quite often, however, phonotactic constraints hold for both the phonological and phonetic levels, and different facets of the phonological system "conspire" to ensure that the constraints will be obeyed. Consider the Tulu forms of Problem 4.1–13. In the data presented no form has a cluster of more than two consonants; the lack of such clusters also holds true for the level of phonological representation. A phonotactic rule precluding clusters of more than two consonants can therefore be postulated, and the underlying representations of lexical items must be constructed in accordance with this restriction. Furthermore, this constraint apparently affects the application of non-phonotactic rules. We saw in Problem 4.1–13 that a stem-final vowel is deleted in Tulu before a suffix; thus [kor-ka] 'let's give!' and [tin-ka] 'let's eat!' are the phonetic manifestations of /koru-ka/ and /tini-ka/ respectively. This rule does not apply, however, in the derivations of [kalpu-ga] 'let's learn!' and [kullu-ga] 'let's sit!', which have /kalpu-ka/ and /kullu-ka/ as their phonological representations. In Problem 4.1–13 a special restriction was added to the vowel deletion rule to prevent it from applying to these forms; it was necessary only to specify that the stem-final vowel must not be preceded by a consonant cluster. Clearly, though, it is more insightful to attribute the non-application of vowel deletion in this environment to the phonotactic rule prohibiting clusters of more than two consonants. If vowel deletion were to apply to /kalpu-ka/ or /kullu-ka/, the non-permissible clusters [lpk] and [llk] would arise.

Let us consider one more example, from Klamath. A phonological rule of Klamath changes a stem-final glide to a long vowel when it is preceded by a consonant and followed by a suffix beginning in a consonant (Problem 4.1–9). The phonetic shape of /nidw-s/ 'guessing' is thus [nidoo-s], and that of /mboty²-tk/ 'wrinkled up' is [mbotii-tk]. The effect of this vocalization rule is to eliminate complicated consonant clusters with internal glides at the phonetic level. Presumably this reflects a phonotactic constraint that also precludes clusters such as /dws/ or /ty²tk/ in the phonemic representations of individual morphemes.

Problem 4.3–6   *Maxakalí*

The following Maxakalí forms (Gudschinsky and Popovich, 1970) can be accounted for by means of three phonological rules which derive the phonetic representations in column II from the phonological representations in column I. Formulate these rules and determine the order in which they must apply. (Two of the rules illustrate the relevance of syllable boundaries to phonological analysis.) Give the derivations of 'toad' and 'rib'. [ë] stands for a mid back unrounded vowel (the unrounded counterpart of [o]), and the diacritic [͜] beneath a vowel symbol indicates that the vowel is articulated as a glide. (Phonetic detail irrelevant to the point at hand has been omitted. The phenomenon illustrated here is actually much more general in Maxakalí than these forms indicate; we will focus our attention on /p/ and /t/ in order to keep the problem relatively simple.)

I	*II*	
/mat.tɨk/	maə.tɨk	'toad'
/pat.kɨp/	paət.kiẹ̆p	'rib'
/ta.pet/	ta.peət	'paper'
/kep.pa/	keë.pa	'in front of'
/pap.tič/	paë̆p.tič	'drunk'
/pip.kɨp/	piẹ̆p.kiẹ̆p	'nail'

Solution

Comparison of the forms in columns I and II reveals that a vowel is inserted before every syllable-final /p/ and /t/ in the underlying representations. This vowel is [ə] before /t/, and [ë] before /p/. Rule (A) accounts for this epenthesis.

> (A) A mid unrounded vowel is inserted before a non-velar stop in syllable-final position; this epenthetic vowel is central before /t/, and back before /p/.

No vowel is inserted before the /p/ of /ta.pet/ 'paper', because this /p/ is a syllable onset, not a syllable coda.

In the phonetic forms for 'toad' and 'in front of', an epenthetic vowel is present despite the absence of a following stop in syllable-coda position. However, the syllable-final stop is present in the underlying representations of these forms. The generality of (A) can therefore be maintained, but another rule must serve to delete the stop that allows (A) to apply. 'Toad' and 'in front of' are the only two forms that contain a consonant cluster consisting of two identical consonants; rule (B) will thus delete the proper consonants.

> (B) The first in a cluster of two identical consonants is deleted.

Finally, the epenthetic vowel in the phonetic forms is pronounced as a glide in some instances but not in others; specifically, the epenthetic vowel is glided when it precedes a consonant that functions as a syllable coda. The gliding rule can be stated formulaically as (C).

(C) VVC. $\longrightarrow$ VY̯C.

That is, the second of two vowels is glided before a consonant in syllable-coda position.

These rules are illustrated in the derivations of 'toad' and 'rib':

$$/\text{mat.tik}/ \text{ 'toad'} \longrightarrow \text{maət.tik} \longrightarrow \text{maə.tik}$$
$$\text{(A)} \text{(B)}$$
$$/\text{pat.kɨp}/ \text{ 'rib'} \longrightarrow \text{paət.kïë̯p} \longrightarrow \text{paə̯t.kïë̯p}$$
$$\text{(A)} \text{(C)}$$

Rule (A) must precede (B), for otherwise (B) would delete the syllable-final stop in 'toad' and 'in front of' before (A) could insert the epenthetic vowel. (B) must precede (C), since (C) does not apply in those forms from which (B) deletes a repeated consonant.

Problem 4.3–7 Tonkawa

PART A The data below (Kisseberth, 1970) is from Tonkawa, an American Indian language of Texas. There are three sets of words, each built on a stem with a single phonological representation. The affixes attached to these stems are [oʔ] 'THIRD PERSON SINGULAR SUBJECT', [we] 'THIRD PERSON PLURAL OBJECT', and [n] 'is...ing'. Posit underlying representations for the stems and formulate three vowel deletion rules that will account for their divergent phonetic shapes. Comment on rule ordering. Give the derivations of 'hoe', 'he hoes them', and 'he is hoeing (it)'.

notox	'hoe'
notx-oʔ	'he hoes (it)'
we-ntox-oʔ	'he hoes them'
notxo-n-oʔ	'he is hoeing (it)'
we-ntoxo-n-oʔ	'he is hoeing them'
picen	'castrated one, steer'
picn-oʔ	'he cuts (it)'
we-pcen-oʔ	'he cuts them'
picna-n-oʔ	'he is cutting (it)'
we-pcena-n-oʔ	'he is cutting them'
netl-oʔ	'he licks (it)'
we-ntal-oʔ	'he licks them'
netle-n-oʔ	'he is licking (it)'
we-ntale-n-oʔ	'he is licking them'

Solution

The three phonological representations are /notoxo/ 'hoe', /picena/ 'cut', and /netale/ 'lick'. Phonetically, any one of the vowels in these stems can be omitted depending on its position in a word. In the two forms without suffixes, [notox] 'hoe' and [picen] 'castrated one, steer', the stem-final vowel fails to appear. Rule (A) accounts for this.

(A) A word-final vowel is deleted.

A second deletion rule elides the second vowel of a word under certain conditions. When the prefix [we] is present, this rule affects the first vowel of the stem. When there is no prefix, it affects the second vowel of the stem. The rule fails to apply to [notox] or [picen], presumably because the second vowel is the final vowel of the word.

(B) The second vowel of a word is deleted in words containing more than two vowels.

Finally, the last vowel of a stem is deleted before the suffix [oʔ]. Since there are no vowel clusters in the data, this rule can be formulated as in (C).

(C) The first of two adjacent vowels is deleted.

The rules are illustrated in the following derivations:

/notoxo/ 'hoe' ⟶ notox
(A)

/we-notoxo-oʔ/ 'he hoes them' ⟶ we-ntoxo-oʔ ⟶ we-ntox-oʔ
(B) (C)

/notoxo-n-oʔ/ 'he is hoeing (it)' ⟶ notxo-n-oʔ
(B)

Rule (A) must precede (B); with this ordering (B) is correctly blocked from applying in the derivation of 'hoe', since this form has only two vowels once (A) has applied.

PART B Not all the words in the data below follow precisely the patterns established in Part A. To account for the exceptional forms, posit appropriate underlying representations for the stems and formulate a phonotactic constraint that holds both for phonological and for phonetic representations. Assume that the phonotactic patterns illustrated by the words in the data are valid for the language as a whole.

nepaxk-oʔ	'he smokes'
nepaxke-n-oʔ	'he is smoking'
we-npaxk-oʔ	'he smokes them'
salk-oʔ	'he pulls sinew from meat'
salke-n-oʔ	'he is pulling sinew from meat'
we-salk-oʔ	'he pulls sinews from meat'

Solution

The stems examined in Part A contained no underlying consonant clusters. However, there is no evidence for an underlying vowel between /xk/ in the stem for 'smoke', nor for one between /lk/ in the stem for 'pull sinew from meat'; no underlying vowel ever appears in these positions phonetically, but every underlying vowel posited in Part A appears phonetically in certain forms. Apparently, then, the correct phonological representations for these stems are /nepaxke/ and /salke/.

Rule (B) unexpectedly fails to apply in the derivations of 'he smokes', 'he is smoking', 'he is pulling sinew from meat', and 'he pulls sinews from meat'. However, it is in exactly these four forms that the application of (B) would produce a consonant cluster consisting of three members: [nepxk-oʔ], [nepxke-n-oʔ], [salk-n-oʔ], and [we-slk-oʔ]. This correlation suggests the formulation of a phonotactic rule for Tonkawa that precludes the occurrence of clusters of more than two consonants. Such a constraint would correctly predict the non-application of (B) in the forms mentioned above. This constraint is consistent with the rest of the data, and it apparently holds for both phonological and phonetic representations.

NON-SEGMENTAL INFORMATION

Many phonological rules apply only in certain environments, as we have seen. The specification of this environment is part of the rule. In many instances, the environment can be specified entirely in terms of segments. This is true, for instance, of the Papago rule that palatalizes a dental stop before a high vowel. It is also true of the English rule that inserts the glides [y] and [w] after the respective vowels [e] and [o].

Sometimes, however, the environmental specification of phonological rules must refer to non-segmental information. Some of this information is purely phonological in character. For instance, many rules take cognizance of suprasegmental phenomena, such as stress and tone. An example is the Mohawk rule (Problem 4.1–3) that lengthens a vowel if it is stressed and is not followed by a consonant cluster. Other rules, such as vowel nasalization in French and the gliding rule of Maxakalí (Problem 4.3–6), make reference to syllable structure.

As mentioned earlier, surface structures are the "input" to the phonological component of a grammar. The surface structure of a sentence comprises not only the phonological representations of individual lexical items but also the grammatical structure of the sentence. Facets of this structure include the division of segment sequences into morphemes; the grouping of morphemes into words; the division of complex words into roots, stems, and affixes; the internal constituent structure of complex lexical items; and "external" constituent structure—that is, the way lexical items are grouped to form a sentence. All this information is in principle available for purposes of phonological description, and certain phonological rules do in fact make reference to it.

Numerous phonological rules make reference to word boundaries, as we have seen. In Turkish the word is the domain within which vowel harmony obtains (Problem 2.1–4, p. 45). In Tonkawa a word-final vowel is deleted (Problem 4.3–7). The segment /č/ becomes [š] in Luiseño at the end of a word (Problem 4.1–10). A homorganic voiced stop is inserted after a word-initial nasal consonant in Maxakalí (Problem 4.2–1). Countless other examples could be cited.

It is somewhat less common for phonological rules to refer to morpheme boundaries, since adjacent segments of different morphemes within the same word usually interact as if they belonged to the same morpheme. One example is a rule of French (Schane, 1968) that deletes the first of two consonants if they are separated only by a morpheme boundary (or by a word boundary in certain types of phrases). Consider the following paradigms for the French verbs *vivre* 'to live' and *dormir* 'to sleep' (not all the segments shown are always rendered phonetically in normal conversational French).

vi-z	'I live'	viv-ɔ̃z	'we live'
vi-z	'you live'	viv-ez	'you (PLURAL) live'
vi-t	'he lives'	viv-ət	'they live'
dɔr-z	'I sleep'	dɔrm-ɔ̃z	'we sleep'
dɔr-z	'you sleep'	dɔrm-ez	'you (PLURAL) sleep'
dɔr-t	'he sleeps'	dɔrm-ət	'they sleep'

Note that each verb root has two alternate phonetic shapes, one in the singular and one in the plural. At the phonological level, however, they can be accorded uniform representations, /viv/ for 'live' and /dɔrm/ for 'sleep'. Thus the phonological representations of the present tense forms of these verbs are as follows:

/viv-z/	/viv-ɔnz/
/viv-z/	/viv-ez/
/viv-t/	/viv-ət/
/dɔrm-z/	/dɔrm-ɔnz/
/dɔrm-z/	/dɔrm-ez/
/dɔrm-t/	/dɔrm-ət/

The phonetic representations are derived by the rule of vowel nasalization and the deletion rule referred to above, which elides the first of two adjacent consonants if they are separated by a morpheme boundary. This rule applies to the singular forms, because the singular endings consist of single consonants. The full root remains in the plural, since the plural endings start in vowels. This deletion rule has considerable independent motivation. For instance, contrast the expressions *petit enfant* [pətit ãfã] 'little child' and *petits enfants* [pətiz ãfã] 'little children'. The underlying representation of the adjective is /pətit/ in the singular and /pətit-z/ in the plural. The stem-final /t/ is manifested phonetically in the first expression, but in the second it is deleted. This deletion is accomplished by the same rule that derives the verb forms above; /t/ is deleted in the plural because it precedes another consonant across a morpheme boundary.

Phonological rules also make reference to the division of complex words into roots or stems and affixes. Problem 4.3–4 illustrated a rule of Walbiri that harmonizes the vowel of a suffix with the final vowel of the stem whenever the latter is high. A rule of Klamath makes the vowel of a prefix agree in quality with the first vowel of a verb stem, as we saw in Problem 4.2–5. In Luiseño the object form of a noun is sometimes marked by a vowel deletion rule that affects only an absolutive suffix (Problem 4.1–10). Problem 4.1–13 demonstrated the necessity for a rule in Tulu that deletes a stem-final vowel before a suffix.

Two aspects of constituent structure (either internal or external) can be distinguished. The constituent structure of a sentence or lexical item includes both the hierarchical structure in which smaller units are grouped to form larger ones, and the categories (noun, verb, prepositional phrase, and so on) to which each unit, large and small, belongs. Both aspects of constituent structure are relevant to the formulation of certain phonological rules, particularly (but not exclusively) those that pertain to suprasegmental phenomena. The reference to constituent structure by phonological rules can be illustrated by the rules that assign stress in English.

The placement of stress in English is in large part predictable by rules (Chomsky and Halle, 1968). These rules are fairly complex, and a systematic examination of them is beyond the scope of this book. However, it is not difficult to show that both aspects of constituent structure mentioned above function in determining the placement of stress in English. To see the relevance of grammatical categories, consider verbs like *permit, progress, convict, export, survey, protest, insert, suspect, torment,* and *combine*. These verbs are all matched by nouns that are derived from them. No affix marks this derivational pattern, but a difference in stress does. All the verbs have weak stress on the first syllable, and strong or ***primary*** stress on the second syllable (there is dialectal variation for some of the forms): *permít, progréss, convíct,* and so on. The corresponding derived nouns, on the other hand, have primary stress on the first syllable and a lesser degree of stress, marked by ['], on the second syllable: *pérmìt, prógrèss, cónvìct,* and so on. Clearly, the phonological rules that assign stress to such words must refer to their grammatical category if the generalization involving placement of stress is to be captured.

Stress assignment in phrases and compounds illustrates the importance for phonological description of the second aspect of constituent structure, the way in which smaller units cluster to form larger ones. In a phrase consisting of an adjective plus noun, the noun normally bears the heavier stress, as in *blùe shírt*. In a compound, on the other hand, the first element bears the heavier stress, as in *blúebìrd*. Consider now the nominal *a racing car washer*. This nominal can have either of two stress patterns—namely, *a rácing càr wàsher* or *a ràcing cár wàsher*. The former is a washer of racing cars, and the latter a car washer who is racing. The two stress patterns are not arbitrarily assigned; rather they correspond to two different meanings and two different constituent structure configurations. These are given in Figures 4.3–1 and 4.3–2.

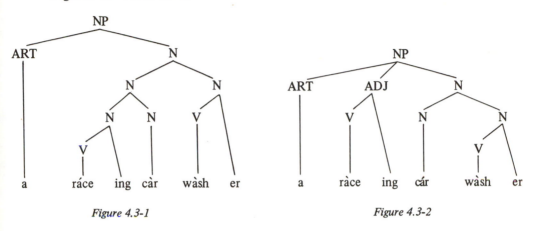

Figure 4.3-1   Figure 4.3-2

In Figure 4.3–1 *racing car* is a compound formed from the nouns *racing* and *car*; *racing car washer* is also a compound, its constituents being the compound noun *racing car* and the noun *washer*. *Racing car* receives stronger stress than *washer* in the larger compound *racing car washer*, since *racing car* is the first element of this compound. Within *racing car*, moreover, *racing* receives primary stress, because it is the first element of the smaller compound. *Racing* is therefore the most strongly stressed element in the nominal. The stress pattern is different in Figure 4.3–2, reflecting a different constituent structure. In this case, *racing* is an adjective that modifies the compound noun *car washer*. As in *blùe shírt*, the noun bears heavier stress than the adjective. Within the noun compound, *car* receives heavier stress than *washer*, since it is the first element. *Car* is therefore the most strongly stressed element in Figure 4.3–2. The two different stress patterns of *a racing car washer* are thus automatic consequences of the interaction of general stress assignment rules with different syntactic structures.

Problem 4.3–8   Desano

Desano is a language of the Tucano family spoken in Colombia and Brazil. Some morphemes in Desano are inherently nasal; that is, they always occur with nasalized vowels and their voiced consonants are nasal in character.

Other morphemes are inherently non-nasal; they never occur with nasal vowels and their voiced consonants are manifested as either oral voiced stops or non-nasal glides. A third class of morphemes is neither inherently nasal nor inherently non-nasal. The manifestation of these morphemes as nasal (with nasal vowels and nasal voiced consonants) or non-nasal (with oral vowels and oral voiced consonants) depends on the surrounding environment. The morpheme /du/, for instance, which is suffixed to nouns that designate round or hollow objects, can be manifested as either [nũ] or [ru].

In the forms below (Kaye, 1971), *N* marks an inherently nasal morpheme, *O* marks an inherently non-nasal or oral morpheme, and *U* marks those morphemes that are unspecified with respect to nasality. Above each underlying representation is an indication of how the morphemes are grouped to form constituents. State the rules that determine whether a morpheme is manifested phonetically as nasal or non-nasal. Can the same principles handle both the simpler and the more complex lexical items given in the data?

Solution

When an inherently nasal morpheme and an inherently non-nasal morpheme combine to form a constituent, each retains its own value for the property of nasality. The word for 'holiday' is thus partly oral and partly nasal phonetically: [bohse-nĩ].

When a morpheme unspecified for nasality (a *U* morpheme) combines to form a constituent with a morpheme that is specified, the former is assimilated in nasality to the latter. Thus /du/ is nasal (manifested as [nũ]) in the word for 'pineapple', since the root /seda/ is inherently nasal; /du/ is non-nasal (manifested as [ru]) in the word for 'ball', for the root /go/ is inherently non-nasal.

The same two principles account for the more complex examples. In the word meaning 'for (me) to dig', /bu/ assimilates to /gi/ rather than /keda/, since it is with /gi/ that /bu/ forms a constituent. This constituent is phonetically non-nasal throughout; because it has a value for the nasality feature, it does not assimilate to /keda/, even though /keda/ and /bugi/ form a higher-level constituent. In the word for 'a small round thing', /di/ assimilates to /bi/ in nasality because the two make up a constituent. Moreover, /du/ assimilates to /bidi/, since /bidi/ and /du/ form a constituent. Consequently, this word is entirely nasal: [mĩnĩnũ].

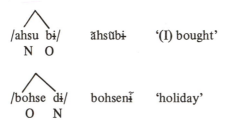

/ahsu bɨ/   ãhsũbɨ   '(I) bought'
  N O

/bohse dɨ/   bohsenĩ   'holiday'
  O   N

/seda du/   sĕnănŭ   'pineapple'
 N U

/go du/   goru   'ball'
 O U

/bɨ da/   mĩnă   'old men'
 U N

/bɨ gɨ/   bɨgɨ   'old man'
 U O

/keda bu gɨ/   kĕnăbugɨ   'for (me) to dig'
 N U O

/eda yo bi/   erañŭmĩ   'he arrives'
 O U N

/bi di du/   mĩnĩnŭ   'a small round thing'
 N U U

/wɨa di du/   wɨariru   'a large round thing'
 O U U

FURTHER PROBLEMS

Problem 4.3–9   Clallam

Clallam is an American Indian language of the Salishan family. The verbs in columns I and II (Thompson, 1969) differ aspectually; those in column II are similar in meaning to English verbs with *be...ing*, while those in column I are more neutral semantically. Formulate a rule that derives the verbs in column II from the corresponding verbs in column I.

I		II	
čkʷut	'shoot'	čukʷt	'shooting'
xčʔit	'scratch'	xičʔt	'scratching'
qʔxʷit	'tie up'	qʔixʷt	'tying up'
tʔcət	'shatter'	tʔəct	'shattering'
ƛʔkʷət	'grasp'	ƛʔəkʷt	'grasping'
čxət	'tear'	čəxt	'tearing'
qʔmʔət	'chop'	qʔəmʔt	'chopping'
mtəqʷt	'put in water'	mətqʷt	'putting in water'
cʔŋʔət	'bite'	cʔəŋʔt	'biting'

Problem 4.3–10   Assiniboine

Assiniboine is an American Indian language of the Siouan family. The forms below (Hollow, 1970) demonstrate the operation of phonological rules that apply at morpheme boundaries within a word. Formulate the necessary rules. Comment on rule ordering. Give the derivations of 'I cause to be black', 'coyote', and 'wolf'. ('Cane' is a semantically irregular combination of 'dry' and 'cause'.)

/saba/	'black'	/saga/	'dry'
/waya/	'I cause to be'	/ye/	'cause'
/yaya/	'you cause to be'	/togeǰa/	'wild'
/xoda/	'gray'	/poγa/	'nose'
/šiǰa/	'bad'	/čīǰanã/	'offspring'
/šũga/	'dog'	/knekneγa/	'pinto'
/ǰukanã/	'small'		

samwaya	'I cause to be black'	sakye	'cane'
samyaya	'you cause to be black'	šũktʰogeǰa	'wolf'
xonwaya	'I cause to be gray'	šũkpʰoγa	'dog's nose'
xonyaya	'you cause to be gray'	šũkčʰīǰanã	'puppy'
šinwaya	'I cause to be bad'	šũkknekneγa	'pinto'
šinyaya	'you cause to be bad'	šũkǰukanã	'coyote'

Problem 4.3–11   Piro ·

The data below (Kisseberth, 1970) is from Piro, an Arawakan language spoken in Peru. The complex lexical items in column II are derived by affixation from the stems in column I. Formulate a rule that accounts for the variation in those morphemes that have more than one phonetic shape. Propose a phonotactic constraint that accounts for the apparent exceptions to this rule.

	I		*II*	
1	yimaka	'teach'	yimak-lu	'teaching'
2	xipalu	'sweet potato'	n-xipal-ne	'my sweet potato'
3	čalu	'fish net'	n-čal-ne	'my fish net'
4	čokoruha	'harpoon'	čokoruh-kaka	'cause to harpoon'
	salwa	'visit'	salwa-kak-lu	'cause him to visit'
	kahli	'clay'	n-kahli-ne	'my clay'
	xinri	'palm'	n-xinri-ne	'my palm'
	yohima	'hide'	yohim-lewa	'hide habitually'
	hiwla	'cook'	hiwla-lewa	'cook habitually'
	hiknoka	'pass'	hiknoka-m-ta	'pass by without stopping'
	kakonu	'build hunting shelter'	kakon-ru	'hunting shelter'

Problem 4.3–12   Korean

PART A This problem (Kim, 1970) concerns phonological processes that affect compounds in Korean. Examine the non-compounds below and formulate two ordered rules that account for their phonetic manifestations. The symbol ['] after a consonant indicates that the consonant is tense.

/ket-ki/	ket-k'i	'walking'
/cap-ta/	cap-t'a	'to catch'
/kuk-pi/	kuk-p'i	'top secret'
/eps-ta/	ep-ta	'lacks'
/neks-to/	nek-to	'the soul also'

PART B Examine the compounds below and formulate two rules to account for their phonetic manifestations. Discuss the ordering of these rules and those formulated in Part A, and give the derivation of 'riverside'. The symbol [+] stands for a boundary between two elements of a compound.

/nay+ka/	nɛtk'a	'riverside'
/cʰo+pul/	cʰotp'ul	'candlelight'
/pay+kil/	pɛtk'il	'waterway'
/may+tol/	mɛtt'ol	'millstone'

PART C Formulate three additional rules to account for the phonetic shapes of the compounds below. Give the derivations of 'boat song' and 'sea water', and discuss the ordering of all the rules posited so far.

/pay+nolay/	pɛnnorɛ	'boat song'
/kʰo+nal/	kʰonnal	'nose line'
/pata+mul/	padanmul	'sea water'
/yo+nala/	yonnara	'the Yo nation'

PART D Formulate any additional rules needed to handle the compounds that follow. Give the derivation of 'palm of the hand'. Summarize the ordering relationships among the rules formulated in Parts A–D in a chart analogous to the one given for Kasem in Problem 4.3–2.

/san+pul/	sanp'ul	'forest fire'
/pam+pi/	pamp'i	'night rain'
/son+patak/	sonp'adak	'palm of the hand'
/tal+pam/	talp'am	'moonlit night'

Problem 4.3–13   Snohomish

Snohomish is an American Indian language of the Salishan family (Hess, 1966). The forms in column II are the "attenuative" forms of the nouns and verbs in column I; the attenuative form of a noun *N* means something like 'little *N*', and the attenuative form of a verb *V* means something like '*V* a little bit'. The attenuative morpheme is a process morpheme that may affect the root in various ways. The derivation of attenuative forms can be described in terms of a series of rules that apply to the stem; a given stem typically undergoes two or more of these rules, the choice being an idiosyncratic property of each stem. Formulate a series of rules for deriving the attenuative forms. List the class of stems that undergo each rule.

I	*II*	
bədaʔ	bibədaʔ	'offspring'
bəščəb	bibščəb	'mink'
tubš	tutubš	'man'
badil	babdil	'mountain'
tudəq	tutədəq	'slave'
luh	liʔluh	'hole'
ləgʷab	liʔlgʷab	'youth'
talə	taʔtalə	'money'
waqʔwaqʔ	waʔwqʔwaqʔ	'frog'
Lubʔ	LuʔLəbʔ	'soup'
tqad	titqad	'close'
pʔəqʷʔ	pʔipʔqʷʔ	'drift'
qʷulub	qʷuqʷulub	'get gray'
čʔaxʷad	čʔačʔxʷad	'club it'
Lalil	LaLəlil	'go ashore'
buus	biʔbuus	'four'
Ləqʷ	LiʔLqʷ	'wet'
qadaʔ	qaʔqadaʔ	'steal'
laqil	laʔlqil	'be late'
kʷagʷičəd	kʷaʔkʷəgʷičəd	'elk'

Problem 4.3–14 Eskimo

The data below (Mattina, 1970) is from the Kuskokwim dialect of Alaskan Eskimo. The back consonants include /k x q x̣/. /k/ is a voiceless velar stop, and /x/ a voiceless velar fricative. /q x̣/ are the same as /k x/ except that they are articulated farther back, toward the uvular region. Accordingly, they are said to be **uvular** sounds; /x̣/, for instance, is a voiceless uvular fricative. Eskimo has four underlying fricatives, /f s x x̣/, and three underlying vowels, /i a u/. Formulate the rules that determine the allophones of the fricatives and vowels (other than the basic allophones). Discuss the ordering of these rules, and show this ordering in a diagram. Give the derivations of 'his hat', '(male's) cousin', 'give it to me', 'belt', 'six', and 'take your hat'. The symbol [ᵊ] after a vowel indicates that the vowel is articulated with a following glide toward the mid central region.

/qaufiáq/	qau̯vi̯áq	'sand'		/naqúufutaq/	nəqóovutəq	'belt'
/kúskukfák/	kúskukfák	'Kuskokwim'		/áqfaqúq/	áqfəqóq	'run'
/tunúfni/	tünúvni	'behind you'		/uŋúfan/	uŋúvən	'heart'
/áfx̣ilnuq/	ávɣ̩ɪlnᴜq	'six'		/nasáx̣luq/	nazáɣluq	'sweetheart'
/táisxu/	tái̯zɣu	'give it to me'		/nátstuq/	nátstᴜq	'go up the hills'
/atssáq/	atssáq	'berry'		/naxístuq/	nayístᴜq	'louse'
/íxtuq/	íxtᴜq	'den'		/úqx̣suntix̣úx/	óqx̣süntɪᵊɣúx	'take your hat'
/uLúufak/	uLúuvək	'cheek'		/aLqáq/	aLqáq	'older sister'
/káiLun/	kái̯Lün	'how'		/ináx̣un/	ináɣun	'ribs'
/kitá/	kitá	'here!'		/tsalí/	tšalí	'some more'
/uqx̣súu/	uqx̣sóɔ	'his hat'		/qúutuq/	qóotᴜq	'tooth'
/uqúq/	uqóq	'fat'		/nitsúiáq/	nitšúi̯áq	'little house'
/ilúŋáq/	ilū̃ŋáq	'(female's) cousin'		/attáutsiq/	attáu̯tšɪᵊq	'one'
/kuík/	ku̯ík	'creek'		/iúxtun/	i̯úxtün	'in Eskimo'
/qilúk/	qɪlū̃k	'bark'		/nuláatsuŋáq/	nulǽætšuŋáq	'(male's) cousin'
/kiáax̣tuq/	ki̯ǽæx̣tᴜq	'look around'		/stámaq/	stáməq	'four'
/ámx̣aq/	ámɣəq	'sleeve'		/ax̣áaiún/	aɣáajún	'god'
/qátx̣aq/	qátɣəq	'chest'		/Lúx̣tuq/	Lóxtᴜq	'fix'
/px̣x̣íq/	px̣x̣íᵊq	'wipe'		/áx̣naq/	áɣnəq	'woman'
/qánx̣tuq/	qánx̣tᴜq	'he spoke'		/tanx̣áx̣liq/	tanɣáɣlɪᵊq	'black bear'
/ix̣náaq/	ɪᵊɣnǽæq	'child'		/kíq/	kíᵊq	'hot'
/kaufíx̣liq/	kau̯víᵊɣlɪᵊq	'red'		/qiáq/	qɪáq	'cry'
/qimúk/	qɪmúk	'pulling'		/áŋlx̣i/	áŋlɣɪ	'big one'
/tsánnit/	tšánnɪt	'grasses'		/tátik/	tátɪk	'forehead'
/qimúxta/	qɪmúxta	'dog'				

Problem 4.3–15 Tera

Tera, a Chadic language, is spoken in northern Nigeria. The data below (Newman, 1968) contains seven nouns, which fall into three classes in regard to the final segment of their phonological representation. Posit phonological representations for these nouns and formulate two ordered rules that derive the proper phonetic forms. One of these rules applies at the end of the sentence (or phrase), and another at the end of a word. These rules interact with a phonotactic constraint that prevents a word from ending in a consonant cluster. The segments [ɓ ɗ] are glottalized implosive stops.

na səɗi	'This is a snake.'	na səɗ ɓa	'This is not a snake.'
na wuɗi	'This is milk.'	na wuɗi ɓa	'This is not milk.'
na ruf	'This is a baboon.'	na ruf ɓa	'This is not a baboon.'
na dəɓi	'This is gum.'	na dəɓ ɓa	'This is not gum.'
na saɓi	'This is a stick.'	na saɓi ɓa	'This is not a stick.'
na gomok	'This is a bushcow.'	na gomok ɓa	'This is not a bushcow.'
na pərsi	'This is a horse.'	na pərsə ɓa	'This is not a horse.'

Problem 4.3–16 Papago

PART A   The forms below (Hale, 1965, and Saxton, 1969) exemplify the distribution of the phonetic segments [ɖ l ṣ s n ñ] in Papago. [ɖ] is an alveolar stop (as opposed to the dental stop [d]); [l s] are alveolars; [ṣ] is retroflex; and [n ñ] are dental and palatal respectively. [ɖ l] bear a special phonological relationship to one another, as do [ṣ s] and [n ñ]. Determine the nature of these relationships on the basis of the following data, and formulate appropriate rules. Recall the Papago rule, discussed earlier, that makes dental stops palatal before high vowels. Assume that no form ends in a consonant at the level of phonological representation. Also assume the existence of a rule that deletes word-final [a] (in most circumstances).

juɖum	'bear'	ñim	'liver'	sidolim	'coiled'
taapnañ	'split!'	čigitoiɖag	'mind'	siʔi	'suck'
baʔiwič	'pass'	wiɖut	'swing'	ṣuug	'mocking bird'
nowi	'hand, arm'	ṣab	'splash'	kiliw	'shell corn'
ñiñiɖ	'wait for'	čipiɖk	'be even'	biǰ	'turn around'
ṣiiʔi	'wolf'	naw	'leaf cactus'	toñ	'hot'
siʔalig	'dawn'	ñuuwi	'buzzard'	siiki	'deer'
ʔilidag	'skin, bark'	ñiʔi	'sing'	naato	'finish'
ṣoñikon	'beat'	siakam	'hero'	huɖuñ	'descend'
noɖagid	'turn'	namkid	'pay'	čihañ	'hire'
ñuukud	'care for'	ṣoʔig	'be poor'	mulin	'break'

PART B   Column I contains verbs, and column II contains nouns derived from these verbs.

I		II	
ǰuuk	'rain'	ǰuuki	'rain'
bɨhɨ	'take'	bɨhi	'something taken'
naad	'build a fire'	naaǰ	'something kindled'
ṣɨlin	'straighten'	ṣɨliñ	'something straightened'
hɨwɨḍ	'blow'	hɨwɨl	'wind'
kooṣ	'sleep'	koos	'sleep'
ñɨʔɨ	'sing'	ñɨʔi	'song'
waʔig	'fetch water'	waʔigi	'fetched water'
wiǰin	'twist'	wiǰiñ	'something twisted'

On the basis of these phonetic representations, there appear to be at least six ways in which a noun can be derived from a verb: (1) by suffixing [i]; (2) by changing [ɨ] to [i]; (3) by changing [d] to [ǰ]; (4) by changing [n] to [ñ]; (5) by changing [ḍ] to [l]; or (6) by changing [ṣ] to [s].

Posit underlying representations for each verb such that a single, general rule (in addition to the rules formulated in Part A) can be given to account for the derivation of all the nouns in column II from the corresponding verbs in column I. State this rule. Give the derivations of the first six verbs and the nouns derived from them. Comment on rule ordering.

Problem 4.3–17   *Yawelmani*

In Problem 4.1–11 aorist and passive aorist forms of Yawelmani verbs were cited that led to the postulation of a rule that shortens a long vowel when it occurs before a consonant cluster or before a single, word-final consonant. The data below (Kuroda, 1967) contains some of the verbs listed in Problem 4.1–11 and some that were not listed.

Aorist	Passive Aorist	
xathin	xatit	'eat'
gophin	gopit	'take care of infant'
giyʔhin	giyʔit	'touch'
muṭhun	muṭut	'swear'
ṣaphin	ṣaapit	'burn'
gobhin	goobit	'take in'
mekʔhin	meekʔit	'swallow'
ʔoṭʔhun	ʔooṭʔut	'steal'
pʔaxatʔhin	pʔaxaatʔit	'mourn'
ʔopothin	ʔopootit	'arise from bed'
hibeyhin	hibeeyit	'bring water'
ṣudokʔhun	ṣudookʔut	'remove'
cʔuyoohun	cʔuyot	'urinate'

The underlying representation of [ṣaphin], for instance, is /ṣaaphin/; /aa/ is shortened to [a] phonetically because a consonant cluster follows. In terms of the analysis of Problem 4.1–11, the underlying representation of [cʔuyot] would be /cʔuyoot/, since the passive aorist suffix has the form /t/ after a vowel; /oo/ thus shortens to [o] because it precedes a single, word-final consonant.

With the new data given above, the analysis of Problem 4.1–11 can be improved in several respects. First, the vowel shortening rule can be stated more simply if reference is made to syllable structure (recall that a sequence of the form *VCV* normally syllabifies as *V.CV*, while a sequence of the form *VCCV* typically syllabifies as *VC.CV*). Second, forms with [hun] and [ut] as the phonetic shapes of the aorist and passive aorist suffixes must be accounted for; these forms were omitted from consideration in Problem 4.1–11. Finally, the asymmetric character of the inventory of phonetic vowels suggests that the underlying vowel system may well differ in important respects from the phonetic system. Phonetically, the following long and short vowels occur.

	UNROUNDED	ROUNDED			UNROUNDED	ROUNDED
HIGH	ii	uu		HIGH	i	u
NON-HIGH	aa	oo		NON-HIGH	a	o

In terms of universal tendencies, it is somewhat unusual for long vowels to correspond to only three of five short vowels; the occurrence of long mid vowels but not long high vowels is also quite unusual.

Propose an analysis that incorporates the improvements suggested above. Give the underlying representations of each verb stem, together with three ordered rules that will derive the proper phonetic shapes. Motivate the ordering of the rules and give the derivations of the aorist and passive aorist forms of 'swallow' and 'steal'. The underlying vowel system should be a symmetrical one that avoids the difficulties cited.

Problem 4.3–18   Lardil

Each Lardil stem below (Hale, *to appear*, b) is given in four different forms. The nouns in the first column are uninflected; these forms are used for nouns that function as subjects. The (non-future) direct object form of each noun is given in the second column, and the third column contains the special inflected noun forms used for the direct objects of future sentences. The nouns in the last column are inflected for "locative" case, a case used in specifying location. The non-future accusative ending has two alternate underlying representations, and the future accusative ending has three; the choice is determined by the character of the last segment of the stem. The locative case ending has a single phonological representation. Lardil has four underlying vowels, as shown in the chart below.

	FRONT	BACK
HIGH	i	u
NON-HIGH	e	a

Posit underlying representations for the inflectional endings; for those endings with more than one underlying representation, state the principles that determine which will be used with a given stem. Posit a single phonological representation for each stem. Formulate four phonological rules that will account for the data, and determine how they must be ordered. Give the derivations of the nominative and locative forms of 'water', 'wife', and 'husband'.

Nominative	Accusative	Future Accusative	Locative	
mela	melan	melaṛ	melaa	'sea'
kela	kelan	kelaṛ	kelaa	'beach'
wanka	wankan	wankaṛ	wankaa	'arm'
kuŋka	kuŋkan	kuŋkaṛ	kuŋkaa	'groin'
ŋuka	ŋukun	ŋukuṛ	ŋukuu	'water'
ŋawa	ŋawun	ŋawuṛ	ŋawuu	'dog'
kaṭa	kaṭun	kaṭuṛ	kaṭuu	'child'
muṇa	muṇun	muṇuṛ	muṇuu	'elbow'
kenṭe	kenṭin	kenṭiwuṛ	kenṭii	'wife'
tʸimpe	tʸimpin	tʸimpiwuṛ	tʸimpii	'tail'
pape	papin	papiwuṛ	papii	'father's mother'
nʸerwe	nʸerwin	nʸerwiwuṛ	nʸerwii	'place'
ṭuŋal	ṭuŋalin	ṭuŋaluṛ	ṭuŋale	'tree'
kentapal	kentapalin	kentapaluṛ	kentapale	'dugong'
keṭar	keṭarin	keṭaruṛ	keṭare	'river'
miyaṛ	miyaṛin	miyaṛuṛ	miyaṛe	'spear'
yalul	yalulun	yaluluṛ	yaluluu	'flame'
mayar	mayaran	mayaraṛ	mayaraa	'rainbow'
karikar	karikarin	karikariwuṛ	karikarii	'butter-fish'
wiwal	wiwalan	wiwalaṛ	wiwalaa	'bush mango'
yukar	yukarpan	yukarpaṛ	yukarpaa	'husband'
wuṭal	wuṭaltʸin	wuṭaltʸiwuṛ	wuṭaltʸii	'meat'
wulun	wulunkan	wulunkaṛ	wulunkaa	'fruit'
paṇtʸipaṇ	paṇtʸipaṇtʸin	paṇtʸipaṇtʸiwuṛ	paṇtʸipaṇtʸii	'hat'

4.4 Suprasegmental Phonology

Suprasegmental phenomena are those that pertain to length, pitch, and loudness. They derive their name from the common practice of transcribing them phonetically by means of diacritics written above the symbols for segments.

INTONATION

Suprasegmental phenomena, also called **prosodic** phenomena, are normally examined in relation to individual lexical items or short phrases. However, many interesting prosodic patterns can be described only in terms of major constituents or entire sentences. Moreover, they are intimately connected with the syntactic and semantic properties of the sentences in which they occur. The prosodic properties of entire sentences, particularly those pertaining to pitch and stress, are referred to as **intonation**. Intonational studies are not so well developed as those which deal with the suprasegmental properties of individual lexical items, and we will restrict our attention to examples that show the close relationship between intonation and the syntactic and semantic structure of sentences.

Intonational differences frequently correlate with sentence types, and sometimes intonation is the only overt marking of these types. In English and many other languages, for example, questions answerable by 'yes' or 'no' occur with rising (or non-falling) intonation, while declaratives and other kinds of questions occur with final falling intonation.

(1) Did Danny buy a cow?

(2) Danny bought a cow.

(3) What did Danny buy?

It is not unusual for non-falling intonation to be the only indication that a sentence is a question rather than a statement. The same rising or non-falling intonation contour is associated with conjoined structures in English; each conjunct except the last is pronounced with this contour.

(4) At the party I saw Jackie, Aristotle, Lyndon, Eldridge,

Tricia, Spiro, and Irving.

Variations in the degree of stress borne by constituents further illustrate the intimate relationship between suprasegmental phenomena and the syntactic and semantic structure of sentences. Some constituents bear noticeably heavier stress than the remainder of the sentence. We may distinguish between *focus* stress, indicated below by a double accent (["]), and **emphatic** or **contrastive** stress, marked with a triple accent (["]). The focus of a sentence is the constituent that conveys new information (it is closely related to the notion comment, discussed in Chapter 3, p. 181). *A novel* is marked as the focus in (5), and *Max* in (6).

(5) Max wrote *a n̋ovel*.
(6) *M̋ax* wrote a novel.

Sentence (5) would be an appropriate answer if someone asked what Max wrote; in this context *a novel* would bear new information, since the question itself presupposes that Max wrote something. Similarly, (6) would be an appropriate answer if someone asked who wrote a novel. Notice that focus stress is consistently associated with certain syntactic constructions. For example, in sentences of the form *It's X that Y*, the constituent in position *X* receives focus stress.

(7) It's *my m̋oney* that he's after.
(8) It's *J̋anet* that I want to marry.

Emphatic stress is heavier than focus stress. It is the special stress used to emphasize an element, often to contrast it with another, as in dialogue (9).

(9) (a) "Raoul is the brains of the outfit."
(b) "No, you fool—*H̏arvey* is the brains of the outfit!"

Just as focus stress implies that the stressed element contributes new information, so the destressing of a constituent implies that the constituent duplicates information already available from the context. Pronouns, for instance, are normally stressed very weakly, since they substitute for full nominals under the condition of coreference. *He* is thus unstressed in (10), as indicated by the diacritic [ˇ], because it is coreferential to the non-pronominal noun phrase *Peter*.

(10) Peter$_i$ said that *hĕ$_i$* had never been so confused.

The destressing of constituents that contribute no new information is not restricted to pronouns. In (11) the entire clause *that Tom was a thief* has relatively weak stress because it duplicates a previously occurring clause.

(11) Eileen McDonald shouted that Tom was a thief, even though everyone already knew *thăt Tŏm wăs ă thiĕf*.

It is interesting to observe that destressing can take place even when the unstressed elements are not repetitions of previously uttered expressions; it is sufficient that the speaker presuppose semantic equivalence. In (12), for instance, *insult* can occur either with weak stress or with normal stress. The choice depends on whether or not the speaker considers calling someone a Republican to be an insult.

(12) Although Norman called Kate a Republican, she decided not to insult him.

LENGTH

Let us turn now to the suprasegmental properties of individual lexical items, beginning with length. To indicate that a segment is pronounced long, any one of the diacritics [‾ : ·] may be used, or else the segmental symbol may be written twice (the practice normally followed in this book). Long [a], for instance, can be written in any of these ways: [ā a: a· aa]. Consonants as well as vowels may be long or short. Long [t], for instance, is usually symbolized [tt]. The articulation of a long segment is greater in duration than that of the corresponding short segment, but it is not equivalent to articulating the short segment twice. Thus the articulation of [tt] does not involve two separate stop closures, but rather a single stop closure of somewhat greater duration than that of [t].

Although phonetic differences in length are found in all languages, length is distinctive only in some. In Problem 4.1–3 we saw that Mohawk has both long and short vowels phonetically, but their distribution is predictable; stressed vowels are lengthened when not followed by a consonant cluster. Length is thus not distinctive in Mohawk and need not be marked in the phonological representations of lexical items. Vowel length is distinctive in Alabaman (Problem 4.1–4), but only in certain environments. Word-final vowels are always long, and vowels are regularly short in word-initial position or when followed by a consonant cluster. At the level of phonological representation, the distinction between long and short vowels must be marked only in those instances where length is not predictable by these general rules.

Length may be distinctive for vowels, for consonants, or for both, although distinctive length is more common with vowels than with consonants. It is perhaps true that no more than two degrees of length (long and short) are ever distinctive, but there is some possibility that three degrees will have to be recognized for some languages. Phonetically, of course, considerable variation in length is possible.

Problem 4.4–1   English

Small differences in vowel length are to be found in English. Determine the status of length on the basis of the words below.

heed	hiid	*sit*	sɪt	*tag*	tææg	*Sid*	sɪɪd
bell	bɛɛl	*lap*	læp	*luck*	lʌk	*eased*	iizd
fat	fæt	*stall*	stɔɔl	*west*	wɛst	*loom*	luum
east	ist	*loop*	lup	*rouge*	ruuž	*weld*	wɛɛld
bear	bɛɛr	*food*	fuud	*heat*	hit	*rib*	rɪɪb

Solution

In this data long vowels appear only before voiced segments, and short vowels before voiceless segments. This difference in length is predictable and consequently not distinctive.

STRESS

In many languages special prominence is accorded one or more syllables in the articulation of lexical items. This special prominence is referred to as *accent* or *stress*. (These terms will be used interchangeably, though the latter is sometimes reserved for accent in which the primary component is added loudness.) Accent may consist in a distinct level of pitch, amplitude, or both. Accent in Classical Greek, for instance, is believed to have consisted in higher pitch. In English stressed syllables differ from unstressed ones by having higher pitch and greater loudness (they are also longer).

The placement of accent in some languages is apparently unpredictable and must be marked as part of the phonological representations of individual lexical items. Frequently, however, it is partially or fully predictable. Accent placement is commonly predictable in relation to word boundaries. For example, in Classical Aztec stress regularly falls on the second vowel from the end of a word (Problem 2.1–9, p. 52); the same is true of Swahili (Problem 2.1–12, p. 55). In French stress occurs on the last vowel of a word (not counting [ə]). For many languages, including Papago, the stem rather than the word is the unit relevant for rules of stress placement. The Papago stress rule formulated in Problem 2.1–3 (p. 43) applied stress to the first vowel of a word. While this is correct for most Papago forms, including all the ones under consideration in Problem 2.1–3, the rule is not fully general; in words with prefixes stress does not appear on the prefix vowel, but rather on the first vowel of the stem, as in [ʔi-hásc̆ud] 'aggrandize himself'. The proper generalization is that the first vowel of the stem is stressed in Papago.

Accent rules sometimes take into account not only the position of a syllable within a stem or word but also its phonological shape. Long vowels are commonly stressed in preference to short vowels, for instance. In Latin words of more than two syllables, the second syllable from the end is stressed if it is "strong"; otherwise the third syllable from the end is stressed. A strong syllable is one containing a long vowel, or a short vowel plus a consonantal coda. Thus *a.mí.cus* 'friend' and *mo.lés.tus* 'annoying' have stress on the next-to-last syllable, but *dó.mi.nus* 'master' is stressed on the third syllable from the end. A similar distinction between strong and weak syllables is crucial for the basic rules of stress placement in English (Chomsky and Halle, 1968).

In languages that employ stress to a significant degree, it is quite common for stress to accompany more than one syllable in complex lexical items. Usually, one syllable bears primary stress, while other syllables bear a stress of secondary intensity or are unstressed altogether. The symbols [′ ^ ` ˘] are employed to indicate varying degrees of stress, ranging (in order) from primary stress to lack of stress. Araucanian words bear stress on every even-numbered syllable, counting from the beginning of a word, as we saw in Problem 4.1–2. The first of these is a primary stress, while the others are weaker, as in [kĭmúfălùwŭlày] 'he pretended not to know'. The co-occurrence within a word of primary and lesser degrees of stress is also quite character- istic of English, though the situation is much more complicated. It is partic- ularly interesting to note that a primary stress in a simple lexical item may be retained as a lesser degree of stress in a complex lexical item derived from it. Compare *élement*, *órchestra*, and *círculàte* with *èleméntary*, *òrchéstral*, and *circulátion*. The rules determining the placement and degree of stress are sometimes quite intricate, and their interaction with other rules often has important consequences for the phonological system of a language.

Problem 4.4–2   Diegueño

Examine the words below (Langdon, 1970) and formulate a rule that predicts the placement of stress in Diegueño.

ʔəmát	'land'	ʔàaṣáa	'bird'
ʔəmúu	'wild sheep'	àakʷál	'he licks'
àakərətíip	'in a row'	kìmáʔ	'dance!'
ʔənáavək	'if we go'	kəṣùučúʔ	'poke the fire!'
ʔiikʷíčvəč	'the man' (subject)	ʔəxána	'is it good?'
ʔiičáčvu	'I think so'	píľvəy	'right now'

Solution

Primary stress falls on the last vowel of a word, excluding from consideration [ə] and word-final short vowels. Weaker stress appears on long vowels that precede the primary stress.

TONE

In many languages vowels that are identical in quality contrast with one another due to differences in pitch. Languages such as these are referred to as **tone languages**, and the distinctive pitches are called **tones**.

Tone systems differ from accentual systems in several important respects.

First, the degree and placement of stress are quite often fully or partially predictable, while tone is distinctive. Second, accent typically occurs on only one syllable of a simple lexical item, and in complex lexical items only one syllable normally bears primary stress; in tone languages, on the other hand, it is not uncommon for every syllable in a lexical item to be characterized by its own distinctive tone. Finally, the degrees of stress that are distinctive in a language are quite restricted in number, the upper limit probably being no more than three (primary stress, secondary stress, and unstressed); the number of distinctive tones that can occur in a single language is considerably higher—six or eight might be the maximum (incomplete data and problems of analysis leave the precise figure in doubt).

Some languages, such as Navaho (Problem 2.2–12, p. 72), distinguish only two levels of tone, typically high versus low. Languages that distinguish three levels of tone (such as high, mid, and low) are exemplified by Ayutla Mixtec (Problem 2.1–11, p. 54) and Nupe (Problem 4.1–5). In languages with three or more distinctive tones, the contour of tones is frequently important as well as their relative pitch. Lushai, for instance, has four tones: high, mid, falling, and rising. Mandarin Chinese also has four tones: high, high rising, high falling, and a low tone that falls and then rises. Occasionally one finds complex tones that involve glottal constriction as well as pitch; this is true of certain dialects of Vietnamese, for example.

Tones, like other phonological properties, are subject to modification by phonological rules. We encountered an Ayutla Mixtec example in Problem 2.1–11, (p. 54). If the first of two adjacent words ends in [ʔ], this segment is deleted and the first three vowels of the second word receive the tone pattern high-high-low, regardless of their underlying tones. Otomi, an Otomanguian language spoken in Mexico, has three tones, high (['']), low (['']), and rising ([ˇ]). A morpheme that has high tone when it occurs in isolation is pronounced with rising tone instead when it combines with other morphemes in a word; compare *cí* 'he eats' and *mǎgàcǐgá* 'I am going to eat' (Wallis, 1968).

Problem 4.4–3   Lushai

In the Lushai forms below (data courtesy of William Bright), the diacritics [' ` ˇ ^] indicate high, mid, rising, and falling tone respectively. (In the case of long vowels, these diacritics are used only on the first of the two identical vowel symbols.) The first column contains declarative expressions. In the second column these expressions are made into yes-no questions by adding the suffix [ĕm] ([ʔĕm] after vowels) to the declarative forms (compare Problem 3.5–4, p. 190). The prefixes [ʔà] and [ʔá] are different phonetic manifestations of the third person singular pronoun. Formulate rules that account for tone variation. Give the derivation of 'does he look?' and comment on rule ordering.

Declarative	Interrogative	
ʔàkál	ʔàkálĕm	'he goes'
ʔàbéy	ʔàbéyĕm	'it sticks'
ʔàhláa	ʔàhláaʔĕm	'it's far'
ʔàsáa	ʔàsáaʔĕm	'it's hot'
ʔáʔên	ʔáʔénĕm	'he looks'
ʔátrân	ʔátránĕm	'he starts'
ʔávây	ʔáváyĕm	'he waves'
ʔánâa	ʔánâaʔĕm	'it's rough'
ʔálêew	ʔálêewĕm	'it glances off'
ʔámêet	ʔámêetĕm	'he shaves'
ʔábàal	ʔábàalĕm	'it's dirty'
ʔázòom	ʔázòomĕm	'he obeys'
ʔánìi	ʔánìiʔĕm	'he is'
ʔávùa	ʔávùaʔĕm	'he beats'
ʔàlĕy	ʔàléyĕm	'he buys'
ʔàʔŏm	ʔàʔómĕm	'he stays'
ʔàsŭy	ʔàsúyĕm	'he scrapes'
ʔàʔăa	ʔàʔăaʔĕm	'he's foolish'
ʔàhŏo	ʔàhŏoʔĕm	'he goes home'
ʔàtĕe	ʔàtĕeʔĕm	'it's small'

Solution

Two rules are required. One of them determines the tone that will accompany the prefix [ʔa]. The other adjusts the tone of a stem when the interrogative morpheme is suffixed.

    (A) The prefix [ʔa] has mid tone ([ˈ]) when attached to a stem with high or rising tone ([ˈ ˇ]). It has high tone ([ˊ]) before a stem with mid or falling tone ([ˈ ^]).

    (B) Before the interrogative suffix [ĕm] (or [ʔĕm]), a short stem vowel with rising or falling tone ([ˇ ^]) receives high tone instead ([ˊ]).

Both rules apply in the derivation of 'does he look?':

$$\text{/ʔa-ʔên-ĕm/ 'does he look?'} \longrightarrow \underset{(A)}{\text{ʔá-ʔên-ĕm}} \longrightarrow \underset{(B)}{\text{ʔá-ʔén-ĕm}}$$

Since the pronoun has high tone in this form, rule (A) must precede (B). The pronoun generally receives high tone before a stem with mid or falling tone, but (B) changes this to high tone. Once (B) applies, therefore, there is no general way to assign tone correctly to the pronominal prefix.

Discussion

On the basis of the present data, there is no motivation for assigning one tone or another to the prefix [ʔa] at the level of phonological representation.

Rising or falling tone is posited for the phonological representation of those stems that exhibit alternation between rising or falling and high tone. The reason for choosing these underlying representations is that it is possible to state a general rule that will change rising or falling tone to high tone in precisely the right instances, while the converse rule could not be general. Not all stems with a high tone before the interrogative suffix have rising or falling tone in the corresponding declarative expression, and for those that do there is no apparent way to predict whether rising or falling tone will appear.

FURTHER PROBLEMS

Problem 4.4–4 Spanish

This problem (see Foley, 1967) concerns stress and plural formation in Spanish. The nouns in column I are singular, and those in column II are their corresponding plurals. Each morpheme represented in the data, including the plural morpheme, can be accorded a single phonological representation. Postulate appropriate underlying representations for these morphemes, as well as a rule that predicts the placement of stress and any other phonological rules that might be necessary. Give the derivations of 'letter', 'month', 'Mondays', and 'coffees', and comment on rule ordering.

I	II	
kárta	kártas	'letter'
íxo	íxos	'son'
mésa	mésas	'table'
rasón	rasónes	'reason'
relixyón	relixyónes	'religion'
muxér	muxéres	'woman'
més	méses	'month'
bós	bóses	'voice'
lúnes	lúnes	'Monday'
kafé	kafés	'coffee'

Problem 4.4–5 Ayutla Mixtec

The data below from Ayutla Mixtec (Pankratz and Pike, 1967) consists of nouns in their unpossessed and possessed forms. The first column shows the noun as it appears in isolation; the other columns show the noun with various possessive suffixes. Posit a single phonological representation for each noun and each suffix. Formulate a series of rules that will derive the phonetic data. Give the derivations of 'my grindstone', 'your grindstone', and 'our candle'. Determine how the rules must be ordered. The diacritics [′ ^ ‵] stand for high, mid, and low tone respectively.

N	'my N'	'your N'	'his N'	'her N'	'our N'	'their N'	
yòsóʔ	yòsóí	yòsóʔ	yòsórá	yòsóáʔ	yòsóéʔ	yòsóñá	'grindstone'
čîtʾà	čîtʾài	čîtʾàûʔ	čîtʾàrà	čîtʾààʔ	čîtʾæʔ	čîtʾàñà	'banana'
lášá	lášái	lášáûʔ	lášárà	lášááʔ	lášǽʔ	lášáñá	'orange'
tôtò	tôtòi	tôtòʔ	tôtòrà	tôtòàʔ	tôtòèʔ	tôtòñà	'clothing'
îkàʔ	îkài	îkàûʔ	îkàrà	îkààʔ	îkǽʔ	îkàñà	'basket'
čîló	čîlói	čîlóʔ	čîlórà	čîlóàʔ	čîlóéʔ	čîlóñà	'knife'
tímáʔ	tímái	tímáûʔ	tímárá	tímááʔ	tímǽʔ	tímáñá	'candle'
kôòʔ	kôòì	kôòʔ	kôòrà	kôòàʔ	kôòèʔ	kôòñà	'snake'

Problem 4.4–6 *Mandarin Chinese*

The Mandarin data below (courtesy of Benjamin T'sou; compare Cheng, 1970) illustrates the operation of rules that modify tone. Each expression consists of two or more morphemes. In column I these morphemes are given with the tones they have when each morpheme occurs by itself, and the sequences in column I can be regarded as phonological representations. The phonetic representations of the expressions are given in column II. Formulate the rules needed to account for the data and determine how they must be ordered. Give the derivation of the last expression. The diacritics [¯ ´ ` ˇ] stand respectively for high tone, rising tone, falling tone, and a low tone that falls then rises.

I	II	
lǎo mǎ	láo mǎ	'old horse'
yī shié shì	yī shiē shì	'department of medicine'
hán shú biǎo	hán shū biǎo	'household thermometer'
dōng nán fēng	dōng nān fēng	'southeast wind'
wó yé yǒu	wó yē yǒu	'I also have'
lǎo má	lǎo má	'old jute'
hǎo jiǔ	háo jiǔ	'good wine'
mǎi mǎ	mái mǎ	'buy a horse'
mǎi lǎo mǎ	mái lāo mǎ	'buy an old horse'
siǎng mǎi lǎo mǎ	siáng māi lāo mǎ	'wish to buy an old horse'
lǎo lǐ mǎi hǎo jiǔ	láo lǐ māi hāo jiǔ	'old Li buys good wine'

Problem 4.4–7 *Lushai*

The Lushai forms below (courtesy of William Bright) supplement those given in Problem 4.4–3. The negative versions of the declarative expressions listed in the former problem are given first, followed by several new sets of expressions. The affix [lòw] is the negative morpheme.

Negative		Negative	
ʔàkállòw	'he doesn't go'	ʔábàallòw	'it isn't dirty'
ʔàbéylòw	'it doesn't stick'	ʔázòomlòw	'he doesn't obey'
ʔàhlálòw	'it isn't far'	ʔánìlòw	'he isn't'
ʔàsálòw	'it isn't hot'	ʔávòlòw	'he doesn't beat'
ʔáʔênlòw	'he doesn't look'	ʔàlĕylòw	'he doesn't buy'
ʔátrânlòw	'he doesn't start'	ʔàʔŏmlòw	'he doesn't stay'
ʔávâylòw	'he doesn't wave'	ʔàsŭylòw	'he doesn't scrape'
ʔánâalòw	'it isn't rough'	ʔàʔăalòw	'he isn't foolish'
ʔálêewlòw	'it doesn't glance off'	ʔàhŏolòw	'he doesn't go home'
ʔámêetlòw	'he doesn't shave'	ʔàtĕelòw	'it isn't small'

Declarative	Interrogative	Negative	
ʔádùʔ	ʔádùʔĕm	ʔádùʔlòw	'he wants'
ʔáchìa	ʔáchìaʔĕm	ʔáchèlòw	'it's bad'
ʔàcĕe	ʔàcĕeʔĕm	ʔàcĕelòw	'it shakes'
ʔáphîat	ʔáphîatĕm	ʔáphîatlòw	'he sweeps'
ʔàdŏo	ʔàdŏoʔĕm	ʔàdólòw	'he tells lies'
ʔàhrïa	ʔàhrïaʔĕm	ʔàhrélòw	'he knows'
ʔàtlĕe	ʔàtlĕeʔĕm	ʔàtlélòw	'it's bright'
ʔàhŭa	ʔàhŭaʔĕm	ʔàhólòw	'he hates'
ʔàzăa	ʔàzăaʔĕm	ʔàzálòw	'it tickles'

Despite phonetic variation, each morpheme can be assigned a uniform phonological representation. Three new rules, plus rule (A) and a refinement of rule (B) of Problem 4.4–3, suffice to account for the data. Postulate the necessary rules, together with appropriate underlying representations for the stems. (In all but a few important cases, the underlying representation of the stem is the same as its phonetic shape in the declarative expression.) Determine how the rules must be ordered. Give the derivations of the three forms of 'it shakes' and the three forms of 'he hates'.

5

Diachronic Analysis

Preceding chapters have dealt with synchronic analysis, the analysis of a single linguistic system at one point in time. Let us turn now to diachronic analysis, the study of language change. The objectives of diachronic analysis are to describe the historical evolution of particular languages and language families, and to formulate a theory of language change. Any adequate theory of language change must correctly specify the kinds of changes which can occur in linguistic systems and must clarify the causes and mechanisms of these changes.

Since language change is the modification through time of a linguistic system, diachronic investigation is most fruitful when two or more historical stages of a language are known in some detail and have been adequately analyzed. This is normally not the case, however, for the simple reason that most languages have not been committed to writing or otherwise recorded for a period commensurate with the time spans over which major structural changes occur. Consequently, diachronic studies must rely fairly heavily on indirect methods to supplement the direct comparison of different stages of a language.

One indirect technique of diachronic investigation is ***dialectal analysis***, the description and comparison of different dialects of a single language. Since dialect diversification and historical evolution are both products of language change, dialects of a language differ from one another in the same kinds of ways that two historical stages of a language differ. Dialectal comparison can therefore shed considerable light on the problems of diachronic study.

Internal reconstruction is another indirect technique of diachronic investigation. It is the attempt to determine certain details of the historical development of a language by means of a careful scrutiny of its structure. Internal reconstruction is important as a supplemental technique in diachronic analysis, but as the sole method for determining the prehistory of a linguistic system its potential is severely limited.

Of far greater importance is the **comparative method**, which might also be called "external reconstruction". In the broadest sense, the comparative method is the systematic comparison of languages thought to be related in order to establish conclusively that they are in fact related and to reconstruct, insofar as possible, the proto language from which they are all descended. The comparative method is inherently much more powerful than internal reconstruction as a tool for reconstructing linguistic prehistory, since evidence from more than just a single language is brought to bear in determining the character of the parent tongue.

5.1 Language Change

Languages are constantly undergoing structural change. Most individual changes are subtle and minor enough, and their diffusion through the speech community gradual enough, that they escape our attention while they are taking place. Given sufficient time perspective, however, the cumulative effect of language change is readily apparent. Diachronic studies typically involve time depths of hundreds or even thousands of years.

EFFECTS OF CHANGE

The most obvious changes, from the standpoint of the language user, are no doubt those that affect individual lexical items. The addition of new lexical items (such as *quasar* and *moon-rover*) to the lexicon of a language is easily accessible to introspection by native speakers, as are changes or extensions of meaning (like the use of *pig* as a derogatory term for policemen or other representatives of the establishment). The loss of lexical items, by contrast, is a gradual process and is thus less likely to come to the attention of native speakers, though speakers can recognize certain words and expressions (such as *brethren*) as archaic. Changes in the syntactic and phonological properties of individual lexical items are also quite likely to escape the attention of native speakers who happen not to be linguists.

Changes that affect the syntactic or phonological rules of a language command more attention from linguists than lexical changes, since they are more general and have greater consequences for a linguistic system. Such changes can consist in the addition or loss of rules, the modification of existing rules, or the reordering of rules.

Many phonological changes originate in the addition of rules to the phonological system. The change of [c] to [s] in the history of Burmese, discussed in Chapter 1 (p. 14), presumably originated in the adoption of a phonological rule of the form [c] → [s]. Changes of this kind may be mirrored in synchronic regularities that are retained by a language for centuries as productive and general rules. French vowel nasalization is a case in point (see Problem 4.1–12, p. 255). This rule, which merges a vowel with a syllable-coda nasal consonant to produce a nasalized vowel, is a productive rule of French phonology and has been for many centuries. The rule was not part of the phonological system of Classical Latin; rather it represents an innovation in the historical evolution of French. French vowel nasalization also illustrates language change through rule modification. In Old French a vowel was nasalized before a nasal consonant regardless of syllable structure; it was not required that the nasal consonant be a syllable coda. Moreover, the consonant was retained phonetically rather than merged with the nasalized vowel. It is apparent, then, that the rule of vowel nasalization has been modified in the development of Old French into modern French.

Language change through the reordering of rules can be illustrated by an example from Finnish (Kiparsky, 1968). Rules (A) and (B) are characteristic of standard Finnish.

> (A) [ee] ⟶ [ie].
> (B) [γ] is deleted intervocalically.

Rule (A) derives [vie] 'take' from the underlying representation /vee/, while (B) applies to /teγe/ and produces the phonetic sequence [tee] 'do'. It is readily seen that (A) precedes (B), since [tee], which is derived by (B), does not subsequently diphthongize to [tie], as it would if (A) followed (B). However, in some dialects of Finnish, the ordering of the two rules has been reversed, so that (B) precedes (A). In these dialects (B) applies to /teγe/ to produce [tee], which in turn becomes [tie] by virtue of rule (A).

Let us return to the evolution of Latin into French for an example of rule loss, this time from the domain of syntax. In Latin subject nominals were marked by means of a special case, the nominative (see Problem 3.6–7, p. 204). This syntactic principle, as well as others pertaining to case, have disappeared from the grammar of modern French, which has lost case inflection entirely (except for certain distinctions in the shape of pronouns). Rule loss will be considered further in the discussion of restructuring below.

Problem 5.1–1   Latin

The forms in the first column below are from Classical Latin, and those in the second column are the corresponding forms from a later stage, called

Vulgar Latin, from which the modern Romance languages ultimately evolved. Describe the phonological changes that link the Vulgar Latin forms with their predecessors in the classical language, insofar as these changes are reflected in the data. Assume for purposes of this problem that the phonological representations of lexical items are the same for Classical and Vulgar Latin. (It is an oversimplification to regard Vulgar Latin as the direct linear descendant of textbook Classical Latin. Nevertheless, the correspondence is sufficiently close that the problem remains correct in its essentials.)

Classical	*Vulgar*	
ásinus	ásnos	'ass'
kálidum	káldo	'hot' (accusative)
kéera	kéra	'wax'
kínerem	kénre	'ash' (accusative)
díikere	díkre	'say'
fúrnus	fórnos	'oven'
kolóorem	kolóre	'color' (accusative)
kírkulus	kérklos	'circle'
dúukere	dúkre	'lead'
pílus	pélos	'hair'
stáare	estáre	'stand'
stríktus	estréktos	'close'
spíina	espína	'thorn'
skúutum	eskúto	'shield'
plakéere	plakére	'please'

Solution

Five phonological changes account for the Vulgar Latin forms. Under the assumption that underlying representations remained constant, each change can be regarded as the addition of a rule to the phonological system of Latin.

(A) Short high vowels become mid vowels.

(B) Long vowels become short.

(C) An unstressed vowel is deleted if a stressed syllable precedes and another syllable follows.

(D) Word-final [m] is deleted.

(E) [e] is inserted before a word-initial consonant cluster beginning with [s].

Problem 5.1–2   French

In modern French the past participle of a verb that occurs with the auxiliary verb *avoir* 'have' agrees with its direct object in number and gender under certain conditions (see Problem 3.7–6, p. 222). A similar rule was operative in Old French, but the details of the rule were somewhat different (Foulet, 1967). Examine the Old French and modern French expressions below, and determine how the participle agreement rule has been modified. The direct objects in these examples are all feminine. Feminine gender is marked on past participles with the ending *e*, and plurality with *s*.

Old French

    (1) la trahison que j'ai fete

        the treachery that I have done FEMININE
        'the treachery that I have done'

    (2) Une espee du fuerre a trete.

        a sword from the scabbard has drawn FEMININE
        'He drew a sword from the scabbard.'

    (3) Grant joie menee avoient.

        great joy brought FEMININE they had
        'They had brought great joy.'

    (4) El chief li a embatue l'espee.

        in the head to him has plunged FEMININE the sword
        'He plunged the sword into his head.'

    (5) celui cui j'amoie et trahie m'a

        he whom I loved and betrayed FEMININE me has
        'he whom I loved and who has betrayed me'

    (6) En a la duchoise menees les dames en sa chambre o soi.

        in has the duchess led FEMININE PLURAL the ladies in her
            room with her
        'The duchess led the ladies into her room with her.'

    (7) J'ai creü vostre parole.

        I have believed your word
        'I believed what you said.'

    (8) Or l'ai lonc tens en vain servi.

        now her have long time in vain served
        'I have long served her in vain.'

Modern French

    (9) les femmes que j'ai vues

        the women that I have seen FEMININE PLURAL
        'the women that I saw'

(10) Je l'ai surprise.

I her have surprised FEMININE
'I surprised her.'

(11) *Je l'ai surpris.

I her have surprised
'I surprised her.'

(12) Il a trouvé l'épée.

he has found the sword
'He found the sword.'

(13) *Il a trouvée l'épée.

he has found FEMININE the sword
'He found the sword.'

(14) Quelle épée avez-vous trouvée?

which sword have-you found FEMININE
'Which sword did you find?'

(15) *Il a vue quelle femme?

he has seen FEMININE which woman
'He saw which woman?'

(16) Il a vu quelle femme?
he has seen which woman
'He saw which woman?'

Solution

In modern French a past participle agrees with its direct object only when
the object precedes the participle, and the agreement is obligatory. In Old
French, on the other hand, agreement was optional, and it could occur
regardless of the linear order of the object and participle. The agreement
rule has thus been modified in two ways. It has become obligatory, and it
has been restricted to apply only when the object precedes.

MECHANISMS OF CHANGE

One of the most important sources of linguistic change is **borrowing**, the
adoption by speakers of one language of certain structural traits of another.
The borrowing of lexical items is extremely common and tends, as we might

expect, to follow the lines of cultural influence. For example, many Arabic loan words are found in Swahili, Turkish, and other languages in Africa and the Middle East, reflecting the predominance of Arabic culture in this area for many centuries. In the recent centuries of British and then American ascendancy, English loan words have been adopted in languages all over the globe. Languages also borrow from one another in regard to phonology and syntax, but less is known about the mechanisms and possible extent of phonological and syntactic influence than about lexical influence. The borrowing of lexical items is undoubtedly an important factor in phonological and syntactic borrowing. For instance, Xhosa, a Bantu language, has a series of *click* consonants; these are "clicking" or "popping" sounds produced by trapping a body of air (usually between the tongue and the roof of the mouth), rarifying this pocket of air by enlarging the cavity, and then releasing the closure so that air flows in rapidly to fill the partial vacuum. These click sounds were borrowed into Bantu from the neighboring Khoisan languages, no doubt through the adoption of loan words containing clicks. Similarly, the borrowing of nouns from Bantu may be responsible for a syntactic innovation in Mbugu, a Cushitic language spoken in Tanzania (Welmers, 1970). Mbugu has adopted the Bantu system of noun classes with characteristic prefixes that are used for agreement purposes (see Problems 2.2–10 and 2.4–6, Swahili, pp. 70 and 91).

Not all linguistic changes are due to borrowing. Innovations can and do occur in the speech of adult speakers, for stylistic or expressive value, for ease of articulation or sentence construction, or for any number of reasons. More important, changes take place during the transmission of language from one generation of speakers to the next. As children learn their native language, changes can occur through either *imperfect learning* or *restructuring*.

Imperfect learning plays a role in every child's acquisition of his native language. Because languages are extremely complex, and because a child must learn his first language on the basis of an unsystematic exposure to linguistic performance that gives him at best an imperfect view of the structure of the language, the linguistic system that the child internalizes can never replicate exactly the one used by his models. If the modifications are minor or subtle enough, they may go uncorrected, or indeed unnoticed. When a child incorrectly learns the meaning of a lexical item, or fails to master all the morphological idiosyncrasies of an irregular verb, he is guilty of imperfect learning. Imperfect learning may also be a factor in rule change, particularly in cases where rules are generalized—that is, extended to apply to a larger class of structures. For example, a number of Uto-Aztecan languages were characterized at one stage in their historical development by a rule backing [k] to [q] before a non-high vowel. In one such language, Mono, this rule was extended so that it affected both [k] and [k^w], deriving [q] and [q^w] respectively before non-high vowels (see Problem 5.4–12 below). Imperfect learning was no doubt one factor in the generalization of this rule. The failure of Mono speakers to master the precise conditions under which the rule applied led to its application before all velar stops instead of just unrounded velar stops.

Restructuring is a reshaping of the rules and representations that account for the surface forms of a language. In contrast to imperfect learning, restructuring may leave the surface forms of the language intact. In imperfect learning, as we have seen, discrepancies between the linguistic system of the child and that of his models are overtly manifested; the rules of a language are modified in subtle, not drastic respects, and the modification of individual lexical items is sporadic, not regular. Restructuring involves more substantial modification of the rules of a language, sometimes with a concomitant readjustment of lexical representations that may be fairly systematic. It must be emphasized that these two mechanisms of change, while quite distinct on the conceptual plane, may in practice be nothing more than two poles of a continuum. In fact, relatively little is known about the effects of the transmission of language from one generation of speakers to the next, so such distinctions must be accepted more as useful concepts for the discussion of language change than as clear-cut categories derived inductively from large numbers of clinical cases.

Let us consider the changes in Latin phonology discussed in Problem 5.1–1. Among the phonological changes that derive the phonetic shapes of Vulgar Latin from their historical predecessors is the deletion of word-final [m]. Another is the deletion of an unstressed vowel that is neither the first nor the last vowel of a word. These two changes serve to derive Vulgar Latin [kénre] from Classical Latin [kínerem] 'ash (ACCUSATIVE)'. (We will ignore the change in vowel quality to simplify matters.) Presumably, both changes originated in the addition of rules to the phonological component of Latin. Because they resided in the incorporation of general rules, the changes affected the phonetic shape of all Latin words to which the rules were applicable; their effects were not peculiar to individual lexical items.

Consider now the language learning situation with which children acquiring Latin were faced once these rules were generally adopted in the language. The segments deleted by the rules did not always occur phonetically, though they were present as part of the phonological representations of lexical items. Consequently, children learning Latin would tend to acquire lexical items whose underlying representations lacked the phonetically absent segments. This development entails a massive and fairly regular revision in the phonological representations of the language. It also entails the loss of the two rules in question, which ceased to be functional once the underlying representations had been modified. This restructuring is schematized in three hypothetical stages in Figure 5.1–1. (The underlying representations in the figure are not to be equated with the most abstract phonological representations that could be postulated—they are simply the most abstract representations relevant to the present discussion.)

Stage 1
Underlying Representation: [kínerem]
Phonetic Representation: [kínerem]

Stage 2
Underlying Representation: [kínerem]
Phonetic Representation: [kénre]
Rules: Word-final [m] is deleted. An
unstressed vowel is deleted if it is
not the first or last vowel of a word.

Stage 3
Underlying Representation: [kénre]
Phonetic Representation: [kénre]

Figure 5.1–1

Naturally, this description is highly schematized and in part speculative; the changes may have spread gradually through the lexicon, and much more may have been involved than the present discussion indicates. This conception of the basic mechanism of the change must nevertheless contain a considerable element of truth, and the changes in question definitely occurred somewhere along the line. The medial [e] and final [m] of [kínerem] do not appear in the phonological representation of its modern French descendant, *cendre* [sɑ̃dr], and the two phonological rules have also disappeared from the language.

A second example of restructuring, from the domain of syntax, is found in the development of French interrogatives in certain dialects, including many dialects spoken in Canada (Patterson, *to appear*). In these dialects the particle *ti* is inserted after the inflected verbal element of a sentence to mark the sentence as an interrogative. Thus the declarative sentence *Je sais ton nom* 'I know your name' can be made into a question by the addition of *ti* after *sais: Je sais ti ton nom?* 'Do I know your name?' This method of marking questions contrasts with question formation in standard French, which lacks the particle *ti*. In standard French, questions with pronoun subjects are formed by permuting the pronoun subject with the inflected verbal element. For instance, the interrogative version of *Il dort* 'He is sleeping' is *Dort-il?* 'Is he sleeping?'

The question particle *ti* owes its origin to restructuring. Expressions such as *dort-il* came to be analyzed by speakers as consisting of a verb, *dor* in this case, plus a particle, *ti* (the pronoun *il* is often simply [i] phonetically). One factor in this reanalysis was no doubt the fact that the *t* of verbs like *dort* is normally not pronounced in the declarative, but only in questions (due to phenomena beyond the scope of this discussion). The occurrence of a syllable boundary between *dor* and *t-il* in *dort-il* probably also facilitated the change.

In any event, once *ti* was reinterpreted structurally as a single morpheme distinct from the pronoun *il*, it could be generalized as an interrogative marker and used to mark interrogation in sentences with subjects other than *il*. In this way, a special question-marking particle arose in a language in which questions were originally marked syntactically by special word order.

Problem 5.1–3   Yaqui

Yaqui is a Uto-Aztecan language spoken in Mexico and Arizona. This problem illustrates the grammatical influence of Spanish on the expression of comparison in Yaqui (see Lindenfeld, 1971). (1) and (2) show how comparatives of equality and superiority are expressed in Spanish. (3)–(5) express the equivalent notions in Yaqui as recorded in the early seventeenth century, when Spanish influence had not as yet made itself felt. (6)–(9) are modern Yaqui sentences that betray a certain amount of syntactic borrowing from Spanish. From these examples determine the changes that have occurred in the expression of comparison in Yaqui, and assess the degree to which Spanish influence is responsible for these changes. (Spanish *que* is phonetically [ke].)

Spanish

(1) Juan es tan grande como Pedro.
John is as big like Peter
'John is as big as Peter.'

(2) Juan es mas grande que Pedro.
John is more big than Peter
'John is bigger than Peter.'

Seventeenth-Century Yaqui

(3) hu oʔoo hume haamučim benasya bʷeʔu
this man these women like big
'This man is as big as these women.'

(4) hu oʔoo čeʔa hume haamučim beppa bʷeʔu
this man more these women over big
'This man is bigger than these women.'

(5) hu oʔoo hume haamučim beppa bʷeʔu
this man these women over big
'This man is bigger than these women.'

Modern Yaqui

(6) hu oʔoo bʷeʔu ke hume haamučim benasya
this man big than these women like
'This man is as big as these women.'

(7) hu oʔoo čeʔa bʷeʔu ke hume haamučim beppa
this man more big than these women over
'This man is bigger than these women.'

(8) hu oʔoo bʷeʔu ke hume haamučim beppa
this man big than these women over
'This man is bigger than these women.'

(9) hu oʔoo čeʔa bʷeʔu ke hume haamučim
this man more big than these women
'This man is bigger than these women.'

Solution

The data reveals three differences between seventeenth-century and modern
Yaqui. First, in the earlier language the compared adjective comes at the
end of the sentence, but it precedes the second nominal in modern Yaqui.
Second, the morpheme [ke] is present only in modern Yaqui and is regularly
inserted between the compared adjective and the second nominal. Finally,
[beppa] 'over' is obligatory in comparatives of superiority in the earlier stage
of Yaqui, but in the modern language it is optional (provided [čeʔa] 'more'
is present).

All three modifications can be attributed to Spanish influence. (1) and (2)
show that the compared adjective precedes the second nominal in Spanish.
Moreover, the Yaqui particle [ke] is identical to Spanish *que*, which also
comes between the compared adjective and the second nominal. (This
borrowing has been inexact, since *como* rather than *que* is used in Spanish
comparatives of equality, while [ke] is used for both types of comparatives
in Yaqui.) Finally, the optionality of [beppa] leads to sentences like (9),
which are exactly parallel syntactically to the corresponding Spanish sentences (except that 'be' is unexpressed in Yaqui). In particular, Spanish *mas
ADJ que NP* is mirrored constituent by constituent in Yaqui [čeʔa] *ADJ*
[ke] *NP*.

FURTHER PROBLEMS

Problem 5.1–4   Swiss German

This problem concerns phonological rules in the Swiss German dialects of
Schaffhausen and Kesswil (Kiparsky, 1968). One of the rules involves **umlaut**,
the fronting of a back vowel. This is an important phenomenon in the history
of Germanic, and it originated as an assimilation of a back vowel to a front
vowel in the following syllable. For purposes of this problem, however, the
Schaffhausen umlauting rule can be stated as in (A).

(A) In the plural a back stem vowel is fronted.

The second pertinent rule of the Schaffhausen dialect is (B).

(B) /o/ is lowered to [ɔ] before a dental or palatal consonant.

(A) and (B) are illustrated in the Schaffhausen derivations of the singular and plural forms of /bodə/ 'earth, floor'. (A) cannot apply in the singular, but (B) can, yielding [bɔdə]. The plural is [bödə] ([ö] represents a fronted or "umlauted" [o]), which is correctly derived if (A) is ordered before (B). (A) applies to /bodə/ to produce [bödə]. (B) cannot apply to the latter form, since it affects only [o], not [ö].

The plural forms of /bodə/ are not precisely identical in the two dialects at the phonetic level. The facts are presented below, along with the Kesswil form for 'frog', which bears on the problem.

	Schaffhausen		*Kesswil*		
Singular	/bodə/	bɔdə	/bodə/	bɔdə	
Plural	/bodə/	bödə	/bodə/	bə̈də	
			/fröšš/	fröšš	'frog'

Assume that the Kesswil dialect developed historically from an earlier system identical to the present Schaffhausen dialect in regard to the phonological processes in question. Also assume that the phonological representations have remained constant. What change occurred in the earlier system to produce the current Kesswil situation? Give the Kesswil derivation of the plural of /bodə/.

Problem 5.1–5 French

On the basis of the sentences below, describe a syntactic rule change pertaining to pronouns that has occurred in the development of modern French from Old French.

Old French

(1) Tenez moy pour vostre annemy?
take me for your enemy
'Do you take me for your enemy?'

(2) Demanderoiz me vos plus rien?
would ask me you more anything
'Would you ask anything more of me?'

(3) J'ai creü vostre parole.
I have believed your word
'I believed what you said.'

(4) Or l'ai lonc tens en vain servi.

now her have long time in vain served
'I have long served her in vain.'

(5) Une espee du fuerre a trete.

a sword from the scabbard has drawn
'He drew a sword from the scabbard.'

(6) Il est chi pour eles remés.
he is here for her remained
'He remained here for her.'

Modern French

(7) Vous avez de l'argent.

you have of the money
'You have some money.'

(8) *Pouvez venir?
can come
'Can you come?'

(9) Je suis très heureux.
I am very happy
'I am very happy.'

(10) *Suis professeur.
am teacher
'I am a teacher.'

(11) Il veut savoir la vérité.

he wants to know the truth
'He wants to know the truth.'

(12) *Aime les enfants.
likes the children
'He likes children.'

Problem 5.1–6   *Maori*

PART A   Listed below are active and passive verb forms in Maori (Hale, *to appear*, b). Each verb stem has a single phonological representation, and the passive suffix has two alternate phonological representations. Posit the appropriate underlying representations and formulate whatever rules are required to derive the phonetic data. What determines which form of the passive suffix will be used?

Active	Passive	
awhi	awhitia	'embrace'
hopu	hopukia	'catch'
aru	arumia	'follow'
tohu	tohuŋia	'point out'
mau	mauria	'carry'
wero	werohia	'stab'
patu	patua	'hit, kill'
kite	kitea	'see, find'

PART B There is reason to believe that the solution for Part A, while correct for an earlier historical stage of Maori, is no longer valid. A restructuring appears to have taken place in this facet of Maori grammar. Specifically, speakers of Maori have reanalyzed the passive forms above so that, for instance, [tia], not just [ia], is taken to be the passive suffix in [awhitia]. Similarly, [kia] is the passive suffix in [hopukia], [mia] in [arumia], and so on. As evidence that such a reanalysis has taken place, it is pertinent to note that consonant-final verbs borrowed from English take [tia] in the passive, not [ia]. Other evidence could be cited. One effect of the reanalysis was to make morpheme and syllable boundaries coincide; another was to render the phonetic shape of each stem the same in the active and the passive. The naturalness of these situations was no doubt among the contributing factors.

Describe in detail the nature of this restructuring. More precisely, describe the modifications that have taken place in the rules and underlying representations, as well as the way in which the various changes are related to one another.

5.2 Dialectal Variation

Language change is a constant process. Over a period of centuries a language changes to a sufficient degree that early and modern speakers, were they to meet, could understand one another only with great difficulty, if at all. Shakespearean English is by no means easily intelligible to uninitiated speakers of contemporary English, but in large measure it can be understood; Chaucerian English, on the other hand, is largely beyond the bounds of comprehensibility, and Alfredian English is almost totally incomprehensible. Similarly, modern French speakers can easily understand the plays of Molière, but they read the medieval *chansons de geste* only with great difficulty at best, and they must learn Latin as a foreign (though related) language.

Linguistic innovations are never adopted simultaneously by all speakers of a language. The diffusion of innovations through the speech community is a gradual process, and one that is not always carried to completion. Dialectal variation results from the incomplete diffusion of linguistic changes. A **dialect** is a variety of speech that differs from that of the rest of the speech community in regard to a number of traits; each point of difference stems ultimately from the failure of an innovation to be adopted by all speakers of the language. When two or more dialects become sufficiently divergent, they are said to be **genetically related languages**. The difference between genetically related languages and dialects of a single language is therefore only a matter of degree.

The various kinds of language changes discussed in section 5.1 are thus responsible not only for the historical evolution of a single language but also for dialectal variation and for the development of families of genetically related languages. It follows that dialects of the same language, and also genetically related languages, will differ from one another in the same ways that earlier and later historical stages of a single language differ. Diachronic study and dialectal study are therefore very closely connected.

Dialects differ in vocabulary, syntax, and phonology. Vocabulary differences include discrepancies in the inventory of lexical items as well as differences in the properties of shared vocabulary items. For instance, the average speaker of British English is unlikely to be familar with the American sports expressions *shortstop* and *tight end*; in addition, most speakers of American English pronounce *schedule* with an initial [sk], in contrast to the British pronunciation with [š]. There is little point in proliferating examples. Speakers are generally rather sensitive to dialectal variation that pertains to phonological rules; in large measure such variation is responsible for "accents". Syntactic rule differences also exist, of course. It was noted previously, for example, that interrogation is marked in certain dialects of French by the suffixation of the particle *ti* to the inflected verb; questions are marked quite differently in standard French.

Two dialects may differ in several ways with respect to rule content. One dialect may lack a rule that is present in another. For instance, as we saw in Chapter 4 (p. 247), the rule that changes initial [s] to [š] before [r] in English is present in certain dialects but absent in others. *Shrimp* /srɪmp/ is pronounced as either [šrɪmp] or [srɪmp] accordingly. Similarly, many speakers of English, but by no means all, possess a rule that changes [ɛ] to [ɪ] before a nasal; in dialects characterized by this rule, *pen* is pronounced like *pin*, *Ben* like *bin*, and *hem* like *him*. Another possibility is for corresponding rules in two dialects to differ in detail (while remaining similar enough to be recognized as variants of the same rule). For example, a syntactic rule of English optionally deletes *to be* in certain environments, allowing *I thought him mad* as a variant of *I thought him to be mad*, *He pronounced us man and wife* as a variant of *He pronounced us to be man and wife*, and so on. The conditions on the applicability of this rule vary dialectally. Thus some speakers permit the reduction of *The grass needs to be watered* to *The grass needs watered*, but many others judge the latter sentence (to be) ungrammatical. A third possibility is for two dialects to have identical rules that are ordered differently with respect to one another. Examples from Finnish and Swiss German were cited in section 5.1.

In both dialectal and diachronic analysis, underlying representations sometimes prove to be more uniform than their surface manifestations suggest. Superficial differences between two dialects, or between two historical stages of a single dialect, can often be shown to reside not in different underlying representations but rather in the rules that relate these underlying representations to their surface forms. English speakers who say [šrɪmp] and those who say [srɪmp] both have /srɪmp/ as the phonological representation of this morpheme, but only the former possess the rule that changes initial [s] to [š] before [r]. Similarly, we can distinguish two English dialects on the basis of whether *to be* deletion is allowed to derive *The grass needs watered* from *The grass needs to be watered*, but these two sentences have the same underlying representation in both dialects and both dialects possess a rule deleting *to be* in certain environments. Diachronic studies have shown that underlying representations often remain fairly constant for long periods of time despite rather substantial surface changes. In the same way, dialects that at first appear to be strikingly different sometimes prove on closer examination to be quite similar at the level of underlying representations.

Problem 5.2–1   *English*

In Problem 4.1–1 (p. 240) rule (A) was established for certain dialects of English; it serves, for instance, to derive [bʌyk] *bike* as the phonetic manifestation of /bayk/.

   (A) /ay/ becomes [ʌy] before a voiceless segment.

Rule (B), which derives [fliDɪŋ] *fleeting* from /flitɪŋ/, was established in Problem 4.1–7 (p. 251).

   (B) /t/ is voiced to [D] when it occurs between two syllabic elements.

Examine the following data from two dialects of English, and determine the nature of the differences between these two dialects.

	Dialect I	*Dialect II*
write	rʌyt	rʌyt
writing	rʌyDɪŋ	rayDɪŋ
bite	bʌyt	bʌyt
biting	bʌyDɪŋ	bayDɪŋ
fight	fʌyt	fʌyt
fighting	fʌyDɪŋ	fayDɪŋ

Solution

In dialect I rule (A) precedes rule (B). Thus the stem vowel of *writing, biting,* and *fighting* is modified to [ʌy] by (A) before (B) voices the following /t/.

Dialect II has the same rules and underlying representations, but the rules apply in the opposite order. Thus (B) voices /t/ to [D] in words like *writing* before (A) can change the quality of the stem vowel, which consequently remains [ay] phonetically.

Problem 5.2–2 Italian

Listed below are corresponding forms from three Italian dialects; I is the standard dialect, II is the regional variety of northern Italy, and III is the Lombard dialect (Wanner, 1970). The underlying representations, which can be assumed to be identical for the three dialects, are listed at the left. Determine precisely how the three dialects differ.

	Dialect I	Dialect II	Dialect III	
/fisso/	fisso	fiso	fis	'fixed'
/kassa/	kassa	kasa	kasə	'cabinet'
/kasa/	kaasa	kaaza	kaazə	'house'
/kosa/	koosa	kooza	koozə	'thing'

Solution

The following five rules are needed to account for the phonetic shapes in the various dialects.

(A) A vowel is lengthened if it is followed by a short consonant.
(B) /s/ voices to [z] intervocalically.
(C) A long consonant is shortened.
(D) /o/ is deleted in word-final position.
(E) Word-final /a/ reduces to [ə].

The three dialects differ in regard to which of these rules they contain. Only rule (A) is operative in dialect I. Dialect II has (A), (B), and (C). All five rules function in dialect III. There are no differences in rule ordering; (A) and (B) must both precede (C) in the two dialects (II and III) which have all three rules.

FURTHER PROBLEMS

Problem 5.2–3 Papago

As demonstrated in Problem 4.3–16 (p. 290), rules (A)–(C) are needed for the most insightful description of Papago phonology.

(A) /ḍ/ becomes [l], and /ṣ/ becomes [s], when followed by [i].
(B) A dental consonant becomes palatal before a high vowel.
(C) A word-final high vowel is deleted after an alveolar or palatal consonant.

All three rules function in the derivation of the forms in column I below, which represent one dialect of Papago. Columns II and III contain corresponding forms from other Papago dialects (Hale, 1965). Analyze this data and determine how dialects II and III differ from each other and from dialect I. Assume the phonological representations, given at the left, to be the same for all three dialects.

	Dialect I	*Dialect II*	*Dialect III*	
/ʔuuṣi/	ʔuus	ʔuus	ʔuus	'stick'
/tini/	čiñ	čiñi	tin	'mouth'
/hiwɨḍi/	hiwɨl	hiwɨli	hiwɨl	'wind'
/ṣuudagi/	ṣuudagi	ṣuudagi	ṣuudag	'water'
/tɨhani/	čɨhañ	čɨhañi	tɨhan	'hire'
/naadi/	naaǰ	naaǰi	naad	'something kindled'
/duuki/	ǰuuki	ǰuuki	duuk	'rain'

Problem 5.2–4   Vietnamese

Listed below are corresponding forms from the Hanoi and Saigon dialects of Vietnamese (Thompson, 1967). These forms illustrate a phonological change affecting final consonants after front vowels. Determine which dialect is more basic, in the sense that the data of the other dialect can be derived from it by means of the adoption of a simple phonological rule. State the required rule. Assume, for purposes of this problem, that restructuring has occurred in the innovative dialect, so that corresponding lexical items affected by the change no longer have identical underlying representations. Using the words for 'frog' and 'self' as examples, present the details of this restructuring in terms of a diagram similar to Figure 5.1–1. The diacritics [´ ^ `] stand respectively for high rising, mid-high trailing, and low trailing tone. (Other tones of Vietnamese include high rising laryngealized, mid-low dropping-rising, and low dropping laryngealized.)

Hanoi	*Saigon*	
xúkxíč	xúkxít	'giggle'
ʔíč	ʔít	'be useful'
ʔít	ʔít	'be a small amount'
mìñ	mìn	'self'
čín	čín	'nine'
ʔéč	ʔét	'frog'
bêñ	bên	'protect'
bên	bên	'side'
kǽk	kǽk	'dime'
dén	dén	'arrive'

Problem 5.2–5 *Walbiri*

PART A In Problem 4.3–4 (p. 273) rule (A) was posited for Walbiri.

> (A) The vowel of a suffix harmonizes with the final vowel of a stem if the stem vowel is high.

This rule accounts for the forms in column I, which represent one dialect of Walbiri. In column II are listed the corresponding forms from a second Walbiri dialect (Hale, *to appear*, b). Formulate a revised version of rule (A) that is appropriate for the description of this second dialect.

	Dialect I	*Dialect II*	
/kaṭi-ku/	kaṭi-ki	kaṭi-ki	'to the man'
/kaṇu-ku/	kaṇu-ku	kaṇu-ku	'to the boy'
/ŋapa-ku/	ŋapa-ku	ŋapa-ku	'to the water'
/yanta-ṇi/	yanta-ṇi	yanta-ṇi	'come hither!'
/yani-ṇi/	yani-ṇi	yani-ṇi	'to come hither'
/yanu-ṇi/	yanu-ṇu	yanu-ṇi	'came hither'

PART B Warramunga, an Australian language related to Walbiri, has still another variant of rule (A). Formulate an appropriate version of the rule on the basis of the forms below. Discuss the phonological representation of the suffix meaning 'to'.

kaṭi-ki	'to the man'
kaṇu-ku	'to the boy'
ŋapa-ka	'to the water'

5.3 *Internal Reconstruction*

Careful attention to the structural details of a language often enables us to draw certain conclusions concerning the nature of an earlier historical stage of that language. Internal reconstruction—reconstruction involving just a single language—is a valuable technique of diachronic investigation because it allows us to determine certain facts about the history of a language even in the absence of written records or knowledge of closely related languages that could be used for comparison.

The potential of internal reconstruction is naturally quite limited, relative to that of the comparative method. One language necessarily casts less illumination on the structure of a parent or *proto language* than several, since a property that leaves traces in one descendant or *daughter language* may disappear completely from another. Moreover, the results of internal reconstruction are in general more tentative than those of the comparative method, since no external corroboration is provided by comparison with other daughters. Nevertheless, the evidence for reconstructions that are based on a single language is sometimes quite compelling, and in some instances they may be supported by the results of subsequent comparative research.

Suppose, for example, that an investigator were to examine modern English with no previous knowledge of its history or of the structure of any related language. One thing that such an investigator might notice is that English is not a highly inflected language, but that the pronominal system shows more inflection than nouns do. Thus one form of a noun is used as a possessive (for example, *Roger's*) and another as a subject or object (*Roger*), but no distinction in form is made between subject and object nouns. Most English pronouns, on the other hand, have separate subject, object, and possessive forms (such as *I*, *me*, and *my*), not to mention a special possessive form used in the absence of an overt head noun (*mine*). If our investigator knew something about universal tendencies of syntactic change, he might well hypothesize that the present English nominal inflections are remnants of an older, more elaborate inflectional system that is best preserved with pronouns and has all but disappeared with simple nouns. Subsequent examination of German and other Indo-European languages would prove his conjecture to be correct.

For another example, consider the Papago rule that palatalizes a dental consonant before a high vowel. Synchronic analysis of Papago shows that this is a productive phonological rule of the language; by positing such a rule and treating the palatal consonants [č j ñ] and the dental consonants [t d n] as allophones of the respective phonemes /t d n/, we account for the fact that the palatal segments do not occur before low vowels, while their dental counterparts do not occur before high vowels. It was stated earlier that [č j ñ] occur only before high vowels. Although this is probably true for relatively abstract levels of representation in Papago, it is not strictly true at the phonetic level. Thus [čiñ] 'mouth' and [naaj] 'something kindled' end phonetically in palatal consonants that are not followed by high vowels. Given this synchronic data, it would not be unreasonable to hypothesize that forms such as these ended phonetically in high vowels at an earlier stage in the history of Papago. The final high vowels triggered the palatalization of the consonants; only after this assimilation occurred did the vowels disappear phonetically. On the basis of internal reconstruction, therefore, we are led to posit historically earlier forms like [čiñV] and [naajV], where *V* stands for a high vowel. In this instance, dialectal evidence can be used to corroborate the analysis. There is another dialect of Papago in which the deletion of a final high vowel takes place only after [s]; in this dialect 'mouth' and 'something kindled' appear phonetically as [čiñi] and [naaji] (see Problem 5.2–3). This constitutes very strong evidence in support of the reconstructions.

As this second example shows, the technique of internal reconstruction sometimes bears a strong and non-accidental resemblance to the process of

positing underlying representations in a synchronic analysis. This similarity
is to be expected, for language change often consists in the addition of new
rules to a language, and the function of rules is to relate superficial and
underlying representations. A rule which serves in a synchronic analysis to
connect abstract representations with their surface forms may in a diachronic
analysis specify the derivation of forms from their historical antecedents.
Moreover, the underlying representations postulated in a synchronic analysis
often prove quite similar to surface forms of an earlier historical stage of the
language. In the example from Papago, there is reason to posit underlying
representations with final /i/ in the words for 'mouth' and 'something kindled'
as part of a synchronic analysis of Papago phonology. This final vowel
corresponds exactly to the final high vowel [V] that is suggested on the basis
of internal reconstruction for an earlier stage of Papago. In a synchronic
analysis this final /i/ is deleted by a rule that erases word-final high vowels
after palatal consonants (see Problem 4.3–16, p. 290). The adoption of this
rule constituted a diachronic change responsible for replacing such forms as
[čiñi] and [naaǰi] with their contemporary phonetic counterparts [čiñ] and
[naaǰ].

To be sure, the synchronic analysis of a language must be justified
independently of diachronic considerations. Although underlying representations sometimes resemble historically older forms, this is by no means always
the case. Congruence in the synchronic and diachronic analyses of a language
is a circumstance that linguists are pleased to encounter, but it can never
be granted a priori.

Problem 5.3–1   Cahuilla

Cahuilla is a Uto-Aztecan language closely related to Luiseño and Cupeño.
The forms listed below (courtesy of William Bright) are prefixed to verbs and
indicate the person of the subject and object; only those forms associated with
singular subjects and objects are included. In the glosses the first pronoun
indicates the person of the subject, and the second the person of the object.
'I-you', for instance, indicates that the corresponding expression is used with
a verb whose subject is 'I' and whose object is 'you'. Synchronically, these
prefixes are slightly irregular, in the sense that the first, second, and third
person forms have slightly different phonetic shapes depending on whether
they designate the subject or the object; thus any given subject-object
marking combination is not the simple sum of the person markers of the
subject and object. However, the data points to an earlier marking system in
Cahuilla that was more regular but that has been eroded by phonetic simplification. Determine this earlier pattern by internal reconstruction and describe
the phonetic simplification that has taken place. (There are no forms for
'I-I' or 'you-you', since these forms are replaced by reflexives.)

neʔ   'you-me'
ne   'he-me'
ʔen   'I-you'
ʔe   'he-you'
pen   'I-him'
peʔ   'you-him'
pe   'he-him'

Solution

First person is associated with either [ne] or [n], second person with either [ʔe] or [ʔ], and third person with either [pe] or zero. In prefixes where the subject and object person markers both have phonetic substance, the object marker precedes the subject marker, and the latter occurs in its shorter form. If we assume that the final vowel has been lost from certain object-subject marker combinations, a somewhat more regular pattern can be postulated for an earlier stage of Cahuilla. These four morphemes, each with constant phonetic shape, can be reconstructed (∅ stands for a morpheme with no phonetic manifestation).

First Person	ne
Second Person	ʔe
Third Person (*Subject*)	∅
Third Person (*Object*)	pe

The object-subject marker combinations constructed from these morphemes are summarized in the following table.

PERSON OF OBJECT

		1	2	3
PERSON OF SUBJECT	1	—	ʔe-ne	pe-ne
	2	ne-ʔe	—	pe-ʔe
	3	ne-∅	ʔe-∅	pe-∅

The modern Cahuilla forms given in the data derive from these reconstructed forms by the loss of the final vowel in sequences with two syllables.

Problem 5.3–2   Classical Aztec

In addition to simple postpositions, Classical Aztec has a series of complex (polymorphemic) postpositions, some of which are illustrated in column I below. Notice that when a postposition is attached to a pronoun, the pronoun occurs in its possessive form. Determine the origin and development of the complex postpositions of column I by means of internal reconstruction. Show the reconstruction of [itik] 'inside'. The expressions in column II are pertinent to the analysis. [ƛi] and [ƛ] are alternate forms of the Aztec absolutive suffix, discussed in Problem 4.1–6 (p. 250).

I	*II*
m-iško	ƛe-ko
	fire-in
your-in presence of	'in the fire'
'in your presence'	
	no-pan
te-išpan	my-on
one's-before	'on me'
'before someone'	
	mo-ƛan
t-išƛan	your-with
	'with you'
our-in sight of	
'in our sight'	mo-nawak
	your-with
n-išnawak	'with you'
my-before	
'before me'	tepe-k
	mountain-in
to-kʷiƛapan	'in the mountain'
our-after	
'after us'	kʷiƛa-ƛ
	shoulder-ABS
no-itik	'shoulder'
my-inside	
'inside me'	iš-ƛi
	face-ABS
	'face'
	iti-ƛ
	belly-ABS
	'belly'

Solution

The complex postpositions all derive from expressions consisting of a simple postposition attached to a noun designating a body part. Thus [iško] 'in presence of' can be reconstructed as [iš] 'face' plus [ko] 'in'; [itik] 'inside' as [iti] 'belly' plus [k] 'in'; and so on. The complex postpositions evidently came into being as distinct lexical items when the body part term and simple postposition, originally separate, were reanalyzed as constituting a unit.

Consider [itik] 'inside'. The meaning 'inside me' at an earlier historical stage of Aztec was apparently expressed literally as 'in my belly'. This form consisted of the nominal [no-iti] 'my belly' followed by the simple post-position [k] 'in'. Letting parentheses indicate constituent structure, we can say that the complex postposition [itik] came into existence when speakers reanalyzed expressions like ((no-iti)k) as (no(iti-k)). The other complex postpositions apparently came into being by means of a similar restructuring.

FURTHER PROBLEMS

Problem 5.3–3   Nootka

The data below (Haas, 1969) is from Nootka, an American Indian language of the Wakashan family. These paradigms consist of various modal expressions containing pronominal elements. By means of internal reconstruction, determine the five pronominal elements that can be posited for an earlier historical stage of Nootka; comment where possible on the changes that have contributed to the phonetic inconstancy of these elements in the contemporary language. Assume for purposes of this problem that the final [š] of certain contrastive forms and the final [a] of the inferential forms belong to the modal base (as discontinuous elements) and are not part of the pronominal inflections. Notice that one form is not known, and that another form has two possible variants. Notice also that certain modal bases are irregular, in the sense that they have more than one phonetic shape. [ḥ] stands for a pharyngealized [h].

	First Person Singular	Second Person Singular	First Person Plural	Second Person Plural	Third Person
Interrogative	ḥaas	ḥaak	ḥin	ḥaasuu	ḥaa
Conditional	quus	quuk	qun	quusuu	quu
Relative	yiis	yiik	yin	yiisuu	yii
Quotative	weeʔisi	weeʔincuk	weeʔinni	weeʔincuu	weeʔin
Contrastive	ʔatasiš	ʔateʔitsk	ʔataniš	—	ʔateʔiš
Inferential	hacsa	hačka	hačʔin hačʔana	hacsuuwa	hačʔa

Problem 5.3–4   French

In modern French plurality is seldom overtly marked on nouns and adjectives. In certain environments a plural suffix [z] of long historical standing may occur phonetically, but for the most part number must be determined from the form of an article, from verb agreement, or simply from the context. However, for a limited class of nouns and adjectives plurality is apparently marked in another way; compare the singular and plural forms below.

Singular	*Plural*	
šəval	šəvo	'horse'
lwayal	lwayo	'loyal'
egal	ego	'equal'

In sets like these plurality appears to be marked by means of a process morpheme that replaces final [al] by [o].

Examine the data below and determine by internal reconstruction whether it is necessary to reconstruct such a process morpheme as a plural marker for earlier stages of French. (The final consonants of the verb forms in the first column are not always manifested phonetically.)

vo-z	'(I) am worth'	mwa	'me'
vo-z	'(you) are worth'	ãfã	'child'
vo-t	'(he) is worth'	garsɔ̃	'boy'
val-ɔ̃z	'(we) are worth'	amwa	'to me'
val-ez	'(you (PLURAL)) are worth'	alãfã	'to the child'
val-ət	'(they) are worth'	ogarsɔ̃	'to the boy'

Problem 5.3–5   Cahuilla

Problem 5.3–1 dealt with verbal prefix combinations of Cahuilla that agree in person with the subject and object. The data was restricted to include only the prefix combinations used with singular subjects and objects. The full set of combinations, including those that agree with plural subjects and objects, are listed below (courtesy of William Bright). Complete the internal reconstruction that was begun for the singular forms in Problem 5.3–1.

PERSON OF OBJECT

			SINGULAR			PLURAL		
			1	2	3	1	2	3
	SINGULAR	1	—	ʔen	pen	—	ʔemen	men
		2	neʔ	—	peʔ	čeʔme	—	meʔ
PERSON OF SUBJECT		3	ne	ʔe	pe	čeme	ʔeme	me
	PLURAL	1	—	ʔečem	pičem	—	ʔemečem	mičem
		2	neʔem	—	peʔem	čemʔem	—	meʔem
		3	nem	ʔem	pem	čemem	ʔemcm	mem

5.4 The Comparative Method

A group of languages that are genetically related constitute a language *family*. The members of a language family are divergent continuations of a single, historically earlier proto language. They are referred to as daughters of this parent language and as *sisters* of one another.

The comparative method is a technique for establishing the genetic relatedness of a group of languages and for reconstructing to some degree the proto language from which they descend. The method was developed by philologists during the nineteenth century and was first applied to the Indo-European family of languages, for many of which written records were available that covered hundreds, or even thousands, of years. Subsequent work has verified that the technique is fully applicable to languages with no recorded history; all that is required is sufficient information regarding the structure of the daughters. To be sure, the method has its limitations. For instance, two or more languages that are in fact genetically related may have diverged so greatly that the method will yield no conclusive results. However, when the results are positive, they constitute virtual proof that the languages in question are related.

In the broadest sense, the comparative method includes any technique for comparing languages in order to ascertain their relationship. The comparison of syntactic and morphological properties is an important aspect of the method in this broad sense, an aspect that will be discussed in the next section. In a somewhat narrower sense, the comparative method is the examination and elucidation of phonological and lexical similarities. These will be our immediate concern.

CORRESPONDENCES

The cornerstone of the comparative method is the notion of **systematic sound correspondences.** Consider the following forms.

English	German	Dutch	Swedish	
maws	maws	möys	muus	'mouse'
haws	haws	höys	huus	'house'
laws	laws	löys	luus	'louse'

These three sets of forms are drawn from four languages that are known to be fairly closely related; many other sets could be added. The words in each set are doubly similar in that they bear a strong resemblance to one another in both form and meaning. Thus the four words for 'mouse' all begin in [m] and end in [s], the four words for 'house' all begin in [h], and so on. Furthermore, even the phonetic differences between the members of each set are systematic. English and German have [aw] as the vocalic nucleus of the word for 'mouse', while Dutch has [öy] and Swedish [uu], but this pattern turns out to be a regular one not confined to a single set of forms. Rather it is character-istic of all the sets; there is a systematic correspondence between English [aw], German [aw], Dutch [öy], and Swedish [uu]. To say that sounds cor-respond is not to say that they are identical, only that they regularly occur in corresponding positions in sets of lexical items that are similar in both form and meaning.

Problem 5.4–1 Indo-European

Listed below are sets of related forms from four Indo-European languages, each of which represents a separate subfamily of the large Indo-European family. The forms in each set are related in sense and are similar phono-logically. Consider just the italicized consonants and state the systematic sound correspondences that they reveal. The forms are given orthographically, but for the most part the italicized consonants have the value of the identical phonetic symbols. Here are the exceptions: Latin $c = [k]$, $qu = [k^w]$; Sanskrit $ś = [š]$; English $th = [\theta]$, $wh = [h]$.

Latin	Greek	Sanskrit	English
*p*ater	*p*atēr	*p*itā	*f*ather
cen*t*um	he*k*aton	*ś*atam	*h*undred
*p*ēs	*p*ōs	*p*āt	*f*oot
*qu*od	*p*oteros	*k*as	*wh*o
*t*rēs	*t*reis	*t*rayas	*th*ree
*c*or	*k*ardiā	—	*h*eart
*t*enuis	*t*anaos	*t*anuḥ	*th*in
de*c*em	de*k*a	da*ś*a	—	'ten'
lin*qu*ō	lei*p*ō	riṇa*k*ti	—	'let'

Solution

The italicized letters represent four systematic sound correspondences.

Latin	Greek	Sanskrit	English
p	p	p	f
t	t	t	θ
k	k	š	h
k^w	p	k	h

Discussion

Even a cursory examination reveals that there is a greater dissimilarity among the forms in each set than among those in the sets from Germanic cited above. The reason is simply that English, German, Dutch, and Swedish are much more closely related to one another than are Latin, Greek, Sanskrit, and English. When genetic relationships are very distant, the correspondences that show the relationships are sometimes very difficult to track down. To reveal them, it is necessary to examine in detail the phonological development of each daughter language, together with the special circumstances surrounding the evolution of each form. Frequently, the correspondences can be observed directly only in those parts of words that have been most stable during the long descent from the proto language (often this is the initial syllable, as in the present problem).

COGNATE SETS

Sets of related items in daughter languages, such as those in Problem 5.4–1, are called **cognate sets**. Lexical items in different daughters are **cognates** if they are continuations of the same lexical item in the proto language. Thus Latin *pater*, Greek *patēr*, Sanskrit *pitā*, and English *father* are cognates, since they can all be traced back to a single root of proto Indo-European.

Cognates in sister languages are related in form by systematic sound correspondences. Typically, each correspondence summarizes the development of a single segment of the proto language in the historical evolution of its daughters. For example, the [p]-[p]-[p]-[f] correspondence for Latin, Greek, Sanskrit, and English represents the evolution of the segment *[p] of proto Indo-European. (An asterisk marks a reconstructed element.) This proto segment remained as [p] in the first three daughters, but it changed to [f] in English (and in the Germanic languages generally). Similarly, the [t]-[t]-[t]-[θ] correspondence represents proto Indo-European *[t], [k]-[k]-[š]-[h] represents proto *[k], and [kʷ]-[p]-[k]-[h] reflects proto *[kʷ]. Each segment or form is a **reflex** of the proto segment or form from which it derives. English [f] is a reflex of proto *[p], for instance, and Sanskrit *pitā* is a reflex of the proto Indo-European root meaning 'father'.

In many instances, the same segment in one daughter will participate in two or more correspondences. For example, as we saw in Problem 5.4–1, Greek [p] participates both in the correspondence [p]-[p]-[p]-[f] and in the correspondence [kʷ]-[p]-[k]-[h]. This situation comes about when two segments that were distinct in the proto language **merge** (that is, become nondistinct) in one of the daughters. The two correspondences at hand reflect proto Indo-European *[p] and *[kʷ] respectively. These segments were distinct in the proto language and have remained distinct (though often represented by a different form) in Latin, Sanskrit, and English, but in Greek the two have merged to [p].

When a single proto segment develops differently in one or more daughters depending on the surrounding environment, the proto segment will be represented in the daughters by two or more correspondences, each relative to a specific environment. An example is provided by the segment *[t] of proto Uto-Aztecan. For the sake of simplicity, let us consider only three daughters, Comanche, Hopi, and Yaqui.

Comanche	Hopi	Yaqui	
tama	tama	tammin	'tooth'
karɨ	qatɨ	katek	'sit'

In word-initial position, *[t] is reflected as [t] in all three daughters, as shown in the cognate set for 'tooth'. However, intervocalic *[t] develops differently. Its reflex is [t] in Hopi and Yaqui, but in Comanche it is [r], as shown by the cognate set for 'sit'. Therefore [t]-[t]-[t] is the correspondence for initial *[t], but the one for intervocalic *[t] is [r]-[t]-[t].

Problem 5.4–2   *Cupan*

Cupan is a subfamily of Uto-Aztecan containing three closely related languages, Cahuilla, Cupeño, and Luiseño. The cognate sets below (Bright and Hill, 1967) illustrate the reflexes of proto Cupan *[l]. List the correspondences that represent this proto segment and state the principles that determine which correspondence will appear in a given phonological environment.

Cahuilla	Cupeño	Luiseño	
haal	hal	hal	'look for'
silʸi	silʸi	şiili	'pour'
kiyul	qəyul	kiyuul	'fish'
qasilʸ	qəşilʸ	qaaşil	'sagebrush'
puul	puul	puula	'doctor'
ʔawal	ʔəwal	ʔawaal	'dog'
mukilʸ	mukʔilʸ	muukil	'sore'
laʔlaʔ	ləʔəl	laʔla	'goose'

Solution

The two correspondences are [l]-[l]-[l] and [lʸ]-[lʸ]-[l]. The latter represents proto *[l] directly after [i], and the former represents *[l] in all other environments.

ESTABLISHING GENETIC RELATIONSHIP

In using the comparative method to determine whether or not two languages are genetically related, it is important to distinguish between native vocabulary (vocabulary descended from the proto language) and borrowed vocabulary. Only native vocabulary bears directly on genetic relationship, since languages that are totally unrelated to one another genetically may borrow lexical items and thereby acquire certain lexical similarities.

There is no single or unfailing technique for determining whether a vocabulary item has been borrowed, but an experienced analyst who is familiar with the languages in question can usually recognize many if not most borrowed lexical items. One key to their recognition is that borrowed lexical items often disobey otherwise general phonotactic restrictions of the borrowing language. For instance, the Luiseño word [mahaar] 'five' ends in [r], and in this respect it differs from native Luiseño words; the word is believed to have been borrowed from Gabrielino, a closely related Uto-Aztecan language that is now extinct. Long lexical items that cannot be broken down into familiar morphemes are also likely to have been borrowed, since most native words of any length are polymorphemic. Many American place names borrowed from American Indian languages can be recognized as borrowings on this basis; *Mississippi, Susquehanna, Waukegan,* and *Chicago* are among hundreds of examples that could be cited. Some borrowed words can be identified as such because they name concepts or products known to have been adopted from speakers of another language. The English word *gnu,* for example, was borrowed from a Bantu language; the direction of borrowing is quite clear since *gnus* are found in Africa but not in Europe or North America. On the basis of these and other considerations, native and borrowed vocabulary can quite often be distinguished.

Once probable borrowings have been identified, the remaining vocabulary can be examined for purposes of establishing genetic relationship. Suppose that two languages show substantial similarity in their native vocabulary, in that a large number of lexical items in the two languages resemble one another in both form and meaning. Suppose further that the phonological shapes of shared lexical items in these two languages are connected by means of systematic sound correspondences. These circumstances constitute virtual proof that the two languages are genetically related. For one thing, such similarities go far beyond those that could be expected in two unrelated languages on the basis of mere chance. Moreover, borrowing is not a plausible explanation; since borrowing is an essentially sporadic process, it is highly improbable that enough borrowed words could go undetected to be responsible for what appear to be systematic similarities that pervade the native vocabulary of two languages. Only the hypothesis of genetic relationship and descent from a common parent language is sufficient to explain both the lexical similarities and the existence of systematic sound correspondences.

Two languages that are divergent continuations of a common parent can of course be expected to share a large number of lexical items similar in both form and meaning. Moreover, the regularity of sound correspondences is explained as a consequence of the common original vocabulary together with the observation that changes in the sound system of a language typically originate by means of the addition, modification, or loss of phonological rules. Since phonological rules affect whole classes of lexical items and are not restricted in their effect to individual lexical items, phonetic divergence attributable to rule changes will naturally be basically regular in character.

RECONSTRUCTION OF SEGMENTS

Once a group of languages have been shown to be related by the demonstration of systematic sound correspondences, the next step in the comparative method is to reconstruct the segmental inventory of the proto language. One segment is reconstructed to underlie each correspondence, with allowance for the fact that some proto segments may be represented by more than one correspondence depending on the surrounding phonological environment. For example, the respective proto Indo-European segments *[p], *[t], *[k], and *[kʷ] are reconstructed for the four correspondences established in Problem 5.4–1. On the other hand, the single proto Cupan segment *[l] is reconstructed for the two correspondences of Problem 5.4–2; *[l] is represented as [lʸ]-[lʸ]-[l] directly after [i], and as [l]-[l]-[l] in other environments.

The choice of a proto segment to underlie a correspondence is straightforward when its reflex is the same in all the daughters. The character of the proto segment may not always be so obvious when the daughters disagree, but it is usually possible to make a motivated decision. The two basic desiderata are to minimize the number of **sound changes** that must be posited to derive the reflexes in the daughter languages and to maximize the naturalness of the changes that are required. Thus by positing proto Indo-European *[p] for the correspondence [p]-[p]-[p]-[f] in Problem 5.4–1, we need only claim that *[p] becomes [f] in English to account for the reflexes in the daughter languages. The choice of any other proto segment would require the postulation of a greater number of changes. The change of [p] to [f] is also more natural than the converse change; it is more common for stops to become fricatives historically than for fricatives to become stops. The change of *[l] to [lʸ] after [i] in Cahuilla and Cupeño (see Problem 5.4–2) is also a phonetically natural change.

Problem 5.4–3   Cupan

Examine the Cupan cognate sets below (Bright and Hill, 1967) and state the sound correspondences that account for the vowels. For each correspondence, reconstruct a proto Cupan segment; reconstruct only one proto segment for two or more correspondences that are environmentally conditioned variants of one another. State the sound changes that must have occurred in the evolution of the daughters on the basis of the proto segments you have postulated. Ignore the difference between long and short vowels, since vowel length in Uto-Aztecan presents special problems beyond the scope of this discussion; treat long vowels as if they were short vowels of the same quality. Omit from consideration the elements enclosed in parentheses.

Cahuilla	Cupeño	Luiseño	
kut	kut	kut	'fire'
ne(ʔ)	nə	noo	'I'
waaviš	waviš	waaviš	'foxtail grass'
nexiš	nixiš	neexiš	'gourd'
pe(ʔ)	pə	po	'he'
ʔis	ʔis	ʔes	'teardrop'
haal	hal	hal	'look for'
tew	təw	toow	'see'
mex(an)	mix(ən)	—	'possession'
wih	wih	weh	'two'
nit	nit	net	'pregnant woman'
yaw	yaw	yaaw	'bring'
puul	puul	puul(a)	'doctor'
pi(ʔ)	pi	pi(ʔ)	'breast'
mu	mu	muu(vi)	'nose'
ma	ma	maa	'hand'
ʔamu	ʔamu	ʔaamu	'hunt'
čaʔiš	čaʔiš	čaaʔiš	'bluebird'
pit	pit	pet	'road'
pal	pal	paal(a)	'water'
teʔ(e)	təʔ(ə)	tooʔ	'borrow'
wex(et)	—	wex(eʔtut)	'pine'

Solution

These six correspondences are represented in the data:

i-i-i	i-i-e
a-a-a	e-i-e
u-u-u	e-ə-o

Clearly *[i], *[a], and *[u] must be reconstructed for the three correspondences in the first column. No sound changes affect these three vowels in the daughters. It is also evident that a fourth vowel must be reconstructed to account for the correspondence [e]-[ə]-[o], but it is not immediately clear which vowel should be chosen. The data at hand provides no conclusive evidence for any of the candidates, but the sound changes are slightly simpler if *[ə] is posited rather than *[o] or *[e]. From proto *[ə], the reflexes can be derived by a change rounding [ə] to [o] in Luiseño, and another fronting [ə] to [e] in Cahuilla. If *[o] were reconstructed, on the other hand, the changes would be more complex; this vowel would have to be unrounded to [ə] in Cupeño, and be both fronted and unrounded to [e] in Cahuilla. The sound changes would also be more complex if *[e] were reconstructed for this correspondence; this vowel would have to be backed to [ə] in Cupeño, and be both backed and rounded to [o] in Luiseño.

Another reason not to reconstruct *[e] for the [e]-[ə]-[o] correspondence is that this vowel is the natural choice to underlie the correspondences [i]-[i]-[e] and [e]-[i]-[e]. The latter represents proto *[e] before [x], and the former represents *[e] in all other environments. A sound change that raises [e] to [i] must therefore be claimed for Cahuilla and Cupeño, and it must also be stipulated that the change fails to occur in Cahuilla when the following segment is [x].

The reconstructions and sound changes are summarized below.

Cahuilla	Cupeño	Luiseño	Proto Cupan
i	i	i	*i
a	a	a	*a
u	u	u	*u
i/e	i	e	*e
e	ə	o	*ə

Cahuilla Sound Changes
   *[e] becomes [i] unless the following segment is [x].
   *[ə] becomes [e].
Cupeño Sound Changes
   *[e] becomes [i].
Luiseño Sound Changes
   *[ə] becomes [o].

Discussion

Naturalness provides another reason for choosing *[ə] rather than *[e] to underlie the correspondence [e]-[ə]-[o]. It is quite common for back vowels to be fronted historically, but the backing of front vowels is less usual. Thus if *[e] were reconstructed for this correspondence, the sound changes required would be in conflict with a universal tendency. The choice of *[ə] is also strongly confirmed by comparative evidence from other Uto-Aztecan languages. For example, in Serrano, which is closely related to Cupan, the corresponding vowel is [ɨ], which is just like [ə] except for a slight difference in height.

The raising of [e] to [i] is also a natural phonological development; the lowering of [i] to [e] is less common. The choice of *[e] rather than *[i] to underlie the correspondence [i]-[i]-[e] is therefore motivated by considerations of both naturalness and simplicity (no simple rule could predict the lowering of *[i] to [e] in Luiseño).

RECONSTRUCTION OF FORMS

Once proto segments have been reconstructed to underlie systematic sound correspondences, the next step in the comparative method is to reconstruct the proto lexical items from which the native vocabulary of the daughters descends. Basically, this step simply involves examining cognate sets to determine which correspondences are represented in each set, and then replacing the representatives of each correspondence with the proto segment that underlies it. Consider the following Cupan cognate set.

Cahuilla	*Cupeño*	*Luiseño*	
pit	pit	pet	'road'

Three correspondences are involved in this set: [p]-[p]-[p], [i]-[i]-[e], and [t]-[t]-[t]. These represent the respective proto segments *[p], *[e], and *[t]. The proto Cupan form for 'road' was consequently *[pet]. This form has remained unchanged in Luiseño, but in Cahuilla and Cupeño it has become [pit] because of the sound change that derives [i] as the reflex of *[e]. Using the symbol > to represent historical changes, we can symbolize the sound change and its effect in Cahuilla and Cupeño as follows:

*e > i
*pet 'road' > pit

Problem 5.4–4   Cupan

Reconstruct the proto Cupan form that underlies each cognate set in Problem 5.4–3. Do not consider parenthesized elements and ignore the difference between long and short vowels. Your first step will be to establish correspondences for the consonants and to reconstruct proto segments to underlie them.

Solution

For each consonantal correspondence, the reflexes in all three daughters are the same. Consequently, the proto Cupan segment will in all cases be identical to the segments in the daughters, and no sound changes need be posited for the consonants represented in the data. Thus *[k] is reconstructed for the correspondence [k]-[k]-[k], *[n] for the correspondence [n]-[n]-[n], and so on.

Here are the reconstructed lexical items:

*kut	'fire'	*yaw	'bring'
*nə	'I'	*puul	'doctor'
*waviš	'foxtail grass'	*pi	'breast'
*nexiš	'gourd'	*mu	'nose'
*pə	'he'	*ma	'hand'
*ʔes	'teardrop'	*ʔamu	'hunt'
*hal	'look for'	*čaʔiš	'bluebird'
*təw	'see'	*pet	'road'
*mex	'possession'	*pal	'water'
*weh	'two'	*təʔ	'borrow'
*net	'pregnant woman'	*wex	'pine'

SUBFAMILIES

Language change does not cease with the differentiation of a parent language into a set of related daughter languages. Each of the daughters is in turn susceptible to progressive dialect differentiation that may lead ultimately to a division into a new generation of daughter languages. For this reason, language families can normally be divided into subfamilies, and sometimes into several echelons of subfamilies. The members of each subfamily can be traced back to a common parent language that is itself a daughter of the next higher proto language in the "family tree". The modern Romance languages, for example, all derive from Latin. Latin in turn is one of the daughters of proto Italic (other daughters include Oscan and Umbrian), which ultimately derives from proto Indo-European.

In applying the comparative method, it is important to determine as soon as possible how, if at all, the various daughter languages cohere as subfamilies. When distantly related languages are compared directly, the discovery of correspondences and other similarities proves quite difficult. A more fruitful approach is to first reconstruct the parent of each subfamily, insofar as this is possible, and then to use these reconstructions as the basis for further comparative work. If the modern Indo-European languages were well known but had not been subjected to historical investigation, it would not be advisable to begin the analysis by directly comparing English, Portuguese, Polish, and Welsh, at least not in a serious attempt to reconstruct proto Indo-European in full detail. It would be more profitable to begin by reconstructing proto Germanic, proto Romance, proto Slavic, proto Celtic, and so on. The direct comparison of languages related only indirectly has some heuristic value, and such comparison may be necessary to initially determine which daughters constitute subfamilies; however, substantial progress requires preliminary comparative work within each subgroup.

In some instances, the way in which daughter languages cohere as subfamilies is readily apparent on even cursory inspection. For example, the lexical and structural similarities of Cahuilla, Cupeño, and Luiseño are so extensive that a brief examination of cognate sets and grammatical descriptions leaves no doubt that the three constitute a special group within Uto-Aztecan. The division of daughter languages into subfamilies is not always so obvious, however.

The basic criterion for establishing subfamilies is shared innovations. If two or more languages have undergone a substantial number of common changes that have not occurred in any other daughters, it is likely that these languages constitute a subfamily and derive from a common parent that does not underlie the other daughters. In general, one does not expect the same innovation to take place independently in several different daughters (though parallel innovations certainly do occur on occasion). When several daughters share a large number of innovations that are restricted to them alone, the most likely explanation is that they constitute a subfamily. The changes in question can be presumed to have occurred in the parent language at a time when the daughters making up the subfamily had not yet been differentiated. This hypothesis is simpler and more likely than that of parallel innovations, since the changes are claimed to have taken place in only one language, the parent of the languages that constitute the subfamily.

Let us consider some examples. We saw in Problem 5.4–1 that [f] is the English reflex of proto Indo-European *[p]. The change of *[p] to [f] is not restricted to English. It is one of a whole series of changes affecting stops in all the Germanic languages; collectively these changes are known as **Grimm's law** (after Jacob Grimm, who did a great deal to document the changes and call them to the attention of scholars). These shared innovations provide motivation for grouping these languages into a subfamily descending from a common parent, proto Germanic.

Within Cupan, there is some evidence for grouping Cahuilla and Cupeño into a subfamily that excludes Luiseño. For example, *[l] has become [lʸ] after [i] in Cahuilla and Cupeño, but this sound change has not occurred in Luiseño (see Problem 5.4–2). Moreover, *[e] has changed to [i] in Cahuilla and Cupeño, but it remains [e] in Luiseño (Problem 5.4–3). These shared innovations support the hypothesis that proto Cupan first divided into two daughters, one of which was the ancestor of modern Luiseño, and the other the parent of Cahuilla and Cupeño. The two innovations occurred in the latter before it diverged into Cahuilla and Cupeño. This hypothesis is consistent with the rest of the data we have considered, for no sound changes have come to light that affect both Luiseño and one—but not both—of the other two Cupan languages.

It must not be supposed that two or a handful of shared innovations are sufficient in themselves to establish conclusively the existence of a subfamily. Parallel innovations do occur. Moreover, it is not at all uncommon to find shared innovations in daughters that are definitely known on other grounds to be related only indirectly; the propagation of changes cannot always be expected to adhere rigidly to the lines of genetic relationship. Only when the number of shared innovations is relatively large can subfamilies be posited with full confidence.

Problem 5.4–5 *Uto-Aztecan*

Given below are cognate sets from six Uto-Aztecan languages, including reconstructed proto Cupan. Consider only the initial consonant and vowel of each form (excluding parenthesized material), and ignore vowel length. State the correspondences to which the data attests. Select a proto segment to underlie each correspondence, and reconstruct the initial consonant and vowel of the proto Uto-Aztecan root that underlies each cognate set. State the sound changes that have affected each daughter, and evaluate whatever evidence there may be for grouping any of these daughters into subfamilies.

Cupan	Cora	Hopi	Papago	Yaqui	Huichol	
*puš	hiʔisi	poosi	wuhi	puusi	hiši	'eye'
*pet	huye	pöhɨ	woog	booʔo	huye	'road'
*nəma	neemʷa	niima	ñim	—	nema	'liver'
*muk	miʔiči	mooki	muuki	muuke	mɨki	'kill, die'
—	(ti)hete	pɨtɨ	wiič	bette	hete	'heavy'
*ʔeŋ	ʔunah	ʔöŋa	ʔon	ʔoona	ʔuna	'salt'
*tama	tame	tama	taatam	tammin	taame	'tooth'
*čivu	cihivi	ciivo	siw	čiibu	ciɨ	'bitter'
*piva	—	piiva	wiw	biiva	—	'tobacco'
*naqa	—	naaqa	naak	nakka	naka	'ear'

Solution

Cupan	Cora	Hopi	Papago	Yaqui	Huichol	Proto Uto-Aztecan
p	h	p	w	p/b	h	*p
t	t	t	t	t	t	*t
č	c	c	s	č	c	*c
ʔ	ʔ	ʔ	ʔ	ʔ	ʔ	*ʔ
m	m	m	m	m	m	*m
n	n	n	n/ñ	n	n	*n
a	a	a	a	a	a	*a
i	i	i	i	i	i	*i
ə	e	ɨ	ɨ	e	e	*ɨ
u	ɨ	o	u	u	ɨ	*u
e	u	ö	o	o	u	*o

*pu	'eye'	*ʔo	'salt'
*po	'road'	*ta	'tooth'
*nɨ	'liver'	*ci	'bitter'
*mu	'kill, die'	*pi	'tobacco'
*pɨ	'heavy'	*na	'ear'

Cupan Sound Changes	*Cora Sound Changes*
*c > č	*p > h
*ɨ > ə	*ɨ > e
*o > e	*u > ɨ
	*o > u

Hopi Sound Changes	*Papago Sound Changes*
*o > ö	*p > w
*u > o	*c > s
	*n > ñ

Yaqui Sound Changes	*Huichol Sound Changes*
*p > b	*p > h
*c > č	*ɨ > e
*ɨ > e	*u > ɨ
	*o > u

On the basis of shared innovations, Cora and Huichol must definitely be grouped as a subfamily, since exactly the same four changes have taken place in the two languages. There is no strong evidence for any other subgrouping; no other combination of languages share more than a single change.

Discussion

Either [p] or [b] may be the reflex of proto *[p] in Yaqui. There is no simple way to predict which will occur on the basis of the limited data for this problem.

[ñ] is the Papago reflex of proto Uto-Aztecan *[n] only before high vowels. The change of *[n] to [ñ] in this environment originated in the addition of a rule to the phonological component of Papago. This rule, which palatalizes dental consonants before high vowels, is still a productive synchronic rule of Papago, as we have seen on a number of occasions.

The choice of proto *[ɨ], *[u], and *[o] to represent the last three correspondences is not so obvious as the other choices. Since Cora and Huichol constitute a subfamily, the two taken together have only one "vote" in determining the quality of each reconstructed vowel. For the first of the three problematic correspondences, then, two daughters have [ɨ], two have

[e], and one has [ə]. *[ɨ] rather than *[e] is reconstructed for this correspondence because the fronting of back vowels is more common than the backing of front vowels, but the choice is a controversial one (see Langacker, 1970). *[u] is the most obvious choice for the next correspondence, since three daughters have [u] as the reflex of this vowel, while [ɨ] and [o] show up in only one daughter each (counting Cora and Huichol as one). *[u] is therefore not available to underlie the final correspondence, for which *[o] would seem to be the appropriate reconstruction. Two daughters have [o], one [u], one [ö], and one [e]. The fronting of [o] to [ö] is a common process; in fact, [ö] was almost certainly an intermediate stage in the development of proto Cupan *[e] from proto Uto-Aztecan *[o]. The raising of [o] to [u] is also quite natural.

CHRONOLOGICAL ORDERING

The sound changes that affect a daughter language are not simultaneous; they take place at different points in the historical development of the daughter from the proto language. It is sometimes possible to determine the relative chronological order of innovations, even in the absence of written historical documentation. The following discussion is somewhat simplified in that it treats segments in isolation from the system of rules and underlying representations that determine their occurrence, but there is reason to believe that this simplification is likely to have practical consequences only in relatively few cases.

Often one sound change can be posited as having preceded another because the opposite chronological ordering would have resulted in the merger of two proto segments that have in fact remained distinct. For example, Problem 5.4–3 showed that proto Cupan *[e] becomes [i] in Cahuilla (except before [x]), and that *[ə] becomes [e]. The two sound changes evidently occurred in this order, for *[e] and *[ə] remain distinct in Cahuilla. If the changes occurred in the opposite order, the two proto segments would have merged; *[ə] would first have become [e], and then [e]—both proto *[e] and [e] derived from *[ə]—would have been raised to [i]. The hypothesis of chronological ordering therefore accounts for the failure of the two segments to merge.

Relative chronological order can sometimes be posited on other grounds as well. Consider Papago [wiič], from proto Uto-Aztecan *[pɨtɨ] 'heavy' (compare Hopi [pɨtɨ], Yaqui [bette], and Huichol [hete]). Besides *[p] > [w], two changes have affected this form in Papago: *[t] has become [č], and the final *[ɨ] has been lost. On other grounds, the palatalization of [t] to [č] in Papago is known to have been conditioned by a following high vowel. We may therefore conclude that *[t] > [č] preceded the vowel deletion chronologically in the evolution of Papago. If the opposite order were assumed, the palatalization would be irregular.

Problem 5.4–6 Uto-Aztecan

Reexamine the sound changes established in Problem 5.4–5 and determine if any conclusions can be drawn regarding the chronological order of these changes.

Solution

The two changes in Hopi must be ordered. Proto Uto-Aztecan *[o] becomes [ö], and proto *[u] becomes [o]. *[o] > [ö] must have occurred first, since under the opposite ordering *[u] and *[o] would have merged in Hopi as [ö].

Three changes affecting vowels took place in the parent of Cora and Huichol: *[ɨ] > [e], *[u] > [ɨ], and *[o] > [u]. The three changes must have occurred in the order stated, for only this ordering prevents merger.

There is no evidence for the chronological ordering of any other changes.

FURTHER PROBLEMS

Problem 5.4–7 Chatino

The cognate sets below (Upson and Longacre, 1965) are drawn from four dialects of Chatino, a language spoken in Oaxaca, Mexico. List the vowel correspondences which the data reveals, and reconstruct a proto segment to underlie each. State the sound changes that have occurred in each dialect and comment on their chronological order. One proto segment has attested reflexes in only two daughters. Speculate on the vowels that would have represented this proto segment in the other two daughters had they been preserved. (Ignore vowel length, and do not try to formulate rules to predict when a proto vowel will be lost.)

Yaitepec	Tataltepec	Zenzontepec	Papabuco	
kʷeʔ	kʷeʔ	kʷeʔ	bee	'crab'
hũ	—	hũ	—	'spin'
kii	—	kii	kii	'fire'
yaʔ	yaʔ	yaʔ	yaa	'hand'
čũʔ	čõʔ	cõʔ	ši	'back'
kuweʔ	kuweʔ	kuweʔ	—	'pig'
—	tʸõʔõ	tãʔã	saaya	'walk'
loo	loʔo	nto	loo	'eye'
ke	ke	ʔike	ike	'head'
—	cõ	cõ	šii	'day'
kihĩ	—	kihĩ	kiti	'skin'
kata	kata	kata	kasaa	'black'
kũũ	—	kõõ	—	'edible root'

ysĩ	—	yuʔsĩ	yuči	'sand'
cẽʔ	ceʔ	cẽʔ	—	'tongue'
tihʸõ	čiʔõ	tihʸã	—	'bone'
šẽ	—	cẽ	še	'wide'
koʔo	koʔo	koʔo	doo	'drink'
—	tukĩ	tukĩ	ruki	'burn'
kičõ	kičõʔ	kicã	—	'hair'

Problem 5.4–8 *Chatino*

List the consonant correspondences illustrated in the Chatino cognate
sets below (Upson and Longacre, 1965), and reconstruct a proto segment to
underlie each. State the sound changes that have occured in each dialect and
comment on their chronological order.

Yaitepec	*Tataltepec*	*Zenzontepec*	*Papabuco*	
kʷihĩ	—	kʷẽhẽ	biti	'bag'
yaʔ	yaʔ	yaʔ	yaa	'hand'
ca	—	ca	ša	'go'
—	seʔ	šẽʔ	—	'nose'
kii	—	kii	kii	'fire'
sti	sti	suti	—	'father'
kʷeʔ	kʷeʔ	kʷeʔ	bee	'crab'
kata	kata	kata	kasaa	'black'
ysĩ	—	—	yuči	'sand'
kʷihi	kʷihi	kʷihi	—	'skunk'
—	cõ	cõ	šii	'day'
haʔ	—	haʔ	daa	'straw mat'
šiʔyu	—	šiʔyu	šiña	'cut'
kʷitʸĩʔ	kʷitʸẽʔ	kʷitʸẽʔ	beča	'louse'
toʔõ	—	tãʔã	saa	'roasting ear'
cẽʔ	ceʔ	cẽʔ	—	'tongue'
kitʸi	—	kitʸi	kiče	'paper'
šti	—	šiti	—	'laugh'
kihĩ	—	kihĩ	kiti	'skin'

Problem 5.4–9 *Indo-European*

Three series of stops have been reconstructed for proto Indo-European: a
series of four voiceless stops, a series of four unaspirated voiced stops, and
a series of four aspirated voiced stops. Each series contains a labialized velar
stop as well as three non-labialized stops. The cognate sets below illustrate

the development of these segments in four subfamilies of Indo-European; Latin, Greek, Sanskrit, and English have been chosen to represent these subfamilies. State the sound correspondences that link the italicized consonants. For each correspondence, reconstruct a proto segment. State the sound changes for each daughter, making each statement as general as possible (some changes may affect more than one segment); these correspondences and the sound changes responsible for the Germanic (English) reflexes of the proto segments constitute Grimm's law. The forms are given orthographically, but for the most part the italicized consonants have the value of the identical phonetic symbols. Here are the exceptions: Latin $c = [k]$, $qu = [k^w]$, $v = [w]$; Sanskrit $j = [j]$, $ś = [š]$; English $th = [\theta]$, $wh = [h]$, $c = [k]$; h directly after a stop symbol in Greek and Sanskrit indicates that the stop is aspirated. The English words and glosses indicate only the approximate semantic value of each cognate set. The precise meaning of each form may vary considerably from daughter to daughter.

Latin	Greek	Sanskrit	English	
*f*erō	*ph*erō	*bh*arāmi	*b*ear	
q*u*od	*p*oteros	*k*as	*wh*o	
*p*ater	*p*atēr	*p*itā	*f*ather	
*h*iems	*kh*eimōn	—	—	'winter'
e*d*ō	e*d*omai	a*d*mi	ea*t*	
*f*acio	ti*th*ēmi	da*dh*āti	*d*o	
lin*qu*ō	lei*p*ō	riṇa*k*ti	—	'let'
dē*f*endō	*ph*onos	*h*anti	—	'strike'
*p*ēs	*p*ōs	*p*āt	*f*oot	
*g*enus	*g*enos	*j*anaḥ	*k*in	
*t*enuis	*t*anaos	*t*anuḥ	*th*in	
*v*eniō	*b*ainō	a*g*amam	*c*ome	
*f*ormus	—	*h*aras	*w*arm	
*g*rūs	*g*eranos	—	*c*rane	
*t*rēs	*t*reis	*t*rayas	*th*ree	
rū*f*us	eru*th*ros	ru*dh*ira	re*d*	
dē*b*ilis	*b*eltion	*b*alam	—	'strong'
*c*entum	he*k*aton	*ś*atam	*h*undred	
—	pē*kh*us	*b*āhuḥ	—	'arm'
*f*rāter	*ph*ratōr	*bh*rātā	*b*rother	
*d*ecem	*d*eka	*d*aśa	*t*en	
*c*or	*k*ardiā	—	*h*eart	
*h*ostis	—	—	*g*uest	
—	kanna*b*is	—	hem*p*	
—	*b*ōs	*g*āuḥ	*c*ow	

Problem 5.4–10 *Burmish*

PART A The Burmish family consists of Burmese, Atsi, and Maru. In the cognate sets below (Burling, 1966), each form can be divided into an *initial*, which consists of the initial consonant or consonant cluster; a *final*, which consists of the vowel or vowel cluster; and in the case of Maru, a final stop. Treating each initial as a unit, determine the correspondences that relate initials in these three languages. Reconstruct a proto sequence to underlie each of these correspondences. State the sound changes that have affected initials in each daughter. The diacritics [' ` ^ ˇ] stand for tones. The precise value of each tone symbol differs from language to language, but the phonetic shape of the tones is not important for purposes of this problem.

Burmese	Atsi	Maru	
θéi	šî	šìt	'die'
sʰòu	—	cʰúk	'stop up'
čʰéi	kʰyí	kʰyìt	'leg'
—	mău	múk	'feather'
—	í	ìt	'rice beer'
nòu	nău	núk	'breast'
yéi	—	γìt	'skin'
pʰôu	pʰàu	pʰúk	'grandfather'
—	čʰí	čʰít	'wash'
tʰôu	tʰáu	tʰúk	'stab'
čʰêi	kʰyì	kʰyít	'dung'
kʰôu	kʰáu	kʰúk	'steal'
čʰóu	kʰyúi	kʰyùk	'horn'
sʰôu	cʰàu	cʰúk	'bad'
nyóu	nyûi	nyùk	'green'
yôu	vùi	γùk	'bone'
čʰóu	—	čʰùk	'sweet'
môu	màu	mùk	'sky'
ŋóu	ŋâu	ŋùk	'cry'
lôu	láu	lùk	'copulate'
pʰóu	pʰáu	pʰùk	'widower'

PART B Reexamine the cognate sets in Part A and establish the correspondences linking the finals in the three languages. On the basis of these correspondences, formulate an argument to justify the choice of *[y] to underlie the [y]-[v]-[γ] correspondence of Part A. Ignore tone.

PART C The final stops that occur in Maru did not occur in the proto language. What determines which stop is added to a given form?

Assume for purposes of this problem that the proto tones were the same as the contemporary Burmese tones. On the basis of the proto or Burmese tones, the tones in Maru can be predicted by general rules. What are these rules?

PART D Assume that the proto finals *[ei] and *[o] underlie the correspondences of Part B. Reconstruct a proto form for every cognate set in Part A for which a Burmese reflex is listed.

Problem 5.4–11   Lolo-Burmese

Listed below are cognate sets from six related languages (Burling, 1967). The family is called Lolo-Burmese. Within this family, Burmese, Atsi, and Maru constitute a subfamily called Burmish. Lisu, Lahu, and Akha belong to a subgroup known as the Lolo languages.

Find the correspondences linking the initial consonants in the forms below (exclusive of parenthesized material). Reconstruct a proto Lolo-Burmese segment to underlie each correspondence. State, as generally as possible, the sound changes that have affected these segments in the various daughter languages. In three instances, the reflex of a proto consonant in one of the daughters is not known. What is the expected reflex in each case? Is there any evidence for grouping Lisu, Lahu, and Akha into a subfamily? Is there evidence for any other subgrouping? [ẓ] is the voiced counterpart of [c]. Tones are not relevant to the problem and have been omitted.

Burmese	Atsi	Maru	Lisu	Lahu	Akha	
teʔ	toʔ	toʔ	dæ	taʔ	daʔ	'ascend'
tʰa	—	tʔoyeʔ	tu	tuhu	tu	'stand'
tʰeʔ	tʰoʔ	—	tʰæ	—	taʔ	'sharp'
pou	pau	patʰoŋ	bü	pi	bŏ	'insect'
—	čʰočʰi	—	čʰü	čʰi	čiha	'deer'
sʰu	cʔu	cʔau	cu	—	—	'boil'
pʰeʔyweʔ	pʰoʔ	—	—	(siʔ)pʰaʔ	(a)paʔ	'leaf'
toun	tum	tam	dule	—	(yɔ)dm	'blunt'
—	(suʔ)čʔup	čʔap	—	—	čuʔ	'suckle'
tʰa	tʔo	tʔo	—	tɛta	(yu)ta	'put'
sʰeʔ	cʰoʔ	cʰoʔ	—	—	caʔ	'join'
sa	co	co	ẓa	ča	ẓa	'eat'
čʰi	čʔi	—	—	—	—	'borrow'
—	cam	cin	—	čo	(lɔ)ẓm	'bridge'
sʰouʔ	cʔup	—	—	(pi)čiʔ	—	'clench fist'
tʰu	tʰu	tʰau	tʰu	tʰu	tu	'thick'
čʰeʔ	čʰoʔ	čʰoʔ	—	—	čaʔton	'navel'
čeihŋeʔ	či	čitau	(a)ɟi	(pɛ)čika	(a)ɟixaɟe	'parrot'
pʰa	pʔo	pʔo	(wu)pa	pa	(xa)pa	'frog'
pʰwenu	pʰuičʔap	(woʔ)pʰoi	(ẓa)pʰi	(vaʔ)pʰi	—	'chaff'
sʰa	cʰu	cʰau	čʰi	čʰu	cu	'fat'

Problem 5.4–12   Uto-Aztecan

Given below are cognate sets from eleven Uto-Aztecan languages, including reconstructed proto Cupan (compare Bright and Hill, 1967; Miller, 1967; and Voegelin and Hale, 1962). Consider only the initial consonant and vowel of each form (exclusive of parenthesized material), and ignore vowel length. Establish the consonant and vowel correspondences, and reconstruct a proto segmental inventory to underlie them. State the sound changes affecting the daughters as generally as possible, and evaluate whatever evidence there may be for grouping the daughters into subfamilies. For each cognate set, reconstruct the initial consonant and vowel of the proto form. The glosses indicate only approximate semantic values; the precise meaning of the members of a cognate set may vary considerably from language to language.

	'bitter'	'breast'	'black'	'husband'	'mother'
Comanche	—	picipɨ	tuhu	—	—
Mono	—	pici	tuhu	kuwa	—
Tübatulabal	—	piil	tuugu	kuuŋan	—
Cupan	*čivu	*pi	*tula	*kuŋ	*yə
Hopi	ciivo	piihɨ	toko	kooŋʸa	yiʔat
Papago	siw	wipi	čuk	kun	jiʔɨ
Tarahumara	cipu	—	rukuawa	kuna	—
Yaqui	čiibu	pippim	—	kuuna	—
Cora	cihivi	—	—	kɨin	—
Huichol	cii	—	tɨɨ	kɨna	—
Aztec	čičiik	—	—	—	—

	'ear'	'die'	'whip'	'tooth'	'eat'	'urinate'
Comanche	naka	—	wɨh	tama	—	—
Mono	nahqa	—	wɨh	tawa	—	sii
Tübatulabal	nanhal	muugin	wɨba	tamant	—	šiʔ
Cupan	*naqa	*muk	—	*tama	*kʷa	*si
Hopi	naaqa	mooki	wivaata	tama	—	sisiwkɨ
Papago	naak	muuki	giw	taatam	baʔa	hiʔa
Tarahumara	naka	muku	wipiso	rame	(aʔ)wa	(i)si
Yaqui	nakka	muuke	—	tammin	bʷa	siʔi
Cora	—	miʔiči	—	tame	kʷaa	siʔisuri
Huichol	naka	mɨki	we	taame	kʷaʔa	šiši
Aztec	nakas	miki	—	ƛanƛi	kʷa	(a)šiša

	'who'	'tail'	'kill'	'heavy'	'hold'	'house'	'heart'
Comanche	hakarɨ	kʷasi	kooi	—	caai	—	su
Mono	—	qʷaci	qoi	—	—	—	suh
Tübatulabal	ʔagi	—	—	pilɨ	—	—	—
Cupan	*hax	*kʷas	—	—	*čakʷ	*ki	*sun
Hopi	haki	kʷasi	qööya	piti	—	kiihi	soona
Papago	—	bahi	koʔi	wiič	ṣaaku	kii	huḍ
Tarahumara	—	wasi	koʔya	bite	—	—	sura
Yaqui	habbe	bʷassia	—	bette	—	—	suula
Cora	—	kʷasi	—	(ti)hete	—	čiʔi	—
Huichol	—	kʷaaši	—	hete	—	kii	—
Aztec	aakin	—	—	etiik	cakʷa	—	—

	'arrow'	'know'	'end'	'tobacco'	'eye'	'fire'
Comanche	huuhpi	—	—	—	pui	ku
Mono	—	—	—	—	puhsi	kuh
Tübatulabal	ʔumušat	maag	yahaawit	—	punẓil	kut
Cupan	*hu	—	—	*piva	*puš	*kut
Hopi	hoohɨ	maat	yaqa	piiva	poosi	koo
Papago	ʔuʔu	maač	daak	wiw	wuhi	kuu
Tarahumara	—	maci	aka	—	busi	ku
Yaqui	huʔiwa	(ye)mahta	—	biiva	puusi	—
Cora	ʔiʔɨri	(ra)mʷaʔaree	—	—	hiʔisi	—
Huichol	ʔɨri	maati	—	—	hiši	—
Aztec	—	mati	yakaλ	—	iišλi	—

	'blood'	'suck'	'excrement'	'sit'	'wing'	'navel'
Comanche	—	—	kʷita	karɨ	ʔahna	siiku
Mono	—	—	kʷita	qahtɨ	—	—
Tübatulabal	—	—	wiilaat	hal	ʔanambɨil	—
Cupan	*ʔəw	—	—	*qa	—	—
Hopi	ʔiŋʷa	—	kʷita	qati	ʔaaŋa	—
Papago	—	siʔi	biit	kaač	ʔaʔan	hik
Tarahumara	—	ciʔi	wita	—	ana	siku
Yaqui	—	—	bʷitta	katek	—	—
Cora	—	ciʔimeh	čʷita	—	ʔana	—
Huichol	—	cici	kʷita	—	ʔana	—
Aztec	esλi	čiičii	kʷiλaλ	—	—	šikλi

	'rain'	'yes'	'reed'	'road'	'liver'	'head'	'carry'
Comanche	—	—	paaka	—	—	co	kʷihi
Mono	—	hɨɨhiʔi	paqa	poyo	—	coh	(cah)kʷipa
Tübatulabal	—	—	paahuul	poht	niimal	comool	wikit
Cupan	—	*hə	—	*pet	*nəma	—	—
Hopi	yokva	—	paaqa	pöhɨ	niima	cökya	kʷisi
Papago	juuk	—	waapk	woog	ñɨm	ṣoñ	—
Tarahumara	uku	—	baka	—	—	coʔma	—
Yaqui	yuku	heewi	—	booʔo	—	čoonim	—
Cora	—	ʔeewi	haka	huye	neemʷa	cuʔume	(raʔa)čʷeni
Huichol	—	ʔeeri	haka	huye	nema	—	(pi)kʷeʔe
Aztec	—	—	aakaλ	ohλi	—	coon	—

	'sleep'	'star'	'bone'	'cold'	'pine'	'dry'
Comanche	—	—	—	—	wokoovi	—
Mono	—	—	ʔoho	(tiʔah)sɨh	wohqo	—
Tübatulabal	—	šuul	—	šiib	wohombool	waag
Cupan	—	*suʔ	—	*səv	*we	*wax
Hopi	—	soohɨ	ʔööqa	siisiŋʷa	löqö	laaki
Papago	koos	huʔu	ʔooʔo	hiip	—	gaki
Tarahumara	koci	—	sipi	—	oko	waki
Yaqui	koče	—	ʔota	sebbe	woko	waake
Cora	kucu	—	—	seeri	huku	wahči
Huichol	kuci	—	ʔume	šeri	huku	waki
Aztec	koči	siiλalin	oomiλ	seewa	—	waaki

	'nose'	'two'	'salt'	'put down'	'name'	'man'
Comanche	muuvi	—	ʔonaavi	tikɨ	—	—
Mono	mupi	wooh	ʔohma	tikɨ	—	—
Tübatulabal	mupit	woo	ʔoŋal	—	—	tahambiš
Cupan	*mu	*weh	*ʔeŋ	—	*təw	*taxa
Hopi	—	lööyöm	ʔöŋa	—	tɨŋʷa	taaqa
Papago	muuwij	gook	ʔon	čɨik	čɨigig	—
Tarahumara	—	—	—	rika	riwa	—
Yaqui	—	wooyi	ʔoona	teeka	tea	takaa
Cora	—	—	ʔunah	—	—	—
Huichol	—	huuta	ʔuna	—	tewa	—
Aztec	—	oome	—	teeka	—	λaakaλ

	'ribs'	'winter'	'not'	'grandmother'	'bite'
Comanche	—	—	—	kakuʔ	kɨh
Mono	—	(ʔɨ)ciʔɨ	qatuʔu	—	kɨh
Tübatulabal	caʔapil	ciiʔjiiʔ	ha	—	kiiʔ
Cupan	*ča	—	*qay	*qa	*kəʔ
Hopi	—	—	qa	—	kɨɨka
Papago	—	sɨpi	—	kaak	kiʔi
Tarahumara	—	—	kaita	—	(i)ki
Yaqui	—	—	kaa	—	keʔe
Cora	(ʔi)caʔapʷari	—	kapu	—	čeʔe
Huichol	—	—	ka	—	ke
Aztec	—	—	—	—	kecoma

	'ant'	'fingernail'	'shave'	'woman'	'big'	'swallow'
Comanche	—	—	sive	—	—	yiʔwi
Mono	—	—	sipa	—	—	yɨhkʷɨ
Tübatulabal	ʔaanint	šulunt	šiip	—	—	—
Cupan	*ʔanat	*sula	*siv	—	*wət	—
Hopi	ʔaanɨ	—	siiva	(siwa)hovi	wiiko	—
Papago	—	huuč	hiwkon	ʔuwi	giʔi	—
Tarahumara	—	sutu	sipa	upi	—	—
Yaqui	—	suttu	—	hubi	—	—
Cora	—	site	—	—	beʔe	yeʔe
Huichol	—	šite	—	ʔiimari	weri	yeʔe
Aztec	—	—	—	—	wey	—

5.5 Grammatical Reconstruction

The comparison of languages for purposes of establishing genetic relationship most often involves analysis of lexical similarities and phonetic correspondences. These, of course, are not the only domains in which comparison and reconstruction are possible. Broadly construed, the comparative method also encompasses syntactic phenomena and phonological phenomena more abstract than phonetic correspondences.

The aims of grammatical and phonological comparison are the same as those of lexical and phonetic comparison—to demonstrate the genetic relatedness of a group of languages and to reconstruct, insofar as possible, the proto language of which they are divergent continuations. The phonological and syntactic traits that are used in the attempt to establish genetic relationship must of course be language-specific. For example, the discovery that two languages share a rule allowing the optional deletion of a subject pronoun would not in itself constitute significant evidence that the languages are genetically related. Subject pronoun deletion occurs in languages all over the world (Navaho, Spanish, and Turkish are but three examples) and thus represents a universal tendency; the hypothesis of genetic relationship is not necessary to explain the similarity.

Similarity in non-universal properties is more suggestive of genetic relationship. Consider possessives in Papago and Huichol. In both languages possessive pronominal elements ('my', 'our', and so on) occur as prefixes on the nouns they modify. Although this is quite common, Papago and Huichol share an interesting exception to this pattern that is anything but universal; the third person singular possessive (and no other possessive) is a suffix rather than a prefix on the modified noun. The fact that they share this idiosyncrasy may be taken as evidence that Papago and Huichol are genetically related. Of course, much more evidence is required (to rule out the possibility of borrowing and to demonstrate that the similarities are too extensive to be attributed to chance), but it is clear that we are dealing with a highly idiosyncratic property, one whose co-occurrence in two languages cannot be attributed to universal tendencies.

In the domain of phonology, shared phonological rules and similar segmental inventories may count as evidence of genetic relationship. For instance, the three Cupan languages, Cahuilla, Cupeño, and Luiseño, share a rule that changes [č] to [š] at the end of a word (compare Problem 4.1–10, p. 254). The fact that all three languages have this non-universal rule in common supports the hypothesis that they are genetically related. Moreover, one can tentatively reconstruct the rule changing [č] to [š] before a word boundary as part of the phonological system of proto Cupan. In the same way, the claim that Turkish and Classical Mongolian are genetically related is substantiated to some degree by the fact that the two languages have very similar rules of vowel harmony (see Problem 2.1–4, p. 45, and Chapter 4,

p. 246), as well as almost identical vowel inventories to which the harmony rules apply. To be sure, individual traits such as these are not sufficient in themselves to prove the relatedness of two languages. The possibility of borrowing must always be considered, and also the chance that such similarities are purely coincidental. The case for genetic relationship is fully convincing only when there is reason to believe that the similarities are extensive enough or of such a character that no other explanation is adequate.

Syntactic comparison involves the comparison and reconstruction of syntactic rules, grammatical patterns, and individual morphemes having special grammatical importance. For example, the genetic relatedness of French and Spanish is suggested by the fact that both have syntactic rules that move object pronouns from post-verbal position (the usual position of object nominals) into pre-verbal position. In both languages, moreover, the rule fails to apply in positive imperative sentences (compare Problem 3.5–7, p. 192). The parallelism in the positioning of possessive affixes in Papago and Huichol, described above, is suggestive of genetic relationship quite independently of any consideration of their phonological shapes; in grammatical reconstruction, patterns can be as important as actual forms.

Naturally, the strongest grammatical evidence for genetic relationship is provided when two languages show strong similarities both in syntactic patterns and in the particular morphemes that enter into these patterns. Consider the following pronominal elements from Samoan and East Futunan, two Polynesian languages (Hamp, 1970).

	Samoan	East Futunan
First Person Singular	ʔou, oʔu	kau
Second Person Singular	ʔe	ke
Third Person Singular	ia, na, ona	ina
First Person Dual Exclusive	maa	maa
First Person Dual Inclusive	taa	taa
Second Person Dual	lua	kulu
Third Person Dual	laa	laa
First Person Plural Exclusive	maatou	motou
First Person Plural Inclusive	taatou	tou
Second Person Plural	tou	kotou
Third Person Plural	laatou	lotou

(The individuals designated by first person *inclusive* forms include the hearer; those designated by first person *exclusive* forms exclude the hearer.) Not only are the corresponding forms in the two columns very similar, but the general pronominal systems are identical. In both languages three numbers (singular, dual, and plural) are distinguished as well as three persons.

Furthermore, both languages display an exclusive/inclusive contrast in the first person dual and plural. Gender does not appear to enter into either system, and neither language appears to make any distinction not made by the other. This simultaneous congruence in form and pattern constitutes very strong evidence that the languages are genetically related.

Problem 5.5–1   Takic

The Takic subfamily of Uto-Aztecan comprises Serrano and Cupan, the latter including Cahuilla, Cupeño, and Luiseño. Proto Cupan *[ə] corresponds to Serrano [ɨ]. Cupeño [ə] sometimes derives from unstressed proto Cupan *[a].

Listed below are postpositions from these four Takic languages. Insofar as possible, reconstruct the postpositions from which they derive, first for proto Cupan and then for proto Takic. It will prove helpful to begin with a certain amount of internal reconstruction.

Serrano		*Cahuilla*		*Cupeño*		*Luiseño*	
pa	'at, in, on'	(y)ik	'(in)to'	ik	'toward'	ŋay	'from'
yɨka	'toward'	pa	'in, on'	pə	'place of'	ik, yok	'toward'
		ŋa	'in, on'	ŋə	'in'	ŋa	'at'
		pax	'from'	ŋəx	'from'		
		ŋax	'from'				
		ka	'toward'				

Solution

Internal reconstruction of Cahuilla results in the postulation of four basic elements: [pa] and [ŋa], both meaning 'in, on'; [x], which means 'from' and combines with either [pa] or [ŋa] to form a complex postposition; and [yika] 'toward'. [yika] does not show up in Cahuilla as a unit. However, the similarity in meaning and partial similarity in form of [(y)ik] and [ka] suggest that the longer sequence should be reconstructed. [yika] is simplified phonetically in Cahuilla to one syllable; either the first or second syllable may be retained, and the two resulting forms have evidently taken on partially distinct meanings.

The postulation of [yika] is partially confirmed by comparison with Cupeño and Luiseño. From *[yika] 'toward', Cupeño [ik] 'toward' is derived by a phonetic simplification similar to that posited for Cahuilla, and the two Luiseño variants can also be derived from this reconstruction. However, Luiseño [yok] would be more easily derivable from *[yəka]. ([o] is the Luiseño reflex of proto Cupan *[ə]; see Problem 5.4–3.) [(y)ik] could also derive from *[yəka], since [ə] might easily assimilate to the preceding [y]. Tentatively, then, *[yəka] 'toward' can be reconstructed for proto Cupan.

Cupeño and Luiseño also confirm the other elements reconstructed for Cahuilla. Cupeño [pə] is cognate with Cahuilla [pa], and [ŋə] with [ŋa], which also is found in Luiseño. [x] is paralleled by [x] in Cupeño and by [y] in Luiseño; there is no immediate explanation for the phonetic difference. The following simple and complex postpositions can therefore be reconstructed for proto Cupan.

*yəka	'toward'	*ŋa	'at, in, on'
*pa	'in, on'	*ŋa-x	'from'

Not all these forms can be reconstructed for proto Takic on the basis of the data given. Serrano [yɨka] 'toward' demonstrates the correctness of proto Cupan *[yəka]. [pa] is the only other postposition attested in both Cupan and Serrano. Consequently, only these two postpositions can definitely be reconstructed for proto Takic.

*yɨka	'toward'
*pa	'in, on, at'

Problem 5.5–2   Nootka-Nitinat

In Problem 5.3–3 a series of modal expressions containing pronominal elements were given for Nootka. The problem was to determine the five pronominal elements that could be reconstructed for an earlier historical stage of Nootka by means of internal reconstruction. Similar paradigms from Nitinat, a language closely related to Nootka, are given below (Haas, 1969). Determine the pronominal elements that can be posited for Nitinat by means of internal reconstruction, as was done for Nootka in Problem 5.3–3. Compare the Nootka and Nitinat pronominal elements, and reconstruct the proto Nootka-Nitinat forms from which those of the two daughters derive. Bear in mind that the simplification of segments in the direction of greater articulatory ease is more common in historical evolution than developments leading in the opposite direction. Nootka [n] and Nitinat [d] can both be taken as reflexes of proto Nootka-Nitinat *[n]. The Nitinat modal bases show a certain amount of irregularity. Assume that the final [š] of the contrastive forms belongs to the modal base (as a discontinuous element) and is not part of the pronominal inflections.

	First Person Singular	Second Person Singular	First Person Plural	Second Person Plural	Third Person
Interrogative	aks	ak	akid	aksuwʔ	aa
Conditional	quus	quusukʷ	quyid	quusuwʔ	quy
Contrastive	ʔatsiš	ʔatʔăkiš	ʔatidiš	ʔatʔasuwʔičiš	ʔatʔaš

Solution

The first person singular marker is [s] in two forms and [s] or [si] in the third, depending on how the modal is divided into morphemes. Similarly, the first person plural marker is [id] in two forms and either [id] or [idi] in the third. The second person plural morpheme is always [suwʔ] (there is no reason to include the following [iči] as part of the contrastive pronominal element), and the third person morpheme is evidently zero. The second person singular is more problematic. This person is marked by zero in the first form, by [sukʷ] in the second, and by either [k] or [ki] in the third. Presumably, [sukʷ] approximates the original pronominal element and has been eroded phonetically in certain forms. The reconstructions are summarized below, with uncertain segments included in parentheses. Given with these Nitinat reconstructions are the Nootka reconstructions established in Problem 5.3–3.

	Nitinat	Nootka
First Person Singular	s(i)	si
Second Person Singular	sukʷ(i)	suk
First Person Plural	id(i)	ini
Second Person Plural	suwʔ	suu
Third Person	∅	∅

Taking account of the [d]-[n] correspondence and universal phonetic tendencies, we can reconstruct the proto pronominal elements as follows:

Proto Nootka-Nitinat

*si
*sukʷ
*ini
*suwʔ
* ∅

FURTHER PROBLEMS

Problem 5.5–3   Numic

Numic is a subfamily of Uto-Aztecan that includes, among other languages, Shoshone, Comanche, Mono, and Southern Paiute. Listed below are the first and second person pronoun forms for these daughters. The synchronic analysis of these pronominal forms involves numerous irregularities, but in comparative terms one can perceive a regular underlying system. Five morphemes can be reconstructed for proto Numic. Singly and in regular combinations, these morphemes underlie the daughter pronouns. Reconstruct these grammatical morphemes and the combinations from which the daughter pronouns descend. Southern Paiute [ŋʷ] is a reflex of proto *[m].

	Shoshone	Comanche	Mono	Southern Paiute
First Person Singular	ni	niʔ	nii	ni
First Person Dual Inclusive	tawih	takʷi	taa	tammi
First Person Dual Exclusive	niwih	nikʷi	—	—
First Person Plural Inclusive	tammin	tamii	taahkʷaa	taŋʷa
First Person Plural Exclusive	nimmin	nini	niihkʷaa	nimmʷi
Second Person Singular	ʔin	ini	ʔii	immi
Second Person Plural	mimmin	mii	ʔiihkʷaa	mʷimmʷi

Problem 5.5–4   Yuman

Listed below are demonstrative stems and suffixes from five languages of the Yuman family, which is a subfamily of Hokan (Langdon, 1968). From the data, four demonstrative elements can be reconstructed for proto Yuman. Each can be reconstructed as a single consonant (the vowels present special problems not relevant to this discussion). The four proto demonstratives differ semantically in regard to relative distance from the speaker (just as, in English, *this* indicates objects closer to the speaker than *that*). Reconstruct the four proto demonstratives, and arrange them in order of increasing distance from the speaker. Yuma [ð] is a reflex of proto Yuman *[y]. Cocopa [ṣ] and Walapai [θ] are reflexes of *[s]. Cocopa [p], Walapai [w], and Diegueño [p] may all represent *[v] under certain conditions.

Yuma

ava	'this (short distance)'
vaða	'this (nearby)'
sava	'that (far away)'
ñaa	'that'
va	'this (nearby)'
sa	'that (far off)'
ñ	'that (location unspecified)'

Cocopa

pii	'this (nearby)'
puu	'that (nearby)'
ṣuu	'that (far away)'
pu	'nearby'
ṣa	'far away'
pa	'close by'
p	'this'
ṣ	'that'

Paipai

ya   'this'
sa   'the, that'
ñu   'nearby'
ya   'the, this'
ñu   'the, this here'

Walapai

va   'this (very close)'
ya   'this (rather close)'
θa   'there (distant)'
ñu   'there (by you)'
wi   'this (close)'
v   'this'
ñ   'that'

Diegueño

pǝyaa   'this'
puu   'that'
ñip   'that (other)'

Problem 5.5–5   *Takic*

One interesting feature of the Takic languages is the optional occurrence, after the first word or constituent of a sentence, of an expression indicating tense, modality, agreement with the subject or object, or some combination of these (compare Problem 3.7–8, p. 224). Examples from Serrano, Cupeño, and Luiseño are given below (K. Hill, 1967, and J. Hill, 1966); such expressions do not occur in Cahuilla, which has evidently lost this grammatical device. Analyze these expressions, and reconstruct their proto Takic antecedents as fully as possible. (The "dubitative" modal ranges in meaning from 'must'—in the sense of probability, not that of obligation—to interrogation.)

Serrano

ni-ʔ	'I, PAST'
ta-ni-ʔ	'I, PAST, DUBITATIVE'
ta-n	'I, DUBITATIVE'
bi-ʔ	'he, PAST'
ta-bi-ʔ	'he, PAST, DUBITATIVE'
ta-m-ç	'they, you (OBJECT), DUBITATIVE'
mi-ʔ	'they, PAST'
ha-čimi-ʔ	'we, PAST, INFERENTIAL'

Cupeño

ṣə-t-pə	'FUTURE, DUBITATIVE, EMPHATIC'
čə-pə	'we, FUTURE'
t-ʔəp	'PAST, EMPHATIC'
ṣə-nə	'I, DUBITATIVE'
n-i	'I, you (OBJECT)'
ṣə-pə	'FUTURE, DUBITATIVE'
m-pə	'it (OBJECT), FUTURE'
ṣə-t	'DUBITATIVE, EMPHATIC'

Luiseño

čam-il	'we, PAST'
xu-n-po	'I, FUTURE, SHOULD'
ṣu-š	'we, DUBITATIVE'
no-po	'I, FUTURE'
xu-š-po	'we, FUTURE, SHOULD'
n-il	'I, PAST'
ča-po	'we, FUTURE'
ṣu-n	'I, DUBITATIVE'

Index
of Languages
and Language
Families

Parenthesized numbers refer to problems. Only the number of the page on which a problem begins is listed with the problem number.

Index of Technical Terms

It would not be practicable to reference here all occurrences of all technical linguistic terms; hardly any sentence in the text lacks one or several technical expressions. This index focuses instead on passages that serve to define terms (implicitly or explicitly) or to reveal fundamental properties of their referents. The technical expressions that are specifically introduced in the text (marked in ***boldface italics***—the numbers of the pages on which they are introduced are similarly marked below) are all included here, as are certain other expressions for which indexing seems useful. However, certain basic terms taken for granted in the text, such as "stop" and "verb", are excluded.

References

IJAL = International Journal of American Linguistics
IUPAL = Indiana University Publications in Anthropology and Linguistics
LG = Language
PIL = Papers in Linguistics
UCPL = University of California Publications in Linguistics

Annear, Sandra S. 'English and Mandarin Chinese: Definite and Indefinite Determiners and Modifying Clause Structures,' Ohio State University Project on Linguistic Analysis, Report 11 (1965), pp. 1–55.

Aquilina, Joseph. *Teach Yourself Maltese.* London: English Universities Press, 1965.

Bailey, T. Grahame. *Teach Yourself Urdu.* Edited by J. R. Firth and A. H. Harley. London: English Universities Press, 1956.

Baker, Carol E. 'Tense Nonsense in Diegueño,' unpublished (1970).

Beeler, M. S. 'Sibilant Harmony in Chumash,' *IJAL* (1970) 36.1, pp. 14–17.

Bright, William, and Jane Hill. 'The Linguistic History of the Cupeño,' in Dell Hymes (ed.), *Studies in Southwestern Ethnolinguistics.* The Hague: Mouton, 1967. Pp. 351–71.

Bucca, Salvador, and Alexander Lesser. 'Kitsai Phonology and Morphophonemics,' *IJAL* (1969) 35.1, pp. 7–19.

Burling, Robbins. 'The Addition of Final Stops in the History of Maru (Tibeto-Burman),' *LG* (1966) 42.3, pp. 581–86.

———. *Proto Lolo-Burmese.* Indiana University Research Center in Anthropology, Folklore, and Linguistics, Publication 43 (1967). Supplement to *IJAL* 33.2.

Chafe, Wallace L. *A Semantically Based Sketch of Onondaga.* *IUPAL* Memoir 25 (1970). Supplement to *IJAL* 36.2.

Cheng, Chin-Chuan. 'Domains of Phonological Rule Application,' in Sadock and Vanek, pp. 39–59.

Chomsky, Noam, and Morris Halle. *The Sound Pattern of English*. New York: Harper & Row, 1968.

Connor, George Alan *et al. Esperanto, The World Interlanguage*. New York: Thomas Yoseloff, 1959.

Dingwall, William Orr. 'Secondary Conjunction and Universal Grammar,' *PIL* (1969) 1.2, pp. 207–30.

Dixon, R. M. W. 'Relative Clauses and Possessive Phrases in Two Australian Languages,' *LG* (1969) 45.1, pp. 35–44.

Drachman, Gaberell. 'Copying, and Order-Changing Transformations in Modern Greek,' Ohio State University Computer and Information Science Research Center, Working Papers in Linguistics 4 (1970), pp. 1–30.

Echeverría, Max S., and Heles Contreras. 'Araucanian Phonemics,' *IJAL* (1965) 35.2, pp. 132–35.

Egerod, Søren. 'Word Order and Word Classes in Atayal,' *LG* (1966) 42.2, pp. 346–69.

Elliott, Dale E. 'Interrogation in English and Mandarin Chinese,' Ohio State University Project on Linguistic Analysis, Report 11 (1965), pp. 56–117.

Fillmore, Charles J. 'Toward a Modern Theory of Case,' in David A. Reibel and Sanford A. Schane (eds.), *Modern Studies in English*. Englewood Cliffs, N.J.: Prentice-Hall, 1969. Pp. 361–75.

Foley, James. 'Spanish Plural Formation,' *LG* (1967) 43.2, pp. 486–93.

Foulet, Lucien. *Petite Syntaxe de l'Ancien Français*. Paris: Librairie Honoré Champion, 1967.

Friedrich, Paul. *On the Meaning of the Tarascan Suffixes of Space. IUPAL* Memoir 23 (1969). Supplement to *IJAL* 35.4.

Gudschinsky, Sarah C., and Harold and Frances Popovich. 'Native Reaction and Phonetic Similarity in Maxakalí Phonology,' *LG* (1970) 46.1, pp. 77–88.

Haas, Mary R. 'Internal Reconstruction of the Nootka-Nitinat Pronominal Suffixes,' *IJAL* (1969) 35.2, pp. 108–24.

Hale, Kenneth. 'Some Preliminary Observations on Papago Morphophonemics,' *IJAL* (1965) 31.4, pp. 295–305.

———. 'Papago /čim/,' *IJAL* (1969) 35.2, pp. 203–12.

———. 'On Papago Laryngeals,' in Earl H. Swanson, Jr. (ed.), *Languages and Cultures of Western North America, Essays in Honor of Sven S. Liljeblad*. Pocatello, Idaho: Idaho State University Press, 1970. Pp. 54–60.

———. 'Navajo Linguistics.' *To appear*, a.

———. 'Deep-Surface Canonical Disparities in Relation to Analysis and Change: An Australian Example.' *To appear*, b.

Hamp, Eric P. 'Fijian-Polynesian Embedded Subject Personals,' *Kivung* (1970) 2.1, pp. 26–34.

Hess, Thomas M. 'Snohomish Chameleon Morphology,' *IJAL* (1966) 32.4, pp. 350–56.

Hill, Jane H. *A Grammar of the Cupeño Language*. UCLA doctoral dissertation, 1966.

———. 'Volitional and Non-Volitional Verbs in Cupeño,' in Robert I. Binnick *et al.* (eds.), *Papers from the Fifth Regional Meeting of the Chicago Linguistic Society*. Chicago: Department of Linguistics, University of Chicago, 1969. Pp. 348–56.

Hill, Kenneth C. *A Grammar of the Serrano Language*. UCLA doctoral dissertation, 1967.

Hockett, Charles F. 'What Algonquian is Really Like,' *IJAL* (1966) 32.1, pp. 59–73.

Hohepa, Patrick W. *A Profile Generative Grammar of Maori. IUPAL* Memoir 20 (1967). Supplement to *IJAL* 33.2.

Hollow, Robert C., Jr. 'A Note on Assiniboine Phonology,' *IJAL* (1970) 36.4, pp. 296–98.

Hyman, Larry M. 'How Concrete is Phonology?' *LG* (1970) 46.1, pp. 58–76.

Javarek, Vera, and Miroslava Sudjić. *Teach Yourself Serbo-Croat.* London: English Universities Press, 1963.

Jones, C. Stanley. 'Hungarian Verbs and Objects and the "A-Over-A" Convention,' *PIL* (1970) 2.3, pp. 399–414.

Kaye, Jonathan D. 'Nasal Harmony in Desano,' *Linguistic Inquiry* (1971) 2.1, pp. 37–56.

Kim, Chin-Wu. 'Boundary Phenomena in Korean,' *PIL* (1970) 2.1, pp. 1–26.

Kiparsky, Paul. 'Linguistic Universals and Linguistic Change,' in Emmon Bach and Robert T. Harms (eds.), *Universals in Linguistic Theory.* New York: Holt, Rinehart and Winston, 1968. pp. 170–202.

Kisseberth, Charles W. 'Vowel Elision in Tonkawa and Derivational Constraints,' in Sadock and Vanek, pp. 109–37.

——. 'The Treatment of Exceptions,' *PIL* (1970) 2.1, pp. 44–58.

——. 'Cyclical Rules in Klamath Phonology,' *Linguistic Inquiry. To appear.*

Koutsoudas, Andreas. 'Doubled Nominals in Lebanese,' unpublished (1968).

——. 'Gapping, Conjunction Reduction, and Coordinate Deletion,' *Foundations of Language* (1971) 7.3, pp. 337–86.

Kuroda, S.-Y. 'Causative Forms in Japanese,' *Foundations of Language* (1965) 1.1, pp. 30–50.

——. *Yawelmani Phonology.* Cambridge: M.I.T. Press, 1967.

Kwee, John B. *Teach Yourself Indonesian.* London: English Universities Press, 1965.

Lamb, Sydney. *Mono Grammar.* University of California (Berkeley) doctoral dissertation, 1958.

Langacker, Ronald W. *Language and Its Structure.* New York: Harcourt, Brace Jovanovich, 1968.

——. 'The Vowels of Proto Uto-Aztecan,' *IJAL* (1970) 36.3, pp. 169–80.

Langdon, Margaret. 'The Proto-Yuman Demonstrative System,' *Folia Linguistica* (1968) 2.1, pp. 61–81.

——. *A Grammar of Diegueño. UCPL* (1970) 66.

Lees, Robert B. 'Turkish Nominalizations and a Problem of Ellipsis,' *Foundations of Language* (1965) 1.2, pp. 112–21.

Lewis, G. L. *Teach Yourself Turkish.* London: English Universities Press, 1953.

Lightner, Theodore M. 'On the Description of Vowel and Consonant Harmony,' *Word* (1965) 21.2, pp. 244–50.

Lindenfeld, Jacqueline. 'Semantic Categorization as a Deterrent to Grammatical Borrowing: A Yaqui Example,' *IJAL* (1971) 37.1, pp. 6–14.

Mattina, Anthony. 'Phonology of Alaskan Eskimo, Kuskokwim Dialect,' *IJAL* (1970) 36.1, pp. 38–45.

McCawley, James D. 'A Note on Multiple Negations,' unpublished (1969).

Mey, Jacob. 'Possessive and Transitive in Eskimo,' *Journal of Linguistics* (1970) 6.1, pp. 47–56.

Miller, Wick R. *Uto-Aztecan Cognate Sets. UCPL* (1967) 48.

Neufeld, Leonard. 'Some Syntactic Rules in Baron Long Diegueño,' unpublished (1970).

Newman, Paul. 'The Reality of Morphophonemes,' *LG* (1968) 44.3, pp. 507–15.

Osborn, Henry A., Jr. 'Warao II: Nouns, Relationals, and Demonstratives,' *IJAL* (1966) 32.3, pp. 253–61.

———. 'Warao III: Verbs and Suffixes,' *IJAL* (1967) 33.1, pp. 46–64.

Pankratz, Leo, and Eunice V. Pike. 'Phonology and Morphotonemics of Ayutla Mixtec,' *IJAL* (1967) 33.4, pp. 287–99.

Patterson, George W. 'French Interrogatives: A Diachronic Problem.' *To appear.*

Perrott, D. V. *Teach Yourself Swahili.* New York: David McKay Company, 1951.

Pizzini, Quentin. 'Predicate Complement Constructions in Samoan,' unpublished (1969).

Postal, Paul M. 'The Limitations of Phrase Structure Grammars,' in Jerry A. Fodor and Jerrold J. Katz (eds.), *The Structure of Language.* Englewood Cliffs, N.J.: Prentice-Hall, 1964. Pp. 137–51.

———. 'Mohawk Vowel Doubling,' *IJAL* (1969) 35.4, pp. 291–98.

Rand, Earl. 'The Structural Phonology of Alabaman, a Muskogean Language,' *IJAL* (1968) 34.2, pp. 94–103.

Rivero, María-Luisa. 'A Surface Structure Constraint on Negation in Spanish,' *LG* (1970) 46.3, pp. 640–66.

Ross, John Robert. 'Gapping and the Order of Constituents,' in Manfred Bierwisch and Karl Erich Heidolph (eds.), *Progress in Linguistics.* The Hague: Mouton, Series Maior 43, 1970. pp. 249–59.

Ruwet, Nicolas. 'Note sur la Syntaxe du Pronom *en* et d'Autres Sujets Apparentés,' *Langue Française* (1970) 6.

Sadock, Jerrold M., and Anthony L. Vanek (eds.), *Studies Presented to Robert B. Lees by His Students. PIL* Monograph Series 1 (1970).

Saxton, Dean, and Lucille Saxton. *Dictionary, Papago and Pima to English, English to Papago and Pima.* Tuscon: University of Arizona Press, 1969.

Schane, Sanford A. *French Phonology and Morphology.* Cambridge: M.I.T. Press, 1968.

Schiffman, Harold F. *A Transformational Grammar of the Tamil Aspectual System.* University of Washington, Studies in Linguistics and Language Learning 7 (1969).

Stenson, Nancy. 'Negation in Diegueño,' unpublished (1970).

Thompson, Laurence C. 'The History of Vietnamese Final Palatals,' *LG* (1967) 43.1, pp. 362–71.

Thompson, Laurence C., and M. Terry Thompson. 'Metathesis as a Grammatical Device,' *IJAL* (1969) 35.3, pp. 213–19.

Upson, B. W., and Robert E. Longacre. 'Proto-Chatino Phonology,' *IJAL* (1965) 31.4, pp. 312–22.

Voegelin, C. F., F. M. Voegelin, and Kenneth L. Hale. *Typological and Comparative Grammar of Uto-Aztecan: I (Phonology). IUPAL* Memoir 17 (1962). Supplement to *IJAL* 28.1.

Walker, Douglas. 'Diegueño Plural Formation,' unpublished (1970).

Wallis, Ethel E. 'The Word and the Phonological Hierarchy of Mezquital Otomi,' *LG* (1968) 44.1, pp. 76–90.

Wang, William S.-Y. 'Two Aspect Markers in Mandarin,' *LG* (1965) 41.3, pp. 457–70.

Wanner, Dieter. 'Substratum as a Special Case of Grammar Simplification,' *PIL* (1970) 2.3, pp. 415–48.

Welmers, William E. 'Language Change and Language Relationships in Africa,' *Language Sciences* (1970) 12, pp. 1-8.

Welmers, William E., and Beatrice F. Welmers. 'Noun Modifiers in Igbo,' *IJAL* (1969) 35.4, pp. 315–22.

F
G 8
H 9
I 0
J 1